D1594313

Palgrave Studies in Cultural Heritage and Conflict

Series Editors
Ihab Saloul
University of Amsterdam
Amsterdam, The Netherlands

Rob van der Laarse
University of Amsterdam
Amsterdam, The Netherlands

Britt Baillie
Centre for Urban Conflicts Research
University of Cambridge
Cambridge, UK

This book series explores the relationship between cultural heritage and conflict. The key themes of the series are the heritage and memory of war and conflict, contested heritage, and competing memories. The series editors seek books that analyze the dynamics of the past from the perspective of tangible and intangible remnants, spaces, and traces as well as heritage appropriations and restitutions, significations, musealizations, and mediatizations in the present. Books in the series should address topics such as the politics of heritage and conflict, identity and trauma, mourning and reconciliation, nationalism and ethnicity, diaspora and intergenerational memories, painful heritage and terrorscapes, as well as the mediated reenactments of conflicted pasts. Dr. Ihab Saloul is associate professor of cultural studies, founder and research vice-director of the Amsterdam School for Heritage, Memory and Material Culture (AHM) at University of Amsterdam. Saloul's interests include cultural memory and identity politics, narrative theory and visual analysis, conflict and trauma, Diaspora and migration as well as contemporary cultural thought in the Middle East.Professor Rob van der Laarse is research director of the Amsterdam School for Heritage, Memory and Material Culture (AHM), and Westerbork Professor of Heritage of Conflict and War at VU University Amsterdam. Van der Laarse's research focuses on (early) modern European elite and intellectual cultures, cultural landscape, heritage and identity politics, and the cultural roots and postwar memory of the Holocaust and other forms of mass violence. Dr. Britt Baillie is a founding member of the Centre for Urban Conflict Studies at the University of Cambridge, and a research fellow at the University of Pretoria. Baillie's interests include the politicization of cultural heritage, heritage and the city, memory and identity, religion and conflict, theories of destruction, heritage as commons, contested heritage, and urban resistance.

More information about this series at
http://www.palgrave.com/gp/series/14638

Jeroen Rodenberg · Pieter Wagenaar
Editors

Cultural Contestation

Heritage, Identity and the Role of Government

Foreword by
Marc Howard Ross

palgrave
macmillan

Editors
Jeroen Rodenberg
Department of Political Science
and Public Administration
VU University Amsterdam
Amsterdam, Noord-Holland,
The Netherlands

Pieter Wagenaar
Department of Political Science
and Public Administration
VU University Amsterdam
Amsterdam, Noord-Holland,
The Netherlands

Palgrave Studies in Cultural Heritage and Conflict
ISBN 978-3-319-91913-3   ISBN 978-3-319-91914-0   (eBook)
https://doi.org/10.1007/978-3-319-91914-0

Library of Congress Control Number: 2018941892

This Palgrave Macmillan imprint is published by the registered company Springer
International Publishing AG part of Springer Nature
The registered company address is: Gewerbestrasse 11, 6330 Cham, Switzerland

FOREWORD

I am pleased and honored to have been asked to write the Foreword to this book, whose subject has been the major topic my own research for more than three decades. Over this time, the vastness of the analysis of the concepts of culture and heritage have meant that I managed to investigate questions about culture and political conflict in a wide range of settings and using a variety of methods of data collection and analysis. The chapters in this book are important in expanding both what we know about the importance of heritage to people and societies, and how cultural contestation challenges our ability to live in a diverse and peaceful world.

Culturally defined expressions and enactments form the content of cultural heritage linking people who share an identity across time and space. Threats to cultural heritage are at the core of cultural contestation. These threats can variously engage a long-established group in a society that feels its heritage and identity are at risk and/or a minority (often one that is newly arrived) in a state that feels it is not getting the respect and recognition it deserves. As cultural contestation intensifies around cultural heritage, it becomes especially difficult to mitigate because the parties in these conflicts often do not readily view identity and heritage as divisible or negotiable.

In recent decades, the combination of increased migration in the world and greater mobilization around minority rights in states with a history in which a single-identity group dominated for a long time has increased cultural contestation in most of the world and has been particularly apparent in Western Europe, the North America, and much of Asia that are the focus of the chapters in this book. Central to understanding cultural contestation around heritage is recognizing that they are fundamentally about inclusion and exclusion in a society and its symbolic landscape which are expressed in the narratives groups recount about themselves, the cultural expressions and enactments they use to do this, and the presence or absence of recognition of a group's heritage on a society's symbolic landscape.

The contributors to this volume examine cultural contestation arising from heritage issues within, and between, a wide range of societies and states, showing how widespread and diverse the forms of cultural contestation around heritage politics are in the world. Indeed, it makes sense from my perspective to see these conflicts as virtually universal in the contemporary world, while at the same time recognizing that there is great variation in the forms and contents of the individual cultural conflicts described in my own work and in the chapters of this book. Variation in the issues around which the contestation occurs and the actions participants undertake vary a good deal and the cases described here provide a wide range of examples of the roles that states play, sometimes as direct participants including as initiators of contestation, and at other times in working toward their mitigation. States play diverse roles in cultural heritage disputes in great part depending upon who controls the state, and because cultural group boundaries are rarely coterminous with those of a state and cross-border issues can greatly affect the positions states adopt, and the actions they take, in a conflict. The reality that states in the world today include multiple cultural groups and most people from most of these live in more than one state makes cultural contestation more widespread and more intense than in the past.

It would be a mistake, moreover, to view cultural groups as stable. Rather, cultural identities are social constructions whose boundaries and defining characteristics can, and do, shift over time. As Donald Horwitz and others have explained, new more inclusive groups can form where once distinctive groups come together around a broader cultural identity, and at other times a larger group can subdivide leaving smaller, distinct entities in its place. This is all very consistent with the perspective of most scholars who widely accept the constructed and changing nature of cultural identities. Yet, at the same time, we should be aware that most people and groups involved in cultural contestation see group identities in essentialist terms and rarely acknowledge or are aware of the ways that these identities shift becoming more inclusive or exclusive over time.

Anthropologists and sociologists have puzzled about the nature and behavior of cultural identity groups for a long time examining their constructed and changing character in a wide variety of societies. Their work has often paid attention to cultural expressions such as festivals, social rituals, monuments, and the importance of group narratives. The work of anthropologists Max Gluckman, Victor Turner, Abner Cohen, and David Kertzer has always been particularly important to me in thinking about these questions as has that of sociologists going back to Emile Durkheim, Maurice Halbwachs, and Joseph Gusfield.

It has taken political scientists longer to recognize the importance of culture in politics. This is probably because, like historians, their predominant focus for a long time was almost exclusively on the structures of government (the state), the policy options political leaders and administrators considered, and the personalities and beliefs of competing political elites. This was not universally the case, however, and there were invariably voices that adopted a broader perspective than the mainstream. Some examples include people interested in political socialization such as David Easton, Fred Greenstein, and especially Richard Merelman, a student of Murray Edelman who initiated the study of symbolic politics and then broadened his work to include the influence of art on political life. Then as the field of political psychology evolved in recent decades, recognition of the importance of narratives, rituals, and political ceremonies in political life became more widespread.

My own investigations led me to recognize that intense cultural contestation often revolves around issues that have little material significance. Examples include intense conflicts over clothing (most often worn by women), flag displays, religious beliefs, monuments and memorials, parades, place names, public holidays, and control over public spaces. The trivial material value of many culturally valued objects such as headscarves and flags obliges us to give significant emphasis, at times, to non-material explanations for the intensity of conflicts around these objects and their connection to threatened identities. In the contestation that occurs, I have learned that attention to what I have called the public and symbolic landscape is especially important in understanding the dynamics of cultural contestation and heritage politics. The public landscape refers to the lands that include the streets, parks, museums, former battlefields, and other areas that ordinary citizens use and view in the course of their daily lives.

A society's symbolic landscape contains both real and imagined space. It includes specific places used by the public as well as abstract (and imagined) spaces associated with heritage and how people understand the past. Visits to specific physical sites often are experienced as emotionally special and are generally associated with narratives and rituals that connect people who see themselves sharing a common past and reinforce feelings of group identity. These places are sacred to in-group members and have an emotional significance for people because of events and people associated with them and these connections are expressed through memorials, statues, and buildings that mark significant historical events. Part of the sacred landscape also is found in cultural objects such as films, theater productions, music, books, religious practices, civic holidays, museum exhibits, paintings, statues, parades, family celebrations, religious practices, and festivals. Cultural contestation can become intense when any of these expressions associated with heritage and group identity become threats to that of another group and especially when they represent exclusion from a political community.

Outsiders often easily dismiss such conflicts as trivial and have trouble taking them seriously. But this is a mistake. What is more important is to consider why the people engaged in these cultural conflicts feel so intensely about them. A first step in doing this involves careful listening to what the parties engaged in cultural conflict say and do in order to better understand why the participants feel so strongly about them. While a common response is to dismiss statements and actions of participants in cultural contestations as foolish, self-serving or even irrational, this is not helpful for figuring out what is needed to mitigate a conflict's intensity. Without outsiders taking seriously what the participants feel and do, movement toward the lowering of tensions will be far more difficult to achieve.

Bryn Mawr, Pennsylvania, US   Marc Howard Ross
                                         Professor of Political Science
                                                Bryn Mawr College
                                              William Rand Kenan Jr.

CONTENTS

Notes on Contributors

Mehmet Calhan is a practitioner in the field of architectural conservation in London.

Dr. Rumana Hashem is a postdoctoral associate affiliated with the Centre for Research on Migration, Refugees, and Belonging at the University of East London.

Dr. Carlos Jaramillo is a cultural heritage practitioner with broad experience in conflict and post-conflict territories, and has been consultant for the UN, UNDP, and UNESCO.

Deniz Ikiz Kaya is a final-year research student at the School of Architecture, Oxford Brookes University (UK).

Elizabeth Kryder-Reid is a Professor of Anthropology and Museum Studies at the Indiana University School of Liberal Arts, IUPUI in Indianapolis, and Director of the Cultural Heritage Research Center.

William Logan is an Emeritus Professor of Heritage Studies at Deakin University, where he was founding director of the Cultural Heritage Centre for Asia and the Pacific.

Dr. Christina Maags is Lecturer in Chinese Politics at SOAS University of London.

Emilia Pawłusz is an early stage researcher in the Marie Curie Initial Training Network Project 'Post-Soviet Tensions' at Tallinn University.

Jeroen Rodenberg is a Lecturer in Public Administration at the Vrije Universiteit Amsterdam.

Dr. Ioan Trifu is Postdoctoral Research Fellow at the Professorship for Japanese Law and Its Cultural Foundations, Goethe University Frankfurt.

Dr. Michelle A. Tisdel is a research librarian at the National Library of Norway.

Desiree Valadares is a Ph.D. student in Architecture at UC Berkeley with a designated emphasis in Ethnic Studies and Peace and Conflict Studies.

Marja van Heese is an art historian and is external PhD-candidate at the Vrije Universiteit Amsterdam.

Biljana Volchevska works at the Centre for International Heritage Activities, The Hague, and is affiliated as an external Ph.D. candidate at the Department of Cultural Studies, Utrecht University.

Dr. Pieter Wagenaar is Assistant Professor in Public Administration at the VU University Amsterdam.

Larry J. Zimmerman is an Emeritus Professor of Anthropology & Museum Studies in the IU School of Liberal Arts at IUPUI.

LIST OF FIGURES

LIST OF TABLES

CHAPTER 1

Cultural Contestation: Heritage, Identity and the Role of Government

Jeroen Rodenberg and Pieter Wagenaar

Burning Flags and Toppling Generals

In the summer of 2017, Charlottesville, VA, was the scene of violent riots. The direct cause was local government's decision to remove a statue of General Robert E. Lee, which provoked a protest march of white nationalists. Human rights and anti-racism movements immediately reacted with counter-marches. In the ensuing riots, a car drove into a group of protesters, killing one and injuring nineteen. The events soon evolved into an intense national debate on the question whether Confederate monuments are 'symbols of hate or heritage' (Kenning 2017). President Donald Trump blamed both sides for the riots, publicly asking whether statues of George Washington and Thomas Jefferson would be next to be toppled (Shear and Haberman 2017). Since the riots statues, plaques and even stained-glass windows depicting Confederate generals, politicians, and judges have been removed from the public space in no less than 26 cities. All in all, almost 40 monuments commemorating the Confederation have been removed by local

J. Rodenberg (✉) · P. Wagenaar
Vrije Universiteit Amsterdam, Amsterdam, The Netherlands

© The Author(s) 2018
J. Rodenberg and P. Wagenaar (eds.), *Cultural Contestation*,
Palgrave Studies in Cultural Heritage and Conflict,
https://doi.org/10.1007/978-3-319-91914-0_1

administrations, acting either on their own accord or reacting to local communities' demands. In a few rare cases, they have been removed by the protesters themselves (Carbone 2017; *New York Times* 2017). Confederate flags have been burnt as well, sometimes as part of art projects aimed at opening up the debate on racism and attributes symbolizing the Confederacy (Thrasher 2015). Yet, at the same time, there seems to be a rise in repositioning dismantled monuments on privately owned lands and in erecting new ones (Tavernise 2017).

The toppling of statues is not unique to the USA. The year 2015 saw the emergence of the *#RhodesMustFall* movement in South Africa. In March of that year, a student of the University of Cape Town threw excrement at a statue of Cecil Rhodes, founder of former Rhodesia who was linked to *apartheid* by protesters. Not long after, the statue was removed by government and a nationwide discussion emerged on the ways in which society deals with monuments, which painfully symbolize racial divides (Shankar 2017).

These recent examples of iconoclasm in the USA and South Africa illustrate how statues can become focal points in processes of 'cultural contestation'. Some groups connect them to positive (hi)stories and use them as building blocks for identity formation. Others see them as witnesses to a dark (hi)story of (post)-colonialism, racism, and social exclusion, to which equally strong feelings are attached. The ensuing claims on the past, the present, and the future lead to fierce societal debates. During such intense cultural contestation, government is often explicitly looked to for guidance. Yet, the various roles it plays in such instances are understudied.

Contested Heritage

Obviously, at the core of cultural contestation is 'cultural heritage'. In this book, which is positioned explicitly in the growing stream of critical heritage studies, heritage is defined not as 'a thing', but as a social and cultural practice, enacted by communities and individuals, in which histories are selected or rejected (compare Smith 2006). Such 'histories' can be connected to objects, landscapes, and cultural expressions and traditions.

Cultural heritage, thus, has to do with meaning-giving. Both the tangible and the intangible are meaningless in themselves. It is the (hi) stories surrounding traditions and artifacts that enact them, which is why heritage is a social construction. When, in processes of meaning-giving, objects and cultural expressions are labeled 'heritage', conservation measures might be taken to save them for future generations. The opposite is also possible, though, when meaning-giving takes a different turn (Graham et al. 2016; Graham and Howard 2008).

As heritage has to do with selecting and neglecting (hi)stories that give meaning to objects and traditions, it is a discursive practice in which some (hi)stories become dominant and institutionalized to the exclusion of others (Hall 2005: 25; Waterton et al. 2006). Smith (2006) draws our attention to the existence of an 'Authorized Heritage Discourse' (AHD), arguing that it is this that constructs heritage practices and the way we perceive heritage in the Western world and even worldwide. AHD focuses on the great moments of national histories and selects tangible and intangible heritage representing exactly these. Because of this, heritage is bound up with processes of identity formation. The great histories of national pasts are not chosen without reason. They are carefully selected expressions of an envisioned national identity (Lowenthal 1985, 1998). At both national and local levels, these narratives give meaning to objects and landscapes, providing communities who relate to them with a sense of place and belongingness (see, e.g., Jones 2005; Waterton 2005). As a consequence, heritage practices have material effects in what is and what is not labeled as heritage and hence preserved or demolished. More importantly, they have social effects as well, in terms of inclusion and exclusion.

Heritage is a zero-sum game (Tunbridge and Ashworth 1996). There are winners and losers, in various different ways. Certain narratives are articulated and become dominant, resulting in objects and cultural traditions being authorized as heritage, at the cost of others. There are those who successfully claim heritage, and those who fail in their attempts, which results in the drawing of demarcation lines between those who belong and those who don't (Smith 2006; Waterton 2010; Graham et al. 2016).

Because there are always several, often conflicting, meanings, which are bestowed on heritage, it is always dissonant (Tunbridge and Ashworth 1996). Heritage is claimed for different uses and with different purposes by individuals, groups, communities, nations, and states. As the heritage of one group can't be that of another, different forms of contestation come into being. Legal fights over ownership are not uncommon, not even between states as the case of the Parthenon Marbles illustrates

(Harrison 2010: 174–182). Economic considerations and the daily practical use of heritage can also be the cause of dissonance. An agricultural landscape, for example, is exactly that to farmers—a means for agricultural production—whereas the same landscape can be labeled as cultural and historical heritage by landscape historians and planners. An example of this is the discussion surrounding the placing of the Dutch *Noordoostpolder* on the UNESCO World Heritage List (Rodenberg 2015). Yet, dissonance can also flow from a heritage's troubled history. There might be feelings of unease that are inherent to it. Holocaust memorials are a prime example, and discussions can arise on how to deal with such 'dark heritage' (Logan and Reeves 2009). Dissonance runs deeper when identity formation and processes of social inclusion and exclusion come into play, as we have seen with the statues in the above.

Although heritage is always potentially contested, this contestation is not always played out. Yet, as soon as feelings of not belonging become too strong and are articulated in public debates, symbols can become focal points in processes of 'cultural contestation'. The discipline of critical heritage studies has identified many instances of this, but is none too explicit on ways of dealing with it. The political sciences do provide answers, though.

Cultural Contestation

Political science deals with conflict resolution extensively and also with ways of solving cultural contestation. Marc Howard Ross offers a way to not only analyze contested heritage, but to also mitigate it. The concept he introduces—and which we have used in the above already—is that of 'cultural contestation'. Cultural contestation is about identities expressed in a society's symbolic landscape. This landscape consists of cultural practices, expressions, and enactments, as well as of objects. As it gives a clear message about who belongs to society and who doesn't, it reveals identity politics and politics of acceptance and rejection. Cultural expressions are vital to a group's identity, and as soon as these expressions become a threat to another group's identity, heavy contestation can occur. As said in the above, cultural expressions and objects are meaningless in themselves. It is groups in society who attribute meaning to them by constructing and articulating narratives. In cases of cultural contestation, several of these narratives are in opposition. And when that happens, emotions can run high (Ross 2007, 2009a, b).

The narratives not only depict images of the in-group, but also of the out-group. Claims of who belongs to society and who doesn't are being expressed, and the stakes are high, as inclusion in a society's symbolic landscape means access to resources and opportunities. Often, the involved parties experience it as a zero-sum game in which looking at a higher authority to resolve the matter is useless, because in many cases at least one of the involved parties doesn't acknowledge its legitimacy (Ross 2009a).

Yet, studying the symbolic landscape and the narratives giving meaning to it can still be fruitful. It brings a deeper understanding of the groups' fears and as a result some guidance for solving the problem. Narratives, after all, as Ross argues, are constructions and can therefore be reconstructed, based on shared experiences and commonalities, which these also show. Mitigation can be achieved if the parties involved are open to one another's narratives, are willing to listen, and try to construct inclusive narratives (Ross 2009a). Ross' ideas on the cultural contestation surrounding contested heritage form the starting point for all the case studies presented in this volume.

ROLES GOVERNMENTS PLAY

Heritage scholars often pay attention to government. They study the social effects of heritage policies and deal with the question of how states and governments use heritage for identity formation or to make political statements (see, e.g., Silberman 1995; Smith 2006; Waterton 2010; Harrison 2010; Laurence 2010; Bendix et al. 2012). The general image we have, however, is that in heritage studies government is rarely at the center of attention. A notable example is the volume edited by Bendix et al. (2012) comprising of ethnographic studies on the role of state bureaucracies in heritage policies and management. As far as we know, studies on the role government plays in cultural contestation are even lacking. Yet, as we have seen in the above, in political science some scholars, most notably Ross, do study it. In his work, Ross shows how governmental actors act in instances of cultural contestation. True is that he does not focus specifically on their role. Yet, even without systematically analyzing the role of government, Ross demonstrates that government, in various ways, is always involved (Ross 2007, 2009a).

In this book, we proceed where Ross has left. In the various chapters, the authors explore the different roles governmental actors play during cultural contestation in different sociocultural contexts and political-administrative systems. Because of the variety of backgrounds of the contributors, we look at the problem from different disciplinary backgrounds. To get a better grip on the case studies presented in this volume, we use a categorization of possible governmental roles, which also functions as the structuring mechanism for the book. In the concluding chapter, we will return to this categorization and reflect on its usefulness.

The first role governmental actors can play, according to our categorization, is favoring certain expressions of heritage over others, by way of listing and subsidizing. There are instances where governments go even further than not favoring, and actively repress social values expressed through minority heritage, denying groups their heritage and identity. The first part of the volume comprises five chapters exploring cases in which it is this role of government that causes cultural contestation. Maags explores how the political-administrative design of the Chinese state, characterized as 'multi-level governance', might be the cause of more subtle forms of resistance. By looking at the formulation of heritage policies of Lancang County, she illustrates how the administrative fragmentation resulted in both administrative contestation and cultural contestation, with a threatened local identity at its core.

William Logan asks attention for the uses of heritage by the Myanmar government. The way Myanmar government deals with ethnic minorities makes it hard to arrive at more inclusive conceptions of heritage. At the root of the problem lies the fact that heritage plays such an important role in the country's nation-building.

Comparable processes have taken place in Bangladesh, as Rumana Hashem argues in her contribution. She explores the causes and consequences of a 27-year ethnic conflict between the Bengali and Jumma people. It is by depreciating certain heritage that the successive governments of Bangladesh have created conflict in the Chittagong Hill Tracts.

Deniz Ikiz Kaya and Mehmet Calhan look at Turkish heritage policies in a historical perspective. Since the establishment of Turkey as a nation-state, its government has used heritage as an instrument for nation-building. However, this could only be done by de-contextualizing and re-contextualizing certain heritage sites. The authors reveal government's role in the ensuing cultural contestation by looking at Greek Orthodox religious heritage.

Michelle Tisdel too takes a historical policy perspective, when looking at Cuban cultural policies from 1902 to the present. During the Republican

Era (1902–1959) and under Socialist rule, Cuban governments persecuted Afro-Cuban religious practitioners. Nowadays, museums showcase Afro-Cuban religious heritage, promoting it as a symbol of cultural blending.

Desiree Valadares zooms in on cultural contestation surrounding natural landscapes. She examines how at Forillon National Park in Quebec government hides the fact that the park's former inhabitants were removed from their homes and how the history of national park policy works socially exclusive.

The second part of the volume deals with contestation on a supranational level. Central in the contributions is the way the use of heritage can lead to interstate contestation. Using Famagusta, Cyprus, as a case study, Carlos Jaramillo examines the difficulties this city faces in formulating heritage policies, due to the heritage system created by UNESCO and the UN. The refusal to recognize the Turkish Republic of North Cyprus as a state by these supranational institutions has prevented the discussion on the future of its cultural heritage. Jaramillo shows how dominant views on cultural heritage at the international level are intertwined with political contestation.

Biljana Volchevska explores the relationship between heritage production and heritage destruction as two coexisting processes at a time of political conflict. She looks at Macedonia, an unstable, multiethnic state, to demonstrate how the obsession with heritage production is related to cultural contestation with Greece.

Marja van Heese discusses what is perhaps the most extreme form of contestation, zooming in on the war over Nagorno Karabakh. She examines cultural contestation between former Soviet states, focussing on the conflict between Armenia and Azerbaijan in the period 1992–1994. The cease-fire, signed on May 5, 1994, formally gives sovereignty over the enclave to Azerbaijan. Yet, Armenian armed forces are in control. Several reports mention the destruction of cultural heritage in the district. According to Azerbaijani authorities, traces of Azerbaijani cultural heritage are erased, for example, by the replacing of Azeri inscriptions on monuments by Armenian ones.

Ioan Trifu explores the ways in which dark heritage has led to cultural contestation between Japan and South Korea. In 2015, Japan announced that it would recommend nineteenth-century industrial heritage for inclusion in the UNESCO World Heritage List. The South Korean government was quick to point out that at these industrial sites Korean civilians had been made to do forced labor during the Second World

War. This attempt at heritage listing, therefore, quickly leads to political conflict between the two states.

The last part of the volume, and of our categorization, consists of four chapters focusing on cases in which governments try to mitigate cultural contestation. Emilia Pawłusz examines the attempt of the Estonian state to reconcile itself with its Soviet past and bring together the different ethnic groups that inhabit the country.

Elizabeth Kryder-Reid and Larry Zimmerman also look at parks. They describe how over the last several years at two government-owned parks in Indiana debates have been held between different groups of stakeholders. An analysis of the debates shows the way these stakeholders deal with their conflicting concepts of cultural heritage.

In the last chapter, Pieter Wagenaar and Jeroen Rodenberg discuss attempts at mitigation by government during the Dutch *Zwarte Piet* (Black Pet) controversy, which has rocked the country for years. The clash between opponents of the figure—who see him as a remnant from a sinister colonial past—and his supporters—to whom he is a vital part of their identity—has been so fierce that government found itself compelled to intervene.

REFERENCES

Bendix, R. F., Eggert, A., & Peselman, A. (Eds.). (2012). *Heritage Regimes and the State*. Göttingen Studies in Cultural Property (Vol. 6). Göttingen: Universitätsverlag Göttingen.

Carbone, C. (2017, October 18). *Which Confederate Statues Were Removed? A Running List*. Available at: http://www.foxnews.com/us/2017/10/18/which-confederate-statues-were-removed-running-list.amp.html. Accessed 19 Dec 2017.

Graham, B., & Howard, P. (2008). Introduction. In B. Graham & P. Howard (Eds.), *The Ashgate Companion to Heritage and Identity* (pp. 1–18). Farnham: Ashgate.

Graham, B., Ashworth, G. J., & Tunbridge, J. E. (2016). *A Geography of Heritage: Power, Culture and Economy*. Abingdon and New York: Routledge.

Hall, S. (2005). Whose Heritage? Un-settling 'the Heritage', Re-imagining the Post-nation. In J. Littler & R. Naidoo (Eds.), *The Politics of Heritage and the Legacies of 'Race'* (pp. 23–35). Abingdon and New York: Routledge.

Harrison, R. (2010). The Politics of Heritage. In R. Harrison (Ed.), *Understanding the Politics of Heritage* (pp. 154–196). Manchester: Manchester University Press.

Jones, S. (2005). Making Place, Resisting Displacement: Conflicting National and Local Identities in Scotland. In J. Littler & R. Naidoo (Eds.), *The Politics of Heritage and the Legacies of 'Race'* (pp. 94–114). Abingdon and New York: Routledge.

Kenning, C. (2017, August 15). U.S. Cities Step Up Removal of Confederate Statues, Despite Virginia Violence. *Reuters*. Available at: http://reuters.com/article/amp/idUSKCN1AV0XE. Accessed 19 Dec 2017.

Laurence, A. (2010). Heritage as a Tool of Government. In R. Harrison (Ed.), *Understanding the Politics of Heritage* (pp. 81–114). Manchester: Manchester University Press.

Logan, W., & Reeves, K. (Eds.). (2009). *Places of Pain and Shame: Dealing with 'Difficult Heritage'*. London and New York: Routledge.

Lowenthal, D. (1985). *The Past Is a Foreign Country*. Cambridge: Cambridge University Press.

Lowenthal, D. (1998). *The Heritage Crusade and the Spoils of History*. Cambridge: Cambridge University Press.

Rodenberg, J. (2015). De bestuurlijke omgang met verleden, heden en toekomst: of hoe de Noordoostpolder geen Werelderfgoed werd. In R. van Diepen, W. van der Most, en H. Pruntel (Eds.), *Polders peilen. Cultuurhistorisch jaarboek voor Flevoland* (pp. 130–154). Lelystad: de Twaalfde Provincie.

Ross, M. H. (2007). *Cultural Contestation in Ethnic Conflict*. Cambridge: Cambridge University Press.

Ross, M. H. (2009a). Cultural Contestation and the Symbolic Landscape: Politics by Other Means? In M. H. Ross (Ed.), *Culture and Belonging in Devided Societies. Contestation and Symbolic Landscapes* (pp. 1–24). Philadelphia: University of Pennsylvania Press.

Ross, M. H. (Ed.). (2009b). *Culture and Belonging in Devided Societies. Contestation and Symbolic Landscapes*. Philadelphia: University of Pennsylvania Press.

Shankar, A. (2017, August 17). *Removing Racist Statues Is 'Taking History to Task' in South Africa*. Available at: https://www.pri.org/stories/2017-08-17/removing-racist-statues-taking-history-task-south-africa. Accessed 19 Dec 2017.

Shear, M. D, & Haberman, M. (2017, August 15). Trump Defends Initial Remarks on Charlottesville: Again Blames 'Both Sides'. *New York Times*. Available at: https://www.nytimes.com/2017/08/15/us/politics/trump-press-conference-charlottesville.html. Accessed 19 Dec 2017.

Silberman, N. A. (1995). Promised Lands and Chosen People: The Politics and Poetics of Archaeological Narrative. In P. L. Kohl & C. Fawcett (Eds.), *Nationalism, Politics and the Practice of Archaeology* (pp. 249–262). Cambridge: Cambridge University Press.

Smith, L. (2006). *Uses of Heritage*. Abingdon and New York: Routledge.

Tavernise, S. (2017, August 30). *A Boom in Confederate Monuments, on Private Land*. Available at: https://www.nytimes.com/2017/08/30/us/confederate-monuments.html. Accessed 19 Dec 2017.

The New York Times. (2017, Augustus 28). Confederate Monuments Are Coming Down Across the United States. Here's a List. Available at: https://www.nytimes.com/interactive/2017/08/16/us/confederate-monuments-removed.html. Accessed 19 Dec 2017.

Thrasher, S. W. (2015, July 4). *You Can't Ignore the Confederate Flag. But You Can Burn It and Then Bury It*. Available at: https://www.theguardian.com/commentisfree/2015/jul/04/confederate-flag-burn-it-bury-it. Accessed 19 Dec 2017.

Tunbridge, J. E., & Ashworth, G. J. (1996). *Dissonant Heritage: The Management of the Past as a Resource in Conflict*. Chichester: Wiley.

Waterton, E. (2005). Whose Sense of Place? Reconciling Archaeological Landscapes in England. *International Journal of Heritage Studies, 11*(4), 309–325.

Waterton, E. (2010). *Politics, Policy and the Discourses of Heritage in Britain*. Houdsmills: Palgrave Macmillan.

Waterton, E., Laurajane, L. Smith, & Campbell, G. (2006). The Utility of Discourse Analysis to Heritage Studies: The Burra Charter and Social Inclusion. *International Journal of Heritage Studies, 12*(4), 339–355. https://doi.org/10.1080/13527250600727000.

PART I

Governmental Favoring and Repression of Heritage

CHAPTER 2

Cultural Contestation in China: Ethnicity, Identity, and the State

Christina Maags

INTRODUCTION

During the past two decades, the protection of traditional cultural practices has taken center stage in international cultural governance. With the adoption of the UNESCO Convention for the Safeguarding of Intangible Cultural Heritage (ICH Convention) in 2003, 171 state parties have committed to implementing domestic "intangible cultural heritage" (ICH) safeguarding measures. ICH refers to "practices, representations, expressions, knowledge, skills—as well as the instruments, objects, artefacts and cultural spaces associated therewith—that communities, groups and, in some cases, individuals recognize as part of their cultural heritage" (UNESCO 2003). Among the earliest signatories, the People's Republic of China (PRC) has eagerly implemented various UNESCO "best practices" of ICH safeguarding. This is surprising as the PRC had previously banned many forms of traditional culture—most notably during the Cultural Revolution. Reflecting UNESCO's best practices, the PRC adopted a national inventory of ICH practices,

C. Maags (✉)
SOAS University of London, London, UK

© The Author(s) 2018
J. Rodenberg and P. Wagenaar (eds.), *Cultural Contestation,*
Palgrave Studies in Cultural Heritage and Conflict,
https://doi.org/10.1007/978-3-319-91914-0_2

13

creating ICH lists on multiple government levels, as well as its own variation of the Living Human Treasures System (UNESCO 2002), the ICH Inheritor program (*chuanchengren xiangmu*) (SC 2005; MOC 2006). Although the PRC's official embrace of traditional culture has unleashed an "ICH fever" among the Chinese populace, enhancing awareness and promotion (Maags 2018), the party-state's ICH safeguarding programs have not only had positive effects. Indeed, the listing of ICH practices on domestic and UNESCO ICH representative lists as well as the ICH inheritor program has created exclusion and inclusion effects which have fueled cultural contestation among local communities (Svensson 2006; Maags 2018). Although these effects have been well documented (Hafstein 2009: 104), few studies examine how administrative implementation mechanisms intentionally and unintentionally create them. This is surprising as academic literature identifies state policy and bureaucracy as a major cause for cultural contestation (e.g., Harrison 2010; Waterton 2010).

Cultural contestation arises between two distinct ethnic or cultural groups, or between the state and such groups. While much has been written about the interests and strategies behind engaging in contestation, Ross (2007) emphasizes that cultural contestation goes beyond these structural or interest-based approaches. In fact, what matters are the groups' identities which are strongly connected to heritage, cultural practices, and expressions, be they tangible such as landscapes, monuments, and artefacts or intangible like rituals, festivals, or language. To capture the role cultural identity plays in cultural contestation, Ross therefore agues for examining cultural expressions as markers of identity and for retracing changes in cultural narratives whether exclusive, thus enhancing the conflict, or inclusive, providing an opportunity to mitigate further conflicts (2007: 1–3).

Following Ross' call for a greater focus on cultural identity and expressions in political science research on cultural contestation, this chapter inquires into the ways government policy and administrative procedures foster cultural contestation between the state and ethnic groups. It seeks to add to the literature by shedding light on the multiple and often ambiguous effects government policy and administration may have on local ethnic culture due to its multi-level structure. It also seeks to show how these effects do not necessarily result in open contestation and conflict, but also take more indirect or subtle forms of resistance. Drawing on a case study of Lancang County in Yunnan Province, PR

China, this chapter will demonstrate how the different interests and strategies within Chinese multi-level governance may on the one hand promote ethnic cultural identities and vernacular practices, while simultaneously brushing over them to pursue economic and political interests on the other, thereby creating local cultural contestation.

The chapter is structured as follows: After providing a review of the scholarly literature on this topic, I will briefly introduce the theoretical and methodological approach which informs this study. The main part of the chapter will demonstrate, firstly, how Chinese changes in policy and administration have provided opportunities for Lancang County to foster its cultural identity and receive national recognition for its cultural practices. Subsequently, the chapter will outline how diverging interests within Chinese multi-level governance result in local, indirect forms of cultural contestation through the establishment of counter-narratives. After a discussion on the ambiguous effects of the Chinese multi-level governance on local community culture, this chapter will end with some concluding remarks on the broader issues underlying ethnic identity and cultural contestations in "state-nations"[1] of the Global South.

THE STATE OF THE ART

A study of the PRC reflects broader issues around ethnicity, cultural identity, and the state unfolding in many post-colonial or post-communist states. Like many other countries, the Chinese state has undergone many ruptures in its development, particularly in the cultural realm. As mentioned above, while the Chinese party-state had criticized traditional culture and religion as superstitious and feudal, resulting in a large-scale repression and destruction of tangible and intangible heritage during the Cultural Revolution (Yuan 1987: 85–95), it has slowly changed its attitude since its Reform and Opening Period commenced in 1978 (Barmé 1999: 236, 256). This attitude change has triggered heightened scholarly interest in the reasons and implications of this change in government policy. Blumenfield and Silverman (2013), for instance, have argued that the Chinese party-state has renewed interest in its past as it may be used as a tool to promote nationalist sentiments among the populace, enhance economic development, and legitimize minority politics (2013: 3–23). Many academic studies have examined the use of heritage as a resource to develop the tourism industry (Shepherd and Yu 2012; Zhu and Li 2013), to enhance nationalism (Gladney 1996; Cheung 2012), and to foster ethnic minority relations (Yang et al. 2008; Zhu 2016), whereas others have studied underlying governmental policies and procedures (Bodolec 2012; Liang 2013; Maags and Holbig 2016).

Studying the governmental impact on local communities, many scholars have demonstrated that government policies and procedures foster cultural contestation between the Chinese state and local communities (Schein 2000; Svensson 2006; Yu 2015). You (2015), for instance, has pointed to the conflicts that emerge between different state and local actors during negotiations on nominating ICH practices for inclusion on ICH lists. She shows that conflicts not only arise due to cultural contestation between local communities concerning whose traditions are to be officially recognized, but also due to the lack of non-state actor involvement in decision-making as local governments control the inscription process, its management as well as the allocation of state funds. Similarly, Chen (2015) has examined local government's interest in using ICH as a tourism resource, arguing that the subjectivity and agency of local cultural practitioners are constrained and weakened through strong state control.

As the People's Republic is home to 56 ethnic minorities (Wang 2015: 4), state control and resulting cultural contestation are at times exacerbated in ethnic minority areas. Echoing Chau's (2005) claim that the party-state seeks to depoliticize religion by reframing it as culture, Liang (2013) has examined how the local government in Dali Bai Autonomous Prefecture in Yunnan Province has made great efforts to inscribe a local religious festival on the domestic ICH items list, particularly associating a supposed fertility cult and sexual promiscuity with the festival.[2] Yet, the party-state's control of ICH inscription and management is also resisted by local non-state stakeholders. In her analysis of Miao village ritual practices, Yu (2015) has found that local communities create and disseminate counter-narratives as well as secretly and publicly perform their rituals which go against official interpretations of the ICH practice.

In PR China, cultural contestation between the state and ethnic groups is thus commonly related to the party-state's desire to control and depoliticize ethnic minority culture and religion on the one hand, while making economic profit on the other. As the examples of cultural contestation and resistance have shown, in an authoritarian state such as China ethnic groups rarely openly contest state policies producing cultural contestations, rather using alternative, more subtle ways of resisting cultural "superscription" (cf. Duara 2010). Moreover, many studies are couched in a narrative of "the state" vs. "the ethnic minority"—which can also be found in Ross' (2007) work. What I want to highlight here, however, is that the state is a multi-layered and fragmented entity in which a plurality of actors pursues very different interests. Building on Ross' notion of cultural contestation, I now turn to incorporating a multi-level governance perspective into his framework of cultural contestation.

THEORETICAL AND METHODOLOGICAL APPROACH

Cultural contestation, according to Ross (2009), can be understood as the "inclusion and exclusion from a society's symbolic landscape and that such inclusion or exclusion tells us about the politics of acceptance, rejection and access to a society's resources and opportunities" (2009: 1). Ethnic and cultural groups seek to express their cultural identity in their symbolic landscape which comprises sacred sites and physical objects as well as music, language, or public celebrations. Ross argues that since scholarship often solely focuses on competing interests, incompatible identities are overlooked. Therefore, he calls for examining symbolic landscapes and how they demonstrate the (perhaps missing) recognition of groups, how different groups refer to each other and themselves in psychocultural narratives, as well as how the control of the symbolic landscape is related to resource allocation (Ross 2009: 1–2; see also Ross 2007).

As domestic heritage politics and the inherent allocation of resources among state and non-state actors are strongly influenced by inscriptions of local tangible or intangible culture on the national level or at the UNESCO, it is necessary to incorporate a multi-level governance perspective in the analysis. This perspective facilitates an analysis of how different government levels interact and helps to explain "the dispersion of central government authority both vertically to actors located at other territorial levels, and horizontally to non-state actors" (Bach and Flinders 2004: 4). This fragmentation of authority both between the central and subnational government levels and between horizontal units and actors is moreover a key feature of the Chinese political system, commonly referred to as "fragmented authoritarianism" (Lieberthal and Oksenberg 1988; Mertha 2009). In this framework, decentralization processes are said to have resulted in a fragmentation between the lines of command, providing subnational governments with greater leeway in policy implementation. Yet, this greater leeway also results in competition between governmental units across the vertical and horizontal lines of authority, leading to diverging policy implementation across government levels and geographical regions (Lieberthal and Oksenberg 1988: 21).

The fact that fragmentation between different government levels leads to competition is important for understanding cultural contestation between the state and ethnic groups, as it demonstrates the plurality of official and vernacular narratives that affect acts of cultural contestation. Moreover, cultural identities and expressions are linked to different scales, be it local, regional, or national. While building on Ross' work, this chapter thus seeks to extend his framework by acknowledging that the processes he described unfold on multiple levels and scales.

The PR China is a significant case study to understand cultural contestation processes across levels or scales. Firstly, as mentioned above, China exemplifies the ruptured and uneven developments in many state-nations across the Global South. Secondly, the Chinese party-state is a key actor in global heritage governance, particularly regarding its inscriptions on UNESCO heritage lists. To date, it has the second largest number of sites on the World Heritage List (52) (UNESCO 2017a) and the largest number of ICH practices on the UNESCO ICH Representative List (39) (UNESCO 2017b). Finally, due to its rich ethnic diversity, the Chinese province of Yunnan is a critical case to understand how ethnic minorities contest cultural identities superscribed by different actors within the multi-level state.

The findings of this chapter are based on a case study of Yunnan Province, with Lancang County at the core. Yet, local cultural contestation processes will be examined concerning decisions made at the national, provincial, and municipal (or prefectural) level. To collect supporting data, I conducted several months of field work and engaged local officials, academics, and cultural practitioners in semi-structured interviews. Moreover, multiple primary (laws, policies, government plans) and secondary sources (newspaper articles, academic studies) in Mandarin Chinese and English inform the study.

Governmental Programs as an Opportunity for Fostering Cultural Identity

Following the ratification of the UNESCO ICH Convention in 2004, the Chinese party-state, through the Ministry of Culture's ICH Department, implemented the Convention by creating ICH lists and an

ICH inheritor program (SC 2005), the Chinese equivalent to a Living Human Treasures program (UNESCO 2002) in 2005. While ICH practices are inscribed on lists to raise awareness, the ICH inheritor program seeks to promote the transmission of ICH practices within local communities by financially supporting selected cultural practitioners (SC 2005; MOC 2008). Government units at all administrative levels with decision-making powers (the national, provincial, municipal, and county level) are asked to create their own ICH lists and ICH inheritor programs, resulting in a multi-level system of ICH safeguarding. After the county level enlists ICH practices and cultural practitioners from lower levels (village or township), the municipal level creates its own ICH and ICH inheritor lists based on county-level programs. Thereby, ICH practices and inheritors can be promoted "up the ladder," eventually becoming national representatives of Chinese ICH (Maags 2018; see also Bodolec 2012: 259).

Because government officials (e.g., county level) who inscribe ICH items (and in part ICH inheritors) on lists at the next (e.g., municipal) level benefit politically and economically, local governments compete to promote their selected cultural practice "up the ladder" (Maags 2018). Firstly, this competition is due to the establishment of such lists and programs on each administrative level. Secondly, as outlined above, the fragmentation of authority between different government units along the horizontal and vertical line fosters competition, as local governments attempt to obtain a promotion or win superordinate level funding (Zhong 2003: 87). As described elsewhere in greater detail (Maags 2018), the multi-level policy implementation and the fragmented authority structure have resulted in cultural contestation between local communities all striving to represent a local ICH, which is prevalent in many localities albeit in different variations, at the next level. As a result, on the one hand, the promotion of ICH practices and inheritors "up the ladder" creates contestation and conflict between local communities (Maags 2018).

On the other hand, the superordinate government levels select from these local ICH practices to forge a regional, provincial, or national cultural identity aimed at promoting social cohesion and pride. Fostering a national identity is especially important as China is home to 56 officially recognized ethnic minorities—a classification devised in the Ethnic Identification Project[3] from 1950s to the 1980s (Wang 2015: 4). To increase social cohesion, the party-state has increasingly selected ethnic minority ICH practices for UNESCO representative lists,[4] seeking to promote the narrative of a "unified multi-ethnic state" and thereby an inclusive multi-ethnic national identity. In this narrative, the party-state emphasizes a supposed historical unity of different ethnic groups to portray the uniting of different ethnic groups as natural and inevitable (Bird 2018: 3). Inscriptions of ethnic minorities' cultural sites and practices on UNESCO lists further substantiate this narrative and according to Shepherd (2009) enhance Chinese political claim over these territories.

With its 26 ethnic groups (Yunnan gov. 2015), Yunnan Province is the most ethnically diverse in the country. Therefore, promoting the narrative of a "unified multi-ethnic state" is particularly important in Yunnan's official documents. In Art. 1 of Yunnan's ICH policy of 2005, for instance, the primary objective of safeguarding ICH is allegedly to promote "patriotism," "strengthen Yunnan's economic and social development," and "preserve national unity" (Art. 1; YNCD 2005). In addition to agriculture and mining, tourism is a pillar industry (Britannica 2016), so safeguarding ethnic minority culture is tantamount to preserving a key resource needed for economic development. Yunnan thus implements central policies in which "Heritage construction is a core feature of regional development strategies, especially in the historically poor and ethnically diverse regions of the southwest" (Evans and Rowlands 2015: 272).

To promote both social cohesion and economic development, Yunnan Province has eagerly pursued provincial ICH; as early as the late 1990s, Yunnan established policies for safeguarding traditional cultural practices (Liang 2013: 61–62). Additionally, it has successfully inscribed 105 ICH practices on national ICH lists (Xinhua 2017) and established 66 ICH environmental protection zones in Yunnan, which are inhabited by 21 different ethnic groups (YBC 2014). Yunnan's eagerness to inscribe ICH practices and zones has at times caused conflict between ethnic groups. To reduce potential cultural contestation and conflicts around the designation of ICH items and safeguarding areas among ethnic groups, all seeking to have their ICH practice listed at the national level and thus enjoy national recognition, the provincial government attempts to recommend equal numbers of ICH practices from each ethnic minority to the national level. However, ethnic sub-groups not identifying with the culture of the larger ethnic group do not feel represented (Blumenfield 2018). As one prominent ICH expert noted, the designation of a territory as "Cultural Landscape of the Honghe Hani Rice

Terraces" in 2013 at UNESCO similarly caused contestation between ethnic groups, as the region is not only inhabited by the Hani ethnic group (Interview 7; see also UNESCO 2013). The designation of ICH practices and zones has thus led to the glossing over of ethnic differences which has created tensions between ethnic groups who contest state programs and inscriptions which violate their cultural identity.

As Yunnan is one of the poorest provinces in PR China[5] (Finance Sina 2016), it is eager to make use of the national financial incentive structure to fund ICH safeguarding. The central government rewards local policy innovation by declaring local best practices as "models" for national emulation and providing these models with additional central funding (Zhong 2003; Heilmann 2008). Yunnan is eager to use its leeway in policy formulation and implementation to be successful in the national competition for central funding. As it is home to many ethnic minorities, which are often allowed more extensive leeway in policy formulation and implementation due to their "self-governing" status,[6] sub-provincial governments can potentially use this greater leeway to compete for national-level funding. One example of such a model unit is Lancang County (in Pu'er municipality) in the very south of Yunnan Province.

Lancang County (*Lancang Lahuzu Zizhi Xian*) is a poor, "self-governing" jurisdiction in the south of Yunnan bordering Myanmar. The county is home to eight different ethnic groups of which the largest group is the Lahu. To promote local Lahu culture, the county government began to develop its safeguarding measures from an early stage on. Following the ratification of the UNESCO ICH Convention in 2003, the county launched its "Lancang Properous County" initiative which is aimed at promoting traditional Lahu culture in the domestic and international realm (Xinhua 2014). This initiative was followed by a series of county-level policies[7] with similar aims in 2008 (revised in 2012) (LCCC 2015a, b). In these and other policies, the Lancang government stipulates that each village in its jurisdiction must establish a cultural performance troupe and a cultural center where local residents can receive lessons in ICH practices and use musical instruments free of charge. Moreover, ICH practices and inheritors are to be promoted for inscription in local and superordinate ICH lists (Interview 42). The county has been very successful. Two of their ICH practices, the Mupamipa legend and the Lusheng dance, were inscribed on the national ICH list in 2006 (China. com 2007a, b). Moreover, due to their safeguarding efforts, Lancang was identified as a "model county" for ICH safeguarding by the central government. These rewards have also contributed to local pride, as an interview with one county ICH official indicates:

This is not meant to sing one's own praise, [but] Lancang is used as a model [lit. "typical example"]. In the whole province, our transmission of ICH items, our work achievements and the atmosphere of our culture are [considered to be] all very good (Interview 42).

As a result of being named a model county, Lancang is able to benefit from the national financial incentive structure.

Along with the promotion of Lahu culture, the county government is disseminating a narrative around Lancang County being a "Global Lahu Cultural Centre." A central theme of their narrative is the Mupamipa (Creating Heaven, Creating Earth) legend which tells the story of Lahu's origin—their journey to the southwest of Yunnan as well as their society, religion, and culture. In this narrative, Lancang is portrayed as the center of Lahu culture. Moreover, this narrative and the Mupamipa legend have been tangibilized through the creation of a symbolic cultural landscape. As, according to legend, the Lahu were born out of a calabash (Interview 42), in recent years, images from the legend, especially the calabash, have been placed across the city (see Fig. 2.1). For instance, a new square has been built in the midst of the city, in which a large calabash decorates the center. According to a local cultural official, the square is to provide public space to perform Lahu cultural practices (Interview 42).

Moreover, a new park has been created which is filled with statues representing events within the Mupamipa legend as well as displaying the Lahu or other ethnic minorities of the region (see Fig. 2.2).

Again, the park incorporates small stages where traditional dances and musical performances can be displayed. The city environment has thus been recreated into a symbolic cultural landscape demonstrating Lahu culture. According to the county government, its main objective behind the rebranding and promotion of ICH practices has been the preservation of Lahu ethnic culture. As a third of the Lahu ethnic minority worldwide[8] live in the county, the county government—whose staff are themselves Lahu—sees itself as the wardens of traditional Lahu culture. They therefore promote traditional dances, songs, and legends which lie at the core of Lahu culture (Interview 42).

The Mupamipa legend, since the 1950s, has been furthermore interpreted according to official narratives which claim a supposed origin of the Lahu in northwestern Qinghai Province to integrate the Lahu into

Fig. 2.1 The calabash in the newly developed Town Square in Lancang County (*Source* Author)

the history of the Chinese state (Ma 2009: 111–114). Although this supposed origin, which scholars such as Ma (2009) contest, is not contested by the Lahu themselves, the Mupamipa legend provides a "politically safe" opportunity to create a narrative and symbolic cultural landscape which highlights and celebrates the distinctiveness of Lahu culture vis-à-vis the dominant Han culture. This celebration of distinctiveness in opposition to the Han majority, historically and at present, furthermore forms the basis of Lahu cultural identity. Ma (2013), for instance,

Fig. 2.2 Statue in the New Park in Lancang depicting the Mupamipa Legend (*Source* Author)

argues that: "The Lahu identity and Lahu culture have been mobilized under the conditions of the arrival of the state powers in the mountains. Without the state's penetration there would have been no political-religion system or Lahu identity, based on detailed historical research on this frontier" (Ma 2013: 9). The promotion of the legend can thus support Lahu cultural identity as well as safeguard local ICH practices.

Overall, Lancang's county government has thus seized the opportunity of the Chinese leadership's greater attention to traditional culture to celebrate its cultural identity and popularize Lahu culture more broadly. While the safeguarding measures foster the preservation of Lahu culture and identity in a rapidly changing environment, the national ICH lists demonstrate national social recognition of Lahu culture which enhances local pride. As one ICH inheritor proudly explained:

> at the moment we have [performed] in Shanghai, Beijing [and these cities]. They have all [experienced] our Lahu singing, our Lahu minority dance, so they know a little, have seen a little. (Interview 45)

The county government has thus been successful in promoting Lahu traditional culture beyond Yunnan, which has fostered local cultural identity and pride. Moreover, national recognition also equals financial support, which is needed to fund the safeguarding measures. Ultimately, national recognition and local safeguarding measures further emphasize the uniqueness and distinctiveness of Lahu culture vis-à-vis the Han as well as other ethnic minorities in the region.

MULTI-LEVEL THREATS TO LOCAL CULTURAL NARRATIVES AND IDENTITIES

Although the nationwide recognition and promotion of Lahu ethnic minority culture can be regarded as a success, as Lancang is now able to showcase its culture and distinctiveness domestically and internationally, this success does not protect them from interests, strategies, and cultural identities promoted at other government levels. In Pu'er, the municipality to which Lancang County belongs, for instance, a different narrative has dominated. In Pu'er municipality, the Deang, Bulang, Hani, and Wa ethnic groups are most numerous (Pu'er gov. 2015; Ethnic China 2016). The regions closer to the municipality's capital have moreover historically been part of an ancient "Tea Horse Road" in China, which linked the tea production in the area to consumers in other parts of China. After Pu'er tea re-gained popularity in the early 2000s (Zhang 2014: 8), the provincial government in Kunming decided to rebrand the municipality along tea culture and production. As a part of this strategy, the municipality which had formerly been known as Simao was renamed Pu'er (the name of the tea) in 2008 (Zhang 2014: 82). Rebranding the municipality's capital along tea culture furthermore included the nomination of its tea mountains as "Ancient Tea Plantations of Jingmai Mountain in Pu'er" for inscription on the World Heritage List. To date, however, the nomination awaits approval (UNESCO 2016). As a result, the Pu'er tea industry has boomed, sparking a subsequent boom in the tourism and cultural industries (PETA 2016).

Thus, in Pu'er a different narrative and symbolic cultural landscape as taken shape. While it celebrates its rich ethnic diversity, its regional identity is strongly linked to tea culture, which is only part of some ethnic minority cultures but not all (Interview 43). Field visits showed that in comparison with Lancang, Pu'er's symbolic cultural landscape is not as much shaped by the display of certain objects such as the calabash, but strongly visible in the transformation of its cultural space. Across the city, tea houses have opened, which celebrate the drinking of tea and tea ceremonies. Pu'er tea and local ethnic minority culture are common sights on billboards and tourism advertisement. Overall, local residents appear to have "rediscovered" Pu'er tea and related cultural practices and rituals.

While Pu'er is said to have started to promote its local tea already since the mid-1990s (Zhang 2014: 42), the provincial government has had a strong influence on the acceleration and expansion of Pu'er's urban rebranding. Already in the mid-2000s, the provincial government issued policies enhancing the development of the provincial tea industry (Yunnan gov. 2005). Soon after Kunming commenced to invest in the Pu'er tea industry by founding state-owned tea enterprises, it developed a brand and marketing strategy for Pu'er tea which was promoted during the 2008 Olympics and 2010 World Expo in Shanghai. For the Pu'er municipal government, this development has been highly advantageous as it strongly seeks to foster its economic development by enhancing its tea, tourism, and cultural industries (PECB 2012).

However, while the promotion of Pu'er as a tea culture destination has been to the benefit of the municipality, it does not necessarily support Lancang County's interests and cultural identity. In 2012, for instance, the provincial government declared that it would establish a historical cultural tourism zone displaying the origin of tea. According to this plan, three adjoining counties within Pu'er municipality, in which Lancang lies at the core, are to be promoted as a "Tea Origin Culture Park" in order to transform the region into one of Yunnan's ten largest historical cultural tourism zones. This park offers tourists the experience of tea culture, entertainment, shops, hotels, and ethnic minority culture. At the time of writing, the provincial government was seeking investors (Yunnan gov. 2015), who in addition to county governments such as Lancang (LCTA 2016) are to fund the establishment of the park.

For Lancang County and its government's dream of becoming a "Global Lahu Cultural Centre," the provincial government's plans create a dilemma. On the one hand, the county is extremely poor (in Yunnan and in national terms) and women have been marrying Han to move out of the region (Ma 2013: 3–12). It could therefore benefit from the economic and infrastructure development which a new tourism zone would facilitate. As noted above, Lancang County is focusing on safeguarding and promoting its performing arts, such as traditional Lahu dances, songs, and myths. An integration into a tourism zone could provide these traditional artists and amateurs with the opportunity to present their art and generate income, thus enabling a sustainable safeguarding of these ICH practices.

On the other hand, Pu'er municipality's cultural identity and narratives directly run counter to Lancang County's plans of establishing themselves as a Global Lahu Cultural Center. As a local ICH official argued, tea culture is not part of Lahu culture but rather related to the Bulang ethnic minority (Interview 43). One ICH official for instance argued that:

> Our (genesis) legend has always continued to develop, we sing it every day and every night. The songs and dances have special characteristics. Speaking of other ethnic minorities, for instance, the Bulang ethnic minority, they like tea, this minorities' ICH projects evolve around tea culture. They have a totally different focus than we do. (Interview 42)

By being incorporated into a larger tourism zone which is linked to a different cultural identity and narrative, Lancang would thus face the challenge of being subsumed under a larger, regional identity which was constructed by superordinate government levels to promote economic development. While the project is still in the making, Lancang appears to react to these 2012 plans by more strongly promoting the county as a "Global Lahu Cultural Centre." It for instance has adopted new local policies (LCCC 2015a, b), is popularizing its culture in TV shows and movies, and is winning national rewards, for instance, "China Village of Folk Culture Art" and "China Cultural Advanced County" (LCCC 2016; People's Daily 2016). It thereby attempts to strengthen its cultural identity and symbolic cultural landscape at a time when competing cultural identities are promoted which might undermine Lahu cultural identity. In doing so, it produces counter-narratives which tell a different story of the locality, running against the broader, regional narratives. In contrast to engaging in open contestation of superordinate plans, Lancang has thus chosen to not directly oppose state-sanctioned narratives and plans, but to subvert them indirectly by maintaining and promoting its own, alternative narratives.

Ambiguous Effects of China's Multi-level ICH Safeguarding System

Whereas the introduction of an ICH safeguarding system in China has provided ethnic groups such as the Lahu with the opportunity to enhance safeguarding and promotion of their ICH practices and thereby to strengthen their cultural identity, simultaneous efforts on other governmental levels may contradict or undermine local. On the one hand, the Lahu's cultural identity has been reinforced by the national recognition and popularization of its cultural practices such as the Lusheng dance and the Mupamipa legend. This national recognition furthermore goes hand in hand with financial support and several awards, as for instance to be named a "model county," and somewhat with a gain in political and economic power. On the other hand, despite its recognition and greater power, it remains to be a poor county which needs to oblige with superordinate development plans, even when they run counter to its own plans and narratives. Here, Lancang County appears to face a dilemma between embracing the development plans it so desperately needs to provide its residents with employment and growth prospects, while fearing that these development plans and related narratives will undermine its own narratives and by extension cultural identity.

Lancang County's response to this dilemma appears to have been to not openly contest any plans or narratives developed by superordinate levels, although the county government might lobby for incorporation or acknowledgment of its own plans and narratives behind closed doors. It rather appears to strengthen its own narratives and cultural identity by further developing their own ICH safeguarding measures and symbolic cultural landscape, e.g., by creating a large square displaying Mupamipa symbols such as the calabash. In doing so, its symbolic cultural landscape and narratives are reinforced and demonstrate a counter-narrative vis-à-vis other, regional narratives which might undermine its cultural identity.

Although local communities across China have also openly contested state narratives and development projects (see e.g., Svensson 2006), a more indirect or covert form of cultural contestation appears to be a common strategy among local ethnic groups and by extension any cultural group, which does not have the power or agency to openly defy and contest superordinate narratives and plans. Yu (2015), for instance, has similarly argued that local Miao communities create and disseminate counter-narratives as well as secretly and publicly perform their rituals which go against official interpretations so that "Vernacular narratives, beliefs, spaces and practices have spread beyond the reach of the state, even as the country undergoes massive economic and social transformation, and the more recent global surge of interest in safeguarding ICH" (2015: 1032). Similarly, Evans and Rowlands (2015) have pointed out that the sustainability of local initiatives "depends on the successful accommodation of the state's political, economic and commercial interests through appropriating *and* contesting the commodification of heritage and negotiating complex relationships between individuals, communities, entrepreneurs and official agencies" (2015: 280, emphasis in original). Cultural contestation in authoritarian China can therefore take more indirect forms in which government plans and narratives are not openly contested, even accommodated to a certain extent, while subtle counter-narratives and measures simultaneously undermine superordinate efforts.

However, many of the studies which elaborate on these indirect forms of cultural contestation portray a dichotomy between local communities and the state in which local communities are fighting against state control and repression. Although this picture accurately depicts many instances of cultural contestation, it is necessary to consider the different actors and administrative levels within multi-level governance systems. Different government levels may pursue different interests and strategies as well as disseminate different narratives. As Yu (2015) has argued, in China central government policy is often contested by local governments, as expressed in the local idiom "Up, there is policy. Bottom, there is countermeasure (shang you zheng ce, xia you dui ce)" (2015: 1022). Cultural contestation therefore may arise due to a locality being caught up in a multi-level governance structure which all have different interests, strategies, as well as narratives and identities. Moreover, the dichotomy between state and society glosses over the fact that government officials are also part of the local community and, especially when their own local cultural identity is concerned, may attempt to use opportunities provided by the state such as ICH lists and financial incentive structures to safeguard their local heritage and create a symbolic cultural landscape which reinforces their cultural identity.

In the case of Lancang County, it appears that local officials have used their available resources and power to safeguard Lahu ICH practices by promoting local ICH practices "up the ladder" of the multi-level ICH inscription system or by establishing culture centers and troupes.

In doing so, they reinforce local cultural and historical narratives and cultural identity, while simultaneously complying with central ICH policies and using heritage as a development strategy for poor, ethnically diverse regions.

Conclusion

The introduction of an ICH safeguarding system in the Chinese multi-ethnic, multi-level state has had ambiguous effects. While the party-state's recent increase in attention toward ICH safeguarding has been, among others, an effort to strengthen nation-building and nationalist sentiments among its populace, governmental programs also generate cultural conflicts among ethnic and cultural groups as well as between these groups and the state. While many conflicts arise due to the artificial classification of ethnic groups during the 1950s and the central strategy of using ethnicity as a resource to develop poor, remote regions on Chinese periphery, this chapter has shown that the multiple levels and scales at which identities are formed similarly create cultural contestations. While some local communities and groups chose to openly challenge imposed or competing narratives and cultural identities, others select more indirect and subtle ways of contestation which are based on creating counter-narratives and reinforcing their local cultural identity and symbolic cultural landscape. Moreover, the dichotomy between "state" and "society" is not always as clear-cut as state officials may be members of an ethnic minority and thus have an intrinsic motivation to use opportunities that the state provides to safeguard and promote their ethnic cultural identity. Since the PRC is an authoritarian state, however, cultural contestation may take more subtle and indirect forms of cultural contestation which are based on counter-narratives and measures.

The Chinese party-state can thus be understood through the notion of the "robustly multinational" state-nation (Stepan et al. 2010). On the one hand, the party-state has engendered "strong identification and loyalty from their citizens" (Stepan et al. 2010: 1) by promoting a national identity through the narrative of a multi-ethnic state (Brady 2012: 3) and fostering a "performance-based legitimacy" (Holbig and Gilley 2010) which promises economic growth and prosperity. On the other hand, the national narrative of a multi-ethnic state continues to be contested by certain groups, for instance, among the Tibetans and Uyghurs (Bhattacharya 2008), who "in the name of nationalism and self-determination, advance claims of independence" (Stepan et al. 2010: 1). However, although Stepan et al.'s (2010) conception of a state-nation is based on democratic systems, many of which are federalist in nature (Stepan et al. 2010: 22) and the Chinese party-state is an authoritarian, centralized state, this chapter demonstrates that China displays similarities with other state-nations in the Global South. Firstly, due to its fragmentation, subnational administrative levels, especially provinces, obtain greater leeway in policy formulation, thereby enabling similar dynamics as in federalist states. Secondly, there are separatist movements among ethnic minority groups and at times open forms of cultural contestation against imposed narratives and identities by the party-state. However, due to the authoritarian nature of the state, it also gives way to more indirect and subtle forms of contestation which simultaneously seek to accommodate and contest state narratives and identities.

To understand the complexities of cultural contestation, particularly in multi-ethnic states, more research needs to be conducted which incorporate alternative explanatory frameworks such as that proposed by Ross (2007) which highlight the role of cultural identity and narratives in these processes. This chapter has sought to build on Ross' framework and to extend it by incorporating a multi-level perspective. While this chapter has briefly related its findings to the literature of state-nations, future studies could demonstrate how cultural contestation emerges and unfolds in different types of state-nations and nation-states to comprehend how the differences in ethnic composition, cultural homogeneity, and political systems have an impact on cultural contestation and with what effects.

Notes

1. Stepan et al. (2010) have argued that state-nations are "multicultural, and sometimes even have significant multinational components, which nonetheless still manage to engender strong identification and loyalty from their citizens, an identification and loyalty that proponents of homogeneous nation states perceive that only nation states can engender" (2010: 4). In contrast to nation-states, state-nations, however, are "robustly multinational" societies as the states "have deep cultural diversity, some of which is territorially based and politically articulated by significant groups that, in the name of nationalism and self-determination, advance claims of independence" (Stepan et al. 2010: 1–4).

2. See also Louisa Schein (2000) on eroticization of ethnic minorities in China.

3. In this "Project," ethnic groups who identified as a separate ethnicity were asked to officially register as an ethnic minority. Yet, ethnic groups who failed to apply for recognition did not obtain ethnic minority status and thus do not enjoy minority rights (Wang 2015: 4).

4. Among the first 10 ICH items the Chinese party-state nominated for the UNESCO ICH list, five represent ethnic minority culture (UNESCO 2017c).

5. Yunnan's provincial GDP ranks 23rd out of the 31 provinces and autonomous regions (Finance Sina 2016).

6. The PRC's Constitution (2004) stipulates that ethnic minorities have the right to pass local regulations and manage their own budget (to be approved by central authorities) and government departments need to be headed by members of the ethnic groups (Art. 112–122) (NPC 2004).

7. These policies include "Traditional Ethnic Folk Culture Protection Regulations" (revised in 2012) as well as the "Lancang Lahu Minority Self-governing County Methods on Strengthening the Implementation of County level ICH Protection and Transmission" (LCCC 2015).

8. The other two-thirds of the Lahu live in other parts of China or in neighboring regions inMyanmar and Thailand, see Ma (2013): 8–9.

References

Bache, I., & Flinders, M. (2004). Introduction. In I. Bache & M. Flinders (Eds.), *Multi-level Governance* (pp. 1–14). New York: Oxford University Press.

Barmé, G. (1999). *In the Red: On Contemporary Chinese Culture*. New York: Columbia University Press.

Bhattacharya, A. (2008). Conceptualising Uyghur Separatism in Chinese Nationalism. *Strategic Analysis, 27*(3), 357–381.

Bird, J. (2018). *Economic Development in China's Northwest: Entrepreneurship and Identity Along China's Multi-ethnic Borders*. London and New York: Routledge.

Blumenfield, T. (2018). Recognition and Misrecognition: The Politics of Intangible Cultural Heritage in Southwest China. In C. Maags & M. Svensson (Eds.), *Chinese Cultural Heritage in the Making. Experiences, Negotiations and Contestations*. Amsterdam: IIAS/Amsterdam University Press.

Blumenfield, T., & Silverman, H. (2013). Cultural Heritage Politics in China: An Introduction. In T. Blumenfield & H. Silverman (Eds.), *Cultural Heritage Politics in China* (pp. 51–71). New York: Springer.

Bodolec, C. (2012). The Chinese Paper-Cut: From Local Inventories to the UNESCO Representative List of the Intangible Cultural Heritage of Humanity. In R. F. Bendix, A. Eggert, & A. Peselmann (Eds.), *Heritage Regimes and the State. Göttingen Studies in Cultural Property* (Vol. 6, pp. 249–464). Göttingen: Universitätsverlag Göttingen.

Brady, A.-M. (2012). Ethnicity and the State in Contemporary China. *Journal of Current Chinese Affairs, 41*(4), 3–9.

Britannica. (2016). *Yunnan.* https://www.britannica.com/place/Yunnan.

Chau, A. Y. (2005). The Politics of Legitimation and the Revival of Popular Religion in Shaanbei, North-Central China. *Modern China, 31*(2), 236–278.

Chen, Z. (2015). For Who to Conserve Intangible Cultural Heritage: The Dislocated Agency of Folk Belief Practitioners and the Reproduction of Local Culture. *Asian Ethnology, 74*(2), 307–334.

Cheung, K. C.-K. (2012). Away from Socialism, Towards Chinese Characteristics: Confucianism and the Futures of Chinese Nationalism. *China Information, 26*(2), 205–218.

China.com. (2007a). *Mapamipa.* http://www.china.com.cn/culture/zhuanti/whycml/200706/13/content_8384459.htm.

China.com. (2007b). *Yi Ethnic Minority Hulusheng Dance.* http://www.china.com.cn/culture/zhuanti/whycml/200706/13/content_8384294.htm.

Duara, P. (2010). The Historical Roots and Character of Secularism in China. In W. Gungwu (Ed.), *China and International Relations: The Chinese View.* London: Routledge.

Ethnic China. (2016). *Puer (Simao) Prefecture.* http://www.ethnicchina.com/Geo/Yunnan/puerintro.htm.

Evans, H., & Rowlands, M. (2015). Reconceptualising Heritage in China: Museums, Development and the Shifting Dynamics of Power. In P. Basu & W. Modest (Eds.), *Museums, Heritage and International Development* (pp. 272–295). New York: Routledge.

Finance Sina. (2016). *Provincial GDPs of 2016 According to Rank.* http://finance.sina.com.cn/china/gncj/2017-02-07/doc-ifyaexzn9124761.shtml.

Gladney, D. C. (1996). *Muslim Chinese: Ethnic Nationalism in the People's Republic.* Cambridge, MA: Harvard East Asian Monographs.

Hafstein, V. (2009). Intangible Heritage as a List: From Masterpieces to Representation. In L. Smith & N. Akagawa (Eds.), *Intangible Heritage* (pp. 93–111). London and New York: Routledge.

Harrison, R. (Ed.). (2010). *Understanding the Politics of Heritage.* Manchester: Manchester University Press.

Heilmann, S. (2008). Policy Experimentation in China's Economic Rise. *Studies on Contemporary International Development, 43*, 1–26.

Holbig, H., & B. Gilley. (2010). *In Search of Legitimacy in Post-revolutionary China: Bringing Ideology and Governance Back* (GIGA Working Papers, 127/2010).

LCCC (Lancang Culture Center). (2015a). *Lancang County's ICH Protection Work Circumstances*. Obtained from the Lancang Culture Center during Field Research in Summer 2015.

LCCC (Lancang Culture Center). (2015b). *Situation of Lancang County's Culture Center*. http://www.lcwhg.net/portal.php?mod=view&aid=19.

LCCC (Lancang Culture Center). (2016). *Deepening and Advancing the Strategy of Prominent County of Lahu Culture' Actively Establishes National Cultural Advanced County*. http://www.pelcxxw.cn/kllh/0254419500359242520.

LCTA (Lancang Tourism Administration). (2016). *Project for Establishing Tea Origin Historic Cultural Tourism in Three Adjoining Counties in Pu'er Municipality*. http://news.jkyscsmc.com/zcnsgddyy/2819.html.

Liang, Y. (2013). Turning Gwer Sa La Festival into Intangible Cultural Heritage: State Superscription of Popular Religion in Southwest China. *China: An International Journal, 11*(2), 58–75.

Lieberthal, K., & Oksenberg, M. (1988). *Policy-making in China. Leaders, Structures and Processes*. Princeton: Princeton University Press.

Ma, J. (2009). Local Knowledge Constructed by the State. Reinterpreting Myths and Imagining the Migration History of the Lahu in Yunnan Province, China. *Asian Ethnology, 68*, 111–129.

Ma, J. (2013). *The Lahu Minority in Southwest China: A Response to Ethnic Marginalization on the Frontier*. New York: Routledge.

Maags, C. (2018). Creating a Race to the Top: Hierarchies and Competition within the Chinese ICH Transmitters System. In C. Maags & M. Svensson (Eds.), *Chinese Cultural Heritage in the Making: Experiences, Negotiations and Contestations*. Amsterdam: Amsterdam University Press.

Maags, C., & Holbig, H. (2016). Replicating Elite Dominance in Intangible Cultural Heritage Safeguarding: The Role of Local Government-Scholar Networks in China. *International Journal of Cultural Property, 23*, 71–97.

Mertha, A. (2009). Fragmented Authoritarianism 2.0. *The China Quarterly, 200*, 995–1012.

MOC (PRC Ministry of Culture). (2006). *National ICH Safeguarding and Provisional Administration Methods*. http://59.252.212.6/auto255/200612/t20061215_13005.html?keywords=%E9%9D%9E%E7%89%A9%E8%B4%A8%E6%96%87%E5%8C%96%E9%81%97%E4%BA%A7.

MOC (PRC Ministry of Culture). (2008). Methods on the Recognition and Management of ICH Representative ICH Inheritors (Draft), http://www.gov.cn/gongbao/content/2008/content_1157918.htm, (accessed 20 May 2018).

NPC (National People's Congress). (2004). *Constitution of the People's Republic of China*. http://www.npc.gov.cn/englishnpc/Constitution/node_2825.htm.

PECB (Pu'er Culture Bureau). (2012). *Pu'er Municipality People's Government's Implementation Opinion on Strengthening the Establishment of a System on Public Culture Services that Benefit the People*. http://xxgk.yn.gov.cn/Z_M_004/Info_Detail.aspx?DocumentKeyID=DB6B9A2EE748417C8618D55A87441B75.

People's Daily. (2016). *Summary of the Great Achievements of Lancang County's Deepening and Progressing "Lahu Culture Famous County" Strategy*. http:// yn.people.com.cn/news/yunnan/n2/2016/0706/c376835-28623182.html.

PETA (Pu'er Tourism Administration). (2016). *Pu'er Tourism News—Number 11*. http://www.puerta.gov.cn/content.aspx?id=479378914048.

Pu'er gov. (Pu'er Municipal Government). (2015). *Pu'er Situation*. http:// www.puershi.gov.cn/pegk/07643077707004600223.

Ross, M. H. (2007). *Cultural Contestation in Ethnic Conflict*. Cambridge: Cambridge University Press.

Ross, M. H. (Ed.). (2009). *Culture and Belonging in Divided Societies: Contestation and Symbolic Landscapes*. Philadelphia: University of Pennsylvania Press.

SC (State Council) (2005). *State Council's Opinion on Strengthening Intangible Cultural Heritage Protection Work*. http://www.gov.cn/zwgk/2005-08/15/content_21681.htm.

Schein, Louisa. (2000). *Minority Rules: The Miao and the Feminine in China's Cultural Politics*. Durham: Duke University Press.

Shepherd, R. (2009). Cultural Heritage, UNESCO, and the Chinese State Whose Heritage and for Whom? *Heritage Management, 2*(1), 55–79.

Shepherd, R., & Yu, L. (2012). *Heritage Management, Tourism, and Governance in China: Managing the Past to Serve the Present*. New York: Springer.

Stepan, A., Linz, J. J., & Yadav, Y. (2010). *Crafting State-Nations. India and Other Multinational Democracies*. Baltimore: John Hopkins University Press.

Svensson, M. (2006). *In the Ancestors' Shadow: Cultural Heritage Contestations in Chinese Villages*. Lund: Center for East and South-East Asian Studies. http://isites.harvard.edu/fs/docs/icb.topic1466881.files/Svensson%20 ancestors_shadow.doc.

UNESCO. (2002). *Guidelines for the Establishment of Living Human Treasures Systems*. http://unesdoc.unesco.org/images/0012/001295/129520eo.pdf.

UNESCO. (2003). *Convention for the Safeguarding of the Intangible Cultural Heritage 2003*. http://portal.unesco.org/en/ev.phpURL_ID=17716&URL_DO=DO_TOPIC&URL_SECTION=201.html.

UNESCO. (2013). *Cultural Landscape of Honghe Hani Rice Terracesi*. http:// whc.unesco.org/en/list/1111.

UNESCO. (2016). *Ancient Tea Plantations of Jingmai Mountain in Pu'er*. http://whc.unesco.org/en/tentativelists/5810/.

UNESCO. (2017a). *China*. http://whc.unesco.org/en/statesparties/cn.

UNESCO. (2017b). *China and the 2003 Convention*. https://ich.unesco.org/en/state/china-CN.

UNESCO. (2017c). *China and the 2003 Convention*. https://ich.unesco.org/en/state/china-CN.

Wang, L. (2015). Identification of Ethnic Minorities in China. *Asian-Pacific Law & Policy Journal, 16*(2), 1–21.

Waterton, E. (2010). *Politics, Policy and the Discourses of Heritage in Britain.* Hampshire: Palgrave Macmillan.

Xinhua. (2014). *Charm of "Cultural Lancang".* http://www.yn.xinhuanet.com/puer/2014-03/27/c_133217966.htm.

Xinhua. (2017). *Yunnan Publishes Fourth Provincial Level ICH Representatives Items Projects.* http://news.xinhuanet.com/gongyi/2017-06/09/c_129629426.htm.

Yang, L., Wall, G., & Smith, S. L. J. (2008). Ethnic Tourism Development: Chinese Government Perspectives. *Annals of Tourism Research, 35*(3), 751–771.

YBC. (2014). *The Situation of Yunnan Province's Ethnic Traditional Cultural Environmental Protection.* http://www.ynich.cn/book-view-51.html.

YNCD (Yunnan Province Culture Department). (2005). *Notice on Implementing the Opinion of the Yunnan Province People's Government Office on Distributing and Carrying out the State Council Document on Strengthening National ICH Protection Work.* http://www.cnnsr.com.cn/csfg/html/20051206000000105299.html.

You, Z. (2015). Shifting Actors and Power Relations: Contentious Local Responses to the Safeguarding of Intangible Cultural Heritage in Contemporary China. In M. D. Foster & L. Gilman (Eds.), *UNESCO on the Ground. Local Perspectives on Intangible Cultural Heritage* (pp. 113–130). Bloomington: Indiana University Press.

Yu, H. (2015). A Vernacular Way of "Safeguarding" Intangible Heritage: The Fall and Rise of Rituals in Gouliang Miao Village. *International Journal of Heritage Studies, 21*(10), 1016–1035.

Yuan, G. (1987). *Born Red. A Chronicle of the Cultural Revolution.* Stanford: Stanford University Press.

Yunnan gov. (Yunnan Provincial Government). (2005). *Yunnan People's Government's Opinion on Advancing the Development of the Tea Industry.* http://law1.law-star.com/law?fn=lar444s769.txt.

Yunnan gov. (Yunnan Provincial Government). (2015). *Pu'er Tea Origin Cultural Park.* http://pelc.yninvest.gov.cn/InvestDetail.aspx?id=3374.

Zhang, J. (2014). *Puer Tea. Ancient Canvas and Urban Chic.* Seattle and London: Washington University Press.

Zhong, Y. (2003). *Local Government and Politics in China. Challenges from Below* (M.E. Sharpe Paperback). London and New York: Routledge.

Zhu, Y. (2016). Heritage Making of Lijiang: Governance, Reconstruction and Local Naxi Life. In C. Brumann & D. Berliner (Eds.), *World Heritage on the Ground. Ethnographic Perspectives* (pp. 78–96). Oxford: Berghahn.

Zhu, Y., & Li, N. (2013). Groping for Stones to Cross the River: Governing Heritage in Emei. In T. Blumenfield & H. Silverman (Eds.), *Cultural Heritage Politics in China* (pp. 51–71). New York: Springer.

CHAPTER 3

Ethnicity, Heritage and Human Rights in the Union of Myanmar

William Logan

Introduction

Heritage is formed and maintained (or neglected and abandoned) within a context of power relations between peoples at local, national and global levels. It is often called upon to serve the interests of the nation state and dominant groups and actors within it. Most states are not nation states in the sense of being mono-cultural political entities; most are multicultural but many to recognize the fact in legal, political and structural terms (Logan 2014). In such circumstances, heritage practices tend to favour the set of social values ascribed to by the dominant group, although these may be contested by those holding other values. Governments play contradictory roles in endorsing particular heritage elements on the one hand and seeking to resolve, assuage or prevent heritage contestation. On the other hand, their intervention sometimes merely aggravates conflicts. In post-colonial societies and states that are coming out of periods of military rule or international isolation, governments have the potential to develop new, inclusive forms of heritage. Very often, however, all one

W. Logan (✉)
Deakin University, Burwood, VIC, Australia

© The Author(s) 2018
J. Rodenberg and P. Wagenaar (eds.), *Cultural Contestation*,
Palgrave Studies in Cultural Heritage and Conflict,
https://doi.org/10.1007/978-3-319-91914-0_3

sees is the reinforcement of the new dominant group's heritage and the continued marginalization of minorities groups and their heritage. This scenario connects with issues of individual and collective human rights, especially when intangible, embodied heritage is concerned.

This paper considers these theoretical assertions in the case of the Republic of the Union of Myanmar, based on field observations and interviews conducted in 2013–2015 in the capital city, Naypyidaw; the former capital, Yangon (Rangoon); the country's second city largest city, Mandalay; and in Shan State. The chapter refers to several initiatives to protect Myanmar's physical heritage, notably through the UNESCO World Heritage system and in Yangon. While these efforts worthwhile, the need to protect inanimate structures is less important safeguarding the intangible heritage of traditional skills and practices belonging to the country's ethnic minorities, especially the Muslim Rohingya people in Rakhine State where evidence points to their being subjected to ethnic cleansing.

A British colony until 1948, independent Myanmar (then Burma) had been one of the first countries to adopt the Universal Declaration on Human Rights (1948) at the United Nations, and it provided the UN with its third Secretary-General, U Thant (1962–1971). The country collapsed in 1962 into a long period military rule following a coup d'état led by General Ne Win and, as a result of the military regime's attitudes and actions, Myanmar became known in the late 1990s and 2000s as having the world's worst human rights record, an international pariah status from which it has only recently begun to re-emerge. The military authorities consistently denied allegations of human rights abuses as they related, for instance, to forced labour on state projects, including restoration of heritage monuments (Nwe and Philp 2002: 153) and rejected international pressures from human rights agencies as interference in Myanmar's internal affairs. The state-sponsored media poured ridicule on the concept of human rights as a Western notion alien to Burmese traditional values.

Following the military junta ceding power to a semi-civilian government in 2011, new ideas about the country's identity, heritage, human rights and governance began to circulate more freely in the print and digital media, books, conferences, consultancies to government agencies and private conversations. Some promising signs that the country might create new, more inclusive conceptions of heritage appeared under President U Thein Sein (2011–2015). Hopes, however, that the victory of the National League for Democracy led by Nobel Peace Prize recipient, Daw Aung San Suu Kyi, in the November 2015 elections would facilitate this have been dashed so far. The recognition of minority group heritage, difficult as it is for government policy makers, has been disappointingly slow. Indeed, in some religious minority cases, most notably the Muslim Rohingya, in the eyes of many observers, the state's interventions have only made matters worse.

ETHNICITY AND GOVERNANCE

The Burman Majority

Inter-ethnic relations have long lain at the heart of Myanmar's governance system and its failings. While Myanmar is a multi-ethnic state, one ethnic group—the Burman, or Bamar—dominate demographically (68% of the total population) as well as economically and politically. Their language, Burmese, is of the Tibeto-Burman linguistic group, and they adhere to the Theravada form of Buddhism. In Myanmar, the various ethnic nationalities are distributed in separate areas that form the geographical basis of governance in the Union. Thus, the Burman are concentrated in the Irrawaddy (Ayeyarwady) River valley and in the coastal strips, with an original homeland in the central dry zone. In the governance structure, they have seven administrative units, called Regions (formerly Divisions), whereas the other main ethnic minority groups have their own States (Fig. 3.1).

The military regime had a Burman basis and this meant that protection of the cultural heritage of the dominant Burman ethnic group was prioritized. Some scholars have argued, in fact, that the military regime appropriated the country's Buddhist heritage of archaeological sites and urban pagodas to bolster its own legitimacy (Philp and Mercer 2002; Philp 2010). By contrast, the cultures of the ethnic minorities, or ethnic nationality groups, as they prefer to be called—the Mon, Kayin (Karen), Kayah, Shan, Kachin, Chin and Rakhine—were seen as expendable, and there is a history of attempts to enforce assimilation.

Yangon—always the largest city, currently with a population estimated at over five million (RUM 2014)—was capital of British Burma and independent Myanmar until the military junta decided to create a new capital at Naypyidaw in November 2005. Yangon lies on the eastern estuary of the Irrawaddy, 40 kilometres from the Andaman Sea, an ideal

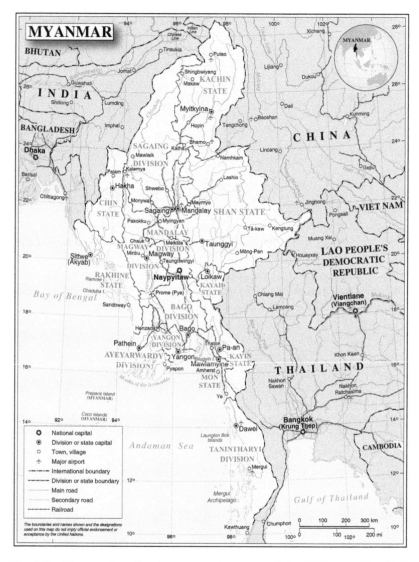

Fig. 3.1 Myanmar's political structure (courtesy of the UN; map No. 4168 Rev. 3, June 2012). Available at: http://www.un.org/Depts/Cartographic/map/profile/myanmar.pdf (accessed 15 March 2017)

location for the trading and administrative town the British needed to exploit Burma's raw materials. The magnificent pre-colonial Shwedagon is Yangon's heritage centrepiece in its setting of hills and the treeline avenues and gardens designed by colonial engineers and architects, while the Sule Pagoda is an impressive feature of the downtown area. Colonial immigration policies aimed to attract labour for the fast-growing city, and Yangon's colonial population became overwhelmingly Indian with sizeable British, mainly Scottish, other European and Chinese components. Burman residents came to dominate in the post-colonial period, but distinctive Indian and Chinese quarters remain in Yangon's downtown. There are also large numbers of Shan, Rakhine and Karen living in Yangon.

The Shan

The Shan are the next largest ethnic group both numerically and in terms of geographical spread. Their language is of the same group as Thai and Lao, although most Shan, apart from those in the extreme east, are now more closely allied to the Burman and use the Burmese language. Shan State itself in fact houses at least eight ethnic groups apart from the Shan themselves and has an exceedingly rich set of local community cultures, especially intangible form such as pottery, weaving, traditional instrument and hat-making and the preparation of traditional foods. Other aspects of cultural heritage importance to the ethnic minority groups in Shan State and elsewhere include language, sacred sites, festivals and indigenous medicine.

As my field work in the northern Shan village of Nam Khan showed, the survival of some of this intangible heritage is threatened due both to the lack of official support and, more importantly, the preference of today's younger generation to work in more lucrative work in the big cities. Instrument-making has been conducted by one family for five generations, with markets extending into China, Thailand, Singapore and even the UK, but the son is a doctor and neither he nor his sister is interested in carrying on the business. There are 16 potteries in Nam Khan and none have children wanting to take over. On the other hand, a number of girls are involved in hat-making and weaving production, again mostly for the Chinese market, and these skills seem better placed to survive into the next generation.

Maintaining the Shan language has been difficult in the past and remains so, although to a lesser extent. Schools are now bringing Shan language into the curriculum alongside Burmese. During my visit to Nam Khan in May 2014, a weekend class of 110 students was observed being taught the Shan linguistic and literary heritage by a group of Buddhist monks trained in Sri Lanka. Meanwhile, gunshots were heard across the Kachin State border nearby where Kachin, Palaung and Shan militia had teamed up against government troops who were ostensibly seeking to stop cross-border smuggling of gems, timber and most probably drugs.

The class was taking place under the cover of a training course in Buddhism, indicating the low level of support for the inter-generational transmission of ethnic nationality cultures from the central government and, especially, the Myanmar army—the Tatmadaw. They do, however, tolerate some locally developed protective mechanisms in various ethnic states, such as the Shan Literature and Culture Association. This association has branches throughout Shan State and in Yangon and Mandalay and has been lobbying authorities at national and State levels to develop language teaching materials for primary schools. Some success has been achieved in influencing national education policy, and the national Ministry of Education has been collaborating with the Ministry of Culture to start teaching eight ethnic languages in relevant parts of the country in 2015 or 2016 (interview U Nyi Moon, Director Department of Archaeology and National Museums, Lashio, 12 May 2014).

Other Ethnic Nationalities

The other main ethnic nationalities might have their own States but the executive governments at State level face many constraints on their capacity to administer their people and areas effectively. Despite the decentralization moves made under President Thein Sein, they are still dominated by a top-down appointment process and ministers have little control over the administrative apparatus (Nixon et al. 2013: v). Budgets allocated by Naypyidaw are small and prepared in a way that reinforces central influence. Since both the ethnic nationality States and the Burman-dominated Regions are constitutionally equivalent, these structural limitations apply to both sets of political units. Because of the ethnic dimension, however, these constraints lead to tensions and conflict in the States in a way that does not occur in the Regions.

However, there is another form of governance that is largely outside the control of the Myanmar state. Extensive sections of the country and their resident populations are controlled to varying degrees by ethnic nationality-based armed groups. Several of these groups, most notably the Kachin, Mon and Kayin (Karen), have developed civil administrative structures in their areas that parallel the Myanmar government system, including for health, land and education (MCRB 2016: 18). In these areas, education has in recent years begun to focus on teaching ethnic minority languages and religion, as part of transmitting indigenous culture to the next generation.

Rakhine State is a special case in having a cultural divide based on religion and language. While Rakhine Buddhists number about two million, the Rohingya Muslims—in fact a Sufi-influenced variation of Sunni Islam (Albert 2017)—number about 800,000–1.2 million (Ware 2015). The Rohingya speak an Indo-Aryan language of Bengali–Assamese lineage that is completely different in origin and linguistic characteristics from Burmese (Ibrahim 2016: 21). These cultural differences are the long-standing cause of hostility towards and oppression of the Rohingya. The Myanmar Center for Responsible Business (MCRB) makes a more general point, arguing that religion and language practices constitute 'a critical cultural heritage…which ethnic minorities are seeking to preserve in the face of a perceived or actual "Burmanization" policy by the central Government intended to suppress ethnic minority cultures, languages and religions' (MCRB 2016: 18).

Ethnic Minorities Without Nationality Status

Some, especially smaller ethnic minorities do not have nationality status and have little political autonomy. This includes Myanmar's Indian and Chinese citizens living in cities like Yangon and Mandalay. Their heritage is touched on below in the context of the protection of Yangon's built heritage. By contrast, other small ethnic communities enjoy considerable autonomy, a notable case being the Kokang Chinese community in northern Shan State (Kyu 2016). They comprise 90% of the population within the section of Shan State between the Salween River and the Chinese border and have been given political status as the Kokang Special Region. They now have a degree of autonomy that underpins a vibrant economy and that should enable better heritage protection.

UNITY AND DIVERSITY

The Burman thus toe a very fine line between asserting neo-colonial and undemocratic central control over the country's other ethnic groups and providing the strong central rule that is probably needed to hold together the seven Burman-dominated Regions and seven ethnic nationality States that make up the Union, to boost the economy and to improve living standards. In this context, cultural heritage has played and continues to play a critical role in Burmese nation-building, especially as seen from the Burman viewpoint. As I have explained in another paper (Logan 2016a: 261–262), a visit to the 'Twelve National Objectives and Nation-Building Endeavours Showroom' in the National Museum in Yangon is instructive in this regard. Here, the government's emphasis on holding the Union together and the use of cultural heritage in the process is seen, especially in its listing of 'four social objectives'. In an attempt to balance the interests of both the Myanmar state and the ethnic nationalities and other groups, all citizens are exhorted to 'Uplift...national prestige and integrity [and] preservation and safeguarding of cultural heritage and national character'.

It is also very clear from my observations and discussions with Burman in Yangon, Mandalay and Naypyidaw that such calls to unity largely fall on deaf ears. While multiculturalism is tolerated, the Burman see themselves as the country's 'real' citizens. In everyday language, this comes out in the way the Burman refer to the Indian and Chinese communities as 'ethnic groups' but do not use the term for themselves. Indeed, the language used to refer to the ethnic minorities in Myanmar is fraught with difficulty. In a MCRB discussion in Yangon in September 2015 the Karen, Rakhine, Chin, Kachin, Mon and Danu participants made clear that the term 'ethnic nationality' was preferred to the more commonly used term 'ethnic minority', which they saw as implying inferior status (MCRB 2016: 5). This is line with the 2008 Constitution which makes no reference to ethnic minorities, or indeed indigenous peoples, instead using the term 'national races'. The Constitution does not, however, define the term but seems to rely on a much disputed list of 135 'national races' that was in turn based on a dubious 1931 colonial census (ibid.). The list includes the majority Burman/Bamar and seven other significant ethnic minority groups, but Myanmar people of Indian, Nepali or Chinese ancestry are not included among the 135, nor are the Rohingya people in Rakhine State.

The ethnic nationalities hold many grievances against the Myanmar state, including the limited opportunities for self-governance; the lack of benefit from the development of resource in their territories; physical abuse and land-grabbing by the Tatmadaw; discrimination in the workplace; inadequate support for their cultures, in particular restrictions on religion and language education. Some of these grievances also apply to ethnic minorities not recognized as ethnic nationalities, such as Myanmar's urban Indians, who are Hindu, but they are most severely felt in ethnic zones, leading to mass displacement and exodus. Such hostility and conflict between the Tatmadaw and ethnic nationality-based militias have exacerbated matters by inhibiting economic development in ethnic areas and contributing to very high poverty rates. An estimated 73% of the population in Chin State live below the poverty line, 44% in Rakhine State and 28% in Shan and Kachin States, compared with the national poverty rate of 26%, which is the worst in Southeast Asia (UNDP 2017; UNICEF 2017).

The conflict between the military government and the non-Burman ethnic militias is extremely complex. On the one hand, the latter often had no feasible means of engaging with the desires and proposals of the military governments and would resort to infighting or break ceasefire agreements when the Tatmadaw conducted military operations in their territories (Paode 2017). On the other hand, it appears that there are elements in the leadership of both the military and the non-Burman States who find advantages, including pecuniary, from its continuation (Hindstrom 2016). Either way, the goal of achieving tangible ethnic reconciliation has proven elusive.

Nevertheless, after President Thein Sein's government took office in March 2011, a process of national reconciliation was pushed vigorously and a ceasefire realized on separate occasions with 14 of the 16 ethnic armed groups. In a fifth round of talks in August 2014, the government side made the major concession of agreeing to the ethnic armed groups' demand for a federal system of government (Weng 2014). In return, the ethnic armed groups agreed to the government's insistence on the principles of non-disintegration of the union, non-disintegration of national solidarity and perpetuation of sovereignty. Daw Aung San Suu Kyi and her NLD government have declared that top priority is to continue the peace process and build a federal democratic union (Mang 2015). Meanwhile, the military have not ceded full authority to the NLD government, the Tatmadaw's commander-in-chief declaring in 2015 that the military will only step out of politics when the civil war was over and peace prevailed (ibid.).

COLLECTIVE RIGHTS TO CULTURAL HERITAGE

To return to the Shan language and literature course referred to above, if stronger application of international human rights principles existed in Myanmar, the course would not have had to operate under cover. As Farida Shaheed, former Independent Expert in the field of cultural rights at the United Nations High Commission for Human Rights in Geneva, advised the UN Human Rights Council in 2011,

> Cultural heritage is linked to human dignity and identity. Accessing and enjoying cultural heritage is an important feature of being a member of a community, a citizen and, more widely, a member of society. The importance of having access to one's own cultural heritage, including linguistic heritage, and to that of others has been emphasized by the [UN] Committee on Economic, Social and Cultural Rights in general comment No. 21 on the right of everyone to take part in cultural life. (United Nations Human Rights Council 2011)

Upholding the collective rights of minorities within Asian states generally seems, however, to face even less commitment than protecting individual rights (Logan 2016b). Indeed, in Asia, collective rights are nearly always narrowly defined and sometimes actively opposed. This is generally because they are seen to be inimical to 'nation-building'. Some Asian states go further and deny that they have any racial or ethnic minority groups at all (Logan 2016c: 165).

There is no doubt that Myanmar's diverse ethnic groups possess a rich set of cultural heritages. To its credit, and despite the fraught political context in the country, the Union has put in place a number of legal and administrative measures to protect some aspects of these heritages, although restrictive conditions apply. The legal protections are contained within the Myanmar Constitution and in legislation.

1. *Constitution*

British rule over Myanmar (then called Burma) ended in January 1948. The various ethnic minorities worked with Burman leaders under General Aung San to amend the 1947 Constitution to establish a genuine federation of states. These principles, laid out in the Panglong Agreement of the same year, were ignored after the 1962 military coup d'état. Following another coup in 1988, Myanmar's military-based

Law and Order Reconstruction Council (SLORC) suspended the 1974 Constitution. Twenty years later, the military government, now the State Peace and Development Council (SPDC), created the country's third and current Constitution. This was ratified in May 2008 following a referendum that was regarded as fraudulent by the opposition, led by Daw Aung San Suu Kyi's National League for Democracy, as well as by external observers.[1]

The 2008 Constitution sets some important principles in relation to cultural heritage albeit within certain conditions. Art. 22 of the Constitution provides for '(i) development of language, literature, fine arts and culture of the national races; and (ii) promotion of solidarity, mutual amity and respect and mutual assistance among the national races; and promotion of socio-economic development including education, health, economy, transport and communication, of less-developed national races'. Article 364 asserts that '[e]very citizen shall, in accordance with the law, have the right to freely develop literature, culture, arts, customs and traditions they cherish'.

Article 364 continues on to set a significant parameter, however, by declaring that '[i]n the process they shall avoid any act detrimental to national solidarity'. Article 390 states that every citizen has the duty to assist the Union of Myanmar in carrying out, inter alia, the preservation and safeguarding of cultural heritage, and Article 365 also provides that 'any particular action which might affect the interests of one or several other of the national races shall be taken…' only after obtaining the 'settlement of those affected'. It is important to note that not only are these protections and the exercise of these rights circumscribed by the notion of 'national solidarity', but the articles apply only to Myanmar citizens. Over a million ethnic minority people, including the Rohingya, are without proper identification documents and are thus denied citizenship.

2. *Legislation*

Only two pieces of cultural heritage legislation currently exist in Myanmar. These are *The Protection and Preservation of Ancient Monuments Law* (Myanmar 2015a) and *The Protection and Preservation of Ancient Objects Law* (Myanmar 2015b). These were passed by the Myanmar parliament (Pyidaungsu Hlattaw) and replace the *Protection and Preservation of Cultural Heritage Regions Law* that the SPDC had enacted in 1998 and amended in 2009. Myanmar's highly conservative cultural heritage management system run by the Department of Archaeology in the Ministry of Culture falls under these laws. Neither law makes reference to minority cultures, although people's use of monuments and artefacts is mentioned. Article 2 of the 1998 law had at least inferred that Myanmar's ethnic nationalities might have significant cultural heritage when it said in Article 2a that 'Cultural Heritage means ancient monument or site which is required to be protected and preserved by reason of its historical, cultural, artistic or *anthropological* value' (my emphasis). The earlier Act also invoked the year 1886 as a cutting off point. The 2015 laws show a little more flexibility in this respect, requiring some forms of cultural heritage to be more than 100 years old rather than nominating a fixed date. However, such a requirement seems to leave many significant twentieth-century monuments, sites and artefacts outside the law and means, for instance, that the laws have little relevance to the urban heritage of Yangon and other cities and towns. There is no mention of intangible heritage or human or cultural rights in either law.

Heritage Initiatives Under President Thein Sein

Under U Thein Sein's presidency, considerable political, economic and social liberalization occurred, at least in the initial years, giving Myanmar renewed acceptance within international community institutions such as the UN and UNESCO. The media was allowed greater freedom and political protests were tolerated. A street exhibition set up to coincide with President Obama's November 2014 visit to Yangon in was allowed to remain for many months (see Logan 2016a: Fig. 14.6). After decades of suppression, interest emerged in developing the Rangoon and other universities.

In the heritage field, three major, new initiatives emerged that gave promise of a more inclusive approach to heritage protection. These relate to the urban heritage of Yangon, World Heritage and intangible cultural heritage (ICH). I have dealt with Yangon's urban heritage in detail elsewhere (Logan 2015, 2016b). Suffice to say here that although efforts are being made to create an adequately skilled heritage planning staff at the Yangon City Development Committee (Yangon's municipal government), much responsibility lies with the Yangon Heritage Trust, a non-government organization founded by Dr. Thant Myint U in 2012. As an NGO, the Trust is vulnerable to resource deficiencies and to opposition from property developers. While there seems to be a broad acceptance by the Burman middle class of the importance of the colonial buildings in downtown Yangon, this may not be true of the majority of the city's residents. To draw local working communities and ethnic minority in-migrants into the process of heritage identification and management is urgent and is likely to bring intangible forms of heritage to the fore.

World Heritage

Efforts in the 1990s to inscribe Bagan on the World Heritage List had fallen into disarray for a host of essentially political reasons. The military government felt its fingers had been burned, rejected the World Heritage system and went about restoration work without advice from the World Heritage Centre or the International Council on Monuments and Sites (ICOMOS). This was extremely damaging to the fabric of Bagan's temples and creates technical problems that will need to be in the World Heritage nomination dossier and management plan currently being prepared.[2]

The Thein Sein government tested UNESCO waters in 2013–2014 with the serial site nomination of the Pyu Cities to the World Heritage List. The Pyu Cities were inscribed at the 38th Session of the World Heritage Committee at Doha in June 2014, although not without some difficulty. The nomination had been negatively viewed by ICOMOS, which recommended deferral, but this was overturned by the Committee, partly because of ICOMOS's bungled report but also partly because of the Committee's good will towards Myanmar, a developing country opening up to the world, transitioning to democracy and, at that point, without any World Heritage inscriptions.

More ethnically inclusive intentions are shown by Myanmar's Tentative List of places it intends to nominate to the World Heritage List in future. There are 14 heritage places on the Tentative List, submitted in two equal batches, the first in 1996 and the second in 2014. The first batch consists mostly of ancient archaeological sites—'Cultural' sites in World Heritage terminology—and relatively well spread across the Union: five in Burman Divisions, including one in the Buddhist part of Rakhine State, and two in Shan State. All of the sites in the second batch are classified as 'Natural': wildlife sanctuaries, national parks, forest reserves and an archipelago. Three are in Kachin State and the remainder in Burman Divisions.

Of course, successful nomination of the proposed sites is contingent upon Myanmar's ability to meet the new World Heritage Committee requirements, especially the UNESCO World Heritage and Sustainable Development policy (UNESCO 2015). Should Myanmar recognize its ethnic nationalities as 'indigenous peoples', their free, prior and informed consent to a site being nominated would also be required. Subsequently, successful management is above all contingent upon the attainment of peace in the relevant political unit(s).

Intangible Cultural Heritage

Moves in the intangible cultural heritage (ICH) field are more fundamentally important to Myanmar's future peace and prosperity than either the work of the Yangon Heritage Trust or World Heritage. ICH, which UNESCO's Intangible Cultural Heritage Convention describes as 'practices, representations, expressions, knowledge, skills' (UNESCO 2003: Article 2), applies to all components of the population and parts of the country. Because this is heritage that is embodied in people rather than in inanimate, tangible places and artefacts and because it is the basis of their self- and collective identity, methods used to safeguard it have to be sensitive to the needs and desires of the ICH holders. The ICH holders have personal and collective rights that should not be trampled upon by governments and their heritage agencies, however, well-intentioned these might be (Logan 2007).

In 2014, a major national project began to collect, catalogue, document ICH across all states in the Union as a preliminary to ratifying UNESCO's (2003) Convention for the Safeguarding of the Intangible Cultural Heritage, which it did in May of that year. The UNESCO Bangkok Office has provided support to the project, beginning with a national workshop in Mandalay, also in May 2014, and extending into a major capacity building project using Italian funds (US$1.4 million) and expertise that ended in 2016 (UNESCO 2016). Most importantly, the project has the potential to identify, record and lead to official recognition of the cultural practices of all ethnic groups across all states of the Union. New lines of dialogue may be opened up between Myanmar's various ethnic groups and strengthen human rights within the country. Several major concerns arise, however, if the project is to succeed. The powerful ethnic politics that underlies the Union state and its functioning cannot at this stage be discounted. Myanmar will need to overcome its poor human rights record so that the project can engage in good faith throughout its duration with the local people who are the ICH holders. The project should extend beyond identification and recording to inter-generational transmission.

HERITAGE AND HUMAN RIGHTS

Some observers (e.g., Einhorn 2014) saw the early positive moves made by President Thein Sein on the human rights front stalling after 2012. Daw Aung San Suu Kyi's government also began by attempting to promote human rights but has so far had very mixed success. In line the recommendations of some scholars, analysts and observers who argued the importance of giving ethnic minorities space at the podium of the State Assembly, the NLD government has appointed members of ethnic nationalities as deputy speaker of the Lower House (Kachin) and speaker and deputy of the Upper House (Karen and Rakhine). In addition, a Chin member of parliament was appointed as the second vice-president of Myanmar. In October 2016, the government framed a new policy of national reconciliation that builds on the ideas of Aung San, Suu Kyi's father, when he negotiated the 1947 Panglong Agreement. The seven points of her policy are to review and amend the political dialogue framework; convene a twenty-first-century Panglong Conference; sign a Union peace agreement based on this conference; amend the 2008 Constitution; hold multiparty democratic elections in accordance with the amended Constitution; and build a democratic federal union (Paode 2017). While this stepped process seems to be generally perceived at home and abroad to be more substantive than the previous military governments' efforts, cultural heritage and cultural rights are not directly addressed.

It is unfortunate that some of the stronger armed ethnic groups refused to sign the Nationwide Ceasefire Agreement brokered in 2015 and did not participate the twenty-first-century Panglong Conference in 2016. Armed fighting continues between the Myanmar Army and ethnic groups in Kachin and elsewhere and there are still very many deaths, injuries and villagers displaced in the war-torn northern region. Paode (2017) concludes that the continuing armed conflict in Myanmar testifies to the 'stiff political differences and antagonism between the Myanmar Army and the non-ceasefire groups' and that the NLD government does not seem to have the necessary power to really pursue national reconciliation.

The Rohingya

With regard to cultural diversity and heritage, none of Myanmar's recent leaders, including President U Thein Sein, the current President Htin Kyaw (appointed March 2016) and Daw Aung San Suu Kyi, has yet to articulate a policy framework for protecting the cultures and cultural heritage of the ethnic minorities. The few public interventions by Daw Aung San Suu Kyi have tended to aggravate rather than assuage inter-ethnic tensions.

Most of the Muslims living in Rakhine State self-identify as Rohingya but are portrayed by Buddhist nationalists led by the Association for Protection of Race and Religion (known by its Burmese acronym, MaBaTha) and by the military as Bengali economic migrants who have entered Myanmar illegally from neighbouring Bangladesh (Lee 2015). The Buddhist nationalists have considerable public support in Burman and other parts of the country for their campaign to protect the religion against perceived threats, particularly Islam (ICG 2014: 8). Ironically, the relaxed freedom of speech since 2011 enables ethno-religious nationalism to flourish as well as the systematic persecution of the Rohingya that has been experienced since at least the 1962 military coup (Ware 2015; Lee 2016). Such persecution includes government policies restricting the Rohingya in relation to travel, marriage, pregnancy outside of marriage as well as economic activity, such as stipulations on work and forced labour. Lee (2015) concludes that 'To many, northern Rakhine State resembles an open prison'.

Most Rohingya have not been recognized as Myanmar citizens since 1982, rendering them effectively stateless and thus marginalized and vulnerable (Lee 2015; Albert 2017). This is despite the fact that they, their parents and grandparents, were almost all born in what is now Myanmar (Ware 2015). Indeed, according to the Rohingya themselves and some scholars, such as Ibrahim (2016: 18–20), many have a history in the coastal Arakan area going back more than a millennium, a very long time before the British imposed the Myanmar political boundary on the area (1886) and at least as long as the Buddhist Rakhine ethnic group migrated into the area from central Myanmar (c. 1000 AD). Others such as Albert (2017) see the Rohingya as moving into the area in pre-colonial and colonial times.

The latest outbreak of violence, beginning in June 2012 and spurred on by Wirathu, a Mandalay-based Buddhist monk, has resulted in 280 killed, rapes, the burning of homes and the displacement of almost 130,000 people.[3] Around 88,000 fled Myanmar in small boats in 2014 and early 2015 (Albert 2017). Ware (2015) cites figures from the Office of the United Nations High Commission for Refugees (UNHCR) that the agency was caring for 140,000 in internal displacement camps in Rakhine State, 47,000 in camps in Malaysia and 33,000 in camps in Bangladesh. According to Ware (2015), there were more than 300,000 illegally living in Bangladesh in 2015 after fleeing Myanmar. A serious flare-up began October 2016 saw more deaths, villages destroyed and, in the three months from August 2017, at least another 620,000 fled into Bangladesh (Associated Press 2017; Kitwood 2017). The number of boat refugees built up quickly, despite moves to block them by some neighbouring states, such as Thailand. Malaysia's foreign minister, by contrast, has described what is going on in Rakhine State as ethnic cleansing and crimes against humanity as have the UNHCR head and Human Rights Watch (Albert 2017; Human Rights Watch 2015). Historian Azeem Ibrahim (2016) goes further to see it as the wiping out of a people and their culture—which he calls a hidden genocide.

The response from the United Nations has been highly critical, especially from its Special Rapporteur on Human Rights, Yanghee Lee. Human rights NGOs such as Amnesty International, Human Rights Watch, along with Médecins Sans Frontières called on Myanmar to change its approach. Foreign governments have reacted in a variety of ways from the strident criticism of Malaysia and the USA under the Obama and Trump Administrations to the more muted criticism from Europe and Australia and silence from China and ASEAN countries. Some foreign scholars and members of the media are condemning Suu Kyi and her government for not having made any public declaration in support of Rohingya rights either before or after the election, and the minority continues to be persecuted (Ponniah 2017; Griffiths 2016; *The New York Times* 2016; Green 2015; Lee 2014).

Daw Aung San Suu Kyi and the NLD have themselves struggled to decide their position. Anti-Muslim sentiment among Buddhists across Myanmar makes it politically difficult for the government to take steps seen as supportive of Muslim rights (ICG 2014: 8; Albert 2017). This has led them into apparently contradictory actions. For instance, in May–June 2016, Suu Kyi asked foreign ambassadors and the UN Special

Rapporteur not to use the term Rohingya and to refer to them instead as the 'Muslim community in Rakhine State' (Slodkowski 2016a). She made the same request of Pope Francis who visited in November 2017 (Pullella 2017). This puts her in the same rank as the military, the Buddhist ethno-nationalists and the Rakhine State's Buddhist majority, all of whom reject the label Rohingya.

The European Union decided to respect her request, whereas the USA indicated it would continue using the term, citing respect for the right of communities to choose what they should be called (Slodkowski 2016b). The EU's softer position was based on the assessment that Suu Kyi's position vis-à-vis the military remains vulnerable and that her government required 'political space' to find a solution to the persecution of the Rohingya. It is, of course, true that Suu Kyi's position is difficult: the NLD may have won the November 2015 election, but a quarter of the seats in parliament are still reserved for the military and several powerful ex-generals remain active behind the scenes. She has to move carefully. While urging against the use of inflammatory terms, she did nevertheless allow the establishment of an Advisory Commission on Rakhine State in August 2016 comprising six local and three international experts and chaired by former UN Secretary-General Kofi Annan to discuss ways to resolve ethnic conflict in Rakhine state (Albert 2017). The Advisory Commission presented its wide-ranging final report in August 2017 (Advisory Commission 2017). It has made recommendations in relation to socio-economic and cultural development, citizenship, freedom of movement, communal participation and representation, internally displaced persons, internal cohesion, the security of all communities and bilateral cooperation with Bangladesh. The Advisory Commission also proposed a ministerial-level appointment whose role would be to coordinate policy on Rakhine State and ensure effective implementation of the recommendations.

At the time of writing (November 2017), Daw Aung San Suu Kyi and the government have yet to respond, although she is promising a repatriation programme for Rohingya now held in refugee camps in Bangladesh. A bilateral agreement with Bangladesh to enable such a programme although the number to be allowed back was not specified nor was the term Rohingya used in the statement issued by Suu Kyi's office (Associated Press 2017).

Conclusion

There are four levels in the political hierarchy of multicultural Myanmar—Burman at the top, State-based ethnic nationalities, the descendants of colonial-era Indian and Chinese immigrants, and the Muslim Rohingya at the bottom. This is reflected in the way the cultural heritage of each group has been treated. While the conception of heritage is now being recast as the regime changes, building human rights into heritage policy, however, requires more wholesome support from the NLD government of Daw Aung San Suu Kyi. If the cultural rights of each layer in the hierarchy and a more inclusive definition of the national heritage could be achieved, it would help defuse inter-ethnic conflict. Interpretations of the past can be opened out so as to recognize the roles played by minority groups in the national story, to engage them more fully in celebration of the nation's achievements, and to recognize injustices done to them in the past (Logan 2007: 42, 49). This may also help to bring Myanmar back in line with the universal principles underlying the UDHR and other international human rights statements.

Instead ethnicity and governance still intersect in Myanmar to deny basic human rights, and heritage practice is complicit in the current arrangement. Of course, we know from hundreds of published case studies that states all round the world use heritage for political purposes as defined by those with political power. The key issue for heritage practitioners, whether in policy-making situations, in academia or out in the field, is to find ways to demonstrate commitment to securing greater social justice. Cultural heritage protection needs to be seen not merely as a technical matter but within the wider social justice and human rights framework (Logan 2008: 439). Such a call to demonstrate commitment is consistent with the rights-based approach to heritage management that is steadily being adopted in UNESCO and its advisory bodies as well as in many of its member states (Ekern et al. 2012; Larsen and Logan 2018). Issues bearing on human rights exist in relation to tangible heritage, such as World Heritage, but are even more critical in relation to intangible heritage since it is living heritage that is both embodied in people and fundamental to their identity and well-being. It is essential to keep the pressure on states to abide by international human rights norms and, in Myanmar's case, to safeguard the heritage of all its peoples and cease activities regarding the Rohingya that have all the hallmarks of ethnic cleansing.

Notes

1. It was the 2008 Constitution that prevented Aung San Suu Kyi from standing directly for the presidency in the November 2015 elections. Specifically, Clause 59(f) disallows anyone from standing whose children are citizens of a foreign country or married to foreigners. Since she has two sons with British citizenship and married to non-Burmese citizens, she was ineligible. The current de jure president is Htin Kyaw. Nevertheless, Aung San Suu Kyi is the de facto head of government and the dominant state figure through her positions as State Counsellor of Myanmar and leader of the ruling National League for Democracy.
2. The Bagan nomination dossier and management plan are due to be completed in 2017 with Japanese funds and submitted to the World Heritage Committee in 2018 (UNESCO 2016). The process was set back by a major earthquake that damaged more than 100 pagodas in August 2016 (*The Guardian* 2016).
3. In March 2017, Myanmar's top Buddhist body, the State Sangha Maha Nayaka Committee, banned Wirathu from giving sermons for 12 months. The Sangha rarely imposes such sanctions but did so in this case because Wirathu 'had delivered hate speech against religions to cause communal strife and hinder efforts to uphold the rule of law' (Murdoch 2017).

References

Advisory Commission on Rakhine State (Advisory Commission). (2017). *Towards a Peaceful, Fair and Prosperous Future for the People of Rakhine* (Final Report of the Advisory Commission on Rakhine State). Available at: http://www.rakhinecommission.org/. Accessed 27 Nov 2017.

Albert, E. (2017). *The Rohingya Migrant Crisis.* CPR Backgrounder, Council on Foreign Relations. Available at: http://www.cfr.org/burmamyanmar/rohingya-migrant-crisis/p36651. Accessed 10 Mar 2017.

Associated Press. (2017, November 23). Myanmar, Bangladesh Sign Agreement on Rohingya Refugees. *The Washington Post.* Available at: https://www.washingtonpost.com/world/asia_pacific/myanmar-bangladesh-sign-agreement-on-rohingya-refugees/2017/11/23/60f86e68-d048-11e7-a87b-47f14b73162a_story.html?utm_term=.f6942d01bff6. Accessed 27 Nov 2017.

Einhorn, B. (2014, November 14). Obama Visits Myanmar, a Success Story That Has Soured. *Bloomberg Business Week.* Available at: https://www.bloomberg.com/news/articles/2014-11-13/obama-visits-myanmar-a-success-story-that-has-soured. Accessed 9 Mar 2017.

Ekern, S., Logan, W., Sauge, B., & Larsen, A. S. (Eds.). (2012). Human Rights and World Heritage: Preserving Our Common Dignity Through Rights-Based Approaches to Site Management. *International Journal of Heritage Studies, 18*(3), 213–225; Updated in Ekern et al. (Eds.). (2015). *World Heritage Management and Human Rights.* London: Routledge, 1–13.

Green, P. (2015, May 20). Aung San Suu Kyi's Silence on the Genocide of Rohingya Muslims is Tantamount to Complicity. *The Independent.* Available at: http://www.independent.co.uk/voices/comment/aung-san-suu-kyis-silence-on-the-genocide-of-rohingya-muslims-is-tantamount-to-complicity-10264497.html. Accessed 9 Mar 2017.

Griffiths, J. (2016). *Is the Lady Listening? Aung San Suu Kyi Accused of Ignoring Myanmar's Muslims.* CNN Cable News Network. Available at: http://edition.cnn.com/2016/11/17/asia/myanmar-rohingya-aung-san-suu-kyi/. Accessed 9 Mar 2017.

Hindstrom, H. (2016, April 1). Burma's Transition to Civilian Rule Hasn't Stopped the Abuses of Its Ethnic Wars. *Time.* Available at: http://time.com/4277328/burma-myanmar-suu-kyi-ethnic-wars/. Accessed 15 Mar 2017.

Human Rights Watch. (2015, May 16). *Burma: Reject Discriminatory Population Bill.* Available at: https://www.hrw.org/news/2015/05/16/burma=reject-discriminatory-population-bill. Accessed 9 Mar 2017.

Ibrahim, A. (2016). *The Rohingyas: Inside Myanmar's Hidden Genocide.* London: C. Hurst & Co.

International Crisis Group (ICG). (2014). *Myanmar: The Politics of Rakhine State* (Asia Report N° 261). Available at: http://www.burmalibrary.org/docs19/ICG-myanmar-the-politics-of-rakhine-state-red.pdf. Accessed 15 Mar 2017.

Kitwood, D. (2017, October 3). "The Boat Crashed and All Tipped Out": Photographing Rohingya Refugees. *The Guardian.* Available at: https://www.theguardian.com/artanddesign/2017/oct/03/the-boat-crashed-to-shore-tipping-everyone-out-photographing-rohingya-refugees-myanmar-bangladesh. Accessed 27 Nov 2017.

Kyu, M. M. (2016). Kokang: The Rise of the Chinese Minority—The New Neo-liberal State? In W. Tantikanangkul & A. Pritchard (Eds.), *Politics of Autonomy and Sustainability in Myanmar* (pp. 13–35). New York: Springer.

Larsen, P., & Logan, W. (2018). *World Heritage and Sustainable Development: New Directions in World Heritage Management.* London: Routledge.

Lee, R. (2014, May 12). A Politician, Not an Icon: Aung San Suu Kyi's Silence on Myanmar's Muslim Rohingya. *Islam and Christian-Muslim Relations.* Available at: http://dx.doi.org/10.1080/09596410.2014.913850. Accessed 9 Mar 2017.

Lee, R. (2015, June 2). Between the Devil and the Deep Blue Sea: The Rohingya's Dilemma. *The Conversation.* Available at: https://

theconversation.com/between-the-devil-and-the-deep-blue-sea-the-rohing-yas-dilemma-42359. Accessed 9 Mar 2017.

Lee, R. (2016). The Dark Side of Liberalization: How Myanmar's Political and Media Freedoms are Being Used to Limit Muslim Rights. *Islam and Christian-Muslim Relations, 27*(2), 195–211. Available at: http://dx.doi.org/10.1080/09596410.2016.1159045. Accessed 9 Mar 2017.

Logan, W. (2007). Closing Pandora's Box: Human Rights Conundrums in Cultural Heritage Protection. In H. Silverman & D. Ruggles Fairchild (Eds.), *Cultural Heritage and Human Rights* (pp. 33–52). New York: Springer.

Logan, W. (2008). Cultural Heritage and Human Rights. In B. J. Graham & P. Howard (Eds.), *Ashgate Research Companion to Heritage and Identity* (pp. 439–454). Aldershot: Ashgate.

Logan, W. (2014). Heritage Rights: Avoidance and Reinforcement. *Heritage and Society, 7*(2), 156–169.

Logan, W. (2015). Heritage in Times of Rapid Transformation: A Tale of Two Cities—Yangon and Hanoi. In G. Bracken (Ed.), *Asian Cities: Colonial to Global* (pp. 279–300). Amsterdam: Amsterdam University Press.

Logan, W. (2016a). Whose Heritage? Conflicting Narratives and Top-Down and Bottom-Up Approaches to Heritage Management in Yangon, Myanmar. In S. Labadi & W. Logan (Eds.), *Urban Heritage, Development and Sustainability: International Frameworks, National and Local Governance* (pp. 256–273). London: Routledge.

Logan, W. (2016b). Collective Cultural Rights in Asia: Recognition and Reinforcement. In A. Jakubowski (Ed.), *Cultural Rights as Collective Rights: An International Law Perspective* (pp. 180–203). Leiden and Boston: Brill Nijhoff.

Logan, W. (2016c). Australia, Indigenous Peoples and World Heritage from Kakadu to Cape York: State Party Behaviour Under the World Heritage Convention. *Journal of Social Archaeology, 13*(2), 153–176.

Mang, L. M. (2015, November 16). National Reconciliation Top Priority and Toughest Challenge. *Myanmar Times*. Available at: http://www.mmtimes.com/index.php/national-news/17636-national-reconciliation-top-priority-and-toughest-challenge.html. Accessed 11 Mar 2017.

Murdoch, L. (2017, March 12). Myanmar Monk Wirathu, Dubbed "Face of Buddhist Terror", Gagged by Authorities. *The Sydney Morning Herald*. Available at: http://www.smh.com.au/world/myanmar-monk-wirathu-dubbed-face-of-buddhist-terror-gagged-by-authorities-20170312-guw9jt.html. Accessed 16 Mar 2017.

Myanmar Center for Responsible Business (MCRB). (2016). *Briefing Paper: Indigenous Peoples' Rights and Business in Myanmar*. Available at: file://F:/Paper_Indigenous_Peoples_Rights_Business_in_Myanmar_Feb2016_ENG.pdf. Accessed 9 Mar 2017.

Myanmar Parliament. (2015a). *The Protection and Preservation of Ancient Monuments Law (The Pyidaungsu Hlattaw Law No. 51, 2015)*. Available at: http://www.unesco.org/culture/natlaws/media/pdf/myanmar/mya_lawprotmon_15_entof. Accessed 16 Mar 2017.

Myanmar Parliament. (2015b). *The Protection and Preservation of Ancient Objects Law (The Pyidaungsu Hlattaw Law No. 43, 2015)*. Available at: http://www.unesco.org/culture/natlaws/media/pdf/myanmar/mya_lawprotcltobjects_15_entof. Accessed 16 Mar 2017.

Nixon, H., Joelene, C., Saw, K. P. C., Lynn, T. A., & Arnold, M. (2013). *State and Region Governments in Myanmar*. Yangon: The Asia Foundation. Available at: https://asiafoundation.org/resources/pdfs/StateandRegion GovernmentsinMyanmarCESDTAF.PDF. Accessed 15 Mar 2017.

Nwe, T. T., & Philp, J. (2002). Yangon, Myanmar: The re-Invention of Heritage. In W. Logan (Ed.), *The Disappearing 'Asian' City: Protecting Asia's Urban Heritage in a Globalizing World* (pp. 147–165). Hong Kong: Oxford University Press.

Paode, A. (2017, March 4). Why Myanmar's New Peace Process is Failing. So Far, the NLD Government Efforts to End Armed Conflicts Have Failed. *The Diplomat*. Available at: http://thediplomat.com/2017/03/why-myanmars-new-peace-process-is-failing/. Accessed 11 Mar 2017.

Philp, J. (2010). The Political Appropriation of Burma's Cultural Heritage and Its Implications for Human Rights. In M. Langfield, W. Logan, & M. NicCraith (Eds.), *Cultural Diversity, Heritage and Human Rights: Intersections in Theory and Practice* (pp. 83–100). London: Routledge.

Philp, J., & Mercer, D. (2002). Politicised Pagoda and Veiled Resistance: Contested Urban Space in Burma. *Urban Studies, 39*, 1587–1610.

Ponniah, K. (2017, January 10). *Who Will Help Myanmar's Rohingya?* BBC News. Available at: http://www.bbc.com/news/world-asia-38168917. Accessed 9 Mar 2017.

Pullella, P. (2017, November 24). *Pope Faces Diplomatic Dilemma in Myanmar Visit*. Reuters World News. Available at: https://www.reuters.com/article/us-pope-asia-myanmar/pope-faces-diplomatic-dilemma-in-myanmar-visit-idUSKBN1DN1D7. Accessed 27 Nov 2017.

Republic of the Union of Myanmar (RUM). (2014). *The Population and Housing Census of Myanmar, 2014. Summary of the Provisional Results*. Yangon: Department of Population, Ministry of Immigration and Population. http://unstats.un.org/unsd/demographic/sources/census/2010_phc/Myanmar/MMR-2014-08-28-provres.pdf. Accessed 13 Mar 2017.

Slodkowski, A. (2016a, June 20). *Myanmar's Suu Kyi Reiterates Stance on Not Using Term 'Rohingya'—Official*. Reuters. Available at: http://www.reuters.com/article/us-myanmar-rights-idUSKCN0Z61AC. Accessed 11 Mar 2017.

Slodkowski, A. (2016b, June 23). *Myanmar: Rohingya Will Not be Called Rohingya by the EU.* Reuters. Available at: http://www.smh.com.au/world/myanmar-rohingya-will-not-be-called-rohingya-by-the-eu-20160622-gppsah.html. Accessed 11 Mar 2017.

The State Peace and Development Council (SPDC). (1998). *The Protection and Preservation of Cultural Heritage Regions Law (The State Peace and Development Council Law No. 9/98).* Available at: http://www.wipo.int/edocs/lexdocs/laws/en/mm/mm013en.pdf. Accessed 15 Mar 2017.

The Guardian. (2016, August 25). *Myanmar Struck by 6.8-Magnitude Earthquake.* Available at: https://www.theguardian.com/world/2016/aug/24/myanmar-struck-by-6-8-magnitude-earthquake. Accessed 9 Mar 2017.

The New York Times. (2016, July 2). *Mob Burns Down Mosque in Myanmar: UN Urges Action on Attacks.* Available at: https://www.nytimes.com/2016/07/03/world/asia/mob-burns-down-mosque-in-myanmar-un-urges-action-on-attacks.html?_r=0. Accessed 9 Mar 2017.

United Nations Development Program (UNDP). (2017). *UNDP in Myanmar.* Available: http://www.mm.undp.org/content/myanmar/en/home/countryinfo.html. Accessed 11 Mar 2017.

United Nations Educational Scientific and Cultural Organization (UNESCO). (2003). *Convention for the Safeguarding of the Intangible Cultural Heritage.* Available at: http://www.unesco.org/culture/ich/en/convention. Accessed 15 Mar 2017.

United Nations Educational Scientific and Cultural Organization (UNESCO). (2015). *World heritage and sustainable development.* Available at: http://whc.unesco.org/archive/2015/whc15-20ga-13-en.pdf. Accessed 5 Mar 2017.

United Nations Educational Scientific and Cultural Organization (UNESCO). (2016) *UNESCO Transparency Portal: Myanmar.* Available at https://opendata.unesco.org/country/MM. Accessed 9 Mar 2017.

United Nations Human Rights Council. (2011). *Report of the Inde$pendent Expert in the Field of Cultural Rights, Farida Shaheed (A/HRC/17/38).* Available at: http://indigenouspeoplesissues.com/attachments/article/10227/A-HRC-17-38.doc. Accessed 24 Nov 2014.

United Nations International Children's Emergency Fund (UNICEF). (2017). *UNICEF in Myanmar.* Available at: https://www.unicef.org/myanmar/overview.html. Accessed 11 Mar 2017.

Ware, A. (2015, September 25). The Muslim "Rohingya" and Myanmar's Upcoming Election. *Australian Outlook.* Available at: http://www.internationalaffairs.org.au/australian_outlook/the-muslim-rohingya-and-myanmars-upcoming-election/. Accessed 9 Mar 2017.

Weng, L. (2014). Burma Govt Agrees to Include Federal System in Ceasefire Deal. *The Irrawaddy.* Available at: https://www.irrawaddy.com/news/burma/burma-govt-agrees-include-federal-system-ceasefire-deal.html. Accessed 10 Mar 2017.

CHAPTER 4

The Obliteration of Heritage of the *Jumma* People and the Role of Government: The Story of the Chittagong Hill Tracts

Rumana Hashem

INTRODUCTION

Contestation over heritage and obliteration of certain forms of heritage leading to ethnic conflict are increasingly noticeable in some of the countries in South Asia, including Bangladesh, India, Pakistan and Sri Lanka. Although Bangladesh rarely enters the discussion in relation to cultural contestation, it is ubiquitous in Bangladesh, especially in the southeast region of the country. Decades of intense cultural expressions of Bengalese and (contested) heritage of both the Jumma and Bengali communities in the Chittagong Hill Tracts (CHT) have become ordinary in

I would like to thank Paul Dudman, the archivist at the Refugee Conflict at the University of East London, for his support and help with proofing of an earlier version of the chapter.

R. Hashem (✉)
Centre for Research on Migration, Refugees and Belonging,
University of East London, London, UK

© The Author(s) 2018
J. Rodenberg and P. Wagenaar (eds.), *Cultural Contestation*,
Palgrave Studies in Cultural Heritage and Conflict,
https://doi.org/10.1007/978-3-319-91914-0_4

Bangladesh. Researchers and scholars including feminists (Ahmed 2011; Guhathakurta 2004), historians and political scientists (Mohsin 1997, 2003; Shelly 1992) and sociologists (Rahman 2011) have analysed the causes and consequences of the conflict in the CHT from a variety of approaches. Some scholars argue that the British Empire and a primordial nationalist ideology of the indigenous peoples were responsible for the conflict (see, for example, Azad 2004), while others (e.g. Abedin 1997, 2003) blame neighbouring India's supremacy over the region and geopolitical issues for the 27-year violent conflict in the region. While much has been written on the conflict itself, little attention has been paid to how culture, that is, contested heritage of communities, contributes to it. What is more, much of the discussion on the role of governments in the processes of contestations in the CHT has so far been over-generalised. Humayun Azad (2004), as one of few, has suggested that when we analyse the ongoing conflict in the CHT we ought to keep all intersectional events, contestations and betrayals of politicians and governments aiding civic-nationalist politics in mind. Yet, the stress of his analysis was on civic nationalism. He paid little attention to the heritage contestation and the role that the Bangladeshi government played in shaping the symbolic landscape. In this chapter, I would, therefore, like to revisit the conflict and examine the role of Bangladeshi government in identity construction and the ensuing cultural contestation. I will therefore explore how 'culture' and heritage, as part of a symbolic landscape to which the Bengali and Jumma communities give meanings through historical narratives, give rise to heavy forms of contestation: namely widespread violence in the CHT.

   This contribution draws on my past research on the gender dynamics of the conflict (Hashem 2014) and shifts the analysis to the role Bangladeshi government plays in identity construction leading to conflict between the Bengalese and the Jummos. I will argue that exclusive expressions of Bengalese culture lead to violent conflict, while government plays a misogynist role in the process, furthering violence even in the post-Accord situation. I will juxtapose theories of identity, arguing that identity is 'in process' (e.g. Bhabha 1994; Hall 2003) with non-essentialist feminist analysis (e.g. Ahmed 2011; Guhathakurta 2004; Mohsin 2003), so as to appreciate the discursive constitution of cultural contestation, and protracted conflict in the region. At the same time, I maintain the suggestion that 'Identities are frequently articulated through, and contested around, collective memories and mundane, everyday cultural practices such as parades, flag displays, language, clothing, religious practices, and public monuments that symbolically connect the past and present and are visible in a region's symbolic landscape' (Ross 2009: 2).

As such, in this contribution I engage theoretically with the concept of intersectional and multi-layered power relations in the construction of identity ('the Self' and 'the Other') in a specific historical and political context.[1] The chapter is organised around the following five parts. First, I define the concepts of culture, ethnicity and religion. Second, I give a precise account of my situated notion and the methodology followed for my analysis. Third, I will briefly sketch the historical background of the CHT and the conflict in the region. Fourth, I will give an illustration of the ongoing contestations over heritages between the two communities, by unravelling the ways that cultural identities have been constructed in Bangladesh. I will pay ample attention to how different governments in Bangladesh failed to resolve the conflict, even contributed to the ongoing cultural contestation, underscoring the disparaging role of government in the obliteration of Jumma heritage in a supposedly secular Bangladesh. Finally, I conclude by arguing that while a situated resolution is needed to end the age-old conflict, the role the government of Bangladesh plays in the contestation and the conflict between the two communities is, indeed, misogynist.

Defining Culture, Ethnicity and Religion

First, it is necessary to define what I understand as 'culture'. Culture' is understood here as an element of group and individual identity and a way in which people belong to or become member of a particular group or community. Culture refers to daily practices and cultural expressions, such as dress, food, festivals, language, livelihood (for instance, Jhum cultivation in the CHT is Jummo culture), monuments and rituals—for example the *Boisabi* festival is a traditional Jumma ritual and representative of its culture. However, culture and ethnicity are different, as are religion and culture. As I will show, the culture of Bangladeshis is traditionally 'Bengali' and related to Hindu heritage. Yet, the religion of Bangladeshi people is predominantly (Sunni) Islam. Likewise, the everyday practices, dress and livelihood of a vast majority of Bangladeshis are similar to Hindu, although they go to mosques for prayers and celebrate Eid-ul-Fitr and Eid-ul-Azha (where animals, for example, cows would be sacrificed for Allah) as part of their religion. The same distinction holds true for the Jummos at large, who share daily cultural practices, but communities and individuals within the Jummos adhere to different religions. This may be difficult to appreciate for some who see religion as a part of culture. We should recognise that cultural expressions do not necessarily include religious expressions, and thus, we should be aware of mixing the two up all too easily. The fact that religion and culture are two separate concepts is vivid in Bangladesh, a country that was born out of struggles over language and cultural nationalism (Hashem 2006).

Secondly, ethnicity needs some further elaboration as well, for in Bangladesh it is an individual's ethnicity which represents the individual's identity. Ethnicity is understood here as 'an inclusionary and exclusionary construct which is formed by people's culture *and* religion' (Hashem 2014: 11). For example, the *Adibasi* (indigenous) people in the CHT belong to different religions but they share the same culture, and form one community on the basis of their ethnicity, as do the Jummo. Jummos represent a larger group consisting of minority ethnicities in Bangladesh. However, culture is only one component of their shared ethnicity, and it does not always represent people's religion, faith and nationality.

Culture and ethnicity are, however, interchangeably used in the literature. Some theorists argue that culture is a 'shared system of meaning that people use to make sense of the world' (Geertz 1973; Ross 1997 and 2002, cited in Ross 2009: 4). Rather than defining culture as a 'system', I define culture as a practice performed by individuals and collectivities who long to belong to certain identical cultures as part of their identity politics.

In the third place, albeit notwithstanding the point made by Ross regarding how cultural expressions shape a societies cultural landscape, I see religion as a separate practice or norm, different from culture. This has been the case for all collectivities, including Bengali and other *Adibasis.*[2]

SITUATING CULTURAL CONTESTATION IN POST-COLONIAL BANGLADESH

Wenona Giles and Jenifer Hyndman (2004: 5) note correctly that '[m] Most contemporary wars occur within the borders of sovereign states, not between countries as they once did. Notions of what constitutes a conflict zone are similarly outdated'. We should look into new ways for understanding every conflict—whether within or between borders—across the globe. While Giles and Hyndman were working within Structural Theories, I situate my analysis within non-essentialist and deconstructive theories by taking the suggestion that we should always look into new ways for apprehending social processes and conflict in culturally, geographically and historically different contexts. As evidenced in the history of Bangladesh, the formation of Bengali identity was made possible through a blood-spattered revival of Bengalese culture against the linguistic control, involving imposition of the Urdu language in place of Bangla, in East Pakistan in 1971. The Bengali people had fought a nine-month war against Pakistan in order to maintain their identity, to achieve freedom of language and Bengali heritage, as these were essentially part of their collective identity. Through war they gained official recognition of the Bangla language and of Bengali heritage (Hashem 2014). In the aftermath of the war, the majority of Bangladeshis continued to strongly uphold their Bengali identity and has imagined a symbolic landscape based solely on Bengali culture (Mohsin 2010). Due to the emotional attachment between Bengali identity and its language, the country was named 'Bangladesh', which translates as 'the land of the Bengali speaking people'. The first government in Bangladesh was formed by the popular political party, the Awami League, which led the war of liberation in 1971. The party's goal was to fulfil the expectations of the majority of Bengalese to favour Bangla and Bengali heritage over others (Hashem 2006). The popularity of the Awami League government meant that the identities and heritage of other existing communities would come second best, or be neglected, or violated, if needed for the purpose of retaining the exclusivity of Bengali culture (Hashem 2006). This exclusiveness of Bengaliness still is powerful for the positioning of those who fought and lost their loved ones in order to gain a cultural identity and form a nation state. As the nation state was born out of cultural struggle, people in Bangladesh found it quite normal that Bengaliness would be prioritised at any cost.

Religion too plays an important role in the construction of identities in Bangladesh. The majority (82%) of Bangladeshis are followers of Islam and they identify themselves as Sunni Muslims, distinguishing themselves from Pakistanis, who are mostly Shi'a Muslims and Urdu speakers (Hashem 2014). Despite their differences, Bangladeshi Muslims often appear highly sensitive about their religion, and the majority of Bengali Muslims are not open to criticism of Islam (Hashem 2016a, b).

The symbolic landscape for the Bangladeshi refers to a nation state comprising of Bengali cultural expressions and Islamic religious praxis. Mosques and Bengali monuments (such as, *Shahid Minar*, Savar's *Smrity Shoudha*) are part and parcel of their symbolic landscape, whereas Hindu temples, Buddhist monuments and Christian churches are perceived as a threat to their identity and excluded from the symbolic landscape by demolition. The level of emotional attachment to the building of a new mosque is often as high as the emotion involved in the destruction of temples and monuments for Buddha or Kali, which subsequently leads to contestations and conflict between Bengali Muslims and other existing communities in Bangladesh. Every time a temple or a sculpture of Buddha has come under attack or has been destroyed, a bloody conflict has occurred in the CHT.

Contrarily, a symbolic landscape for the Jummos would mean a place of autonomy solely for the Jumma people where they can practice their own religion (Buddhism) and culture, including the right to speak in their mother language and the right to practice Jhum cultivation up the hills. The account of Aseem Mong, a 28-year-old young man, for example, shows how identities of the *Adibasi* communities in the CHT are constructed:

> We saw ourselves as small *jati* [nations]. Sometimes we identify ourselves as a Mong *jati*, other times a Jummo and other times a Bangladeshi *jati*. Sometime we prioritise our culture, rituals, livelihood and a place such as Bandarban; sometimes religion, language and political values; other times country and culture; and most of the time all of these. When I say that I am a Mong, I focus on my language and rituals which are different than Bengali. [...] It is totally different and very difficult for any Bengali to understand our livelihood, and it is literally impossible to co-exist with Bengalese in the same place.[3]

Aseem's account shows that his identity is not fixed and it is fluid and in process as he and his community maintain different elements of identities depending on the context. However, what he also makes clear is that there is a limit to this fluidity of identity and that he cannot see how the Bengalese and his community could coexist or share the same landscape. The culture and religion that he and his community belong to are contesting with Bengali culture, and that makes it difficult for them to share the same landscape with Bengalese. Aseem's fear that it is difficult for a Bengali person to appreciate *Adibasi* livelihood is in fact evidenced in the history of the CHT as will be discussed below.

What follows will unravel contestations over heritage between the two communities—Bengalese and the Jumma. A situated gaze at the conflict in the CHT could reveal narratives of how the conflict is identity based and why each side (the majority of Bengalese and the Jummos) fears to recognise the shared parts of their narratives or why the Bengalese find it hard to acknowledge the rights of other communities in Bangladesh. Data for this research were collected through the use of semi-structured and open-ended interviews, archival research and secondary literature review. As any form of qualitative inquiry is a social construction, this inquiry has been co-constructed between the participants of the research and the author. The claims made within this chapter are negotiated through the voice of the participants and the author. The author's own positioning is informed by a discursive and intersectional feminist standpoint which recognises that minority identities—whether based on culture, class, ethnicity or merely religion—are often subject to complex forms of oppressions and politics of belonging which requires a situated gaze to understand.

Finally, the analysis is informed by a wide range of interdisciplinary conceptualisations—from political anthropology to international relations and from political science to sociology. Such a framework, I argue, is needed to be responsive to the need to replenish the critical and creative demand of conflict analysis, and to be responsive to what can be opened up and what could be thought differently, conceptually as much as practically, about the possibilities for what could and should be done next to resolving the protracted conflicts and violence that we live in (Hashem 2014). This article coincides with Yuval-Davis's argument that relying on a situated notion is important for any analysis because a 'situated gaze, situated knowledge and situated imagination [...], construct how we see the world in different ways' (Yuval-Davis 2011: 4).

IDENTITIES AND THE HERITAGE OF *ADIBASI* IN PRE, DURING AND AFTER COLONIALISATION IN BENGAL

Historically, the culture of the Jumma people is different from that of the Bengalese, as is its identity, vision and symbolic landscapes. The separate way of life of the aboriginals, known as *Adibasi* in Bangladesh, can be traced back four hundred years to the age of Indian colonisation (Shelly 1992). Before the British conquest of Bengal, they collectively lived in a secluded area of India—thereafter the Chittagong Hill Tracts, a home to 13 multilingual collectivities. About 600,000 people[4] had made a distinct living based on *Jhum* cultivation[5] in the hills in a region consisting of 5093 square miles in the south-eastern part of East Bengal (thereafter Bangladesh), bordering the Arakan and Chin states of Myanmar as well as Tripura and the Mizoram states of North India (Chakma 1983; Roy 2000).[6] As followers of Buddhism, with some Hindus, the 13 collectivities—namely Chakma, Marma, Tripura, Mru, Murong, Bowm, Khumi, Tanchangya, Ryang, Khyang, Lushai, Uchay, Pankho and Sak— had organised themselves into independent societies and maintained identities that were distinct from the majority of the Indian population in terms of culture (language, dress code, mundane and social norms) and religion (Mohsin 1997: 11–24). Having held multilingual identities, they spoke more than 10 different languages, while the most spoken languages in the region are Chakma, Marma and Tripura (CHTC update 2000; Shelly 1992).

In relation to a social division based on gender and sexuality, the *Adibasi* culture was, by and large, equal before the Bengali settlement (Shelly 1992). Although class and caste divisions existed in invisible forms, *Adibasi* society was matriarchal. On the whole, its culture is noticeably distinctive from that of the Bengalese and of people who lived in the plains. While Bengalese and other Indians are traditionally followers of either Hindu or Islam, the heritage of south-eastern *Adibasi* people (thereafter Jumma) is known as Jumiyan and Buddhist. In terms of identity, they saw themselves as non-violent residents of the hills who did not desire to be bothered by the government from the plains. Due to their distinctive culture, the *Adibasis in* the hills lived in an isolated society before the partition of India. They formed an independent society, refused to be governed by the East India Company, and resisted British regulations for income tax, which led to eight years of intermittent warfare in 1777 in the Hill. Despite victory, the British government/ East India Company had eventually moved away from the province, appreciating the tremendous resistance of the *Adibasis* who wished to stay a non-state people. Initially, the British ruled the province following Mughal administration which lasted for about 65 years (Mohsin 1997). The distinct cultures of the Hill population and their irresistible resilience, conversely, made it difficult to govern the area for long.

The persistent resistance of the aboriginals resulted in the 1860 annex of the Hill Tracts allowing the *Adibasis* to form an autonomous administrative district called 'The Chittagong Hill Tracts'.

In 1900, the colonial government enacted Regulation 1 of the 1900 Act by establishing a further protective law, called the Chittagong Hill Tracts Manual 1900, that 'restricted the movement and settlement of Bengalese and non-aboriginals into the area and imposed restrictions on land transfers from the Hill people to the Bengalese' (Mohsin 2010: 158–159). This reform is seen as the 'single most "positive step" by the British Empire in Bengal' (CHT Commission 2000: 84) and became the 'safeguard' to the Hill *Adibasis*. The law enabled the aboriginals to preserve their traditions, and sociocultural and political institutions by recognising the self-governance of the *Adibasi* in the CHT with respect to their customary laws, traditional ways of life, as well rights on common ownership of land (Roy 2000). It was believed that conflict in the Hill region would be prevented by this law.

Nevertheless, conflict began soon after the controversial partition in 1947 was executed. While originally the partition was based on religious fractions between the Muslim League and the Hindu Congress, and the CHT was presumed to be part of India, in the end the CHT was given to East Pakistan—albeit the aboriginals wanted to join India. Thus, the partition did not reflect their aspirations but rather resulted in ambiguity, making a pathway for new 'ethnic conflict' which became apparent soon after the British had left the region. As culture and religion are at the heart of identity, the contrasting cultural and religious identities of the aboriginals and the Muslims in Pakistan resulted in a mutually exclusive relation. During Yahya's reign, the implementation of a massive hydroelectric project resulted in conflict, although non-violent. Intense conflict between the government and aboriginals in the CHT had begun after Bangladesh gained independence. With the formation of the new state, the Awami League government felt it important to ensure the exclusivity of Bengali identity, and hence refused to recognise that the identities of aboriginals in the CHT could be compatible with Bengalese. This misrecognition of aboriginal identities and the exclusive cultural expressions of Bengalese resulted in an intense conflict, and when the CHT came under military control in 1975, the region faced a two-decade-long armed conflict.

Prior to the armed conflict, when the constitution of Bangladesh was approved, which only recognised Bangla as an only official language and which defined all existing aboriginal communities other than Bengalese as '*upojati*' (the sub [-ordinate] nation) and as 'tribal' (minority ethnic group or minority of the nation), the 13 collectivities came together to form one community and identified themselves as Jummos or Jumma people in 1973. This collective identity of the aboriginal communities was constructed based on *Jumyian* livelihood—a symbolic landscape that they believed would enable practicing Jumma rituals—Buddhism and Jhum cultivation (Hashem 2014). The Jumma people had declared that they would fight until the CHT gained autonomy. From 1975 to 1997, widespread violence prevailed following the resettlement of 40,000 Bengalese in the CHT through a government-sponsored plan (CHT Commission Report 2000). Although Sheikh Hasina's reign took a significant initiative to settle the conflict later by calling upon the leaders of the Jumma and introducing the Chittagong Hill Tracts Accord 1997— which was signed by the government and the leaders of the Jumma people on 12 December 1997 and was designed to prevent conflict by insuring protection for the rights and heritages of both communities— it has hardly ever functioned. The mutual distrust between the competing parties is as high as ever, violent conflict continues to the present day, and the semi-autonomous administration that the 1997 agreement promised has never been fully implemented (Amnesty International Report 2005, 2011, 2013).

WHY GOVERNMENT INTERVENTIONS FAIL

Experts have identified a number of reasons why government's intervention in the conflict is failing and why violence has been so widespread after the signing of the CHT Accord in 1997. The problem apparently lies in both the political arrangements and the mutual distrust between the conflicting parties. The issues surrounding the political arrangements for expressions of identities and the poor level of implementation of the CHT Accord 1997 can be described as threefold failings of the government: firstly, persistent militarisation of the province in the post-Accord situation; secondly, the continued involuntary resettlement of Bengalese who find the CHT a difficult place to make home; thirdly, the inability to recognise the Bangladeshi citizens' dissimilar and multiple identities, and consequently the failure to develop political arrangements for their cultural expressions and equal rights as citizens of Bangladesh.

Militarisation of the Post-accord CHT

As Mohsin notes, 'the relationship between the Bengalese and the Jumma people is historically marked by distrust, animosity, and a certain degree of ambiguity' (Mohsin 2010: 158). However, the militarisation of the CHT in the aftermath of the signing of the CHT Accord 1997 has put the level of (Jumma people's) mistrust and ambiguity even higher. Although one of the important conditions of the signed CHT Accord 1997 had been the immediate removal of the military from the area, this demand of the Jummos is yet to be fulfilled. According to the government, the reason for keeping the military in the towns in all three districts is to keep some control over the geopolitical landscape. As the hills are surrounded by the borders of Arakan and Chin states of Myanmar as well as Tripura and the Mizoram states of North India, government is concerned that the country would face external threats in the absence of state security forces. A second reason for retaining the military is to ease 'communal violence', as explained by the Additional District Commissioner in Khagrachari.[7] The Bangladeshi government fears conflicts between the competing communities in the province.

As the competing communities are framed in mutually exclusive cultural expressions, both sides often refuse to coexist and get involved in violent conflict (see, for example, Amnesty International Report 2013; CHTC International 2011). Incidents of random attacks on Jumna and the vandalising of Buddhist temples by the Bengalese during the *Boisabi* festival of the Jummos or on the eve of Ekushey February—the International Language Day when Bengalese pay tribute to the martyrs of the 1952 movement for (Bangla) language isn't news to Bangladeshis (Hashem 2014). In this sense, the government has a valid reason to keep the military in the area to prevent riots. The Jumma people, however, see the presence of the military as a threat to their everyday life. Aseem Mong, for example, told:

[..] the main problem in Bandaraban [a district in the CHT that he is a resident] is that military would pop up in market places or in your house and pick up an innocent member of the community or the family as/when they like. This is why people cannot stand military. The presence of military in the CHT is just provoking anger among the Jummos. Peace will never come this way, just telling you.

Likewise, a 16-year-old girl, Suporna Chakma, in Khagrachari told that she is as angry with as scared of the military because she has heard brutal stories of military violence. Her aunts and grandparents have told her that during the two decades of intense conflict, soldiers have raped Jumma women and committed various other forms of human rights violations in the area. Suporna concludes her account by throwing a question: 'How do the government even think that the military who indiscriminately abused our people would now be so sympathetic to protect us? They are not here to prevent conflict. They are the ones that cause conflict and spread violence'.[8]

What these accounts substantiate is that the continual presence of military in the area has rather exacerbated the 'feeling of animosity' of the Jummos, as Mohsin (2010) notes correctly. There are incidences of military violence including gender-specific abuse and rape of women which have occurred in post-Accord CHT as well. Notably, the organising secretary of Hill Women's Federation, Kalpana Chakma, was abducted by a military officer from her mother's house in 1996—incidentally Kalpana's abduction occurred at the same night when the Awami League government won the national election after two decades (Hashem 2016a, b). This is why the government's policy of keeping the military in the area for peace-keeping reasons has been repeatedly questioned by experts. However, it is a fact that the hardcore on each side tends to fight over things so intensely that the police is often unable to deal with it. Besides, a fraction of the Jumma who wanted to fight for independence in spite of the agreement of 1997 is still out there. Therefore, military presence is important from the government's perspective. Nevertheless, as Guahthakurta (2004) maintains, peace is hard to achieve by militarisation of the province. In order to prevent conflict, the government should rather take a dialogical approach and engage in a constructive and meaningful discussion with the Jummos. The government chose to deploy the military which turned into the suppression of one particular community, instead.

THE ONGOING BENGALI RESETTLEMENT IN THE HILLS AND RENEWED VIOLENCE

Despite historical distrust and animosity between the two communities, the government continues to expand Bengali settlement in the hills, which aggravates the hostility on both sides. The Bengalese, forcibly sent to the hills from the plains, find it often hard to make homes in the CHT, while the *Adibasis* in the Hill find this unjust as the settlements often cause displacement of their people or loss of traditional land. The government maintains that the Bengalese settle in government-owned land, of what they call *Khash Jamin*. But to the Jummos these lands are their communal property which belongs to them and to their ancestors as much as to their spirits (Mohsin 2010). They relate to the land in a way that land is sacred and untouchable, hence not to be commodified. When their land has been taken away and given to strangers who come involuntarily from the plains and do not see the hills a place to live in, they feel wounded. Besides, Bengalese, being in control of the trade and commerce of the region, see the Hill people as incompatible or as a threat. The agreement of 1997 was designed to rehabilitate the displaced Jummos and to limit Bengali settlements. Nevertheless, the involuntary settlement programme of Bengali people in Jumma villages continues. The competing parties rarely trust each other. Each side continues to fear the 'other' and sees it as seeking total victory. Every time a new group of Bengali arrives in the CHT, tensions arise followed by fresh conflict. A conflict during a rally of a Hill students' forum and the burning of a Buddhist temple continued for weeks and months (see, for example, Ahmed 2011; Amnesty International Report 2011).

According to the government, the resettlement programmes are designed to advance and integrate the aboriginal population. However, critics have pointed out that as the cultural contestation has been obvious since the colonial era, government should have never sponsored Bengali settlement in the CHT (Muhammad 1997, 2010; Rahman 2011; Roy 2000). The Chittagong Hill Tracts Manual—the 1900 Act 1 which the East India Company enacted to enable the CHT to be a secluded region where migration from outside the hills would be restricted and where administration of the plains would not apply—should have been maintained. Contestation in the CHT occurs so regularly because of the poor political arrangements. Apparently, the expansion of the Bengali resettlement programme is doing a disservice to the CHT Accord 1997 itself. Such a programme merely intensifies conflicts between the two communities, which seem to be too different to coexist.

Placing Bangla First: An Absurd Demand and Misrecognition of Multiple Identities

As was discussed earlier in the history of the CHT, the collective identity of the Jumma people had been constructed in 1973 in independent Bangladesh following a constitutional bias. Prior to Bangladesh's independence, the 13 aboriginal collectivities identified themselves as small cultural groups, namely Chakma, Marma, Tripura, Mru, Murong, Bowm, Khumi, Tanchangya, Ryang, Khyang, Lushai, Uchay, Pankho and Sak. They had lived in the CHT since ancient times without contestation. But the constitution of Bangladesh which was approved by the majority of the parliament in 1972 has defined Bangla as the 'first and only' official language of the state and hence has failed to recognise the original identities of non-Bengali communities.[9]

In fact, language occupies a central position in the construction of identity and nationhood of the Bengalese. Bangladesh as a state predicates itself on the linguistic/cultural identity of its majority Bengali population (Mohsin 2010). The war of liberation in Bangladesh started from a social movement for Bangla language, held in Dhaka on 21 February 1952 when four frontline protesters were shot dead as the police opened fire on the students' protest. The day has been nationally celebrated as a day of glory of the Bengalese, and a pledge to defend the Bangla language as the foundation and symbol of the landscape has been reminded every year on Language Day since. Protecting Bangla language, Bengali identity and Bengali culture has been seen as the most important role of the government. The government has, therefore, approved a constitution of Bangladesh, which proclaims Bangla to be the basis of the nation. According to article 3 of the constitution, Bangla is the official language of the state and the medium of instruction. Likewise, all citizens of Bangladesh are to be known as Bengalese through article 6, part 1 of the constitution.[10] However, this constitution was opposed by the lone representative of non-Bengali population, Manobendra Narayna Larma, who pointed out that he was a Chakma man and not a Bengali, but also a Bangladeshi citizen. How would it be possible for him to be identified as a Bengali? In response to his objection, he was advised to identify himself and the people that he represented in the parliament as Bengalese (Hashem 2014). Despite the fact that this lone representative walked out, to later meet the Prime Minister with a delegation from the CHT, the government failed to respond to his demand. The delegates were asked by the Prime Minister, Sheikh Mujib—known as the 'Father of the Nation' in Bangladesh—to forget their indigenous identity and try to become Bengali. He said: '*tora Bangali hoya ja* [You must try becoming Bengali]'.

In order to keep their popularity with the majority of the Bengalese, the government consciously promotes the national culture, that is Bengali heritage, through the supposedly secular (socialist-Islamic) constitution. Article 23 for instance states: 'The state shall adopt measures to conserve the cultural traditions and heritage of the people, and so to foster and improve the national language, literature and the arts that all sections of the people are afforded the opportunity to contribute towards and to participate in the enrichment of the national culture'.[11] As Shelly (1992) notes, while Bangladesh itself was born out of a social and political movement for culture, especially the linguistic expression of Bengalese which defied the supremacy of the Urdu language and the Shi'a Muslim heritage in East Pakistan, the government of independent Bangladesh imposed its own brand of identity upon other communities soon after the independence. The refusal to acknowledge the existence of *Adibasi* identities and the exclusive cultural expression of the Bengalese in turn forced the 13 collectivities to form a separate identity based on Jumma culture. Consequently, an endless ethnic conflict and violence prevail across the CHT.

Despite the CHT Accord 1997, there is no peace in the CHT because of a lack of education programmes for the Jummos. No changes have been made in the rights to education and language of the people in the CHT or elsewhere in Bangladesh. Bangla has been the only official language for instruction and the only medium of education across the country. The non-Bengali pupils in the CHT, especially children in primary schools, find it incredibly hard to acquire education in Bangla. The community advocates and activists have urged the government to set up some schools that would provide education in their mother language for their children (Dewan 2010). However, the government has yet to respond. This deprivation of education has become a major reason for conflict.

Besides, the most cynical approach of the government is the claim that there are no indigenous people in Bangladesh and that the Bengalese are the most ancient residents in Bengal (CHT Commission 2011a, b Amnesty International 2013). This is an ahistorical claim and a fallacy which misrecognises the existence of multiple indigenous identities in

Bangladesh and also humiliating to all aboriginal communities. Despite heavy criticism by constitutional scholars and the civil society movement for using the correct term to recognise indigenous people in the constitution of Bangladesh, the Sheikh Hasina government remains adamant.

CONCLUSION

Throughout this chapter, we have seen that the exclusive framework of government in Bangladesh has become apparent in 1972 when the so-called secular constitution of Bangladesh misrecognised citizens' multiple identities, and the *Adibasis* were asked to become Bengali. Instead of appreciating the cultural contestations, the governments in Bangladesh have followed disparaging policies, which have favoured the majority of Bengali Muslims, simultaneously hurting and misrecognising the heritage of other communities, in this case the Jumma people. As exclusive cultural expressions have continued until the present day, creating spheres for violent conflict in the Chittagong Hill Tracts, a situated resolution is needed.

The illustrations above have demonstrated that although the 1900 Act 1 enabled self-governance in the CHT, this was not appreciated by the government in Bangladesh. Due to populist movements for Bengaliness, the government failed to consider *Adibasi* language and identities as compatible with Bangla, and therefore refused to give it official recognition. The cultural and religious exclusivity of the Bengalese, their intolerance, resistance and social divisions on the basis of identities contributed notably to the policies of the governments and provided for the construction of conflict. The discussion above shows how the exclusive cultural expression of the majority of Bangladeshis, reflected in the government's policies, enabled destruction of the heritage of the Jumma peoples in a so-called secular state.

The question arises what alternatives there were. We should note that there are other options, such as preventing violence by limiting new settlements of Bengalese in the CHT, recognising the languages of all collectivities through constitutional approval, introducing education in Jumma languages and most significantly withdrawal of the military from the CHT. These are demands by the people in the CHT, including many Bangladeshis who signed the global petition for peace in the CHT in 2010. There hasn't been a government, from the Mujib government to the Hasina reign today, who has shown any sincere initiative to listen to the other side of the story.

Even if it claims to be a secular society, the symbolic landscape of Bangladesh is solely Bengali and exclusive of other cultures and identities, which became apparent in November 1972. Although it was expected that Bangladesh would recognise all religious and all cultural and social groups, the constitution of Bangladesh only reflected the aspirations of the Bengali people and upheld the exclusivity of Bengaliness. It is, apparently, the government in Bangladesh that needs to take a role in mitigation by listening to both parties, neutrally, for the purpose of conflict resolution and for the shaping of a cultural landscape that suits all.

NOTES

1. In this study, the term 'Self' is understood not only as individual self but also in a collective sense relating to collective identity. I use the word in a collective sense in most of the chapters with a few exceptions. This discussion is furthered at the end of this chapter where I discuss my notion of identity.
2. Collectivity refers to a group that shares a collective identity based on their shared culture or ethnicity or religion or class. Adibasi is a Bangla phrase. Adibasi stands for aboriginal or indigenous people in Bangladesh.
3. Pseudonym has been used to protect identity of participants. Interview held on 8 August 2011 in my residence in London. The participant spoke in fluent Bangla and fluent English, and thus, no interpreter was required. He switched between languages as he spoke.
4. Although the official statistics in Bangladesh do not match the demography, Roy (2000) argues that the original population in the Chittagong Hill Tracts (before the Bengalese moved in) is 600,000. There are, however, debates about the accuracy of the demographic information, and varied statistics are found in various historiographical literatures about the CHT. I refrain from engaging in these debates and follow the statistics found in the *Adibasi* literature authored by *Adibasi* people (such as Roy 2000).
5. Based on subsistence farming in contrast with the wet rice cultivation system in the plains, they practiced mixed farming of plough cultivation in the fertile valleys and crop rotation methods (shifting cultivation) on the hill slopes. This shifting cultivation is known as *swidden agriculture* or (in the language of the Hill) *jhum chash*. The aboriginals developed their own farmland and practiced *jhum* cultivation using buffaloes and ploughs.
6. See annotation 1 for a map of the CHT. It is believed by many Bangladeshis that these people had come from countries such as Myanmar, China and Mongolia. However, this argument is not relevant to this study, as I refrain from engaging with the concept of 'indigenous' and 'settlers'. I call these people *adivasi* and Buddhists in recognition of their original positions in society.

7. Interview held on 14 January 2013 at Khagrachari, CHT.
8. Interview held on 19 January 2003 at Khagrachari, CHT.
9. Notably, there had been 46 different communities who lived in East Pakistan, thereafter Bangladesh, at that time.
10. The Constitution of the Peoples Republic of Bangladesh. Government of Bangladesh, 1972.
11. The Constitution of the Peoples Republic of Bangladesh (as amended up to 30 April 1996). Government of Bangladesh, 1996. p.16

REFERENCES

Abedin, Z. (1997). *The CHT: That Sheds Blood.* Dhaka: Sunzida Anzuman.
Abedin, Z. (2003). *The Chittagong Hill Tracts: An Indian Intervention.* London: Eastern Publishers.
Ahmed, H. S. (2011). *First Anniversary of Baghaihat and Khagrachhari Attack.* Retrieved March 29, 2011, from https://picasaweb.google.com/117438218115668820753/FirstAnniversaryHumanChainForBaghaihat Attacks.
Amnesty International. (2005). *Communal Violence in the Post-conflict Chittagong Hill Tracts in Bangladesh.* London: Amnesty International's International Secretariat.
Amnesty International. (2011). *Indigenous Land Dispute Turns Deadly in Bangladesh: Amnesty International Public Statement.* London: Amnesty International's International Secretariat.
Amnesty International. (2013). *Pushed to the Edge. Indigenous Rights Denied in Bangladesh's Chittagong Hill Tracts.* London: Amnesty International's International Secretariat.
Azad, H. (2004). *Parbytta Chattrygram: Sobuj Pahar er vetor die Hingsher Jharnadhara (The CHT: The Stream of Envy into the Green Hill).* Dhaka: Agami Prokashani.
Bhabha, H. K. (1994). *The Location of Culture.* London: Routledge.
Chakma, (1983). 'We Want the Land and Not the People': Genocide in the Chittagong Hill Tracts. *Survival International Review* (43).
Chittagong Hill Tracts Commission. (2000). *'Life Is Not Ours': Land and Human Rights in the Chittagong Hill Tracts Bangladesh.* Amsterdam and Copenhagen: The Chittagong Hill Tracts Commission (CHT Commission).
Chittagong Hill Tracts Commission. (2011a). *CHT Commission on Using the Correct Term to Recognize Indigenous People in the Constitution of Bangladesh. Honourable Deputy Leader of the House and Chairperson of The National Committee for Implementation of the CHT Peace Accord.* Dhaka: Chittagong Hill Tracts Commission.
Chittagong Hill Tracts Commission. (2011b). Renewed Violence in the CHT and the Need for Implementation of the CHT Accord: A Memorandum to

the Prime Minister from the CHT Commission Expressing Concern Over the Recent Violence in Ramgarh. Prime Minister Government of the People's Republic of Bangladesh [e-mail] (E-mail communication, 24 April 2011). Dhaka: Chittagong Hill Tracts Commission.

Chittagong Hill Tracts Commission International. (2011). Letter to Prime Minister of the Government of Bangladesh: Concern Over Reports of Renewed Violence in Langadu, Rangamati, Chittagong Hill Tracts. S. Hasina International CHTC Expresses Deep Concern Over Renewed Violence in Langadu, Rangamati, CHT. A Letter of Concern Sent to the Prime Minister of the Government of Bangladesh by the Co-chairs of the International CHT Commission (CHTC). pp. 1–3. Dhaka: Chittagong Hill Tracts Commission Secretariat.

Dewan, I. (2010). Matribhasha (Mother Language). In N. Mohaimen (Ed.), *Between Ashes and Hope: Chittagong Hill Tracts in the Blind Spot of Bangladesh Nationalism* (pp. 167–168). Dhaka: Drishtipat Writers Collective.

Giles, W., & Hyndman, J. (2004). Introduction: Gender and Conflict in Global Context. In W. Giles & J. Hyndman (Eds.), *Sites of Violence, Gender and Conflict Zones* (pp. 1–23). Berkeley, Los Angeles and London: University of California Press.

Guhathakurta, M. (2004). *Ethnic Conflict in a Post-accord Situation: The Case of the Chittagong Hill Tracts, Bangladesh.* Paper presented at the Conference on Ethnic Identity and Ethnic Conflict in Multicultural Societies.

Hall, S. (2003). Cultural Identity and Diaspora. In J. E. Braziel & A. Mannur (Eds.), *Theorizing Diaspora: A Reader.* Oxford: Blackwell.

Hashem, R. (2006). Proshongya vashar shadhinota o narir khomotayan (The Role of Language and Culture in the Empowerment of Hill Women). In Dipayan Khisha (Ed.), *Mawroom* (pp. 39–56).

Hashem, R. (2014). *Gender and Armed Conflict: The Chittagong Hill Tracts, Bangladesh.* (Unpublished Ph.D. Thesis). University of East London, United Kingdom.

Hashem, R. (2016a, May 12). Witnessing Horror in Father's Dreamland. *International Humanitarian Ethical Union blog* [Online]. Available from http://iheu.org/witnessing-horror-in-fathers-dream-land-tribute-to-a-believ-erin-free-speech/. Accessed 12 July 2017.

Hashem, R. (2016b, June 12). The Missing Lines in Bangladesh Profile: Post Editorial. *The New Age* [Online]. Available from http://newagebd.net/234949/missing-lines-bangladesh-profile/. Accessed 18 Feb. 2017.

Mohsin, A. (1997). *The Politics of Nationalism: The Case of the Chittagong Hill Tracts Bangladesh* (2nd ed.). Dhaka: The University Press Limited.

Mohsin, A. (2003). *The Chittagong Hill Tracts, Bangladesh: On the Difficult Road to Peace.* London: Lynne Rienner.

Mohsin, A. (2010). Language, Identity and State. In N. Mohaimen (Ed.), *Between Ashes and Hope: Chittagong Hill Tracts in the Blind Spot of Bangladesh Nationalism* (pp. 157–166). Dhaka: Drishtipat Writers Collective.

Muhammad, A. (1997, December 2). '*The National Minorities in Bangladesh*'. Paper Presented at the *Regional Seminar of Economists*, jointly organised by Bangladesh Economic Association and Department of Economics, Chittagong University, Chittagong.

Muhammad, A. (2010). The Case of National Minorities. In N. Mohaimen (Ed.), *Between Ashes and Hope: Chittagong Hill Tracts in the Blind Spot of Bangladesh Nationalism* (pp. 21–23.). Dhaka: Drishtipat Writers Collective.

Rahman, M. M. (2011). *Struggling Against Exclusion: Adibasi in the Chittagong Hill Tracts, Bangladesh.* Lund Dissertations in Sociology, 95. Lund: Media-Tryck, Lund University.

Ross, M. H. (2009). *Cultural Contestation in Ethnic Conflict.* Cambridge: Cambridge University Press.

Roy, R. C. (2000). *Land Rights of the Indigenous Peoples of the Chittagong Hill Tracts, Bangladesh* (No. 99). Copenhagen: International Work Group For Indigenous Affairs.

Shelly, R. M., (Ed.). (1992). *The Chittagong Hill Tracts of Bangladesh: The Untold Story* Dhaka: Centre for Development Research, Bangladesh.

Yuval-Davis, N. (2011). *The Politics of Belonging: Intersectional Contestestations.* London: Sage.

CHAPTER 5

Impediment or Resource? Contextualisation of the Shared Built Heritage in Turkey

Deniz Ikiz Kaya and Mehmet Calhan

INTRODUCTION: THE CONTEXTUALISATION OF HERITAGE

Cultural heritage is considered as a source of identity, an inheritance, an assemblage of values that are ascribed to certain tangible and intangible assets of shared cultural pasts, which are selected and shaped based on the demands of the present (Ashworth et al. 2007). Logan (2012: 233) points out that these multiple layers of values are "attributed, not inherent", and so cultural heritage is subject to contestation as a result of the construction and deconstruction of memory and identity. Acting as a mediator between the past and present, this shared heritage thus fosters both cooperation and contestation between social groups, systems and administrative forces. Hence, they create both impediments to and opportunities for conflict mitigation.

Based on his studies on the psychocultural narratives of ethnic conflict, Ross (2007) illuminates the significant role of cultural expressions

D. I. Kaya (✉)
School of Architecture, Oxford Brookes University, Oxford, UK

M. Calhan
London, UK

© The Author(s) 2018
J. Rodenberg and P. Wagenaar (eds.), *Cultural Contestation*,
Palgrave Studies in Cultural Heritage and Conflict,
https://doi.org/10.1007/978-3-319-91914-0_5

in connecting individuals to groups and formulating group identities. Analysing the dynamics of cultural contestation, he highlights that certain cultural expressions, narratives and landscapes are capable of bringing parties in conflict closer together, while others can escalate the tension. Drawing on the contemporary conflict theory, Kriesberg (2003) explains that culture can be used as a tool to reshape narratives and identities and to redefine instances of conflict in a more constructive way. McEvoy (2011) also investigates how such cases of cultural contestation can be redefined and managed by the governing parties to favour their political narratives and priorities in the post-conflict regions. Regarding the fact that cultural identities can be constructed, Ross (2009) hence emphasises that they can also be reconstructed through the elaboration of more inclusive narratives. The contextualisation of cultural attributes and symbolic landscapes as "shared" assets among groups in contestation is thus highly important to facilitate conflict mitigation.

While the notion of "shared built heritage" is associated to countries with colonial pasts, it generally refers to heritage properties with multiple identities and varying uses based on the changing demographics throughout their history. The *ICOMOS International Scientific Committee on Shared Built Heritage* define it as "historical urban and rural structures and elements, resulting from multicultural and/or colonial influence"; thus, the notion of "shared" refers to a mixing, an interaction, a confrontation of multiple values and identities (ISCHSBH 2012). Heritage is recognised as a cultural process through which societies use the past—a "discursive construction" with material consequences. As a human condition, it is omnipresent, inter-woven within the power dynamics of any society and intimately bound up with identity construction at both communal and personal levels (Harvey 2001). Hence, heritage is not an innate or primordial phenomenon; people created or converted it into symbolic form, and in many cases, it is associated with religion (Olwig 2005). Although all heritage sites are contestable, the interpretation and representation of human suffering and past injustices can create significant dissonance or disagreement, as it is evident at many sacred places all over the world, especially with reference to the contested religious identities.

In this regard, a complex array of political and sociocultural logics contribute to this interplay that shapes the production, representation and governance of heritage. Tunbridge and Ashworth (1996) emphasise that cultural heritage is inherently "dissonant", which is open to multiple parallel and competing interpretations accounted by different social groups. This dissonance derives, first, from remembering uncomfortable historical facts within a process of making religious identity and then determining how the meaning of religious identity will be presented and communicated in public. Accommodating dissonance means recognising the complicated histories of communities and their places, while simultaneously accepting parallel and competing accounts of the past (Singh 2008). The idea that religious and political conflict goes hand in hand in the de-contextualisation or destruction of heritagescapes that play a symbolic role in forming identities.

Referred as the "authorised heritage discourse" by Smith (2006), the national governments usually dominate the designation and registration of official heritage sites through imposing a mainstream heritage and thus eliciting one type over the other. Hence, the power dynamics associated with nation-building and identity formation often foster dissonance in the recognition of conflicting histories of communities and their heritage. Graham and Howard (2008) further asserts that in this globalisation era, different representations of cultural heritage are also constructed to market destinations as an avenue to foster tourism development and to provide diverse income opportunities through implementation of various development policies by national and local governmental bodies. Winter (2015) suggests that such political and socio-economic complexities structuring the national governance of heritage emerge as ramifications of the "globalisation of heritage politics". Hence, the contents, interpretations and representations of cultural properties are selected, shaped and modified according to the contemporary demands and purposes of national governments.

The shifting ideologies, discourses and policies of governments, in this regard, play a key role in creating and recreating novel images and narratives of the already-existing cultural idioms through diverse ways of contextualisation, especially in countries with multi-ethnic and multi-denominational identities like Turkey. Following the establishment of an ethnocentric nation state at the beginning of the twentieth century, the interpretation and representation of the shared built heritage have created certain disagreement, specifically evident in the sacred places of contested religious identities belonging to minority groups. The long-standing conflicts of interests have been exacerbated by the competitive and often contradictory concerns of development and governmental policies, which have manipulated the use of religious heritage in the context of commercialisation of spirituality (Timothy and Conover 2006). Under the influence of dominant political, socio-economic and cultural paradigms, hence, the significance and meaning attributed to the contested heritagescapes are initially taken out of their original contexts (de-contextualised) and then are ascribed novel set of values and discourses (re-contextualised) over the years in Turkey.

In this context, this chapter analyses how the Turkish government imposes often contradictory contexts and narratives on the local heritage practices and examines the processes of de- and re-contextualisation of Greek Orthodox places of worship in Asia Minor that have been vandalised, neglected or adaptively reused in accordance with the national interest and policies, thus revealing government's role in cultural contestation. In association with the comprehensive analysis of psychocultural narratives by Ross (2007), this chapter studies the evolution of narratives and the transformation of the contested religious heritage in accordance with the official framing of the past and present by the national government. Thus, the aim is to address the material culture of the "other" and its association to politics and the role of the government in the contextualisation and use of the shared built heritage, as well as the delineation of the approach of local communities towards these contested buildings in the contemporary daily life. It further intends to understand and explain the complexities emerging from the shift in the ideological and administrative approach of the Turkish government in parallel to the international trends of governance towards the interpretation, representation and utilisation of the shared built heritage inherited from culturally and ethnically distinct communities. For this purpose, initially, the relevant national legislative acts and policies adopted by the government since the establishment of the Turkish Republic in early twentieth century will be examined. Through illustrating three cases of former Greek Orthodox churches located in Izmir, the trajectory of political and sociocultural approaches to the "Other" heritage will be assessed, and the complexities arising from the conflicting actions of diverse national and local actors will be identified.

Being the microcosm of Turkey's ethnic mixing for centuries, the city of Izmir in Western Turkey is a clear manifestation of the governance and political aspects of heritage. Hence, this multiple case study recounts the connection of heritage politics and development through consideration of debates over the preservation and regeneration of the contested architectural heritage. It has broader implications for the theoretical framework of heritage applicable to similar layered and contested sites. In conclusion, this chapter makes an original contribution to the cultural contestation and heritage governance discourses through the study of novel cases and introduction of a distinct perspective that examines the complexities associated with the role of governments in the de-contextualisation and re-contextualisation of the shared heritage in a region of political dissonance.

HERITAGE POLITICS IN TURKEY AND THE CASE OF IZMIR

In countries accommodating multinational identities, such as Turkey, the interpretation, representation and governance of the shared built heritage have shown great variety based on the political use of heritage. The centrality of politics for contested heritage sites in Turkey is illustrated particularly by the highly politicised and state-controlled approach towards the religious heritage belonging to various minority groups. Hence, it is important to portray how values of heritage have become entangled in Turkey's century-long quest for an identity and how they have changed over time within the historical context of Turkey's heritage politics.

Western Asia Minor accommodated indigenous Greek and Jewish populations and was inhabited by Turkish, Armenian, Sephardic and Ashkenazi Jewish and Levantine communities till the midst of the twentieth century. These ethnically diverse communities conveyed their own culture and religions to the cities where three Abrahamic religions and their fractions coexisted and constituted the main characteristic of the neighbourhoods for centuries. Unlike ghettos existed in European cities, these habitats were not segregated by physical boundaries (Bugatti 2013). Izmir, the biggest cosmopolitan city in Western Asia Minor, for instance, was comprised of numerous different communities with overlapping linguistic, ethnic and religious identities till the beginning of the twentieth century.

The transition of the Ottoman Empire into nation states was materialised in significant state-led modifications implemented at urban centres, especially in cities that had a multicultural character like Izmir. The transformation of these urban centres stemmed from both practical reasons such as the need for post-war reconstruction and the ideological request of building a national identity (Amygdalou 2014). Intrinsic to the character of growing nation-building ideals, the heritage discourse of the period developed within a "camouflaging context", a metaphor introduced by Shaw and Shaw (2003: 78) to describe the approach towards antiquities as a representation of modernity demonstrating progress and civilised history. Closely associated with the role of heritage in the politics of identity, this cultural camouflaging discourse has evolved from the Ottoman legacy of pragmatic Westernisation towards the Kemalist legacy of ethnocentric nation-building in the early twentieth century following the constitution of the new Turkish Republic (Atakuman 2010).

Within this evolved camouflaging context, the hegemonic heritage discourse of the Republican period has acclaimed the Turkish style of Islam and created new metaphors, such as "cradle of civilisations", "mosaic of cultures", and "bridging East and West", which signify the Turkish modernisation programme of formulating a condition of being "in between", a unification of Western materialism and Eastern spirituality (Yazıcıoğlu 2007). Examining how the national and local authorities, along with European architects invited, such as Henri Prost, are engaged in the development of urban modernity in the post-war Izmir in the early twentieth century, Amygdalou (2014) demonstrates how a variety of interpretations of the west and the "Other" based on the approach towards the conservation of the architectural heritage have been incorporated into the realm of national representation. Hence, this "bridge" metaphor serves perfectly to the ideal of creating a superior identity that synthesises Eastern and Western paradigms.

Following the conquest of the city by the Turkish army in 1922, Izmir was destroyed by a massive fire, resulting in the devastation of the Armenian and Greek neighbourhoods. The destruction was coupled with a massive demographic change caused by the compulsory population exchange between Greece and Turkey. The exodus of Christian Greeks as well as Armenians had already started at the end of the Independence War of Turkey in 1922. The Jewish community of Izmir gradually descended to its current approximate figure of 2000 right after the WWII. The transition of the Empire into the Turkish state also endangered the prosperity of the Levantine community, which has reduced to around 1500 in Turkey as of the beginning of the twenty-first century (Uras 2002). Consequently, the legacy of Izmir as a cosmopolitan town of diversity and tolerance gradually diminished in the Republican era, to be replaced by interstate hostility towards the tangible and intangible heritage attributes of the "Other".

At this point, it should be noted that even though religious freedom is under constitutional protection in Turkey, its practice has not been fully consistent with the constitutional act. Grigoriadis (2009) points out that the principles of reciprocity and equal citizenship for minority member under nation states have been subjected to political manipulations of the national governments. The reciprocity principle entails that each state is committed to fulfil its conventional obligations only to the extent that these obligations are fulfilled by its counter-signatory state. Based on this principle, Oran (2008) argues that the reciprocity degenerated into retaliation and then to reprisal, leading to frequent violations of religious freedom whenever national interests were allegedly threatened. Hence, in the times of conflict and contestations, the religious heritage of the associated minorities had been the first to be affected under the acts of vandalism.

Atakuman (2010) highlights that in realm of the "camouflaging" discourse, the governmental approach towards displaying diversity and tolerance has been presented through carefully chosen "fossilised" sites that have been selected for representing the past cultures of Asia Minor that are not contested by any of the living community groups. The early inscriptions of the archaeological site of Hattusa, former capital of the Hittite Empire, and the Mount Nemrut on the UNESCO's World Heritage List to represent the diversity of cultural heritage in Turkey, instead of the archaeological site of Ani, an Armenian heritage site that has just recently been designated as a World Heritage Site, are a clear manifestation of such selective approach towards the national representation of cultural diversity. The intention thus has been to avoid the emergence of dissonance through the neglect and suppression of living sites of contestation, specifically the religious built heritage of the "Other".

In the advent of Turkey's accession to the European Union since the early twenty-first century, this attitude has gradually yielded towards a discourse that embraces a trope of multiculturalism. Sahin Guchan and Kurul (2009) explain how this restructuring period has resulted in new institutionalisation arrangements and increase in resources for conservation practices. The accommodation of culture and tourism functions within the same ministry in Turkey has resulted in the proliferation of tourism-related activities. The government has promoted the conservation and revival of certain selected Christian sacred sites as part of religious tourism development plan. In addition to economic interests, the impositions by the international community have also bolstered investments for the preservation and regeneration of the Christian heritage in Turkey that had been previously devalued.

In this context, the following case study examines how the religious built heritage sites of the "Other" in Izmir have been contextualised, de-contextualised and re-contextualised in tandem with the evolution of the heritage politics and discourse in the past 150 years in Izmir. The results of this study clearly illustrate an analogy between the power dynamics and heritage conservation practices towards the shared built heritage in Turkey.

ANALYSIS OF THE SHARED BUILT HERITAGE IN IZMIR

Since the interpretation and representation of cultural heritage are a dynamic process, depending on how the power groups within a society associate themselves to their multicultural descent or reject it, their imposition on the de-contextualisation and re-contextualisation of the shared built heritage is manifested in the multi-layered association of meanings (Yenisehirlioglu 1998). The approach of this selective heritage has been an embodiment of ideology, a manifestation of the state's attempt to shape the physical environment.

The centrality of politics for places of worship representing living sites of contestation is clearly portrayed by the highly politicised, publicised and government-induced conservation and adaptive reuse practices of the religious heritage of the "Other" in the province of Izmir, which have been examined as a case study for this chapter. Hence, for this study, site visits were conducted in order to locate and document the monumental buildings belonging to the Christian and Jewish minorities in Western Asia Minor, and focused interviews were conducted with the local administrative bodies, leaders and members of the clergies and local community groups. Visual documents, archival sources, official documents and oral histories were collected during these site visits. While most of the historical written sources have been missing due to historical fires and migration, the lack of original documents made it hard to trace the location and knowledge about religious monuments. Additionally, one of the obstacles encountered during the data collection process has been based on the validity and reliability of the local sources and interviewees engaged due to the high degree of false information and lack of apathy in regard to the shared heritage attributes.

Based on the data gathered from the aforementioned sources, initially, an inventory of the still existing places of worship belonging to the minority groups in Izmir is conducted, which specifies the name, location, construction date and ownership status of the buildings, as well as documenting their current use and state of conservation. These details on the remaining religious heritage are outlined in Table 5.1 and used as a basis for their further assessment. Secondly, the historical evolution and the change in the uses of these heritage sites are documented in Table 5.2. Then, three of these places of worship are selected to be further analysed to depict the historical development of the buildings and to examine how these religious buildings have been used and adapted in time in association with the changing ideologies and political concerns of the national governments. These case buildings are hence chosen to represent shifts in the political approaches manifested in distinct methodologies of architectural conservation employed in tandem with the changing heritage discourse. This multiple case study analysis has contributed to the overall assessment and mapping of the evolution of governmental approaches towards the religious heritage of the "Other" and its effect on the uses and perception of the heritage attributes.

In this context, the first step has been the designation of the religious heritage of the "Other" in the province of Izmir and documentation of their current conservation status. As presented in Table 5.1, this shared built heritage is widely dispersed within the province to the various districts of the city, delineating the former neighbourhoods and urban centres of different ethnic communities. Most of these sanctuaries are located in the historical centre of Izmir, known as Konak today. Some of the suburban areas of the time, such as Buca, Bornova and Karataş, have been incorporated into the provincial area of the city since then. Most of the churches were constructed in the early twentieth century and served to the Catholic and Protestant communities in the city. Albeit the construction dates of the existing churches seem relatively new, many of them were rebuilt in the aftermath of natural disasters and fires.

Currently, there is only one church serving the Greek Orthodox congregation, which was allocated for a 100 years by the Dutch Protestant Church. The total number of Catholic and Protestant churches that still maintain their original function in Izmir is eleven. Among them, two Protestant Churches which were constructed and established during the Republican period are not included in this study. According to the interviews made with some of the priests of the Roman Catholic

Table 5.1 List of the registered Christian and Jewish places of worship located in the province of Izmir based on the *Inventory of Immovable Cultural Properties in Izmir*, 2012 (Calhan 2014)

Name	Date	Current use	Ownership	Description	Location
Churches					
1	Çarşı Mosque	End of 19th C.		Municipality of Aliağa		Aliağa
2	Hagios Haralambos Church					İnklap Ave. Çeşme
3	Church	19. C.	Cultural	Private ownership		Dalyan Çeşme
4	Church	19. C.	Park	Private	Some foundation traces are visible	Kilise Yolu St. Çeşme
5	Pazaryeri Mosque	1874	Mosque + Commercial			Sakarya St. Alaçatı Çeşme
6	Ruin	19th C.	Unoccupied			Diyarbakır St. Alaçatı Çeşme
7	Ruin	1883	Unoccupied	Min. of Finance		Sakarya Çeşme
8	Church Portal	19. C.	Unoccupied	Private	Church portal only	Köste Ave. Çeşme
9	Eski Mosque	Byzantine	Mosque			Foça
10	Martyr Georgios Convent		Unoccupied	Grade I natural site		Asmadere Yeni Foça
11	Church Wall		Unoccupied	Private	One of the main outer walls survived	Hamam St. Kınık
12	Church Annex		Unoccupied		Outer walls survived	
13	Agios Konstantinos	Beg. of 19. C.	Municipality of Menemen	Cultural Centre		Çınarlı Çıkmazi kinik Mermerli Menemen

(continued)

Table 5.1 (continued)

Name		Date	Current use	Ownership	Description	Location
14	Church	Beg. of 19. C.	Unoccupied	Min. of Finance		109/1 St. Menemen
15	Armenian Church					Mermerli Menemen
16	Demetrius (Aşağı) Church		Church	Min. of Culture and Tourism		İstiklal Şirince Selçuk
17	Virgin Mary Church	6th C.	Church	Virgin Mary Foundation		Bülbül Mount Yamacı Selçuk
18	St. Jean Church	5th C.	Church	Min. of Culture and Tourism		Ayasuluk Hill Selçuk
19	St. John the Baptist (Yukarı) Church	1805	Church	Min. of Culture and Tourism		İstiklal Şirince, Selçuk
20	Convent Ruins	Byzantine	Monastery Ruins	Min. of Culture and Tourism	Only some walls survived	İstiklal Şirince Selçuk
Synagogues						
21	Synagogues			Min. of Finance	Partially demolished during bus terminal construction	Üç Kemer Ave. No: 3 Bergama
22	Synagogues and Annex		Beer House	Min. of Finance	Roof collapsed	Elektrik Fab. Ave. Bergama
23	Synagogues	18. C.	Workshop/office		Heavily transformed	Atatürk Ave. Tire

Table 5.2 The change in the uses of the religious heritage of the "Other" in Izmir from nineteenth century onwards

		Name	Timeline
			1800 · · · 1939 · · · 1900 1912 1923 · · · 1960 · · · 2000 2014
IZMIR			
Greek Orthodox Church	1	Agios Voukolus	
	2	Agios Konstantinos & Eleni	
	3	Agios Ioannis Theologos	
	4	Agios Ioannis Prodromos	
	5	Evangelismos Theotokou	
	6	Profiti Elia Monastery	
	7	Agia Paraskevi	
	8	Metamorfosis Sotiris	
	9	Agios Ioannis sten A. P.	
	10	Timios Stravros (Doğanlar)	
	11	Analipsis Sotiris	
Roman Catholic Church	12	St. Polycarpe	
	13	St John's Cathedral	
	14	St. Maria	
	15	Holy Rosary	
	16	St. Antoine	
	17	St. Helen	
	18	Notre Dame de Lourdes	
	19	St. Maria	
Anglican	20	St. Mary Magdalene	
	21	All Saints	
	22	St. John the Evangelist	
P.	23	Agia Photini (Dutch P.)	
Synagogue	24	Ashkenazi	
	25	Beit Hillel	
	26	Beit Israel	
	27	Bikur Hollim	
	28	Algaze	
	29	Etz Haim	
	30	Hevra	
	31	Kahal Kadosh	
	32	Los Foresteros	
	33	Portugal	
	34	Rosh Ha Har	
	35	Sinyora	
	36	Shalom	
THESSALONIKI			
Mosque	1	Alaca Imaret Mosque	
	2	Hamza Bey Mosque	
	3	Yeni Mosque	
	4	Rotunda	
	5	Monasteriotes' Synagogue	

Church	Synagogue	Mosque	Destroyed	Unknown
Cultural	Administrative	Housing	Commercial	Military

Churches (St. Maria, St. Helen, Notre Dame de Lourdes, St. John the Evangelist and St. Maria), the congregations that show up regularly on Sunday masses comprise of approximately twenty members in each. They mainly include elder Levantines and expats living in the city. Foreign and exchange students also constitute a small portion of that number.

While the great fire of Izmir diminished the Greek Orthodox and Armenian churches, there was a considerable amount surviving outside the fire zone. But the exodus of the Greek and Armenian communities in the aftermath left these buildings without heirs. As with the beginning of the Republican Era, the new urban regeneration and reconstruction plans embodying largely the areas affected by the fire paid little attention to the safeguarding of the historical urban fabric and the existing monuments poor in shape were mainly neglected (Bugatti 2013). Many of them did not survive due to the late registration of such buildings as cultural properties to be protected and as a result of the rise in urban development schemes. Hence, there are only a limited number of Greek Orthodox churches still existing in Izmir today.

Table 5.2 depicts comprehensively the development of the existing religious buildings and their functional changes in time. Regarding this chart, it is observed that while almost all of the Roman Catholic and Protestant churches, as well as synagogues, have maintained their original functions as places of worship, many of the Greek Orthodox churches have been adaptively reused to accommodate new functions over time. Closely related with the political and cultural shifts in the policies and diplomatic stances on Greece, this reuse approach towards the Greek Orthodox churches reflects the association of still-standing non-Muslim sites as a reminder of the city's multi-ethnic past. It is also important to note that the ownership of the churches did not change hands even though they were underused and struggled to maintain themselves.

As it is portrayed in Table 5.2, some of the reused Greek Orthodox churches were converted into mosques (Agios Ioannis Prodromos, Evangelismos Theotokou, Metamorfosis Sotiris) in the first half of the twentieth century. This transformation is a clear demonstration of the identity formation ideals following ethnocentric nation-building in the early Republican era and its manifestation on the state-led transformation of architectural heritage representing multi-ethnicity and diversity. It is also observed that some of the former Greek Orthodox churches were allocated administrative functions were adapted to be used as public schools in the second half of the twentieth century. In a study of Zeren and Erdogmuş (2011), three schools—Cumhuriyet, Selçuk Yaşar Alaybey and Ankara Primary Schools—were identified to be located on the sites of former churches, built over the foundations of Greek Orthodox churches in the district of Karsiyaka. Three churches listed in the inventory of the study were also constructed on the sites of former Greek Orthodox churches in mid-twentieth century. It should be noted that the same era was marked by the Turkish/Greek dispute over the Cyprus issue. Hence, it is clear that national political trends and diplomatic stances have had a direct impact on the use of contested sites and the discourse towards the shared built heritage.

As part of the European Union accession process in the twenty-first century, the government's attempts to "Europeanise" the heritage discourse and conservation policy have resulted in substantial increase in the resources that are allocated to conservation and tourism development. This period has evoked a rising interest in the shared built heritage assets and in their promotion as a market for entrepreneurial conservation activities and international tourism.

In parallel with these trends, the Greek Orthodox buildings that had lost their original functions and communities were allocated new uses and renovated by the local administrative bodies. These new reuse and regeneration programmes undertaken by the local governmental bodies, such as the Izmir Metropolitan Municipality or the Directorate for Culture and Tourism, have been distinguished from the former intervention that had been employed without provisions. The recent architectural conservation schemes have been developed based on a conservation area plan, and new functions designated for the shared heritage sites have conveyed public use purposes. Additionally, the adaptive reuse interventions have been compatible with the contemporary principles of historic conservation that intends to preserve the integrity and authenticity of sites, while the earlier attempts paid little attention to the integrated conservation of the area and the remains as a whole.

Among these still-remaining Greek Orthodox churches that have been renewed to thrive new functions over time, three of them are further assessed as case studies in order to have a closer look at the impact of national political discourse on the shared heritage attributes. These buildings are selected based on the criteria of representing various functional changes in association with the shifts in heritage politics and maintaining a good conservation status. For this purpose, site observations

and content analysis of the archival records and the interviews are conducted with the members of the clergy and the local community. Based
on the data gathered, the following chart (Table 5.3) that highlights the
construction date, functions, ownership and conservation status of the
selected buildings is depicted.

As portrayed in Table 5.3, the Greek Orthodox churches that are
selected to be further analysed are the Agios Voukolos, Agios Ioannis
Prodromos and Timios Stavros (Doganlar) churches located within
the province of Izmir. Constructed on the former site of an ancient
church, the Agios Voukolos Church is among the best preserved

Table 5.3 The historical evolution of the three case buildings

Name of the Church	Agios Voukolus Greek Orthodox Church	Agios Ionnis Prodromes Greek Orthodox Church	Timios Stravros (Doganlar) Greek Orthodox Church
Photo			
Location	Konak, Izmir	Adatepe Buca, Izmir	Doganlar Bornova, Izmir
Date and Known Functions	1886–1922: Church 1927–1984: Relics Museum (later changed to Archaeology Museum), Opera house 2010–present: Cultural Centre	1854–1922: Church 1922–: Masjid 1970–present: School	1866–1922: Church 1930s–1940s: School 1940s–: Carpenter workshop
Ownership	Izmir Metropolitan Municipality	–	Izmir Metropolitan Municipality
Accessibility	Open to access	Open to access	Open to access
State of Preservation	Good, restored in 2010	Demolished in 1970s, only the entrance gate still remains	Restored in 2014

Orthodox churches still existing in Western Asia Minor as a result of its compatible former uses (Levantine Heritage 2011). It was used by the Eastern Orthodox Armenian community until the mass migration in 1922, which was then turned into a relics museum, and later to the Archaeology Museum. The building was very recently restored to be used as a cultural centre, and the conservation practice was supported by a generous grant provided by the Izmir Special Provincial Directorate of Administration and was operated by the Izmir Metropolitan Municipality. As part of the restoration work, the former church was reinforced, the original surfaces of the exterior masonry walls that had previously been covered in plaster were cleaned, and the original decoration and motives were revealed.

The Agios Ioannis Prodromes Church was initially built in 1796, but then reconstructed in 1854 (Levantine Heritage 2011). Following the migration of the Greek community in 1922, the church was converted into a masjid to be used by the Muslim community instead. The historic building was proposed to be demolished to be replaced by a mosque complex, but this proposition was opposed by a campaign held by the local community members, and the historic site was thus transformed into a primary school property. Hence, the school was built on the former church plot. The only remains of the former church include the marble arched portal and the exterior garden walls surrounding the property. Nevertheless, the contemporary building maintains the existing ruins of the church.

The third case is the Timios Stavros Church, which was originally constructed as a small rural church serving the Levantine communities living within the area. In the early Republican era, the building was converted into a carpenter's workshop and storage space. Since then, the former church accommodated numerous functions changes and interventions. Recently, it was allocated a public use by the Izmir Metropolitan Municipality and restored to serve as a community centre for women and children (Calhan 2014). The stone masonry building covered by a timber vault as a superstructure still maintains most of its original building structures and elements and hence is in a good conservation status. The periodical shifts in the use and conservation attempts of these selected Orthodox churches clearly demonstrate the direct association between the heritage politics and approach towards the shared built heritage and the national trends of foreign relations and internal affairs. This relation is mapped out and further discussed in the following concluding section.

Regarding its Jewish heritage, Izmir is the only city in the world in which an unusual cluster of synagogues with a certain medieval Spanish architectural style is still preserved. These nine medieval style synagogues constructed mainly in the seventeenth century are located in close proximation to one another, creating a unique historical architectural ensemble. Contrary to their plain façades, the interiors of these sanctuaries are elaborately decorated and rich in ornamentation (Calhan 2014). Currently, some of these synagogues have been left to ruin as a result of the absence of their congregations, while some are relatively in good condition despite the lack of maintenance. Since the beginning of the twenty-first century, a number of studies and initiatives have raised awareness on the significance of this heritage on the verge of collapse, and the Kemeraltı synagogues have been designated as a preservation priority project in the city. Its publicity has attracted more funding for conservation efforts from sources such as the municipal government and the Chamber of Commerce. The Izmir Project, led by the Mordechai Kiryati Foundation, has been a collaborative regeneration project conducted by the local government and supported by the Jewish community to restore the seven extant synagogues of the Central Izmir Complex. As part of this public–private partnership, it is also planned to establish an on-site museum and educational centre of local Jewish history (World Monuments Fund 2014).

A broader image of the Christian and Jewish heritage sites in Izmir reveals how past sufferings during the formation of the Turkish state lead to the erasure of the marks of specific community groups and sites of contestation, in a city which was once hailed as one of the greatest multicultural societies in history. The survey and inventory of the religious buildings belonging to the minority groups in Izmir clearly demonstrate the powerful role of the national government and the policies it adopts in manipulation of heritage politics and discourse for public relations, as well as in the shaping of the historic environments that once represented multiculturalism and diversity. These cases examined also manifest the shift in the contextualisation of the heritage rhetoric describing the goals of architectural conservation for the shared built heritage based primarily on political and secondarily on economic interests. They demonstrate how such contested sites of worship have recently been marketed as an instrument to embrace a trope of multiculturalism and to indicate religious tolerance in relation with the international politics, a gesture towards improving the relations between the Republic of Turkey and

Greece, and as a potential pilgrimage destination for faith tourism. They also show how sanctuaries of touristic interests are more likely to be preserved in compatible with the contemporary conservation approaches, while others have been renewed to use the existing space in a more pragmatic way which doesn't always happen to be compatible. The results of this multiple case study are further discussed in the following conclusion section.

Conclusion

This study analyses the relationship between the national political trends and their impact on the preservation of the shared built heritage in Turkey, while pointing out an analogy on the basis of their conservation and use over time. Focusing on the religious architectural heritage of the "Other" in Izmir, it examines their historical evolution and shifts in the conservation rhetoric and practices in tandem with the political priorities of the government. It is closely associated with the following statement by Ross (2007: 41), "as conflicts evolve, contested cultural expressions and their significance shift". In this case hence, the national government emerges as at the main actor determining the processes of cultural contestation. In accordance with the definition of dissonant heritage by Tunbridge and Ashworth (1996) that acknowledges the existence of multiple parallel and often competing interpretations of sites of contestation by different social groups, three phases associated with the governance, interpretation and representation of tangible and intangible attributes of religious heritage of the "Other" in Turkey are thus identified and presented in Table 5.4.

Regarding this chart, three phases are classified that exposes the shifts in the attributes towards the shared architectural heritage, their uses and the changes in the perception of the values attributed to them. These phases are identified as destruction, adaptation and acceptance, respectively, which are also periodically associated with three stages in the evolution of the Republican era that are inclined towards various political and economic trends. In this context, the initial phase is associated with the nation-state building and ethnocentric identity formation ideals following the establishment of the Republic of Turkey in 1923. This period is marked with the dismissal of generations of accumulated memories of tolerance and coexistence and is expressed with a hostile attitude towards the shared heritage in Izmir during the times of conflict. The destruction of certain monuments symbolising the "Other" cultures, coupled with

Table 5.4 Evolution of attitudes towards the religious heritage of 'Other' (based on Murzyn and Gwozdz 2003: 191)

Phase	Historic period	Material heritage/ uses of heritage	Perception of heritage/ values attached to it
I. Hostility, destruction	Establishment of the Republic of Turkey, Nation-state building, ethno-centric identity formation	Removing Ottoman symbolism, irresponsible usage, devastation by fire and demolishment	Hostility, de-contextualisation, inadaptability, attempt at "de-Ottomanisation", cultural camouflage, Modernisation approach
II. Adaptation, partial assimilation	Twentieth century; 1950s— Cypriot dispute between Turkey and Greece	Caring for heritage based on its use value, mid-20th century— adaptive reuse for public usage	Indifference, adaptation, slow familiarisation
III. Acceptance, internation-alisation/Europeanisation, reconstruction	Early twenty-first century—EU accession, political and eco-nomic concerns	Care, extensive regeneration programmes, revival of shared heritage	part of identity, curiosity of the past, representation of diversity and tolerance

the great fire, facilitated the erasure and the de-contextualisation of the memory of the shared past and its tangible assets. Referring to the "cultural camouflage" metaphor induced by Shaw and Shaw (2003), this era is also characterised with a "de-Ottomanisation" attitude that promoted the transformation of the built heritage through the adoption of Modern urban policies and development plans conveying economic values. Based on the reciprocity principle introduced by Oran (2008), and the hostile political climate between Turkey and Greece, the nation-building heritage politics of the period resulted in the destruction, decay or incompatible use of shared heritage, specifically the Greek Orthodox churches that became redundant after the loss of the local community.

The second phase symbolising the period of adaptation and partial assimilation coincides with the re-contextualisation of the shared heritage to create new allusions of certain sites of contestation and their adaptation to thrive novel functions. It is important to highlight that this era witnessed certain interruptions in the adaptation processes during periods of political dissonance between Turkey and Greece. For instance, the Cypriot dispute that was aroused in the 1950s–1960s provoked negative attributions ascertained to former Greek Orthodox churches, resulting in physical and functional changes that often threatened the authenticity and integrity of the sites. Associated with these adverse accounts and narratives of the shared past, the religious heritage belonging to the former Greek communities was regenerated and adapted based on their use value. While the Greek Orthodox churches were converted into mosques or masjids in the early Republican era as part of the assimilation process, they were then renewed to accommodate public uses, as schools or museums, in the mid-twentieth century.

In the advent of European Union accession, the heritage politics in the twenty-first century has entailed a discourse in the context of acceptance and tolerance, coupled with the commercialisation of the shared past as tourism destinations. This era is hence marked with the re-contextualisation of the religious heritage of the "Other" as a reminder of the multicultural identity and diversity that once existed. The national and local governmental bodies have contributed greatly to the reformation of the urban identity of the city as a multicultural city of tolerance that "bridges East and West" (Yazıcıoğlu 2007). They have adopted new development and governmental policies that have boosted investments in conservation practices, which have also promoted the use of religious heritage in the context of commercialisation of spirituality (Timothy and Conover 2006). In this period, numerous Greek Orthodox churches have undergone extensive conservation and restoration activities, mainly operated by the local administrative units.

At this point, however, it should be noted that the presence of minority communities or shared built heritage has still been sparingly mentioned in the official Turkish historiography despite all the internationalisation efforts. While the rhetoric of official governmental bodies when referring to the shared heritage has invoked the trope of multiculturalism to describe the multilayered sites, dissonant narratives have usually taken over in this multicultural rhetoric that elicits one layer over the other. Watenpaugh (2014), for instance, exemplifies this selective approach with a reference to the archaeological site of Ani whose Armenian past has been either silenced or actively repressed. Hence, it can be concluded that this process of re-contextualising the shared built heritage in Turkey has rather been sporadic. It proves the existence of stigma in terms of the interpretation, contextualisation and representation of the shared religious heritage and the identity politics of today.

Consequently, this study demonstrates how fragile the politics of heritage are and how amenable to political manipulation/exploitation cultural heritage is. The hegemonic ideology of authenticity on heritage conservation is usually contested and entangled within the complexities of local diversity, specifically for the sacred places of the shared past. The central governments have long recognised the significant role of cultural heritage in nation-building, identity formation and economic development, and they have established legal instruments and national policies to spread the knowledge and control the practices of heritage conservation (Oakes 1993; Nyiri 2006). As demonstrated with this study, the architectural heritage is thus instrumentalist in the service of political priorities and narratives of ideologically charged historiography. This multiple case study examining the physical and functional alterations that former Greek Orthodox churches have undergone over time is a great manifestation of how choices in regard to the conservation of the shared built heritage cannot escape political manoeuvres. Hence, dissonance emerging from variations in the interpretation and representation of such sites of contestation should thus be acknowledged and engaged for reconciliation.

In conclusion, this chapter makes a significant contribution to the discourse on heritage governance and cultural contestation through the introduction of novel cases and a distinct perspective that examines the complexities associated with the role of governments in the de-contextualisation and re-contextualisation of the shared heritage through the conduct of a multiple case study in a region of political dissonance.

REFERENCES

Amygdalou, K. (2014). Building the Nation at the Crossroads of 'East' and 'West': Ernest Hebrard and Henri Prost in the Near East. *Opticon 1826, 16*(15), 1–19.

Ashworth, G. J., Graham, B. J., & Tunbridge, J. E. (2007). *Pluralising Pasts: Heritage, Identity and Place in Multicultural Societies.* London: Pluto.

Atakuman, C. (2010). Value of Heritage in Turkey. *Journal of Mediterranean Archaeology, 23*(1), 107–132.

Bugatti, E. (2013). Urban Identities and Catastrophe: Izmir and Salonica at the End of the Ottoman Empire. *The Geographical Review, 103*(4), 498–516.

Calhan, M. (2014). *Shared Built Heritage: From Burden to Resource— A Comparison Between Izmir and Thessaloniki on the Basis of Conservation and Use of the 'Other' Religious Heritage After the Mass Migrations of the Twentieth Century.* Unpublished M.Sc. thesis, RLICC, University of Leuven, Leuven.

Graham, B., & Howard, P. (Eds.). (2008). *The Ashgate Research Companion to Heritage and Identity.* London: Assignee.

Grigoriadis, I. N. (2009). Reciprocity as Race to the Bottom in Religious Freedom. In K. A. N. K. Ö. Othon Anastasakis (Ed.), *In the Long Shadow of Europe: Greeks and Turks in the Era of Post-nationalism* (pp. 167–190). Leiden: Martinus Nijhoff.

Harvey, D. C. (2001). Heritage Pasts and Heritage Presents: Temporality, Meaning and the Scope of Heritage Studies. *International Journal of Heritage Studies, 7*(4), 319–338.

ICOMOS Shared Built Heritage. (2012). *Cultural Heritage Connections* [Online]. Available at: http://www.culturalheriageconnections.org/wiki/ICOMOS_Shared_Built_Heritage. Accessed 14 Nov 2015.

Kriesberg, L. (2003). *Constructive Conflicts: From Escalation to Resolution.* Lanham, MD: Rowman & Littlefield.

Levantine Heritage. (2011). *Levantine Heritage* [Online]. Available at: http://www.levantineheritage.com. Accessed 5 June 2016.

Logan, W. (2012). Cultural Diversity, Cultural Heritage and Human Rights: Towards Heritage Management as Human Rights-Based Cultural Practice. *International Journal of Heritage Studies, 18*(3), 231–244.

McEvoy, J. (2011). Managing Culture in Post-conflict Societies. *Journal of the Academy of Social Sciences, 66*(1), 55–71.

Murzyn, M. A., & Gwozdz, K. (2003). Dilemmas Encountered in the Development of Tourism in a Degraded Town: The Case of Schömberg in Lower Silesia. *Prace Geograficzne, 111*, 183–198.

Nyiri. P. (2006). *Scenic Spots: Chinese Tourism, the State and Cultural Authority.* Washington: University of Washington Press.

Oakes, T. S. (1993). The Cultural Space of Modernity: Ethnic Tourism and Place Identity in China. *Environment and Planning D: Society and Space, 11*(1): 47–66.

Olwig, K. R. (2005). Introduction. In D. Lowenthal & K. R. Olwig (Eds.), *The Nature of Cultural Heritage, and the Culture of National Heritage—Northern Perspective on a Contested Patrimony* (pp. 1–7). Abingdon, Oxon: Routledge.

Oran, B. (2008). Reciprocity in Turco-Greek Empire and Modern Turkey Relations: The Case of Minorities. In S. Akgonul (Ed.), *Reciprocity Greek and Turkish Minorities Law, Religion and Politics* (pp. 35–38). Istanbul: Bilgi University Press.

Ross, M. H. (2007). *Cultural Contestation in Ethnic Conflict*. Cambridge: Cambridge University Press.

Ross, M. H. (2009). Culture in Comparative Political Analysis. In M. I. Lichbach & A. Zuckerman (Eds.), *Rationality, Culture and Structure* (pp. 134–161). New York: Cambridge University Press.

Sahin Guchan, N., & Kurul, E. (2009). A History of the Development of Conservation Measures in Turkey: From the Mid-19th Century Until 2004. *METU Journal of the Faculty of Architecture, 26*(2), 19–44.

Shaw, S. J., & Shaw, E. K. (2003). *Reform, Revolution and Republic: The Rise of Modern Turkey, 1808–1975*. Cambridge: Cambridge University Press.

Singh, R. P. B. (2008). The Contestation of Heritage: The Enduring Importance of Religion. In B. Graham & P. Howard (Eds.), *Ashgate Research Companion to Heritage and Identity* (pp. 125–141). London: Ashgate.

Smith, L. (2006). *Uses of Heritage*. London: Routledge.

Timothy, D. J., & Conover, P. J. (2006). Nature Religion, Self-spirituality and New Age Tourism. In D. J. Timothy & D. H. Olsen (Eds.), *Tourism, Religion and Spiritual Journeys* (pp. 139–155). London and New York: Routledge.

Tunbridge, J. E., & Ashworth, G. J. (1996). *Dissonant Heritage: The Management of the Past as a Resource in Conflict*. Chichester: Wiley.

Uras, G. (2002). Levantenler İzmir'in rengi-tadı. *Hurriyet, 7* 9.

Watenpaugh, H. Z. (2014). Preserving the Medieval City of Ani: Cultural Heritage Between Contest and Reconciliation. *Journal of the Society of Architectural Historians, 73*(4), 528–555.

Winter, T. (2015). Heritage Diplomacy. *International Journal of Heritage Studies, 21*(10), 997–1015.

World Monuments Fund. (2014). *Central Izmir Synagogues* [Online]. Available at: http://www.wmf.org/project/centralizmir-synagogues. Accessed 6 Aug 2014.

Yazıcıoğlu, G. B. (2007). Archaeological Politics of Anatolia: Imaginative Identity of an Imaginative Geography. In L. Popova, C. Hartley & A. Smith (Eds.), *Social Orders and Social Landscapes* (pp. 218–252). Cambridge: Cambridge Scholars Publishing.

Yenisehirlioglu, F. C. (1998). Decontextualisation and Decontextualisation of Ottoman Cultural Heritage in Post-Ottoman Nation States. In M. Korzay, et al. (Eds.), *International Conference on Heritage Multicultural Attractions and Tourism* (pp. 119–140). Istanbul: Bogazici University Press.

Zeren, M. T., & Erdogmuş, B. (2011). 19. yuzyil Kordelyası'nda gayrimuslim dini yapilari. *Ege Mimarlk, 7*, 18–22.

CHAPTER 6

From House-Temples to Museum Showcase: Afro-Cuban Religions, Heritage and Cultural Policy in Cuba

Michelle A. Tisdel

INTRODUCTION

Fredesvinda Rosell was the owner of Palacio de los Orishas, a renowned house-temple in a small provincial town. Many years ago, she began opening her doors to visitors who wanted to observe the cultural expressions of Afro-Cuban religions, such as Regla de Ocha, in its ritual setting. The religions have thrived in Cuba for centuries, and times under very adverse conditions—from the colonial slave society through the turbulent years of Cuban socialism. Under the socialist government, state museums have promoted a one-size-fits-all narrative about Afro-Cuban religions. Today, a growing number of ritual houses seek opportunities to share personal stories and alternative narratives about their traditions and sacred biographical objects to the public. This is not only an extension of their ongoing imitation, collaboration, and competition with museums. Below, I argue that their strategic narrative practices are a consequence of a simmering cultural contestation about Afro-Cuban religions and heritage.

M. A. Tisdel (✉)
National Library of Norway, Oslo, Norway

© The Author(s) 2018   105
J. Rodenberg and P. Wagenaar (eds.), *Cultural Contestation*,
Palgrave Studies in Cultural Heritage and Conflict,
https://doi.org/10.1007/978-3-319-91914-0_6

Hamlish (2000) argues that under state socialism, the museum is "a site for asserting hegemony" over the construction of the past (138). Through cultural policy and institutions, the government can use heritage to break with the past while establishing relevance to it. The museum, as Hamlish notes, serves to "resolve the contradictions inherent in constructing a past that is both distant and immediate, through the inversion of two seemingly distinct discourses" (2000: 138).

Studies of museums under Cuban socialism highlight the legitimating power of museums in the symbolic landscape. One approach highlights the concerns and perspectives of source communities, such as "sacred stances," toward Santería (Wirtz 2004) and "alternative" narratives (Tisdel 2006, 2008). These interrogate the relationship between political and secular perspectives of "suspicion" and folklore depicted in museums and related narratives of inclusionary discriminations and "bundles of silence" (Tisdel 2006, 2008; cf. Trouillot 1995; Wirtz 2004).[1] Other perspectives highlight changing national and political narratives in museums and the expansion of the Cuban museum network as consequences of socialist cultural policy (Gonzalez 2014, 2016a, b, c, d; Tisdel 2006, 2008). These observations are similar in that they identify tensions between public and hidden transcripts, as well as depictions of continuity and change in socialist Cuba. These perspectives on Cuban museums and heritage also draw attention to the government's role in shaping discourses on the past through heritage and cultural policy.

In Cuba, museums have become principal venues for meaning making that can reflect and shape perceptions of society (Ross 2007, 2009). In the 1960s and 1970s, Cuba's socialist government implemented a new cultural policy that promoted inclusive representations of national identity and cultural heritage. Although the state embraced a new narrative about African-derived religious expressions and promoted it in museums, the narrative nevertheless avoids certain irreconcilable claims (Ross 2007, 2009) about race, national identity, and citizenship in Cuba. Thus, socialist cultural policy has implications for Afro-Cuban source communities.

Below, I focus on the government's role in cultural contestation surrounding narratives about Afro-Cuban religions. I also examine alternative narratives about Afro-Cuban religions that religious source communities create. Unofficial and forgotten narratives of source communities draw attention to consequences of cultural contestation, such as an ongoing delegitimization process about official statist heritage.

DATA AND OUTLINE

The empirical data below draws on more than a decade of ethnographic research on Cuban museums, cultural policy, and Afro-Cuban heritage. The empirical examples consist of three different narratives about Afro-Cuban religions and source communities in Cuba: narratives in a local history museum, a forgotten metanarrative, and the personal narrative of the late Fredesvinda Rosell, proprietor of Palacio de los Orishas.

The chapter begins with a brief description of Afro-Cuban religions and source communities (Peers and Brown 2003). Then, I explore religious objects as biographical objects (Hoskins 1998) that source communities and museums employ in heritage narratives. The discussion of heritage narratives and cultural contestation addresses heritage and narrative as meaning making processes. Here, the focus on symbolic landscape highlights conflicting claims, as well as psychocultural narratives and dramas that relate to identity and representation (Ross 2007, 2009).

A presentation of exhibitions at el Museo Municipal de Regla (the Municipal Museum of Regla) introduces the state's dominant narrative about Afro-Cuban heritage. The next section discusses the socialist government's racial and cultural policies and consequences for Afro-Cuban religions and source communities. Sawyer's (2006) perspectives on race cycles and inclusionary discrimination provide a theoretical framework for understanding the government's role in cultural contestation. Perspectives on the political role of museums (Hamlish 2000), a usable past (Watson 1995), public and hidden transcripts (Scott 1990), and historical production under state socialism (Watson 1994a) highlight the museum's role in meaning making and cultural contestation.

The next section addresses source communities and alternative narratives about Santería and Afro-Cuban heritage. I draw attention to alternative narratives that have shaped images of Afro-Cuban heritage and source communities, and suggest how they relate to issues at the core of cultural contestation. I discuss the alternative narrative that Fredesvinda Rosell promotes at Palacio de los Orishas and reexamine perspectives on cultural contestation, the "arts of resistance" (Scott 1990), and representations of society under state socialism (Watson et al. 1994). Then, I relate Fredesvinda's insight to a metanarrative about religious practitioners and material culture in the nineteenth and twentieth centuries. Ideas about criminology, ethnology, and folklore influenced the circulation of religious objects from source communities to police warehouses and then to museum showcases. I suggest that the metanarrative represents unaddressed psychocultural dramas and narratives related to cultural contestation.

AFRO-CUBAN RELIGIONS

Afro-Cuban religions draw upon African and European religious and cultural influences.[2] They incorporate notions of personhood and the divine that different "black Atlantic nations" (cf. Matory 2005) began cultivating in Cuba, during the colonial era. Some characteristics include divination, spirit possession, blood sacrifice, offerings, healing, music, and dance. In the colonial era, practitioners of Afro-Cuban religions included slaves, free Africans, and creoles.[3] They were reflective actors with multiple interests, and their actions changed the complex institutional, ritual, and iconographic systems of their religion (Brown 2003: 8).

In the nineteenth and twentieth centuries, powerholders in Cuba associated Afro-Cuban religions and source communities with crime, witchcraft, sorcery, violence, and moral delinquency. In the mid-nineteenth century, Afro-Atlantic religious traditions underwent a "selective reorganization" that resulted in innovation, revision, reform, and "cultural blending" (Brown 2003: 15). Below, I focus on cultural contestation about representations of Regla de Ocha, also called Santería (cf. Brown 2003).

REGLA DE OCHA AND SOURCE COMMUNITIES

Currently, approximately 80% of the Cuban population practices Santería.[4] Practitioners cultivate personal relationships with deities called *orichas*, as well as ancestor spirits. They honor and communicate with them through the performance of ceremonies and daily rituals. Divination, food and drink offerings, prayer, and the maintenance of altars comprised of sacred objects are important rituals. *Orichas* can intervene in the lives of devotees to guide, protect, and assist them. Practitioners can also petition the *orichas* to influence and resolve situations. The two branches of Santería, Ifá and Ocha, have different divination and initiation practices. In the former, *babalawos* are followers of the diviner-oricha, Orunmila, and initiated into the exclusive male order of the Ifá divination system. In the Ocha tradition, an *oriaté* is the "master of ceremonies" for rituals.[5]

Santería practitioners—*santeros* (male) and *santeras* (female)—are representatives of source communities, which refers to "cultural groups from whom museums have collected" (Peers and Brown 2003: 2). The term describes the former owners of ethnographic objects, and groups that museums describe, represent, and display in any form. "Knowledge communities" describe practitioners, priests, and scholar-practitioners (current and former) who possess specialized knowledge of religious systems and traditions. In Santería, the basic unit of a religious branch is the house of a *santera*. It is a "ritual house" or "house-temple" (casa-templo). At home, *santeros* maintain altars and interact with their most sacred religious objects as part of everyday life (Gullestad 1996). Religious branches expand by initiating new practitioners and ritual houses where the *fundamentos* or physical manifestations of the *orichas* become the center of new religious family networks.

Sacred Objects and Biographical Objects[6]

Material objects are central to the practice, form, and substance of Santería (Dornbach 1977; Brown 2003). Ordinary, natural, manufactured, found, or purchased objects can become sacred altar objects, divination tools, and attributes of deities. Stones can be material manifestations of gods, while shells, palm nuts, and coconuts serve as divination tools. Practitioners cultivate personal relationships with their *orichas*, whose physical manifestations or *fundamentos* (foundations) situated inside vessels that conceal and protect them. The vessels are often wooden or porcelain soup tureens. The physical manifestations of the *orichas* are perhaps a practitioner's most sacred religious items. Practitioners care for the *orichas*, for example, by "feeding" them with offerings and "dressing" them by adorning the altars and the vessels of the *orichas* with symbolic objects and decorative fabric. On particular occasions, practitioners create thrones to celebrate and pay respect to their *orichas*, such as on the annual Feast Days of the Catholic Saints that serve as emissaries of the *orichas*.[7]

Sacred objects are central components of meaningful life events that sustain the relationship between practitioners and the *orichas*. Material objects make possible initiation ceremonies and the drumming ceremony known as *bembé*, *toque de santo*, and *tambor*, which honors the *orichas*. Beaded necklaces called *ilekes* are essential to the first ritual of initiation. Initiates place Eleguá figures near the front door of their homes to protect them from negative spirits and influences.

NARRATIVES, HERITAGE, AND CULTURAL CONTESTATION

For practitioners, sacred objects can serve as "biographical objects," which according to Hoskins (1998) actors use as metaphors or references to personal experience, memory, and the past. Hoskins uses the term to describe objects that people use in narrative and formative processes of self-representation, identification, and "self-historicizing" (Hoskins 1998: 7). Biographical objects play a central role in contested narratives about Afro-Cuban religions.

I use *narrative* to describe a retrospective account of an experience in the past—the result of *narrative practice*. Narratives enable the construction and reconstruction of self and society (cf. Bruner 1984). The articulation of content to a listener or viewer is another important function of narratives and narrative practice (Hoskins 1998; Bruner 1984). The narrative is a vehicle for its content. Retrospective accounts of the past can facilitate the discovery and articulation of information and meaning. These perspectives help to understand the role of sacred altar objects in narrative representations that source communities and museums construct about Afro-Cuban religions and heritage.

According to Smith (2006), heritage is not a thing; rather it is a verb, as Harvey (2001) argues. I also use heritage to describe processes consisting of action, negotiation, decision-making, performance, and other practices that create and recreate cultural meaning and social values that people use as building blocks for identity processes (Smith 2006). As (Harvey 2001 and Smith 2006) note, heritage concerns the past and how we use it to construct concepts of individual, group, and national identities Harvey (2001, cf. Smith 2006). Heritage also refers to a particular rhetoric and discourse about the past and its material references and manifestations (Smith 2006: 14). This applies to religious and biographical objects in museums and ritual houses. "Authorized heritage discourse" describes a particular use of concepts and language that favors material objects, sites, places, and other references to the past that society protects and celebrates to pass on to future generations (Smith 2006: 29). Such discourse shapes representations, transcripts, and meaningful components of a public field that Ross refers to as the symbolic landscape (Ross 2007, 2009).

I use heritage narratives to describe cultural and social narratives that construct ideas about the past. When investigating the role of such narratives in cultural contestation, it is useful to consider the relationship between experience and representation (Hoskins 1998: 6). To interrogate the government's role in cultural contestation about Afro-Cuban religions, I consider how statist heritage narratives represent life as *lived*, life as *experienced*, and life as *told* (Hoskins 1998: 6).

> The first refers to what happens to a person; the second to images, feelings, sentiments, desires, and the meanings the person might ascribe to these events; and the third to a narrative, influenced by the context in which it is told, the audience, and cultural notions of storytelling. (1998: 6)[8]

Narratives about a group's cultural expressions can reveal and promote conflicting views of society and social groups (Ross 2007, 2009; Smith 2006) and as lives *lived, experienced,* and *told* (Hoskins 1998: 6).

Heritage narratives can reveal dissonance (Smith 2006: 35), incompatible perspectives about social organization, and non-negotiable claims between and about different social groups and actors (cf. Ross 2009). For Ross, understanding "incompatible identities" and conflicting interests can shed light on "underlying issues of cultural and identity contestation" (2009: 2). Modifying narratives about a group's cultural expressions can facilitate constructive conflict management (Ross 2007: 4). This depends, however, on the nature of the narrative, the modification, who modifies it, and the power relations influencing the social context.

"Psychocultural narratives" describe explanations for events—large and small—in the form of short, commonsense accounts (stories) that often seem simple (Ross 2009: 8). Such narratives, while not homogenous, can meet the emotional needs of a group. The familiar symbols can link people together, reinforce a familiar understanding of the world, and offer reassurance in a time of emotional distress (Ross 2009: 8–9).

For Ross, "competing" and seemingly "irresolvable" claims about group's "historical experience and contemporary identity" can trigger conflicts he refers to as "psychocultural dramas" (2009: 13). These controversial events are about "nonnegotiable cultural claims," such as perceived threats or rights that relate to ideas central to a group's core identity (ibid.). Ross notes that it is important to understand the symbolic and practical "triggers" of psychocultural drama, as well as how they influence meaning and emotions that mobilize actors and source communities (cf. Ross 2009: 15).

Museums, Meaning Making, and Cultural Contestation

In Cuba, heritage and state museums are products of cultural policy, which is an important meaning making practice for the socialist government (cf. Ross 2009: 4; Wedeen 2002). In the City of Havana, there are at least five museums with significant collections about Afro-Cuban religions.[9] They portray the traditions within a dominant framework that acknowledges the religions as unique contributions to society but does not address the adverse conditions that source communities endured. To understand how this representation emerged as a "script" or approved heritage discourse requires exploring power relations that shape meaning making and lead to actions that might constitute cultural contestation in Cuba.

Ross (2009) and Wedeen's (2002) approach to culture emphasizes cognition, semiotic practices of meaning making, and systems of shared meaning (Ross 2009: 3–5). For Ross, culture describes a "worldview containing specific scripts that shape why and how individuals and groups behave as they do" (2009: 3). The system of shared meaning does not indicate shared opinion or values, even though it can support identification markers that distinguish one from outsiders (Ross 2009: 3–5). Wedeen's notion that the effects of institutional arrangements, structures of domination, and strategic interests are also part of culture (2002: 714) aligns with my approach to studying consequences of Cuban cultural policy and Afro-Cuban heritage (cf. Tisdel 2006, 2008).

Cultural contestation reveals concerns about "inclusion and exclusion from a society's symbolic landscape" and "the politics of acceptance, rejection, and access to a society's resources and opportunities" (Ross 2009: 1). In this framework, symbolic landscape refers to a constellation of emotionally important and visible venues, such as museums, that include representations of different groups (cf. Ross 2007, 2009). Ross raises key questions about inclusion and exclusion.

> Who is present and who is absent in public representations? What are the qualities of those people and objects portrayed in it? Who controls the representations and to what extent are they contested? How is hierarchy portrayed and what qualities are associated with particular positions within a society? (Ross 2009: 7)

In a landscape of charged symbols, museums can reflect and project ideas about social relations. In the following section, we explore exhibitions at the Municipal Museum of Regla as examples of the state's dominant heritage narratives about Santería.

THE STATIST NARRATIVE: AFRO-CUBAN RELIGIONS AND HERITAGE AT THE MUNICIPAL MUSEUM OF REGLA

The Municipal Museum of Regla (est. 1982) is a polyvalent local history museum, the most common type of state museum in Cuba. Its exhibitions highlight local personalities and history that state heritage authorities deem noteworthy. The exhibitions illustrate the socialist government's official narrative about Afro-Cuban religions. This state institution promotes four kinds of narratives depicting Afro-Cuban religions, particularly Santería altar objects, classified as "religious ethnology."[10]

Ño Remigio Herrera: The Slave and the Babalawo

The first display is a presentation of Ño Remigio Herrera (ca. 1811–1905), Obara Melli Adechina, who was captured in Nigeria and sold into slavery in Cuba around 1830. Herrera was a slave for about two decades before his associate, Ño Carlos Adé Bí, acquired funds to purchase his freedom in the early 1850s (Brown 2003). By the turn of the twentieth century, he was one of Regla de Ocha's most important religious figures. This is the only narrative that describes the life events of a practitioner. Herrera's photograph is the centerpiece of the presentation, which associates Cuban slavery with Santería. Several biographical and sacred objects from Herrera's ritual house (ilé) accompany the photograph. The display included other sacred items, such as a white beaded necklace (ileke) representing Obatalá.[11] Of particular note is the Eleguá figure, the messenger representing the crossroads and trickster. The object, about 10 inches tall, is an amorphous stone that resembles a head. Eleguá figures are often made of cement or shell and can have cowry shells as eyes and a mouth. Herrera's Eleguá and sacred objects are rare examples of late nineteenth- and early twentieth-century Afro-Cuban material culture. Among the objects are a machete, shackles, and irons, important references to Transatlantic Slavery, Cuban slaves, and Afro-Cubans. At the Museum of Regla, Remigio Herrera is the human face of Regla de Ocha and Cuban slavery. The wall text in the adjacent room of religious ethnology echoes this association (Fig. 6.1).

Religious Ethnology

The second representation consists of attributes belonging to different *orichas*. These objects include the porcelain soup tureens (*soperas*) and other vessels containing the sacred stones that are the *orichas'* material foundation (*fundamento*) and the living "life force" (*aché*). There are necklaces (*ilekes*), and bracelets (*idé*), metal bells (*llamadoras*) for calling the *orichas*, divination shells, and protective charms (*amuletos*). The hand-painted text panels define concepts, such as "material culture," and explain historical details. One text panel reads, "To Regla came Spaniards and Africans belonging to various ethnic groups. From Africa came basically Ibibios, Bantu, and Yoruba."[12]

A Realist Representation

The third example is an installation of thrones, and illustrates the use of sacred objects in daily life and rituals, in this case the annual celebration, known as a "saint's party" (*fiesta de santo*) or "saint's birthday" (*cumpleaños de santo*). This party honors the *oricha* of an initiate on the anniversary of her initiation into the religion or "rebirth" as a "child," of the *oricha*. Hanging beside the thrones are two ceremonial costumes (*ropa de santo*) that an initiate wears twice, during initiation and then again for burial. The small wooden cabinet with its door ajar contains an Eleguá figure. Adjacent stands a large wooden armoire (*canastillero*) with doors and four shelves. On each shelf of the large armoire is a porcelain vessel representing an *oricha* and surrounding it an array of objects signifying the colors and qualities of the deity. The installations illustrate how we might encounter the items in the home of a practitioner. In eras when the authorities persecuted Afro-Cuban religious practitioners, closing cabinet doors concealed and protected sacred and biographical objects.

The marginalization of religions and source communities is part of the historical record in Cuba. It also represents a psychocultural drama (cf. Ross 2009) and connects the social history of past and present source communities. Colonial authorities tolerated Afro-Cuban religions and Republican governments criminalized and sought to eradicate them (Trujillo y Mongas 1882; Castellanos 1937). Scholars have documented the criminalization and repression of Afro-Cuban religions and practitioners well into the socialist era (Hagedorn 2001; Palmié 2002; Brown 2003; Bronfman 2004). For some practitioners, this is central to the social history and heritage of Afro-Cuban religions.

Fig. 6.1 Ño Remigio Herrera Adechina, ca. 1891. The photo is part of a permanent exhibition at the Museo Municipal de Regla (*Source* Wikimedia—public domain in a source country on January 1, 1996 and in the U.S.)

Discrepancies between the social history of practitioners and heritage representations about them are crucial to understanding cultural contestation and the power involved in Afro-Cuban heritage production under state socialism. A former resident of Regla noted that in the 1960s, the socialist government prohibited the famous procession that Herrera's *cabildo* had performed for nearly a century in Regla. Such details were neither part of the guided tour nor the exhibitions that portray Regla as a cradle of Santería and other Afro-Cuban traditions. The Museum of Regla is a site of official heritage production and part of the symbolic landscape. These examples reflect a standard narrative, approved heritage discourse, and an example of a public transcript (Scott 1990) about Afro-Cuban religions and heritage.

STATE SOCIALISM, RACIAL POLITICS, AND RACE CYCLES

The Municipal Museum of Regla and its exhibitions are products of socialist cultural policy. The state cultural policies that redefined Afro-Cuban religions as national heritage were part of racial and cultural politics that the socialist government implemented. When the revolutionary government assumed power in 1959, creating national unity and eliminating racial and economic inequalities were high priorities.

The government implemented anti-discrimination and desegregation laws that challenged racial hierarchy. While the government initiated a dialogue on racial inequality, it also controlled public discourse on race and racism and suppressed the critical voice of black Cuba when it seemed to challenge the government's nationalist ideals. This constitutes a limited gain and an example of "inclusionary discrimination" (Sawyer 2006).

Sawyer (2006) explains that when racial and ethnic inclusion exists alongside discriminatory practices, "inclusionary discrimination" emerges. When inclusionary discrimination is present, race determines the terms of inclusion, not the possibility of inclusion (2006: 19). For Sawyer, such practices can indicate a "modularity of racial inequality" in which sociopolitical improvements occur, but the central racial hierarchy persists (ibid.).

Cuban scholar Carlos Moore has criticized the government for focusing on ending racial segregation (Moore 1988: 21) more than giving a voice to marginalized groups. Moore writes:

> Castro's speeches reconfirmed two permanent features of his approach to race relations: a commitment to an integrationist stance steeped in white liberal paternalism and a firm refusal to allow the racial question to escape that framework. In other words, it was out of the question for Blacks themselves to define the content of their own oppression, or define the terms of their ethnic emancipation. (Moore 1988: 28)

The government considered articulations of ethnic identity antirev-olutionary and antinationalist. To further address the race issue and strengthen national unity, the government discouraged the use of eth-nic labels and encouraged "Cuban" as the new multiracial category. This logic suppressed racial fraternity rather than promoted it. Political views that encouraged self-representation for marginalized groups were unwelcome.

The government closed ethnic-based civic, fraternal, professional, and mutual aid organizations that it considered in conflict with new nationalist ideals. Many Cubans of color perceived stricter regulation of Afro-Cuban religious organizations as an "attack" on the black mid-dle class (Moore 1988: 48–49; de la Fuente 2001: 280). For some, the clubs were the last refuges for the expression of autonomous polit-ical demands. Thus, black citizens lost control over important tools of self-representation in public life (cf. Moore 1988).

According to de la Fuente, "The revolution's integration program left little room for racially defined voices or institutions to persist, much less to thrive" (2001: 280). The regime's racial politics seemed con-sistent with ideologies of Latin American exceptionalism, which uses a history of race mixing and ambiguous racial categories as reasons to deny that race is a useful analytical and political category (Moore 1988: 25; Sawyer 2006).

The regime change constituted a critical event and ignited a "race cycle" (cf. Sawyer 2006). Race cycles theory is useful for understand-ing how racial ideology and state formation interact in periods of crisis and state consolidation in post-revolutionary Cuba. Sawyer posits that mechanisms such as state crisis, regime change, racial ideology, trans-national politics, and critical events influence domestic racial politics. Such mechanisms lead to transformations in racial politics and then state consolidation. Each mechanism provides opportunities for gains for marginalized groups, but the extent and duration of the gains are lim-ited because of conflicting state priorities. Eventually, the mechanisms influencing the changes reach an "equilibrium position of stagnation" (Sawyer 2006: 3).

SOCIALIST CULTURAL POLICY AND AFRO-CUBAN HERITAGE

Cultural policy is an expression of statist principles and a tool of govern-ance. Thus, cultural policy and heritage are neither arbitrary nor inevitable. They emerge from a series of decisions, conclusions, and processes that produce one particular result instead of another (Lewis and Miller 2002; McGuigan 2003; Mercer 1999; cf. Shore and Wright 1997). To understand the role of power in cultural policy and heritage production, one must identify and interrogate the kinds of claims that the socialist government and its representatives make to legitimacy (Scott 1990: 11).

Cultural policy quickly became an important mechanism of racial politics in socialist Cuba. In 1961, the government sponsored a six-month seminar on ethnology, "folklore," and culture and then established the National Institute of Ethnology and Folklore (INEF) (Hagedorn 2001; Moore 1997; Pedroso 2002; Daniel 1998; Brown 2003). According to Moore, the new institute's task was to "research the full impact of Afro-Cuban music, dance, mannerisms, national psychology, and traditions" (Moore 1988: 99). The government-supported studies of Afro-Cuban folklore, based on Ortiz's (1940) notion that Afro-Cuban traditions were examples of transculturation and national culture.

By establishing the institute, the government engaged in the study and knowledge production about Afro-Cuban religions, promoting them as folklore. Nevertheless, Moore and other critics viewed the study of Afro-Cuban religions as contradictory and the beginning of the "regime's struggle to stamp out Afro-Cuban religious fraternities" (Moore 1988: 100). At one point, the government expressed:

> Religious sects of African origin will be continuously researched. Studies will be centered on those sects which have come into conflict with the Revolution. (Moore 1988: 100)

Like criminologists and governments of the previous era, the revolutionary government viewed Afro-Cuban religions and their practitioners as objects for reform and assimilation. Cultural policy seemed wrought with new complexities and contradictions. The government funded the study and staging of Afro-Cuban folklore, while it targeted religious practitioners and discouraged their traditions.

> Religious rituals appeared on stage, converted into folkloric ballets. In the 1960s, during the anti-discrimination campaigns and the state's recognition of Afro-Cuban folklore, arrests of religious leaders and job discrimination became common. After 1972, religious festivals and celebrations required permits and authorization from state officials. (Moore 1988: 100)

In February 1962, the government announced racial and gender discrimination had been eliminated (cf. Moore 1988; de la Fuente 2001). The regime explained that Cuban socialism would eliminate racial and gender inequality, which it noted were products of liberal capitalism class privileges (de la Fuente 2001: 279).

In the 1970s and 1980s, cultural policy continued to reframe Afro-Cuban music, dance, and religions as folklore and national heritage, while divorcing these expressions from their history and current realities of racial inequality. In 1977, regulations for Law No. 1 defined "ethnographic and folkloric objects and documents" and "ethnographic objects and musical instruments" as national cultural patrimony. In 1987, Resolution 2/87 (1987) declared national heritage the collection of "African cult" objects and utensils of the late Arcadio Calvo Espinosa, a resident of the municipality of Guanabacoa in the City of Havana.[13] Afro-Cuban religions have remained part of daily life and social history for many Cubans; thus, the resolutions essentially define aspects of social life and family history as national heritage. While museums collected religious objects, created exhibitions, and promoted narratives about Afro-Cuban religions, the revolutionary government continued to persecute and sanction practitioners. The official heritage narratives in museums do not reference these psychocultural dramas that shaped Afro-Cuban religions and source communities.

CONTESTATION, POWER, AND HERITAGE TRANSCRIPTS

In Cuba, heritage narratives that emerge from state cultural policy are examples of "public transcripts," which Scott describes as the "open interaction between subordinates and those who dominate" (1990: 2). Examining how actors respond to and implement state policies allows one to interrogate the interaction between governance, policy, and subjectivity. This can reveal the consequences of cultural policy for source communities and other citizens, for example, how policies can create new citizens, subjects (Shore and Wright 1997: 12), and new representations of them.

Scott posits that there are cultural patterns to domination and subordination (1990: 4). Disguise and surveillance play a key role in the power dialectic of dominant and subordinate groups (ibid.). Situations of domination will produce a public transcript that conforms to the values and preferred imaginings of the dominant group, according to Scott (ibid.). Noting that the effects of power relations are most visible in the public domain, Scott suggests that the public transcript of the subordinate group accommodates the hegemony and legitimacy of the dominant group, rather than challenging them (1990: 4). Thus, public transcripts do not represent "the whole story" and may reflect merely a tactical respect and approval (1990: 3). They serve as a "mask" that disguises intentions and meaning, and from behind this shield, groups engage in mutual surveillance.

Hidden transcripts, however, describe "discourse that takes place beyond direct observation by powerholders" (Scott 1990: 4). Hidden transcripts include "offstage" gestures, speech, and practices that endorse, challenge, or modify the content of public transcripts (Scott 1990: 4–5). Social actors create public and hidden transcripts for different audiences and under different power constraints. Let us visit the house-temple of Fredesvinda Rosell to reinforce this perspective.

FREDDY'S NARRATIVE: SOURCE COMMUNITIES AND AFRO-CUBAN HERITAGE

State museums are not the only promoters of narratives about Afro-Cuban heritage in Cuba. Religious practitioners are the original custodians of Afro-Cuban religious cultural expressions. Source communities articulate different practical and symbolic concerns in their narratives about Afro-Cuban religions (Tisdel 2006, 2008). Narratives in state museums share the symbolic landscape with the personal memories and histories of past and present source communities. Today, source communities cultivate narratives about religious traditions as *lived* and *experienced* and as complex interpersonal and transcendental relationships.

Palacio de Los Orishas

Fredesvinda Rosell (Freddy) established Palacio de los Orichas (Palace of the Orichas) in 1980 as a memorial to her late husband, Rigoberto Duque Rodriguez, a renowned Santería priest. The religious objects and altars in her house-temple consist of their sacred biographical objects (cf. Hoskins 1998). They are inseparable from their personal history, as well as the lineage of their ritual house, and community of practitioners. Freddy's narrative about Santería in revolutionary Cuba constitutes a reconstruction of self and society. The house-temple and the sacred objects inside serve as biographical objects and the anchor for Freddy's self-historicizing narrative (cf. Hoskins 1998). Her unofficial narrative references different concerns than the statist narrative that the museum promotes (Fig. 6.2).

At Freddy's house, a text panel hangs on the porch, next to the front door. The text constructs the "initial framing" of her narrative and altars of sacred objects (cf. Macdonald 2002).

> Palace of the Orishas
>
> Rigoberto Rodriguez Duque, one of the most prestigious babalosha of Cuba, was born in Madruga on February 20, 1910. He was initiated into the Lucumí religion (Regla de Ocha or Santería) in 1937 under the sign of the Holy Caridad del Cobre Oshun Yemayá. He was the first one to introduce initiation in his native town. He dedicated his life and beliefs entirely to do good for needy souls. In his career as a santero, he traveled the world and reached distant Nigeria in Africa. An untiring defender

Fig. 6.2 Palacio de los Orishas in Madruga, Cuba. Photo: Michelle A. Tisdel (2002)

of Regla, he converted his house or "Ilé osha" into a true sanctuary that brings together the exceptional values of the Lucumí religion.

Upon his death on 1 March 1975, he left an unforgettable wake of love among those who had the privilege to know him. His wife, la Oloyaá Fredesvinda Rosell (Freddy) continued the tradition and her inclination as a cultural promoter has allowed her to offer important contributions to national and universal culture. Today visitors from all borders arrive at the house of Freddy to know Palace of the Orishas and to pray for peace, happiness, and the good fortune of the people of the world.

Freddy reframes Santería as a *lived* and *experienced* aspect of life in the past, through the self-historicizing text that memorializes her husband Rigoberto and his legacy. The text refers to life events, as well as sentiments and meaning Freddy ascribes to religious practice (Hoskins 1998: 7). In contrast, the narrative in the museum reflects cultural notions of public storytelling under Cuban socialism.

During informal interviews, Freddy also described the social context in which they performed rituals and ceremonies in Cuba under the socialist government. Often, church officials begrudgingly attended to the needs of Santería practitioners when the rituals required a visit to the local Catholic Church for prayer, confession, or blessing. For decades after the Revolution, Freddy and the other practitioners intentionally waited until nighttime to transport their sacrificial animals, food, and other supplies to the house-temple, to avoid detection by the authorities. The local authorities required practitioners to obtain a police permit to organize ceremonies. In those days, she noted, people even avoided obtaining the necessary permit. Ceremonies with legal permits that the police and municipal authorities knew about were more susceptible to police interference than illegal religious activities carried out secretly.

Freddy's narrative includes several sentiments about Santería as an experience, a life lived, and as her "personal patrimony." Her account of avoiding the police reconstructs what happened to them and suggests what it means for her. These reflections resonate with the accounts above that describe religious practice as lived and experienced. Freddy's articulation of these unofficial truths is a measured action that mitigates cultural contestation. Her memory constitutes a hidden transcript and defines an unofficial usable past that challenges the statist narrative. This unofficial social narrative also represents a psychocultural narrative about a psychocultural drama for religious practitioners (Figs. 6.3, 6.4, and 6.5).

Fig. 6.3 Religious
artifacts representing
Eleguá at Palacio de los
Orishas. Photo: Michelle
A. Tisdel (2002)

Fig. 6.4 Religious
artifacts representing
Yemayá at Palacio de los
Orishas. Photo: Michelle
A. Tisdel (2002)

Freddy declined several invitations from heritage authorities to join
the network of state museums. She explained her choice to remain independent as follows.

> Before there were municipal museums or a Cultural Heritage Council, this
> was my private patrimony. I do not want to incorporate myself under their
> hands. I get along happily . . . here in my house.[14]

Fig. 6.5 Religious
artifacts representing
Changó at Palacio de los
Orishas. Photo: Michelle
A. Tisdel (2002)

As this example shows, heritage is multi-sited. Source communities are agents of heritage that references their ritual houses, personal history, and memory. As Brown (2003) argues, temple-houses are historical religious institutions and sites of innovation and social life. Socialist cultural policy has softened pre-revolutionary cultural contestation through the legitimization of Afro-Cuban religions and cultural expressions as national heritage. Through her self-historicizing narrative, Freddy capitalizes on the status of Afro-Cuban heritage instead of opposing the official narrative. Thus, Freddy reclaims a crucial role for house-temples and hidden transcripts in the delegitimization of official heritage representations.

HISTORY, MEMORY, AND OPPOSITION

The cultural contestation surrounding Afro-Cuban heritage in post-revolutionary Cuba is part of an ongoing "delegitimization" of official history and heritage in Cuba.[15] This is a common form of opposition under state socialism, as Watson and others have noted (Watson et al. 1994). As Watson notes, "official history" is often associated with "official reality" and perceived as untrue (1994: 16). There can be a shared understanding that official truth is not true. Personal memory can become "more reliable than the official narrative, which is so often contradicted by experience," according to Watson (ibid.).[16] As Palacio de los Orishas illustrates, to understand further the government's role in cultural contestation, we must discuss the alternative narratives, memory, and history of source communities. These represent arts of resistance (Scott 1990), psychocultural narratives (Ross 2007, 2009), and responses to authorized heritage discourse (Smith 2006). My data suggest that for some practitioners, notions of descent, ancestry, and heritage emphasize the materiality of race and physical bodies as important markers of Afro-Cuban religion and culture (Tisdel 2008: 110–111). Some members of religious source communities identify as descendants of African slaves and religious practitioners. For them, religion is a meaningful marker of personal identity. Individuals that perceive themselves as custodians of an inherited tradition express concerns about official heritage representations.

One perspective is that the government's emphasis on folklore distorts the historical value of Afro-Cuban heritage. Another concern is depictions that make Afro-Cuban religions synonymous with slavery. These obscure the complexity of Afro-Cuban traditions and heritage (Tisdel 2008: 110). Another concern is that official representations ignore the importance of Afro-Cuban religions in everyday life. One practitioner argued that museums are important, but the family and house-temples are equally important social institutions. "They have become promoters of cultural patrimony," he argued because Afro-Cuban religion is located in the home. Fredesvinda and Palacio de los Orishas illustrate this point.

Her alternative representation of Santería is also part of a circular metanarrative that begins in the ritual houses of source communities in the late 1800s. The Museum of Regla celebrates Afro-Cuban heritage in this period, employing narratives about Remigio Herrera, slavery, and religious artifacts. Nevertheless, like other state museums that I have observed, official narrative practice constructs a "usable past" for Afro-Cuban heritage by avoiding competing and irresolvable claims that draw attention to psychocultural dramas and narratives. The following metanarrative includes examples of marginalization and inclusionary discrimination that constitute psychocultural dramas and narratives that span from the era of Remigio Herrera to Fredesvinda Rosell and her ritual house.

A Metanarrative: Forgotten Psychocultural Dramas and Narratives

Police, criminologists, and social scientists shaped dominant narratives about Afro-Cuban religions at the end of the eighteenth century. Many of the oldest collections of Afro-Cuban religious objects in Cuba's public museums in Havana are the confiscated property of source communities that the authorities of colonial, Republican, and socialist governments acquired under adverse circumstances. As early as 1863, African-based religions began to spread to poor white populations (Trujillo y Mongas 1882; Brown 2003), causing prominent social scientists, and criminologists to compare African-based religions to contagious diseases, such as yellow fever. In the twentieth century of the republican era, Afro-Cuban populations, religions, and other cultural expressions were objects of political debate about racial equality and the terms of black citizenship (cf. Bronfman 2004; Palmié 2002).

Fernando Ortiz, Crime, and Heritage

Criminologists studied Afro-Cuban religious source communities and their biographical objects to investigate primitive psychology and criminal pathology. They sought to assimilate and reform practitioners and to eradicate the religions and their "criminal environments." When police raided ritual houses and religious ceremonies, they confiscated sacred objects, which they regarded as criminal evidence. Police and criminologists were some of the first non-practitioners to "collect" and study Afro-Cuban religious objects, and confiscated objects were stored and studied in evidence warehouses (Pedroso 2002). This includes Fernando Ortiz. The celebrated ethnologist began his study of Afro-Cuban religions as a lawyer and criminologist. His work emboldened the campaign against these religions in the early 1900s (cf. Bronfman 2004; Brown 2003; Castellanos 2003; Palmié 2002).

In 1906, he referred to ritual houses as "centers of contagion" (cf. Brown 2003: 58; Roche y Monteagudo 1908; Ortiz 1906: 1–22, 223). Ortiz associated the religions with crime and regarded their sacred necklaces, musical instruments, ethnomedicine, divination tools, such as coconuts and cowry shells, as criminal evidence. Biographical and sacred objects circulated from source communities to police storages and then to criminology museums where criminologists studied them as objects of criminal ethnography (cf. Montaldo 2013; Roche y Monteagudo 1908; Trujillo y Mongas 1882).

> Once those swindlers are gone, their feasts, dances, and savage rites ended, their temples destroyed, their impotent deities confiscated, all the tentacles of the witchcraft that chain its believers to the barbaric bottom of our

society cut, then, free of hindrances, they will be able to alleviate their still not de-Africanized minds of the weight of confused superstitions and rise to successive zones of culture. (Palmié 2002: 242; cf. Ortiz 1973 [1906])

Ortiz suggested a stricter legal framework for the criminalization of Afro-Cuban religions, including special courts for prosecuting religious practitioners, fines, short imprisonment of religious leaders, and mandatory physical labor (cf. Castellanos 2003). In the 1920s, Ortiz turned to salvage ethnology and focused on Afro-Cuban traditions as part of a search for Cuba's historical origins and authenticity (Bronfman 2004: 112).[17] Ortiz eventually celebrated Afro-Cuban religions as examples of transculturation, the merging of two or more cultures that forms a new culture and cultural expressions (cf. Ortiz 1940). This reframed Afro-Cuban religions as complex *Cuban* phenomena rather than external primitive *African* expressions.

Given the scope and trajectory of Ortiz's interest in Afro-Cuban religions and cultural expressions, it is interesting to note that there is a Fernando Ortiz collection of Afro-Cuban ethnographic objects at el Museo Casa de África and a parallel collection of Afro-Cuban musical instruments that bear his name at el Museo de la Musica in the City of Havana. A small display about Ortiz at el Museo de Humboldt describes him as the "third discoverer" of Cuba because he "discovered" Cuba's Afro-Cuban heritage.[18] Ortiz's "discovery" of the historical merits of Afro-Cuban cultural expressions represented a possibility to embrace new narratives that could challenge racial ideology and hierarchy (Bronfman 2004: 111).

Ortiz and the Search for a Usable Past

The cultural contest about Afro-Cuban heritage draws attention to an inversion of different discourses about inclusion and representation under state socialism. A central characteristic of socialist cultural policy in Cuba is the role that "inversion" (ibid.) plays in defining and articulating a "usable past" that is both immediate and distant to politics and social life under previous governments (cf. Watson 1995; Hamlisch 1995). This action draws attention to dissonance (Smith 2006) in the symbolic landscape, such as incompatible identities, competing interests, and triggers that emerge around issues of representation and experience in everyday life (Ross 2007, 2009). The selection and deselection of facts and perspectives shape the form and content of inversion and other mechanisms of historical production (cf. Trouillot 1995). Thus, a common characteristic of cultural policy and heritage in Cuba and other socialist societies is hegemonic or "official" representations that promote statist values. Although the socialist government promoted a narrative that included Afro-Cuban religions in representations of national heritage, it avoids core issues and concerns that highlight similarities between distant and immediate conflicts (cf. Hamlish 2000: 139).

One of the core issues of the cultural contestation about Afro-Cuban religions is the discord between the psychocultural narratives that the dominant group uses to address the psychocultural dramas of the subordinate group. The cultural pattern and power dialectic shaping cultural contestation about Afro-Cuban religions are a product of socialist racial and cultural politics. At the core of this conflict is a new psychocultural drama and narrative—inclusionary discrimination and Cuban exceptionalism (cf. Sawyer 2006). The institutional arrangements, structures of domination, and strategic interests (Wedeen 2002) of cultural policy reinforce the statist worldview containing specific transcripts that shape why and how source communities and the government address heritage and cultural contestation (Ross 2009).

COMPETING AND IRRESOLVABLE CLAIMS

Is the statist script at the Museum of Regla evidence of a persistent racial hierarchy that has affected black Cuba disproportionately? Does the forgotten metanarrative about Ortiz and Afro-Cuban source communities reveal what Ross calls a non-negotiable or irresolvable cultural claim about the "historical experience and contemporary identity" of source communities (cf. Ross 2009: 13)? The paradox of inclusionary discrimination illustrates how new heritage logics and narratives can reinforce old social hierarchies that exacerbate cultural contestation. This socialist period of racial policy formation represents another psychocultural drama for religious source communities. For Ross, "competing" and seemingly "irresolvable" claims exacerbate conflicts and trigger the emotions associated with psychocultural dramas (Ross 2009: 13). The implementation of racial and cultural policies illustrates how these acts of meaning making evoke, build, and reinforce strong emotions. In the years following the Cuban Revolution, issues of race, citizenship, cultural identity, and self-representation mobilized actors and source communities (cf. Ross 2009: 15).

Conclusion

Although altering narratives about a group's cultural expressions can mitigate cultural contestation (Ross 2007, 2009), the degree of success depends on the nature of the power relations that shape the social and political context and meaning making practices, such as heritage. Since the 1960s, Cuba's socialist government has employed cultural policy, cultural institutions, and heritage narratives to render visible previously marginalized social groups (Ross 2009: 7). The heritage narrative that state museums promote about Afro-Cuban religion is a poignant example of the government's role in cultural contestation. The social history of Afro-Cuban religions and source communities includes racial inequality, marginalization, and assimilation, as well as associations to slavery, folklore, and heritage. The heritage narrative that public museums promote is the result of racial and cultural policies that the government implemented from the 1960s through the 1990s. These policies defined and institutionalized new heritage narratives about Afro-Cuban cultural expressions, but did not address concerns about representation and experience, or core issues that relate to notions of race, cultural heritage, and national identity.

For some source community members, the social history of Afro-Cuban religions and cultural expressions are inseparable from their lived experiences and personal cultural identity. Many members of current source communities are both actual and ritual descendants of persecuted religious lineages that extend back to the colonial and republican eras (cf. Tisdel 2008). As Ross notes, cultural contestation reveals concerns about inclusion and exclusion from a society's symbolic landscape. Such conflicts also concern the "politics of acceptance, rejection, and access to a society's resources and opportunities" (Ross 2009: 1). For Ross, the symbolic landscape is a constellation of emotionally important and visible venues. As examples and promoters of the government's cultural policy, state museums are important but not exclusive sites of meaning making in the symbolic landscape (Ross 2007, 2009).

Museums and Heritage Narratives

The statist heritage narrative at the Museum of Regla, for example, uses sacred objects to construct ideas about the past as *told*. This narrative associates Afro-Cuban religions to colonial slavery and folklore but without addressing issues of racial inequality and social marginalization. Thus, official heritage narratives represent a particular kind of discourse about psychocultural dramas and narratives that relate to Afro-Cuban religions (cf. Ross 2007, 2009). The metanarrative about Afro-Cuban religions and practitioners also illustrates aspects of the social history related to the source communities and their sacred or biographical objects. These psychocultural dramas and narratives represent facts that the state's approved heritage discourse (Smith 2006) deselects and avoids. Unofficial narratives that practitioners create about their religion, however, use the same biographical objects to create self-historicizing accounts that construct the past as lived and experienced (cf. Hoskins 1998). The narratives of practitioners often highlight different historical concerns, conflicting interests, and psychocultural narratives (Ross 2009) that offer meaningful explanations about aspects of society. The narratives that practitioners construct may also address psychocultural dramas, as Ross notes, that relate to issues at the core of identity for source communities (Ross 2009).

Contested Racial and Cultural Policy

The official narrative about Afro-Cuban religions is the result of the socialist government's racial and cultural policies. The narrative reflects the government's approved heritage discourse and constitutes a psychocultural narrative (Ross 2007, 2009) or public transcript (Scott 1990) about Afro-Cuban religions and heritage. The official narrative also reflects the government's historical and political concerns about race and national identity. The same policies that shaped the heritage narrative resulted in practices of social control and culturalassimilation that targeted Afro-Cuban religions and source communities. As Sawyer argues, race cycles create opportunities for gains that benefit marginalized groups, but the extent and duration of the gains are limited because of conflicting state priorities (Sawyer 2006). The social policies that targeted race-based institutions and religious organizations were not race neutral. They exacerbated the loss of sociocultural institutions that source communities associated with self-representation and Afro-Cuban identity. This also triggered a psychocultural drama that resembled the cultural patterns and power dialectics at the core of Afro-Cuban social history.

According to Sawyer (2006), when racial and ethnic inclusion exists alongside discriminatory practices, "inclusionary discrimination" emerges. Inclusionary discrimination draws attention to issues of representation and experience that play a particular role in the social history of Afro-Cuban religions and source communities. The government uses inclusionary discrimination to create a usable past and to create both distance and relevance to the past (cf. Hamlish 2000). The result is a heritage narrative that promotes Afro-Cuban religions as examples of national culture but excludes aspects of the persistent unsavory social history that characterizes these traditions and source communities.

Sawyer's (2006) notion of inclusionary discrimination addresses what Ross describes as non-negotiable or irresolvable cultural claims about a group's "historical experience and contemporary identity" (cf. Ross 2009: 13). The paradoxical nature of the official narrative illustrates how modifying narratives about a group's cultural expressions, nevertheless, can reinforce old social hierarchies. The race cycle of racial and cultural policy formation represents another psychocultural drama for religious source communities. As Ross notes, "competing" and seemingly "irresolvable" claims exacerbate conflicts and trigger the emotions associated with psychocultural dramas (Ross 2009: 13). The racial and cultural policies illustrate the government's role in influencing acts of meaning making that reinforce strong emotions and shape heritage. Psychocultural dramas and narratives about Afro-Cuban religions trigger emotions about issues at the core of Afro-Cuban identity for many practitioners.

Source Communities and Heritage

On the surface, cultural contestation about representations of Afro-Cuban heritage seems almost non-existent. There appears to be widespread acceptance of the state's portrayal of Afro-Cuban religions as examples of national culture. Nevertheless, for Fredesvinda and many practitioners, issues such as race, cultural identity, and self-representation are core issues that relate to Afro-Cuban social history and personal cultural identity (cf. Ross 2009: 15). Unofficial narratives that practitioners create about their religion also use sacred biographical objects to construct the past as lived and experienced. These unofficial narratives highlight different historical concerns and conflicting interests. They also represent psychocultural narratives (Ross 2009) that serve as meaningful explanations about aspects of society. The alternative narratives of practitioners also address concerns that trigger dramatic emotional events or psychocultural dramas that relate to issues at the core of identity for source communities (Ross 2009).

Cultural contestation about Afro-Cuban religions does not mobilize large groups of source communities to organize and protest explicitly the government's dominant narrative. Nevertheless, cultural contestation motivates source communities to create alternative psychocultural narratives, hidden transcripts, and notions of a usable past that articulate their unofficial truths. Another unexpected consequence of delegitimization is that source communities imitate, collaborate, and compete with museums as promoters of heritage narratives about Afro-Cuban religions. Fredesvinda Rosell and Palacio de los Orichas illustrate this practice. Instead of opposing the state's dominant narrative about Afro-Cuban heritage, Freddy capitalizes on the role of museums as sites of meaning making in the symbolic landscape. By using her house-temple and sacred biographical objects as the anchor of her self-historicizing narrative, Freddy refocuses the heritage narrative on personal memory, unofficial history, and the role of Afro-Cuban religions and the temple-home in everyday life.

As Watson argues, historical production under state socialism can have unexpected consequences, such as delegitimization of official history and official facts (cf. Watson 1994b). Cultural contestation and emergent unofficial heritage narratives reflect this process of delegitimization. It is tempting to agree with the assertion that "sometimes a dominant narrative leaves no room for negotiation" (Ross 2009: 10). Nevertheless, evidence from Cuban museums and source communities suggests that both source communities and the government employ public and hidden transcripts that soften cultural contestation rather that exacerbate it. The government could use cultural policy to address issues related to non-negotiable claims and incompatible identities. This might mitigate further the persistent cultural contestation and the unexpected consequences of the current delegitimization process.

NOTES

1. The current "double moral" that Wirtz (2004) discusses is part of a historical pattern and metacultural stances that Hagedorn (2001) and Daniel (1995) also discuss and illustrate.
2. African-based religions include Regla de Ocha (Regla de Ifá, Lucumí or Santería), Palomonte Mayombe (Conga), Ararrá (Dahomey), and the Secret Society of the Abakuá (Carabalí). Matory (2005) refers to these traditions as black Atlantic religions. According to Brown, Afro-Cuban religions emerged from "ethnic" formations called "nations" and their institutions, including clubs and mutual aid societies known as *cabildos*, *socidades*, and *casas* (2003b: 15).

3. Creole describes people of African or European descent born in Cuba. From about the 1860 s, some working- and lower-class white creoles, as well as Chinese and Filipino laborers, sought out different Afro-Cuban religions as beneficial social networks for economic and other reasons (Brown 2003: 59).
4. Religiones africanas en Cuba. http://www.ecured.cu/Religiones_africanas_en_ Cuba.
5. See Brown (2003) for a detailed discussion of the divergent cosmological models, ritual structures, and historical relationship between Ocha and Ifá branches of Santería.
6. For a thorough overview and discussion of the sacred altar objects, their cultural influences, artistic merit, and religious functions in Santería, see Brown (2003).
7. Practitioners honor the *orichas* and Catholic Saints that they view as emissaries of the *orichas*. Catholic Saints share similar attributes with the *orichas* and rule over corresponding domains of life and nature.
8. See also Bruner (1984: 7).
9. El Museo Municipal de Regla, La Casa de África, El Museo Municipal de Guanabacoa, El Museo de la Musica, and El Museo de la Asociación Yorubá de Cuba are in the City of Havana.
10. I conducted field research at the museum in 2001–2002 and in 2013. In 2013, the museum added a third room dedicated to the tradition of Palo Monte and other traditions. See also Brown (2003: 250–252). The municipal town of Regla also has a significant Chinese presence because of Asian indentured labor and migration to Cuba and the Caribbean in the 18th and 19th centuries (cf. Cosme Baños 1998).
11. The father of the *oricha* pantheon representing whiteness, purity, and tranquility (Brown 2003: 370).
12. My translation. The Spanish text reads: "A Regla llegaron españoles y africanos pertenecientes a various grupos étnicos. De Africa llegaron fundamentalmente Ibibios, bantúes y yorubas."
13. These objects constituted the core of the religious ethnology collection at the Municipal Museum of Guanabacoa (cf. Tisdel 2006; Brown 2003).
14. Personal communication with Rosell in 2002. See also (Tisdel 2006: 388).
15. See also Hamlish's (1995) analysis of Chinese national museums and history.
16. Studies that address opposition and delegitimization in Mongolia (Humphrey 1994), Soviet Georgia (Jones 1994), and China (Hamlish 1995) corroborate this evidence.
17. La fiesta afrocubana del Día de Reyes (1924) is an example. He believed that the recovery of forgotten folklore could facilitate and reconstruct a sense of national identity (Bronfman 2004: 112).
18. I observed this in 2002. The museum text referred to Christofer Columbus and Alexander von Humboldt as the first and second discoverers of Cuba. The first "discovered" "America" and the second discovered its nature and geographical attributes.

134   M. A. TISDEL

REFERENCES

Bronfman, A. (2004). *Measures of Equality: Social Science, Citizenship, and Race in Cuba, 1902–1940 (Envisioning Cuba)*. Chapel Hill: The University of North Carolina Press.

Brown, D. (2003). *Santería Enthroned: Art, Ritual and Innovation in an Afro-Cuban Religion*. Chicago: University of Chicago Press.

Bruner, E. M. (1984). The Opening Up of Anthropology. In E. M. Bruner (Ed.), *Text, Play and Story: The Construction and Reconstruction of Self and Society*. Prospect Heights, IL: Waveland.

Castellanos, I. (1937). *Medicina Legal y Criminologia Afro-Cubanas*. Habana: Molina y CIA.

Castellanos, J. (2003). *Pioneros de la Etnografía Afrocubana: Fernando Ortiz Rómulo Lachatañeré, Lydia Cabrera*. Miami: Ediciones Universal.

Cosme Baños, P. (1998). *Los Chinos en Regla 1847–1997: Documento y Comentarios*. Santiago de Cuba: Editorial Oriente.

Daniel, Y. (1995). Rumba: Dance and Social Change in Contemporary Cuba. In D. C. Hine, J. McCluskey, Jr., & D. B. Gaspar (Eds.), *Blacks in the Diaspora*. Bloomington: Indiana University Press.

Daniel, Y. (1998). Rumba: Social and Aesthetic Change in Cuba. In N. E. Whitten, Jr. & A. Torres (Eds.), *Blackness in Latin America and the Caribbean* (pp. 483–494). Bloomington: Indiana University Press.

de la Fuente, A. (2001). *A Nation for All: Race, Inequality, and Politics in Twentieth Century Cuba (Envisioning Cuba)* (L. A. Pérez, Jr., Ed.). Chapel Hill: The University of North Carolina Press.

Dornbach, M. (1977). Gods in Earthenware Vessels: Gods and Their Representation in the Afro-Cuban Santeria Religion. *Acta Ethnographica Academiae Hungaricae, 26*(3–4), 285–308.

González, P. A. (2014). Museums in Revolution: Changing National Narratives in Revolutionary Cuba Between 1959 and 1990. *International Journal of Heritage Studies, 21*(3) , 264–279. https://doi.org/ 10.1080/13527258.2014.939102.

González, P. A. (2016a). Communism and Cultural Heritage: The Quest for Continuity. *International Journal of Heritage Studies, 22*(9), 653–663.

González, P. A. (2016b). Monumental Art and Hidden Transcripts of Resistance in Revolutionary Cuba, 1970–1990. *Journal of Latin American Cultural Studies, 25*(2), 271–296.

González, P. A. (2016c). The Organization of Commemorative Space in Postcolonial Cuba: From Civic Square to Square of the Revolution. *Organization, 23*(1), 47–70.

González, P. A. (2016d). Transforming Ideology into Heritage: A Return of Nation and Identity in Late Socialist Cuba? *International Journal of Cultural Studies, 19*(2), 139–159.

Gullestad, M. (1996). *Everyday Life Philosophers*. Oslo: Scandinavian University Press.

Hagedorn, K. J. (2001). *Divine Utterances: The Performance of Afro-Cuban Santería*. Washington, DC: Smithsonian Institution Press.

Hamlish, T. (1995). Preserving the Palace: Museums and the Making of Nationalism(s) in Twentieth-Century China. *Museum Anthropology, 19*(2), 20.

Hamlish, T. (2000). Global Culture, Modern Heritage: Re-membering the Chinese Imperial Collection. In S. Crane (Ed.), *Museums and Memory* (pp. 137–158). Stanford, CA: Stanford University Press.

Harvey, D. C. (2001). Heritage Pasts and Heritage Presents: Temporality, Meaning and the Scope of Heritage Studies. *International Journal of Heritage Studies, 7*(4), 319–338.

Hoskins, J. (1998). *Biographical Objects: How Things Tell the Stories of People's Lives*. New York and London: Routledge.

Humphrey, C. (1994). Remembering an "Enemy": The Bogd Khaan in Twentieth-Century Mongolia. In R. S. Watson (Ed.), *Memory, History, and Opposition Under State Socialism* (pp. 21–44). Santa Fe: School of American Research Press.

Jones, S.F. (1994). Old Ghosts and New Chains: Ethnicity and Memory in the Georgian Republic. In R. S. Watson (Ed.), *In Memory, History, and Opposition Under State Socialism* (pp. 1–20). Santa Fe: School of American Research Press.

Lewis, J., & Miller, T. (Eds.). (2002). *Critical Cultural Policy Studies: A Reader*. Oxford: Blackwell Publishers.

Macdonald, S. (2002). *Behind the Scenes at the Science Museum*. Oxford: Berg.

Matory, J. L. (2005). *Black Atlantic Religion: Tradition, Transnationalism, and Matriarchy in the Afro-Brazilian Candomblé*. Princeton, N.J: Princeton University Press.

McGuigan, J. (2003). Cultural Policy Studies. In J. Lewis & T. Miller (Eds.), *Critical Cultural Policy Studies: A Reader* (pp. 23–42). Oxford: Blackwell Publishing.

Mercer, C. (1999). Cultural Policy: Research and the Government Imperative. In D. Boswell & J. Evans (Eds.), *Representing the Nation: A Reader* (pp. 394–403). London: Routledge.

Montaldo, S. (2013). The Lombroso Museum from its Origins to the Present Day. In P. Knepper & P. J. Ystehede (Eds.), *The Cesare Lombroso Handbook* (pp. 98–112). New York: Routledge.

Moore, C. (1988). *Castro, the Blacks, and Africa. Vol. 8, Afro–American Culture and Society Monograph Series*. Los Angeles: Center for Afro-American Studies, University of California.

136 M. A. TISDEL

Moore, R. (1997). *Nationalizing Blackness: Afrocubanismo and Artistic Revolution in Havana, 1920–1940*. Pittsburgh: University of Pittsburgh Press.

Ortiz, F. (1940). *Contrapuneto Cubano del Tabaco y el Azúcar*. Havana: Jesús Montero.

Ortiz, F. (1973) [1906]. *Hampa Afro-cubano: los negros brujos. Apuntes para un estudio de etnología criminal*. Miami: Ediciones Universales.

Palmié, S. (2002). *Wizards and Scientists: Explorations in Afro-Cuban Modernity and Tradition*. Durham and London: Duke University Press.

Pedroso, L. A. (2002). Las exposiciones de cultos afrocubanos y la necesidad de su reconceptualización. *Catauro: Revista Cubana de Antropología, 3*(5), 126–141.

Peers, L., & Brown, A. K. (2003). Introduction. In L. Peers & A. K. Brown (Eds.), *Museums and Source Communities: A Routledge Reader* (pp. 1–16). London and New York: Routledge.

Roche y Monteagudo, R. (1908). *La policía y sus misterios: adicionada con "La policía judicial," procedimientos, formularios, leyes, reglamentos, ordenanzas y disposiciones que conciernen a los cuerpos de seguridad pública / con un prólogo de Rafael Conte*. Habana: Imprenta La Prueba.

Ross, M. H. (2007). *Cultural Contestation in Ethnic Conflict*. Cambridge: Cambridge University Press.

Ross, M. H. (2009). *Culture and Belonging in Divided Societies: Contestation and Symbolic Landscapes*. Philadelphia: University of Pennsylvania Press.

Sawyer, M. Q. (2006). *Racial Politics in Post-revolutionary Cuba*. Cambridge: Cambridge University Press.

Scott, J. C. (1990). *Weapons of the Weak: Everyday Forms of Peasant Resistance*. New Haven and London: Yale University Press.

Shore, C., & Wright, S. (Eds.). (1997). *Anthropology of Policy*. London: Routledge.

Smith, L. (2006). *Uses of Heritage*. London: Routledge.

Tisdel, M. (2006). *Cuban Museums and Afro-Cuban Heritage: Fragments and Transitions in Daily Life*. Unpublished Ph.D. thesis, Department of Anthropology, Harvard University.

Tisdel, M. (2008). Three Interpretations of Materiality and Society: Afro-Cuban Heritage and the Cuban Slave Route Museum. In H. Glørstad & L. Hedaeger (Eds.), *Six Essays on the Materiality of Society and Culture* (pp. 87–125). Staviksvägen: Bricoleur Press.

Trouillot, M.-R. (1995). *Silencing the Past: Power and the Production of History*. Boston: Beacon Press.

Trujillo y Mongas, J. (1882). *Los Criminales de Cuba y D. José Trujillo: Narración de los Servicios Prestados en el Cuerpo de Policía de la Habana*. Barcelona: Fidel Giró (Establlicimiento Tipográfico de).

Watson, R. S. (1994a). *Memory, History, and Opposition Under State Socialism*. Sante Fe, N.M: School of American Research Press.

Watson, R. S. (1994b). Memory, History, and Opposition under State Socialism: An Introduction. In R. S. Watson (Ed.), *In Memory, History, and Opposition Under State Socialism* (pp. 1–20). Santa Fe: School of American Research Press.

Watson, R. S. (1994c). Making Secret Histories: Memory and Mourning in Post-Mao China. In R. S. Watson (Ed.), *In Memory, History, and Opposition Under State Socialism* (pp. 65–85). Santa Fe: School of American Research Press.

Watson, R. S. (1995). Palaces, Museums, and Squares: Chinese National Spaces. *Museum Anthropology, 19*(2), 7–19.

Wedeen, L. (2002). Conceptualizing Culture: Possibilities for Political Science. *American Political Science Review, 96*(4), 713–728.

Wirtz, K. (2004). Santeria in Cuban National Consciousness: A Religious Case of the Doble Moral. *Journal of Latin American Anthropology, 9*, 409–438. https://doi.org/10.1525/jlca.2004.9.2.409.

CHAPTER 7

Dispossessing the Wilderness: Contesting Canada's National Park Narrative

Desiree Valadares

THE TONIC OF WILDNESS

Cultural narratives of North American identity have long hinged on wilderness, the mythology of uninhabited nature, and the vastness of a virgin landscape. The idea of national parks as spaces of ecological purity and sources of national pride relate to this nostalgic search for an authentic and unspoiled landscape. In 1995, William Cronon stirred controversy with his article, "The Trouble with Wilderness, or Getting Back to the Wrong Nature." In it, he declared that the time had come to rethink the very notion of wilderness, which had served as the unexamined foundation on which so many of the "quasi-religious values" of modern environmentalism rest. Cronon, along with his contemporaries, asserted that the false nature–society and wilderness–settlement binaries were problematic in environmental histories.

Western preconceptions of nature and wilderness underwent sweeping changes in America in the 1800s. "Wilderness environmentalism" originated with ideology embedded in two intellectual movements: the

D. Valadares (✉)
UC Berkeley College of Environmental Design, Berkeley, CA, USA

© The Author(s) 2018
J. Rodenberg and P. Wagenaar (eds.), *Cultural Contestation*,
Palgrave Studies in Cultural Heritage and Conflict,
https://doi.org/10.1007/978-3-319-91914-0_7

Romantic Sublime and the Post-Frontier (Primitivist) Ideology, and environmental philosophers like Ralph Waldo Emerson, Henry David Thoreau, John Muir, and Aldo Leopold, along with painters like George Catlin from the Hudson River School (1820–1880), were instrumental in influencing Western attitudes. Their collective sentiments were loosely encapsulated in the Wilderness Act of 1964, whose passage was a historically important event in American environmental politics. The Act states:

> A wilderness, in contrast with those areas where man and his own works dominate the landscape, is hereby recognized as an area where the earth and its community of life are untrammeled by man, where man himself is a visitor who does not remain.

The Wilderness Act of 1964 became a powerful legislative instrument to memorialize America's wilderness heritage and to enshrine vignettes of a "primitive America" symbolic of "a once-virgin land" (Cronon 1995). This idealization of uninhabited wilderness not only underscores what national parks actually preserve, but also exposes the degree to which older cultural values continue to shape current environmental and preservationist thinking (Spence 1999). Other scholars have argued that the ideals that built the national park system and its public support are founded in unrealistic, elitist, and largely undemocratic notions of nature that are reflective of the "narcissism in American conceptions of wilderness" (Tweed 2010). Through individual case studies on national parks, these scholars draw attention to inadvertent results associated with the creation of park boundaries and the role that the society-nature opposition has played in legitimizing the human domination of wilderness in the name of progress.

Despite these realities, national parks have long held illustrious roles in North American cinema. The portrayal of these instruments of nation building highlights the ways in which media influences our notions of landscape (Carr 2000). *The Enduring Wilderness/Jardins Sauvage* (1963), a National Film Board of Canada documentary directed by Ernest Reid, proudly depicts Canada's ecological diversity through a "scenic tour" of the country's most spectacular terrestrial and aquatic ecosystems. Released one year prior to the Wilderness Act of 1964, the film portrays Canada's national parks as pieces of land "preserved in its original state" where the wilderness is "no longer feared." The narrator proudly denotes that wilderness has been tamed—"dominated by the expanding pattern of man" for the "benefit, education and enjoyment" of all Canadians. These ecologically rich spaces are likened to natural museums that house collections of scenic curiosities and offer everyone, regardless of age, "the thrill of discovery." This romantic idea, according to environmental historian Roderick Nash, originated in cities where people experienced nostalgia for when human life was closely intertwined with nature. In the film, Henry David Thoreau is famously quoted from his classic text, *Walden*, first published in 1854, as saying:

> We need the *tonic of wildness*... At the same time that we are earnest to explore and learn all things, we require that all things be mysterious and unexplorable, that land and sea be infinitely wild, unsurveyed and unfathomed by us because unfathomable. We can never have enough of nature... We need to witness our own limits transgressed, and some life pasturing freely where we never wander.

As an antidote to the high pressures of modern life, nature's contemplative properties are highlighted in *The Enduring Wilderness/Jardins Sauvage* (1963) through alternating scenes portraying illusory, tranquil landscapes contrasted with the hustle of city life—glorious and awe-inspiring one moment and dangerous and harrowing the next. Like Thoreau, James B. Harkin, the first Commissioner of Canada's national parks, was also a strong proponent of nature's "inexhaustible vigor." He too valorized the restorative and therapeutic benefits of nature and justified the creation of the country's national parks system on this premise, stating that:

> National parks are maintained for all the people – for the ill that they may be restored; for the well that they may be fortified and inspired by the sunshine, the fresh air, the beauty, and all the other healing, ennobling agencies of Nature. They exist in order that every citizen of Canada may satisfy his craving for nature and nature's beauty; that he may absorb the poise and restfulness of their forests; that he may fill his soul with the brilliance of the wild flowers and the sublimity of the mountain peaks; that he may develop the buoyancy, the joy, and the activity that he sees in the wild animals; that he may stock his brain and mind with great thoughts, noble ideals; that he may be made better, be healthier, and happier.

Similarly, Dayton Duncan and Ken Burns' 12-hour PBS documentary, *The National Parks: America's Best Idea* (2009), further elaborates on the mystique of the wilderness and the associated spiritual and meditative benefits. In this six-part series, national parks are framed as a proud American tradition which "extol the virtues of American democracy." They are imbued with a sense of monumentality—a quality that evokes a powerful sense of natural wonder and national pride, and their creation is justified and enforced as a political duty. The romance and mythology about wilderness is depicted through a series of scenes featuring uninhabited spaces set aside for contemplation, reflection—as a means of regaining serenity and equilibrium. The narrative emphasis on spectacular and monumental scenery links God to nature and to the nation-state, thereby promoting wilderness as a uniquely American cultural and moral resource and as the basis for national self-esteem, state-building, and expansion. Here, national parks are unabashedly endorsed as "statements of national greatness in environmental wealth" (Bella 1986). Environmental historian Alfred Runte attributes this "scenic nationalism" to cultural insecurity since North America lacked the cultural monuments and antiquities of Europe. Instead, the west's untrammeled wilderness, which was "colossal and full of savage grandeur," became a point of pride and national identity (Bella 1986).

The North American "natural" landscape can be seen as a symbolic landscape too, expressing specific social values, constructing an identity for burgeoning North American nations. Ross (2009) in particular asks: "How do people make sense of complex, emotionally powerful events and why do different, seemingly contradictory, accounts of what seems to outsiders to be the same event so frequently coexist?" For Canada and the USA, the acquisition of territory for the creation of national parks remains a complex and deeply contested narrative that is virtually neglected in both films. It is often overshadowed by the cultural rhetoric of wilderness, ecological integrity, and associated landscape aesthetics—the picturesque, sublime, and pastoral (Campbell 2011). Both documentaries minimize race, class, and gender consequences in order to promote national parks as a physical and political construction of the nation-state through an imagined national unity that further silences alternative and difficult histories, including the bitter, conflict, and contentious debates over land use in heritage sites, protected areas, and conservation zones. It is this cultural contestation over landscape that forms the focus of this article.

Dispossessing the Wilderness: The Naturalization of a Vation

The democratic principles enshrined in the national park ideal were intended as an expression of the highest American code of government—"equality for all" (Kopas 2007). Despite this, the North American park model was rooted in an autocratic conservation bureaucracy and an exclusionary policy regime. The scientific, economic, and political paradigms that underpin the conceptual basis of environmental and cultural heritage policy have acted as powerful ideological determinants of conservation practice (Dahlberg et al. 2010). Critiques of this practice often engage with issues of power, scale, equity, and human rights from the perspective of political ecology and post-colonialism.

Establishing national parks has not been an innocent conservation practice. Access to parks was often controlled by powerful groups representing dominant value systems. Historically, these "gatekeepers" emerged from religious orders, the monarchy, and the gentry. Over time national parks were managed by equally powerful government agencies such as the US National Park Service and Parks Canada whose economic policies, political motivations, and imposition of behavioral norms dramatically affected the accessibility of parks and their user groups. This "emparkment" of nature is a vivid paradox as newly established national parks were often enshrined under legislative authority in such a way that they represented an ideal of the wilderness as "sanitized, ordered and homogenous" (Hermer 2002). The resultant "artificial, restrictive and alienating" landscape typically excluded human habitation and conservation policy managed encroachment into park boundaries through strict law enforcement. This "pleasure ground ideal" emerged from a twentieth-century tourist culture which was deeply embedded in the institutions of colonialism and Western power that catered to upper-class sensibilities and eugenicist ideologies (Byrne and Wolch 2009). The prevailing early philosophy of wilderness conservation also collided with pre-existing visions of agrarian landscape development and alternative moral economies of resource use. This conflicting view of the natural world failed to recognize wilderness as ancestral homeland and sacred place for many indigenous and aboriginal people. Instead, native peoples were viewed as "an unfortunate blight" and "an affront" to the sensibilities of tourists (Kopas 2007). This preservation ideal was predicated on native dispossession and broader efforts to assimilate indigenous people into civilized society. Policies of aboriginal displacement gained traction in the founding of America's first national parks, namely Yosemite, Yellowstone, and Glacier, from the 1870s until the 1930s (Spence 1999). These became precedents for the exclusion of native peoples from other holdings within the national parks system in both, the USA and Canada.

In recent years, the number of conservation-induced displacement cases from around the world has led to an emergent subfield of scholarship that centers on the plight of "conservation refugees," particularly those of color, rural, indigenous, and marginalized, that are subject to territorial conflict associated with the exclusionary fortress of nature, wildlife, and heritage conservation (Dowie 2009). Often, legal processes of exclusion are applied beyond the boundaries of parklands, protected areas, and cultural heritage sites whereby the natural environment becomes interwoven into a complex exclusionary framework with long-lasting race, class, and equity implications. Environmental justice activism, emanating from within indigenous communities, tends to emphasize the interconnectedness of people and their environments and "the narrowness and short-sightedness" of a conservation approach that would separate "the well-being of ecosystems from those who depend on them" (Scott 2014). Other scholars in this subfield explicitly assert the importance of integrating indigenous people into conservation areas under contracts that actively involves them in the protection and co-management of biological diversity.

This principle of "co-operative co-management" was tested in protected areas in northern Alaskan Communities in the early 1980s. The movement toward co-management had strong beginnings in the 1980s with international policies and strategies such as the World Conservation Strategy (1980) and Our Common Future (1987) whose vision statements linked the aesthetic, utilitarian, and ecological traditions of Western wilderness protection with the broader processes of social development, economic development, and, most importantly, cultural survival. This model of co-management exposed the conflicting goals of the US National Park Service in regard to wilderness preservation and human habitation. Author Theodore Catton's case studies on "inhabited wilderness" in Glacier Bay, Denali, and Gates of the Arctic reveal this anomaly in the spectrum of national park management in the contiguous United States (Catton 1997). Legislation like the Alaska Native Claims Settlement Act (1971) and the Alaska National Interest Lands Conservation Act (1980) set out explicitly to preserve not only the land but, to a certain extent, also the lives of Native Alaskans living on that land "so as not to upset" the intricacies of the local ecosystem. State legislation in Alaska, thus, implied that nature and culture are deeply intertwined, if not inseparable.

Canada's Earliest National Parks

In Canada, the establishment of the country's first national parks was not without consequence on the lives of many indigenous (First Nations, Inuit and Métis) peoples and their land, hunting, and fishing rights. The first state-sanctioned park Banff Hot Springs Reserve in 1885 was established on unoccupied Crown land in the Western provinces. The Stoney Indians who previously hunted on this land, were excluded from its boundaries as evidenced in one 1895 report that explicitly cited the first commissioner recommending that "the red men be kept out permanently" (Kopas 2007). The exclusion of Stoney people from what became Banff National Park served the interest of game conservation, sport hunting, tourism, and the larger government project of Indian assimilation. In the creation of Banff National Park, conservation ideology was buttressed by broader commercial interests and exclusion was aimed to achieve particular social and economic objectives motivated by widely held beliefs about Canada's indigenous people.

Moreover, nineteenth-century Canadian legislation did not provide an explicit environmental or conservation policy mandate for its national parks. Instead, the Canadian government unambiguously created national parks to generate revenue for the newly constructed transcontinental railway and the federal treasury (Kopas 2007). The rationale for creating these earliest mountain parks on frontier land in Western Canada was explicitly driven by a focus on economic development and less by the need to preserve wilderness—a divergent view on the American national park ideal. Parks Canada historian C. J. Taylor argues that Canada's national parks were "fundamentally resource reserves," which permitted the controlled exploitation of a range of resources such as minerals, timber, and water as well as scenery (Taylor 1990). Thus, rather than protecting environmental values, Canada's earliest national parks created a monopoly to protect the commercial and touristic values associated with land reserved for the natural monument.

It was only under the influence of James B. Harkin, the first Commissioner of the world's first park agency—the Dominion Parks

Branch (later, renamed Parks Canada) in 1911 and successive acts like the Forest Reserves and Park Act (1911) and the Canada National Parks Act (1930) that provided the leadership and legislative framework on which environmental protection and wildlife conservation policy could be further developed and enhanced. Though legislative reforms were passed in the early twentieth century, the Canadian government first began to seriously consider environmental concerns in the mid-1960s as changing public attitudes gave the semblance of public support that government bureaucrats needed to achieve their environmental conservation agendas (Bella 1986). In the 1960s and 1970s, the increased professionalization of wildlife biology, the establishment of interpretive services in national parks, political regimes and changing social attitudes of bureaucrats, citizens and interest groups, indigenous peoples, and legal authorities were particularly influential in the decisions shaping the state of Canada's national parks.

The Emparkment of Nature

Canada's National Parks System Plan was perhaps one of the more ambitious plans for environmental conservation conceived by the Trudeau government in the late 1960s. In addition to strengthening federal control over provincial and territorial lands, the System Plan aimed at representing the physical, biological, and geographic features of each of Canada's 39 terrestrial natural regions within the national parks system. In 1970, the Parks Branch had devised its first classification method for a national parks system that would be based on the varying physiographic characteristics of the country. *The National Parks System Planning Manual* (1970) outlined the use of physiographic criteria for parks planning and selection that was guided by a rationally based, consistent set of unifying principles for all of Canada's national parks whereby the ideological value of wilderness was used as a tool to promote national unity. This was the first federal document to describe the totality of the national parks in terms of their specific "representation" of Canada's ecosystems (Mortimer-Sandilands 2000).

Despite the efforts of the National Park System Plan to spread "the nature-value of the nation more equitably around the country," this plan perpetuated the federal government's goal of expanding its territory under the guise of environmental protection (Mortimer-Sandilands 2000). Ecological language was used to "contest and refute community resistance, land appropriation, and competing kinds of use" associated with the creation of new national parks in the Atlantic provinces. Canada's System Plan was a conceptualization of a state-centered agenda to institute a "chain of national natures with relatively identical meanings" that the government could facilitate, regulate, and promote. In the late 1960s, Chrétien and the Trudeau government put a high priority on the need to establish a national park in Québec "to forge a richer Canadian Union" and inadvertently to suppress French–English tensions and separatist sentiments. National parks in Canada thus became symbolically loaded bearers of unity where wilderness was inextricably tied to cultural naturalism.

As a result, several provincial governments in Eastern Canada were responsible for transferring clear titles to land to the federal reserve through expropriation or eminent domain. The Québec government was initially hesitant to hand over clear title to the federal government citing inconsistencies with Québec's Napoleonic civil code. Québec's reluctance to cede its land was the result of two opposing cultural trends: the Anglo-Saxon movement for conservation and the French Canadian desire for geopolitical expansion through agricultural colonization. As a province, Québec's chief interest was to create its own network of parks in order to protect and proclaim its province's "territorial integrity" (Germain 2007). At that time, Québec already possessed a series of provincial parks beginning with Parc de la Montagne Tremblante (1894), Parc des Laurentides (1895), Parc de la Gaspésie (1937), and Parc du Mont Orford (1938). It was not until the Québec Parks Act in 1977 that a legal framework was established to ensure protection and development of the province's natural heritage. The impetus to establish and support the expansion of national parks by Canada and by Québec reflected these governments' respective cultural ideologies. For the nation-state, the political usage of national parks, as mandated through the National Parks System Plan, served to "merge Canada's several cultures into a unique identity" (Germain 2007). This need to maintain national unity and to sustain a Canadian national identity is repeatedly stated in park policies, federal status reports, and management plans. On the contrary, the creation of national parks in Québec was attributed to geopolitical values and broader provincial goals to meet international standards in order to actualize the Québécois nation. As a result, many rural communities in the eastern region of Québec supported the idea for a national park and were swayed by the promise of enhanced economic, education, and recreation possibilities.

The non-consensual taking by the state of privately owned property, for a public purpose, in exchange for compensation became reconfigured as a widely accepted park-creation tool when dealing with difficult or uncooperative provincial governments. While expropriation serves a necessary role in land use and urban planning, it can be argued that Canada's weak legal framework for the protection of legal and substantive rights of property owners (in the case of national parks establishment) upset the delicate balance between the protection of private-property rights and the promotion of the public interest. Settled communities and local villages in Québec and the Atlantic provinces were expropriated in the interest of conservation, resource, and sovereignty politics. Many of the dispossessed faced an indifferent and unresponsive conservation bureaucracy (Sandlos 2005). These culturally powerless groups were marked by difference in ethnicity, language, gender, and economic status. Beginning in 1970, 225 French-speaking Canadians were expropriated while 1000 individual lots lying within the boundaries of Forillon were razed. The expropriations in the territory of Forillon National Park were unprecedented and incredibly divisive due to the great upheaval caused by disrupting long-standing ethno-cultural communities and local fishing traditions. The lack of communication on expropriation procedures and the absence of a definitive relocation program contributed to a climate of insecurity, tension, and anger among citizens and in the media. The revised details regarding the establishment of the park did not match the expectations of citizens many expressed their anger with the hurried and ill-conceived process to evacuate the territory planned for the national park (Babin 2013).

A relatively simple approach to "clearing out" is described in government archives as the Parks Branch often chose the land it thought appropriate and then instructed "the provinces" to expropriate the land leaving landowners to settle for "meager sums" (MacEachern 2001). The creation of Cape Breton Highlands (1936), Prince Edward Island (1937), Fundy (1948), Terra Nova (1957), Kejimkujik (1960), and Forillon (1970) national parks left many landowners with no choice but to accept the government's financial offers and to relocate to nearby communities. Locals were angered with the arbitrary way in which they were treated and their forced removal fostered negative relationships for years and sometimes generations. Many also publicly expressed their discontent with the low compensation offered in exchange for their properties. The Hyman Fonds at the Library and Archives Canada in Ottawa, for example, contains several letters from former residents of the newly created Forillon National Park pleading for additional compensation for their homes and for concessions to relocate their interior furnishings and personal belongings. Most unsettling are the settlement records of expropriation and personal letters condemning the government practice of burning houses by work crews that included members of other expropriated families in the region. These homes, located within the boundaries of the parkland, were burned to the ground—"a procedure that guaranteed no one could profit" from dismantling or moving of a building that was regarded as government property (Rudin 2011). This haunted many and remains a bitter memory for former residents.

The National Film Board's *For Future Generations* (1987), directed by Boyce Richardson, profiles this growing opposition of local communities in the late 1960s. Particularly contentious was the case of Kouchibouguac National Park (1970) in New Brunswick where expropriations disrupted the lives of more than 1000 Acadians whose families had fished and farmed the land for generations. Two other independent documentary films produced nearly thirty years apart, Kouchibouguac (1979) and Kouchibouguac L'histoire de Jackie Vatour et des Expropriés (2006) introduce Jackie Vautour, a local fisherman, who instigated the fight for justice. According to public historian Ronald Rudin, civil disobedience against the forced removal of a population from its land would have been exceptional in any Canadian context; but Vautour's struggle had particular cultural resonance for Acadians, whose history had been marked by the first modern example of "ethnic cleansing" and their removal at the hands of the British in the eighteenth century (Rudin 2011). Vautour, the leader of the resistance, refused to leave his land on Kouchibouguac until his house was bulldozed in 1976. In an act of defiance, Vautour returned to his land two years later and remains a squatter to this day.

The public outcry, mass resistance, and significant media attention associated with the founding of Forillon and Kouchibouguac in 1970 were influential in starting critical dialogue over the legitimacy of expropriation as a preferred tool for securing parklands in Canada. Unfairly indemnified, several people, whose properties were expropriated, initiated legal proceedings in the following years to obtain better compensation for their lands. At the time, many questioned the legality of the methods for assessing property values which according to them systematically underestimated the value of their possessions. Many residents felt disadvantaged since they had no knowledge of their rights nor did they possess the financial means to procure judicial support. In response, the Newfoundland legislature enacted provincial policy called the Family

Homes Expropriation Act (1970) to prevent future expropriation battles. This provincial legislation stipulated that none of the 125 families, living within the boundaries of this newly designated park, were
required to move (McNamee 2010). Following this act, the Gros Morne
National Park (1970) was created. Today, the park holds seven communities that continued to live within this national park's boundaries.
Based on the success of the Family Homes Expropriation Act (1970) in
Newfoundland, Parks Canada began to consider alternatives for national
park establishment and expansion. Subsequent federal legislation like the
National Park Policy (1979), National Parks Act amendments in 1988,
the Guiding Principles and Operational Policies (1999) and Bill C-27
(2007) recognized the importance of both, ecological and cultural integrity in Canada's national park system (McNamee 2010). In 2000, the
Canadian Parliament amended the National Parks Act with a similar legislative prohibition and now, land that is required to establish national
parks is acquired only on a willing seller–willing buyer basis.

Conclusion

The broader concept of national parks as unpopulated wilderness was
increasingly challenged in the ongoing struggle for decolonization.
Cultural contestation and indigenous political activism around the issue
of national parks also resulted in a change in attitudes toward local stakeholders and land claim agreements. Kouchibouguac Acadians and northern aboriginal groups banded together to successfully argue before the
House of Commons and the Senate Committees that the establishment
of national parks outside the umbrella of unresolved land claims would
amount to an expropriation of Aboriginal title (Stevens 2014). The
National Parks Policy (1979) formalized this new approach by recognizing the existence and importance of First Nation rights in potential
and existing park locations. The Guiding Principles Operational Policies
(1994) further emphasized the need to reduce territorial inequalities and
foster cooperation with local First Nations through dialogue and formal agreements, as well as respect for land rights and wildlife resources
through land claims and court decisions. Successive legislative changes
and amendments to the National Parks Act in 1988 and in 2000 also
permitted hunting, fishing, and harvesting in designated sections of
select parks in Northern Canada like Vuntut and Ivvavik.
    From this brief overview, it is evident that national park ideologies
arise within a complex and deeply contested landscape. National parks

are not ideologically neutral spaces (Byrne and Wolch 2009). Early wilderness ideals were complicit in the dispossession of peoples and policies of forced removal in the interests of conservation were neither universally applied across the country nor solely targeted at Canada's indigenous peoples (Piper 2013). The rhetoric of cultural superiority, which stemmed from feudal principles of land ownership, resulted in the placing of differential values on the landscape. The study of national parks is one way to understand the evolving framework of the Canadian state, conservation thought, and practice and its political character. It is also a way of understanding the making of a nation whose national parks serve as a microcosm for the history of conflict and misunderstanding that has long characterized these unequal power relationships between dominant state-building legislation and more vulnerable native peoples, local populations, and culturally powerless groups. Seeing it through the conceptual lens of Ross' idea of cultural contestation, it can be argued that Canada's national parks are both a physical landscape and a symbolic landscape used for identity formation whereby natural and cultural elements are inscribed with literal and symbolic value that result in an exclusion of communities and in some instances, a denial of access and subsistence rights in these landscapes held as a natural resource by the Canadian state. In order to represent a more accurate account of their creation, national park agencies must position these cultural landscapes within the broader canon of social, cultural, political, and environmental histories to convey histories of contestation and preserve material traces that bear witness to these struggles. As Ross (2009) argues, central to this process is the development of new narratives, ones which do not directly challenge older ones, but which reframe them in more inclusive terms that deemphasize the emotional significance of differences between groups and identify shared goals and experiences.

References

Babin, A. (2013) L'expropriation du territoire de Forillon : étude du processus décisionnel des responsables étatiques fédéraux et provinciaux, 1968–1975. Unpublished Masterthesis: Universite Laval.

Bella, L. (1986). The Politics of Preservation: Creating National Parks in Canada, and in the United States, England and Wales. *Planning Perspectives, 1,* 189–206.

Byrne, J., & Wolch, J. (2009). Nature, Race, and Parks: Past Research and Future Directions for Geographic Research. *Progress in Human Geography, 33*(6), 743–765.

Campbell, C. E. (2011). *A Century of Parks Canada, 1911–2011.* Calgary: University of Calgary Press.

Carr, E. (2000). Park, Forest and Wilderness. *George Wright Forum, 17*(2), 16–30 (Taking Stock: Changing Ideas and Visions for Parks).

Catton, T. (1997). *Inhabited Wilderness Indians, Eskimos, and National Parks in Alaska.* Albuquerque: University of New Mexico Press.

Cronon, W. (1995). The Trouble with Wilderness; or, Getting Back to the Wrong Nature. In *Uncommon Ground: Rethinking the Human Place in Nature* (pp. 69–90). New York: W. W. Norton.

Dahlberg, A., Rohde, R., & Sandell, K. (2010). National Parks and Environmental Justice: Comparing Access Rights and Ideological Legacies in Three Countries. *Conservation and Society, 8*(3), 209–224.

Dowie, M. (2009). *Conservation Refugees: The Hundred-Year Conflict Between Global Conservation and Native Peoples.* Cambridge, MA: MIT Press.

Germain, A. (2007). *Seeking Common Ground: The Politics of National Parks in the Torngat Mountains, Arctic Canada,* paper presented at the Association of American Geographers Annual Meeting, San Francisco, April 18, 2007.

Hermer, J. (2002). *Regulating Eden: The Nature of Order in North American Parks.* Toronto, ON: University of Toronto.

Kopas, P. S. (2007). *Taking the Air: Ideas and Change in Canada's National Parks.* Vancouver, BC: UBC Press.

MacEachern, A. A. (2001). *Natural Selections: National Parks in Atlantic Canada, 1935–1970.* Montreal, QC: McGill-Queen's University Press.

McNamee, K. (2010). Filling in the Gaps: Establishing New National Parks. *George Wright Forum: Parks Canada Agency, 27*(2), 142–150.

Mortimer-Sandilands, C. (2000). The Cultural Politics of Ecological Integrity: Nature and Nation in Canada's National Parks, 1885–2000, *International Journal of Canadian Studies / Revue internationale d'études canadiennes,* 39, 161–189.

Piper, L. (2013). Knowing Nature Through History. *History Compass, 11*(12), 1139–1149.

Reid, E. (1963). *The Enduring Wilderness/Jardins Sauvage.* National Film Board of Canada.

Richardson, B. (1987). *For Future Generations.* National Film Board.

Ross, M. H. (2009). Cultural Contestation and the Symbolic Landscape: Politics by Other Means? In M. H. Ross (Ed.), *Culture and Belonging in Devided Societies: Contestation and Symbolic Landscapes* (pp. 1–24). Philadelphia: University of Pennsylvania Press.

Rudin, R. (2011). The First French-Canadian Parks: Kouchibouguac and Forillon in History and Memory. *Revue de la Société historique du Canada* [Journal of the Canadian Historical Association], *22*(1), 161–200.

Sandlos, John. (2005). Federal Spaces, Local Conflicts: National Parks and the Exclusionary Politics of the Conservation Movement in Ontario, 1900–1935, *Journal of the Canadian Historical Association / Revue de la Société historique du Canada*, *(16)*1, pp. 293–318.

Scott, D. (2014). What is Environmental Justice? Environmental Justice. In M. Brydon-Miller & D. Coghlan (Eds.), *The SAGE Encyclopedia of Action Research*. London: Sage.

Spence, M. D. (1999). *Dispossessing the Wilderness: Indian Removal and the Making of the National Parks*. New York: Oxford University Press.

Stevens, S. (2014). *Indigenous Peoples, National Parks, and Protected Areas: A New Paradigm Linking Conservation, Culture, and Rights*. Tucson: University of Arizona Press.

Taylor, C. J. (1990). *Negotiating the Past: The Making of Canada's National Historic Parks and Sites*. Montreal: McGill-Queen's University Press.

Tweed, W. C. (2010). *Uncertain Path: A Search for the Future of National Parks*. Berkeley: University of California Press.

PART II

Cultural Contestation Between States

Famagusta, Cyprus: Cultural Heritage at the Center of Political and Cultural Contestation

Carlos Jaramillo

INTRODUCTION

What do we really see when we observe structures, statues, or buildings linked to the past? Hints, witnesses, traces, and testimonies of the life we (humans) have lived. Although heritage has historically been formed by a variety of influences or characteristics, the current conceptualization of cultural heritage recognizes (only) single narratives to be capable of endorsing national identity. This perspective, which values heritage on the basis of a certain range of time or event, demonstrates the limitations of our perspective on the past. It also overlooks the reality that new heritage expressions are often triggered by change. And since change is often violent in nature, it manifests via conflict (in most cases a form of contestation). In point of fact, from a historical perspective, societal conflict is often represented by cultural heritage expressions that

C. Jaramillo (✉)
Bucaramanga, Colombia

© The Author(s) 2018

157

J. Rodenberg and P. Wagenaar (eds.), *Cultural Contestation*,
Palgrave Studies in Cultural Heritage and Conflict,
https://doi.org/10.1007/978-3-319-91914-0_8

reflect that conflict and the changes it has brought about. The overall contextualization of cultural heritage can be viewed against this backdrop (the complex relationship between conflict and heritage).[1] Thus, it is useful to understand this connection as well as the impediments to its acknowledgment.

Heritage derives much of its societal impact from the fact that it has survived, and may continue to survive, numerous epochs and cycles of destruction, reconstruction, and alterations that, in some instances, were brought about through imposition and force. The tendency to assess heritage within two narrow frameworks—(1) the highly selective memories embedded by history into the present context; and (2) the political meanings attached to heritage—represents one of the principal difficulties in the current international approach to cultural heritage, in particular with regard to sites that challenge common patterns, logic, and order. The inability, or unwillingness, to acknowledge both that conflict is a historical constant in the shaping of heritage and that heritage is inevitably grounded in distinct political and social structures (rather than in the present or in the future) is a significant obstacle to the development of cultural heritage in forgotten or ignored, conflicted and contested areas. And Famagusta, Cyprus is a prime example of this.[2]

In terms of Famagusta, it is imperative to reassess heritage to acknowledge the relevance the past four decades have had as a unique era impacting its heritage content, as well as that of North Cyprus, generally. Indeed, it is impossible to give sites like Famagusta (and similar places) a role as witness in the current configuration of society. But Famagusta represents the sum of all the considerations that have gone into the formation of heritage and that have been dismissed over the past six decades (coinciding with the emergence of the concept of cultural heritage) since North Cyprus became a contested territory in 1974. Three fundamental aspects of cultural heritage doctrine help explain the difficulties Famagusta and North Cyprus have, over the years, encountered when dealing deal with cultural heritage, its intervention and transit from pre-conflict to date. These aspects are (1) the political component of cultural heritage; (2) its selective endorsement of the past; and (3) the subordination of cultural heritage acknowledgment to nation and identity.

From Monument to Cultural Heritage: Politicization of the Past

The principle that gave birth to cultural heritage scholarship and the industry surrounding it is that past events are relevant to the present—that there are important sets of memories societies should not forget and that should be commemorated.

For centuries, a singular term dominated the discussion when referring to memories of the past: *Monument*.[3] Only during the past few decades has this transformed into the contemporary approach and nomenclature: *Cultural Heritage*. For good or ill, this terminology is intimately connected to international politics and power, as opposed to societal memory. What's more, the legal framework for the concept of cultural heritage, along with the influence of UNESCO, has connected the concept directly to conservation while turning it away from memory. Cultural heritage, as opposed to Monument, favors aspects of nationality, identity, and collectiveness that institutionalize the dismissal of memories, along with minorities and contested territories.

The works of Werner Von Truetzschler (2005) and Jukka Jokilehto (2005) illustrate the considerations that have been fundamental to the development of the concept of cultural heritage. From their discussions, it is possible to deduce three important points. First, as a concept, cultural heritage developed and emerged from within UNESCO and its consultant organizations (ICOMOS and ICCROM), with governments as the only recognized counterparty. This means that cultural heritage's doctrinal foundations were premised on the political system of the UN member states and that the meaning, definition, and characterization of heritage align with that which nations allow in terms of their boundaries, forms of government, national narratives, recognized ethnicities, religions, gender, and human rights approach. Second, cultural heritage, as defined and dictated within UN agencies, is insufficient for purposes of framing, assessing, promoting, and developing contested heritage and heritage sites, such as Famagusta, i.e., those located in contested territories where diverse considerations outside the framework (e.g., pluralism, mobility, connectivity, memory, diasporas, conflict, and transborder forms of culture) give meaning to heritage. Third, since cultural heritage is an expression that captures moments and events that have presumptively enriched the narrative of a nation and its corresponding national memory, there is a propensity for heritage practitioners to favor the simplistic and rigid method of heritage preservation (an approach focused on conservation that restores the 'authentic' features of the heritage asset) over one that considers cultural heritage as a witness, not only to past events and times, but also to those of the present and future yet to occur.

Implicitly, cultural heritage must mean more than the mere act of preservation, a process which is confined by our limited vision of the past and ambivalence about the future. This is borne out by Famagusta. But to understand Famagusta and its relevance to a contemporary approach to cultural heritage, it is essential to understand the context in which cultural heritage expressions there have been left ignored for decades—this despite their relevance to the construction of memory, to representation of cultural expressions, and to life, itself. To do this requires an examination of the evolution of cultural heritage, from its origins as a concept, into a doctrine based on sovereignty and the international system of nations. The system has transmogrified into an uncontested body of 'truths' that not only preclude the existence of realities outside the UN system of nations, but also of recognition of interactions between cultural heritage and other systems in the territory where it exists (e.g., contested territories).

The Impact of 'Nationality' and 'Identity' on Cultural Heritage in Contestation

To understand the current, ambivalent status of Famagusta, it is necessary to assess how and to what extent the UNESCO framework impacts that status, especially since considerations of Nationality and Identity of the cultural heritage site are preconditions for recognition and classification within the organization. However, it is also critical to note that the UNESCO framework does not address a variety of considerations involved in the recognition of Famagusta as vital heritage—considerations that illustrate how identity is constructed or deconstructed there. Nevertheless, the purpose of this section is not to propose an improvement to the functioning of the UN system and its organizations. Rather, it is to reflect upon heritage sites that have been left contested by various cultures, powers, and/or societies. In so reflecting, it is important to acknowledge key terms in current legislation, such as Identity and Nationality, as they are strategic points that have prevented the development of a realistic perspective on cultural heritage, especially in Cyprus. There is a need to respond to the difficulties in Famagusta and to scrutinize the core aspects of the conceptualization of cultural heritage as they relate to unresolved ethnic, religious, and political issues.

A broad view of scholarship pertaining to cultural heritage practice, beginning in the nineteenth century, reveals how the concept of 'identity' has been, and remains, superfluous. Our understanding of identity, which has changed (and will continue to do so) over time, depends on political context, governability, and religion, among other factors. The evolution of the concept leads to the acceptance of multifaceted and more inclusive perspectives, of differing narratives flowing simultaneously alongside one another. Since cultural heritage is an act of recognition and social construction, the 'identity' of that which is collectively recognized must be scrutinized.

The notion of 'identity' is found in political rhetoric, historical expositions, and even popular culture. But a crucial part of identity is inextricably linked to the particular nation. The use of identity to reinforce the concept of nation and a predominantly occidental vision of the world is present in UNESCO's conceptualization of heritage. That alone represents a significant challenge to defining Cyprus' sense of culture, history, and the construction of its self-identity. The understanding of identity and its linkage to territory, ethnicity, religion, and other key concepts that configure the 'social realm' serve as one of the central foundations of a tailored definition of culture, citizenship, and diversity.[4] Identity, as a nebulous and highly contested notion, rests at the very core of various political, economic, and social predicaments. It also permeates pertinent issues in cultural heritage. In the case of Famagusta, the concept of identity represents an important bridge between events that shaped its past as well as its prospects for the future; it also serves as a basic starting point in understanding the complexity of Famagusta as heritage in a contested territory. Simply put, the development of identity is intimately linked with recognition and assertion of its location in a nation-state, as well as political maneuvering—two fundamental, but problematic processes in North Cyprus.

The context in nineteenth-century Europe was one of colonization and industrialization, and this set the milieu in which 'westerners' explored and produced their own corpus of knowledge. This systematic and widely structured epistemic production has been attached to

Orientalism—the creation and definition of the (non-Western) 'Other' in comparison with the (Western) 'Self.' In other words, it referred to a comprehensive attempt to produce binary identities. The fields of history, sociology, anthropology, and even cultural heritage were not immune to this. In fact, the building of history and cultural analysis with a 'western' perspective emerged as a consequence of this, as noted in the following: '[…] the nature of archaeology research is shaped, to a significant degree, by the roles that particular nation-states play, economically, politically, and culturally, as independent parts of the modern world-system' (Habu et al. 2008: 2). Furthermore, nationality has been a term that has complicated the definition of cultural expressions; its influence (as we have seen) has redefined those expressions, not for what they are, but for what they represent. Thus, it is necessary to consider the question of whether North Cyprus can be differentiated, in heritage terms, from the Republic of Cyprus. If differentiated, the two territories face the erasure of traces that prove the imbrication of north and south, and along with that, the destruction of the heritage that gives testimony to it. If the two are not differentiated, the neglect of cultural heritage highlights its manipulation over the years to serve a purpose different from culture. Neither option can explain the limbo Famagusta finds itself in. But this dilemma validates that fact that the governance of heritage (and the role of the de facto government of the north, as well as the Republic of Cyprus in dealing with cultural heritage) is political.

Throughout the second half of the twentieth century, western arguments pointed to Cyprus as a crossroads between East and West in order to argue a Hellenistic origin of the current Cypriot identity and culture. The focus over the past two decades has been on proving the supremacy of the Hellenistic influence while dismissing multiple historical influences and polarizing the political discourse on cultural grounds. The insistence on proving the origins of Cyprus' culture speaks volumes about its political polarization and the broad project of dismissing the recognition of events over the past 43 years.

Study of the past should not be driven by religious or political affiliation; it should only attempt to understand and explain the past and provide evidence for trajectories yet to be explored. Apparently, in the context of Famagusta, the political agenda greatly overpowers both scholarly and scientific attempts to study its culture, history, and heritage.

In the formation of nations and nationalistic ideas of state, governments are inclined to dismiss any form of threat that questions the soundness of the national concept. In addition, the UN desires to pre-serve the geopolitical *status quo* and to prevent dismemberment of nations. Thus, during transition periods after formation, nation-states were compelled to overlook diversity within, focusing instead on the construction of national unity—of cultural homogeneity and harmony. In various circumstances, the creation of the nation, and the suppression of minority cultures in defense of the dominant one, emerged through violent and bloody means. In many places, the tools used to reinforce the concept of nation—ethnic cleansing, religious and class supremacy, gender exclusivity—have not exemplified virtue. In this same context, forms of cultural heritage have been flagged to enhance patriotic and nationalistic arguments and, in the same manner, permitted exclusion and marginalization, manipulating the cultural content of national assets to deliver grandiosity or supremacy of a chosen class. This is essentially what happened in Cyprus, where non-recognition of the contested terri-tory in the north has exacerbated nationalistic discourses.

Famagusta *vis-à-vis* Contestation

In order to highlight the concept and the idea of contestation in Famagusta, its cultural heritage can be viewed through three different lenses that are commonly understood owing to their presence throughout history: (1) as a reflection of contestation (war memorials); (2) as contested expressions of current political affairs (the fall of the Berlin Wall); or most commonly (3) as an argument that validates contestation (the destruction of the al-Nuri Mosque in Mosul, Iraq). The interaction between cultural heritage and contestation is deeply linked to the value we give to cultural heritage. What is clear is that at no time does the production and/or development of cultural heritage cease (with or without contestation).

Throughout the period during which the concept of cultural heritage has developed, the field of preservation has grown in parallel. The set of values accorded heritage assets (beginning with the concept of 'monument') has evolved. They resulted originally from an assessment of whether an asset is historic, aesthetically pleasing, or socially and eco-nomically valuable, and have transformed into one of whether it is of 'cultural significance.' This evolution emerged from the need to stand-ardize the system of values, to balance all aspects in order to give each the same importance. It also served to establish a connection between cultural significance and 'fabric,' the physical expression of heritage.

Randall Mason argues, 'In significance, preservationists pack all their theory, ideology and politics—and their wonder at the capacity to use historic fabric to reflect on the past' (Mason 2004; see furthermore Mason et al. 2012). In approach, Mason agrees that by preserving heritage sites and their significance, current scholarship has identified conservation as synonymous with the representation of memory and history.[5] But what exactly is 'significance,' and for whom is heritage significant?

Efforts at establishing criteria based on importance, significance, or value collide with the problem of subjectivity. This typifies the difficulties for a site like Famagusta, not only because it is difficult to conclude for whom it is significant, but because it is unclear from which time frame it should be viewed. If significance is a form of interpretation, then who are the stakeholders, and in which framework need it be structured?

In contrast, if cultural heritage were viewed as a dynamic concept, allowing for overlapping historical periods, the discussion would expand to permit the addition of memories to heritage sites in recognition of heritage as a witness—not a protagonist—of events and facts.[6] In that vein, Jeremy Wells would argue that it is necessary to return to the set of values embedded in heritage, in particular the values that are connected to the sociocultural and experimental setting of the heritage asset (Wells 2010). Famagusta, itself, raises additional arguments that should be considered whenever one is assessing a site whose significance extends beyond one single society, community, boundary, physicality, and/or history.

Famagusta, which transformed from Christian (French, Genoese, Venetian) to Muslim (Ottoman), then back to Christian (British), is problematic for those who would frame a site with one identity, or one (or any) nationality. This fact alone becomes a starting point from which we can assess the current shape of the political world and from which we can begin to understand the role of cultural heritage in delivering discourses with deep political content. In a number of diverse countries, culture has been incorporated into society's welfare, which necessarily compels it to align closely with political, religious, legal, and social discourses of the majorities. The case of Cyprus is not exempt from the intricacies of identity and western discourse. As a part of the larger Mediterranean region, the history of the island of Cyprus reveals dramatic transitions across numerous regimes. Famagusta was, and still is, at the center of these political transitions and conflicts. In addition, the long history of external occupation and subjugation in Cyprus has yielded a tenuous and ill-defined identity.

Perhaps because of its insular location, Cyprus never received the attention and interest that did other conflict locations in Europe, such as the Balkans during the political reshaping of that region starting in the 1990s. Furthermore, the unresolved transitional territory in North Cyprus closed the door to partial agreements, including mitigation of further deterioration to cultural heritage located in the north. The 1974 events redefined the way Cyprus has been studied for decades. The historic and continuing (current) exacerbation of ethnic differences, and its development into an armed conflict, has facilitated a multidimensional understanding of Cyprus that went beyond the sociological level. The unresolved Cyprus issue offers a clear perspective on the current framework of nations and its limited capacity to resolve its contested territory.

To give Cyprus's cultural heritage a context, it is necessary to stand back and look at the island through an alternative lens, one that helps us recognize additional components to heritage, and redefine attributes such as nationalism and identity. As the cultural heritage Technical Specialist of the Study on cultural heritage in Cyprus tasked to deal with the Bi-communal Committee on cultural heritage in Cyprus, I was a keen observer of the overall political dilemma that drives the two communities (Turkish and Greek Cypriots). Those who argue for the Greek-Cypriot community as the inheritor of Cypriot origins (or Greece as Cyprus' mother nation) do not accept a discussion on how to recognize the heritage of the 'Other' as its own. Most importantly, a discussion on how to dismantle the 'cultural ban' on cultural heritage scholars working in the northern part of Cyprus was never an option. The assumption of national identity overlaps with ethno-national heritage, and both cultural heritage and ethnicity are part of the inherited asset belonging to the citizens.[7] This, in principle, obliges a redefinition of identity, nationality, and ethnicity that is inclusive and participatory in order to replace the polarized vision currently separating something that is indivisible. In the case of Famagusta, the identity of the site has yet to be defined; it demands careful assessment within the context of the unresolved political issues that have caused an acute fracture between Famagusta and the people who live there.

Given the connections between the current situation in Famagusta and the conceptualization of cultural heritage, as well as UNESCO's role in the development of the term, there is a need for a fresh, dynamic, and updated approach to cultural heritage, both in the case of Famagusta and the entire sector. Famagusta proves the difficulties of securing a site that cannot satisfy the number of webs, attachments, and conditions that come with the internationalized politics of culture.

Narratives were, and still are, influenced by political contexts, especially those associated with colonial, imperial, and national discourses. It is well documented that archaeology has always been deeply linked to occidental approaches to the culture, history, and economic values that constrain the recognition of other forms of heritage, such as spiritual or symbolic expressions. As such, archaeology, as well as traditional history, is limited to that which can be scaled in western terms, divorcing the present from the past, and communities from their own definition of the universe. Scholars in this field still remain heavily dependent on the grand narratives that were initiated by these occidental approaches. It is on these terms that the construction of 'identity' needs to be assessed, that is, in light of the several historic influences representing important inputs into what we currently call identity. When supporting the recognition of cultural heritage on the grounds of identity, the current international framework endorses certain historic influences on a particular community. But it fails to consider either the multiplicity of layers composing the community or its definition of the Self (composed of the coexistence of multifaceted visions of the community's past, present, and future) *vis-à-vis* the Other. As such, the international framework does not explore, though it may recognize, the obscure concept of Identity. Instead, the international framework protects the current system of nations, as if nations were forever fixed and uncontested.

The complicated Cypriot political setting gave birth in 2008 to the Bi-Communal Committee on cultural heritage in Cyprus. (The BCCH is an institutional figurehead designed to facilitate the work on cultural heritage in North Cyprus, particularly at sites located in relatively benign settings, such as buildings without contested ownership; privately owned, military occupied; or simple vernacular architecture. It is comprised of institutional representatives from the Turkish and Greek communities.) The BCCH has patterned its approach, in part, on the mechanisms implemented in Kosovo by the Council of Europe following the 2004 events (also known as the 2004 Kosovo riots). During the Kosovo riots, a number of houses and churches from the Kosovan Serb community were burned and looted, people were killed, and some were disappeared. In my role as the cultural heritage Technical Expert for the United Nations Development Programme-Partnership For the Future Cyprus (UNDP-PFF) in 2010, I was exposed to conditions similar to those I had experienced in Kosovo in 2005. There, in conjunction with the events of 2004, cultural heritage carried significant political weight during the status talks on the future of Kosovo. It did so through a plan (the Ahtisaari Plan) drafted in 2007 by the United Nations Mission in Kosovo supported by twelve principles: (1) respect for a multiethnic society, (2) design of a national constitution, (3) promote international status, (4) protection and promotion of the rights of members of communities, (5) develop a decentralized government, (6) implementation of a justice system, (7) protection and promotion of religious and cultural heritage, (8) protection of refugees, (9) follow the principles of sustainable economic development, (10) reinforce the security sector, (11) promote international presence, and (12) guarantee the presence of the OSCE. The events framed a political initiative. The formation of a multilateral group to facilitate the recognition, respect, and protection of heritage linked to the Serbian Orthodox Church and the Kosovan Serb population was an expression of goodwill from the de facto government in Kosovo and an important milestone for status definition (a process that began in 2007 and which, to date, has gained for Kosovo recognition as an independent state by 108 UN member states). A similar experience has been envisioned for Cyprus since the formation of the BCCH by international agencies (UNDP and the European Union) in 2008 (some 35 years after the conflict broke out in Cyprus).

The 1990s Balkan War that preceded the experience in Kosovo resulted in the formation of several new countries in the region, all home to a complex ethnic composition, as well as a difficult governing environment, which included difficulty in managing heritage expressions. To forge a post-2004 compromise between the government of Kosovo and institutions dealing with cultural heritage of Serbian roots, the Reconstruction Implementation Commission for the Balkans (the RIC) came into being.[8]

The RIC for the Balkans is a political commission headed by the Council of Europe, and its principal participating partners include the Serbian Orthodox Church; the Institute for the Protection of Monuments (Serbia); the Ministry of Culture, Youth, and Sports (Kosovo); and the Institute for the Protection of Monuments (Kosovo). It includes a Technical Unit that is financed and controlled by the Council of Europe and the European Commission; the RIC Technical Unit presides over the financial and technical aspects of the reconstruction of buildings. Additional functions, such as training, are provided

by additional partners in the region. These efforts aimed to synchro-
nize action in order to provide a feasible environment for intervening in
the cultural heritage located in Kosovo. However, in a political maneuver taken during Kosovo Status Talks, Serbia introduced a legal road-
block to the complete independence of Kosovo. It did so by proposing
a group of medieval sites located in Kosovo (The Dečani Monastery,
The Patriarchate of Peć Monastery, the church of the Holy Virgin of
Ljevisa, and the Church of Holy Apostles) for World Heritage Site designation under the protection of Serbia. This posed a legal impediment
to the complete independence of Kosovo because the World Heritage
Convention is an international agreement that generally corresponds to
legislation that honors and protects aspects of geographic boundaries,
including cultural and natural resources. In the case of Serbia, the fact
that there are enclaves located in Kosovo that have been given World
Heritage status means that parts of Kosovo are under Serbian dominion, which imposes these additional impediments to full independence of
Kosovo, as well as impeding the exercise of sovereignty, security, governance, self-determination, and full international representation.

In Cyprus, The BCCH represents a structure similar to that which
was created in the Balkans. The BCCH was created in 2008, and
resources from the European Commission have been pledged to support
work on a number of buildings located principally in North Cyprus.

As was the case in the Balkans, the situation in Cyprus reveals the
political implications of cultural heritage when it comes to overlapping
political and religious interests. Assessing the situation in Cyprus requires
both the recognition of North Cyprus as an independent state and the
recognition of a religious community as an important stakeholder.
(In Cyprus, this is the Cypriot Orthodox Church; in Kosovo, it is the
Serbian Orthodox Church.) Furthermore, it presents a scenario in which
divided communities (Christians and Muslims) shape the context of the
work in cultural heritage. This was also true in the Balkans. But in addition to these similarities linking the two situations, there are important
differences, of which five are central: (1) The institutions in Kosovo committed important resources to the work on cultural heritage that included
buildings from all backgrounds, but especially Orthodox structures. By
contrast, in Cyprus, the governmental institutions (from both sides of the
island) have failed to engage their resources; instead, the Bi-communal
Committee on cultural heritage, using resources from the European
Commission, has shouldered the weight; (2) In Cyprus, the presence of

Turkish nationals, Turkish military forces, and the continued occupation of areas in North Cyprus makes Turkey an important stakeholder, one that has not been included in the work on Cultural Heritage; (3) Unlike Kosovo, the technical aspects of the work (such as significance of structures and their features) have not been detached from the political implications of cultural heritage; rather, Cyprus emphasizes cultural heritage by prioritizing sites that are either neutral in terms of ethnic and religious connections or have strong ethnic backgrounds; (4) The technical aspects of the work are neither assessed nor endorsed by an independent expert from outside the conflict; and (5) The Council of Europe and the Technical Co-operation and Consultancy Programme, together with the Regional Programme in Southeast Europe and its Local Development Pilot Projects, intend to link heritage development among regions and countries that share features, landscapes, and customs. In the case of the Balkans, the characteristics shared by neighboring countries have been addressed through transnational projects to boost the economy of developing areas. These include the sharing of borders, linking east and Western Europe, and trying to envisage Europe as a whole, factors that, from a geographical standpoint, do not exist with regard to Cyprus. The Balkans represent an approach to the issues arising from conflict and post-conflict that guarantees the accuracy of mechanisms, involvement, and results. In Cyprus, this approach is still in an embryonic stage, not only because of its insular, island location, but also because Turkey (its closest neighbor) still plays a role in North Cyprus that permeates North Cypriot society, be that as a force in the economy, in its social composition, education, and culture or in its military. This is a persistent condition that has been problematic for the Republic of Cyprus.

The most important shared dynamic in the Cypriot and the Balkan experiences as it pertains to overcoming the difficulties the political component of heritage brings is a commitment to preserve public buildings that are considered of heritage value but which do not have private ownership. That is, they are owned by the Orthodox Church (Cypriot or Serbian), by institutions, or are public.[9] Public resources, coming either from European institutions, donors, NGOs, or form any other source, have been pledged so as not to favor individuals. Internal or external resources can be invested solely in public assets that are detached from profitability, commercial ownership or individual benefit.

But the structure designed via the BCCH, admirable as it is in its efforts, leaves one question remaining, a question which illustrates writ large the problem of cultural heritage vis-à-vis Famagusta. How can the approximately 240 privately owned buildings that constitute the majority of heritage assets in Famagusta be rehabilitated when these buildings represent over 90% of Famagusta?

The process in Kosovo, as well as the one currently unfolding in Cyprus, offers as many benefits as limitations. Thus, further consideration is necessary in order to align the process with the principle that in representing a society, cultural heritage is concerned, not only with great visual structures and buildings, but with ordinary, everyday places like kitchens, dormitories, courtyards, shops, and butcheries, where, throughout history, people have spent most of their time. Great structures are the consequence of wealth, vision, or simply the need not to be forgotten; this is less an expression of society than of its leaders. Kosovo, and Cyprus, as well, will eventually need to face the fact that a community unable to stand on its own principles concerning memories embedded in cultural heritage and to commit to rehabilitation and development in relation to those principles, is a community that is unclear on what, if any, type of society it wants to be. Principles should be crafted by regular people, not by politicians or politics; these principles should then filter up to society's representatives, not vice versa. Cultural heritage has become greater than the framework designed for it. Heritage has contributed—in meanings, uses, and arguments—to our perspective on our own past and future. It has served to force discussions on aspects of decolonization, gender, and human rights, among others, while openly clashing with official narratives of the present. Constrained by this framework, Famagusta, a site in permanent change, has never fit and thus never been fully recognized. But a site determined by change and conflict cannot expect to be fully understood and acknowledged in its heritage content under the current system.

The work of the BCCH has provided a process by which critical aspects of contestation that remain ambiguous—land, property, governance, and citizenship in North Cyprus—can be avoided for the present. This leaves to be assessed the greater portion of cultural heritage expressions, represented by vernacular architecture urban and rural landscapes, and any other expression that lies in private hands. From these, it is possible to recover the memories that characterize a particular community. These expressions, which constitute the heritage area of Famagusta, often lie outside the scope of multilateral banking support, institutional representation, financial conditions, or even basic public services, such as running water, sewerage, or electricity.

We must understand that laudable endeavors of institutions like the BCCHC in Cyprus are by their nature limited and by no means represent an answer to the issues arising from the location, political milieu and over four decades of contestation in Famagusta. To the contrary, the BCCHC in Cyprus highlights both the difficulties of maneuvering in the setting where cultural heritage has been conceptualized and its limitation in accepting the evidence of change produced in Cyprus since 1974.

CONCLUSION

When analyzing Famagusta and its relevance as a cultural heritage site in Cyprus (along with its connections to other Mediterranean sites and therefore its importance for European history), it is inevitable that the political component of such analysis (in the present, as much as in the past) will be highlighted. In sum, Famagusta is the end-result of political changes throughout time, reflected in buildings, urban structures, archaeological sites, and landscapes. But cultural heritage is a concept that emerged within a political setting (the United Nations). It serves political aims (UN member state's foreign policy) and facilitates political changes, when needed (UN Security Council Resolutions). The development of parallel management structures such as the BCCH in 2008 is a worthy action; however, ultimately, this measure reflects the impossibility of dealing with cultural heritage in a contested territory within the framework designed under the umbrella of UNESCO and accepted as doctrine worldwide. The risk of sidestepping current instruments on acknowledgment (by national governments), management (by authorities), and preservation (by experts) of cultural heritage as it has been agreed is the sustainability of cultural heritage and its stakeholders. As such, cultural heritage is a political tool used to recognize state boundaries, rights, and responsibilities, and therefore to prevent contestation. However, there are substantial issues that arise from how we acknowledge cultural heritage that reflects change. (1) Cultural Heritage is, in essence, a mirror of the past, an ever longer past crowded with change and evolution. Still, the structure, conceptualization and definition of what is cultural heritage, generally endorses current political *status quo*, leaving limited space for discussing culture throughout contestation. (2) To avoid the intricacies of dealing with political instability or unresolved political status, the cultural heritage system has created commissions, committees, and expert groups, to endorse politically unfeasible actions on cultural heritage sites that are ungoverned or ungovernable.

(3) A direct consequence of periods of political contestation is the risk of acknowledging a contested territory and its heritage expressions as endorsement for separation. (4) Cultural heritage is a sector deeply connected to conservation and preservation; however, it plays additional roles in society's development, apart from current doctrine. In transitional territories, such as those afflicted by war, contested borders and contested territories, it complements concepts such as memory, history, and remembrance.

In many ways, cultural heritage demonstrates the strong links among property, territoriality, and inheritance, and therefore politics and power. Efforts to address the cultural heritage of Famagusta, from its beginnings until today, lack the comprehensive inclusion of cultural and political contestation as a determinant of heritage construction, which it needs in order to prevent further deterioration, and possible manipulation, of the idea of heritage-history in Cyprus since 1974. The absence of such conceptualization heavily impacts cultural heritage, leading, in some cases, to its destruction, and in others, to the development of contemporary expressions that may have appeared and lay unrecognized only because they are a representation of contestation. In contemporary times when the international community has made efforts to enhance human rights protections and to memorialize war crimes and other values that give evidence of evolution in the right direction, the apparent disconnection between cultural heritage and events during periods of political and cultural contestation points toward the dismissal of evidence necessary to build inclusive and fair societies.

NOTES

1. Though there is more to the development of heritage than simply conflict, I limit myself to this aspect since it most clearly illustrates my contentions.
2. The island of Cyprus had a civil war in 1974, since then, the northern part of the island has remained contested without international recognition. The political situation over the past 43 years has proven to be of heritage impact, damaging built heritage, neglecting sites, unrecognizing and dismissing heritage located in the contested areas. At the same time, new and contemporary cultural expressions have developed, with potential heritage content. Both, traditional and new forms of heritage remain uncertain in Northern Cyprus up to date.

3. It is important to keep in perspective the etymologic definition of 'monument,' which is embedded memory: 'MONUMENT: (Lat. monumentum, from moneo, to remind), anything durable made or erected to perpetuate the memory of persons or events.' See cairn; Cromlech; Sepulchral; Mounds; Pillar; Obelisk; Pyramid; Arch; Triumphal; Brasses; Tomb; Stupa; Mausoleum, & c." (*Chamber's Encyclopedia*, vol. VI, 1860).

4. For the purpose of this work, the applicable definition of Cultural Diversity is the one developed by UNESCO in its Convention on the Protection and Promotion of the Diversity of Cultural expressions: 'Cultural diversity is a driving force of development, not only in respect of economic growth, but also as a means of leading a more fulfilling intellectual, emotional, moral and spiritual life.'

5. 'There are problems, though, with the use and conceptualization of significance. The overriding one is that the preservation field fails to fully appreciate its contingent nature. By making the fixing of places and their meaning the primary emphasis of preservation, we have unduly objectified and scientized our understanding of memory and historicity' (Mason et al. 2012: 64).

6. Mason (2004) explains it thusly: '[S]ignificance...as an expression of cultural meaning...must be expected to change, involve multivalence and contention, and be contingent on time, place, and other factors.'

7. See also Scott (2002) on national identity: 'State strategies involving the projection onto a world stage of narratives of "national destiny," strategies which have often been developed in response to the experience of colonialism, are closely linked to concepts of ethno-national heritage and patrimony which are derived from notions of private family inheritance and the unbroken "genealogical chain."'

8. Among their populace, these new countries counted a wide number of ethnicities, including Romas, Egyptians, Bosniaks, Croats, Albanians, and Serbs, among others, all of which, together, reshaped the political map of Eastern Europe. Exacerbation of ethnic issues and the Kosovo riots led to the formation of a technical committee to assess damages. This body was formed by the Council of Europe, the European Commission, the Kosovo Provisional Institutions of Self-Government (PISG), and the Serbian Orthodox Church. An Implementation Committee was established, and it produced a Memorandum of Understanding with the participation of the Serbian Orthodox Church and the Kosovo Provisional Institutions of Self-Government (PISG). After failure, a new RIC was proposed in 2005, followed by a second Memorandum of Understanding seeking compromise between the Serbian Orthodox Church and Kosovo institutions in the reconstruction of selected religious sites.

9. Cultural heritage is characterized by a fundamental and dual character. On the one hand, it is public in its recognition (by governments), and on the other hand, it is private in its ownership (as a commercial asset). Traditionally, Cultural heritage has fallen under a cultural umbrella by which it is common for stakeholders to concentrate only on the negative condition of sites, such as deterioration, loss of significance, and alterations that diminish their heritage content. The positive impact of cultural heritage on the local and national economies, by contrast, is measured and assessed by other disciplines, such as economics and planning. Scholars of cultural heritage have generally set aside the valuation of heritage, assuming that heritage is a priceless asset that needs to be conserved at all costs. This general restriction (as being framed solely by the cultural sector) as applied to cultural heritage further debilitates any comprehensive attempt to assess the impacts of heritage to the wider economic spectrum.

REFERENCES

Chamber's Encyclopedia, vol. VI. (1860). *s.v. "Monument".* Edinburgh: Chamber's Encyclopedia. https://archive.org/details/cu31924087904664. Accessed 6 Mar 2017.
Habu, J., Fawcett, C., & Matsunaga, J. M. (2008). Introduction: Evaluating Multiple Narratives. Beyond Nationalist, Colonialist and Imperialist Narratives. In J. Habu, C. Fawcett, & J. M. Matsunaga (Eds.), *Evaluating Multiple Narratives. Beyond Nationalist, Colonialist and Imperialist Narratives* (pp. 1–11). New York: Springer.
Jokilehto, J. (2005). Definition of Cultural Heritage: References to Documents in History. *ICCROM Working Group 'Heritage and Society'.* http://cif.icomos.org/pdf_docs/Documents%20on%20line/Heritage%20definitions.pdf. Accessed 6 Mar 2017.
Mason, R. (2004). Fixing Historic Preservation: A Constructive Critique of "Significance". *Places: Forum of Design for the Public Realm, 16*(1), 64–71.
Mason, R., Tumer, E. A., & Kilinç Ünlü, A. (2012). *The Walled City of Famagusta: A Framework for Urban Conservation and Regeneration.* World Monument Fund. http://www.wmf.org/digdeeper?type_1[wmf_publication]=wmf_publication&field_dig_deeper_related_proj_nid=HISTORIC+WALLED+CITY+OF+FAMAGUSTA&field_country_value_many_to_one=All. Accessed 6 Mar 2017.
Scott, J. (2002). World Heritage as a Model for Citizenship: The Case of Cyprus. *International Journal of Heritage Studies, 8*(2), 99–115.
UNESCO. *Cultural Diversity.* http://portal.unesco.org/culture/en/ev.php-URL_ID=34321&URL_DO=DO_TOPIC&URL_SECTION=201.html. Accessed 6 Mar 2017.

Von Truetzschler, W. (2005). *The Evolution of "Cultural Heritage" in International Law'*, *15th ICOMOS General Assembly and International Symposium: 'Monuments and Sites in Their Setting—Conserving Cultural Heritage in Changing Townscapes and Landscapes'*. ICOMOS workshop, Xi'an, China.

Wells, J. (2010). Historical Significance Through the Lens of Contemporary Social, Cultural, and Experiential Values. *Heritage Studies and Cultural Landscapes*. http://heritagestudies.org/files/Wells%20-%20Contemporary%20Values%20in%20HP.pdf. Accessed 6 Mar 2017.

CHAPTER 9

The War Over Nagorno-Karabakh and Its Lasting Effects on Cultural Heritage

Marja van Heese

INTRODUCTION

The war over Nagorno-Karabakh (NK) broke out in 1988 when it was part of Azerbaijan Soviet Socialist Republic (SSR) in the South Caucasus. Its beginning can be traced to October 1987 and protest rallies against a nuclear power plant outside Erevan, which turned into a rally on the Karabakh issue and led to hopes for a resolution and NK's unification with the Armenia SSR. Following the dissolution of the Soviet Union in December 1991, the conflict turned into a full-scale internationalized internal armed conflict by 1992 and spread to adjacent districts in the Republic of Azerbaijan, where Karabakh Armenian forces conducted large-scale operations (De Waal 2003, 2010).

In May 1994, a ceasefire agreement was signed by the Defence Ministers of Armenia and Azerbaijan as well as by the head of the Karabakh Armenian armed forces. This agreement is still in force (Potier 2001; Broers 2005). Since 1994 peace talks have been mediated by the OSCE Minsk Group, which includes representatives of the

M. van Heese (✉)
Vrije Universiteit Amsterdam, Amsterdam, The Netherlands

© The Author(s) 2018
J. Rodenberg and P. Wagenaar (eds.), *Cultural Contestation*,
Palgrave Studies in Cultural Heritage and Conflict,
https://doi.org/10.1007/978-3-319-91914-0_9

177

governments of Armenia and Azerbaijan, the co-chairs of France, the Russian Federation and the USA, as well as members of six other countries. Despite the efforts of many parties, a solution of the conflict over Nagorno-Karabakh is not foreseen in the near future. Since 2013 more (civil) unrest and a rising number of incidents have been observed, with reports of killed or injured persons along the Line of Contact and the Armenia–Azerbaijan border. In April 2016, there was a violent flare-up involving the use of heavy artillery and anti-tank weapons. Since then there has been an increase in the use of arms from both the Armenian and Azerbaijan sides (De Waal 2017; International Crisis Group 2017).

The conflict has caused many deaths and wounded many people and has led to large numbers of refugees and internally displaced persons. In addition, the conflict over the territory of NK and seven adjacent districts has left devastated towns, ruined landscapes and destroyed cultural properties.

In Shusha for example, with a high number of museums and a large number of architectural buildings, heavy fighting took place involving the use of tanks and artillery. In 1992, boxes of Grad rockets were placed by Azerbaijanis in the interior of the nineteenth-century Ghazanchetsots cathedral in Shusha, one of the largest Armenian churches in the world, in order to defend the city (De Waal 2003: 179). Nor did the Armenians respect cultural properties, as they dismantled and sold bronze busts of musicians and poets from Shusha that were important to the Azerbaijani people.

The region was once rich in ages-old architecture, including historical and architectural monuments like mosques, cathedrals, fortresses and monasteries, as well as archaeological monuments. Most museums were founded in the 1960s and in the 1980s (as in Shusha, Lachin and Agdam). They were mainly dedicated to History and to the inhabitants who were influential in literature and music. The area was renowned for its textiles and carpet-weaving, traditional bread making and horse-breeding. Among the most well-known museums were the Shusha Branch of Azerbaijan State Museum of Carpets, Arts and Crafts in Shusha and the Bread Museum in Agdam. Many memorials commemorate different events in the past, especially regarding the two World Wars. Also monuments known as khachkars and mural paintings are part of the cultural legacy. In the districts and villages, many cultural establishments such as libraries, houses of culture and social clubs were set up during the Soviet period.

The Caucasus region has a long and ancient history, and many events and wars over its territories have determined the course of its past and its peoples. The area is a crossroads between different cultures, hence there is a large diversity of languages, ethnicity and religions. The strategic position of the area and its natural resources made it attractive not only for rulers in the past, but also in the present geopolitical arena (Cornell 2001a, b; De Haas 2006).

Different opinions circulate as to the causes of the present conflict. Many researchers have found a relationship between the beginning of the conflict and the involvement of the Russian Empire in the region in the nineteenth century. As a result of the Russo-Persian wars and the concluded peace treaties of Gulistan (1813) and Turkmanchai (1828), Persia handed over to Russia most of the territories of the present-day Republics of Azerbaijan and Armenia, including Karabakh. In this way Russia could control the South Caucasus and deprived Iran and Turkey of its influence over the region (Altstadt 1992).This marked the start of migration flows and a shift in the population. The Russian occupation lasted until the dissolution of the Soviet Union, with a short period of independence for Armenia and Azerbaijan in the period 1918–1920, which was marked by ethnic strife and conflicting attempts to control NK (Kaufman 2001: 50).

The Soviet rule left deep marks on the cultural situation. Its centralized and state-financed cultural policy enabled it to control cultural development and cultural activities and use them for propaganda and ideological purposes, although there was some tolerance for national identity in the fields of culture and language. The national identity was kept alive by, *inter alia*, the policy of ethnicity-registration in passports (Joffé 1996 [2003]). The cultural system initiated in the 1940s remained virtually the same until the 1980s, when changes became possible with the introduction of perestroika and glasnost.

Following the collapse of the Soviet Union the newly established republics were confronted with weak state structures, an unstable political situation due to political disagreements, and a bad economic situation. The result was a feeling of insecurity for many inhabitants. In the search for a new definition of national identities and more security, aspects such as religion, ethnicity, language, national history, family and social organization, as well as regional affiliation, became focal points (Cornell 2001a, b; Hille 2010).

The aim of this chapter is to examine how such a large-scale destruction of cultural property has taken place despite the existence of an international legal framework for the protection of cultural heritage, in which respect for mutual cultural heritage is the main goal. The theories of Stuart Kaufman, Marc Howard Ross and Svante Cornell are viewed against the background of the conflict and the afflicted cultural property. In addition, the status of the afflicted properties in the occupied territories is taken into account, as well as the responsibilities and obligations towards the protection of cultural heritage by the actors in the conflict.

The spelling of geographical names and names of cultural monuments depends on the Armenian or Azerbaijan context. The choice of names can be interpreted as a political statement, therefore pre-1988 spellings and names common in western writing on the subject are used for all geographical features in the areas of conflict.

THEORETICAL BACKGROUND

There are a number of studies which have explored the roots of the many conflicts in the former Soviet Union. The above-mentioned Cornell, Kaufman and Ross have studied past events and their role in the narratives, myths and symbols in relation to the present conflicts. Narratives can be selectively used to justify behaviour and according to Ross are kept alive in the collective memories by cultural performances and rituals.

Cornell (2002) investigated whether territorial control or autonomy was a contributing factor to the violent ethnic conflicts in the South Caucasus since the 1980s, and how these conflicts could explode. An underlying theory in his work is that of Gurr and Harff, who posited that the chances for ethnic conflict increase when there are perceived group disadvantages, a strong group cohesion within an ethnic group, and when they are represented by leaders with a political agenda. Cornell took into account several factors in a conflict situation that could be triggered by either internal or external catalysers. In his study Cornell selected 10 indicators as causes for violent conflict with respect to nine ethnic groups over several territories in the South Caucasus: cultural differences; national conceptions; past conflicts and myths; rough terrain; relative demography; existence of ethnic kin; economic viability; radical leadership; external support; and autonomous status. Although his study is a quasi-quantitative approach in which only the observable causal effects are discussed, it showed that in almost all cases the relationship between autonomy and conflict was supported, and that the catalysing factors (external support and autonomous status) seem to have a significant relationship with the background factors. Only in the conflict over NK did it turn out that all 10 factors were relevant.

Stuart Kaufman (2001) argues that more attention should be paid to the myths and symbols that underlie ethnic conflicts. He believes that the idea of ethnic symbolism is useful in understanding conflicts because it combines the logic of hatreds, manipulative elites and economic rivalries. Ethnic symbolism is about the stories, expressed in myths and symbols, that ethnic groups tell about who they are. Myths and symbols can be emotion-laden and used by the leaders in a conflict. Ethnic wars occur when the politics of ethnic symbolism become extreme, i.e. when they provoke hostile actions which lead to a security dilemma. In his study of the conflict over Karabakh he concludes that the conflict is a clear example of the symbolic politics of mass-led violence, and that the violence started despite the determined opposition of the leaders at the time of Armenia, Azerbaijan and the Soviet Union, who failed to manage the conflict.

Marc Howard Ross (2007) also uses features such as past events, narratives, fears and threats to identity and explain ethnic conflicts. According to Ross, culture is expressed in a wide variety of symbolic forms, such as clothing or games, in physical forms such as monuments and sacred sites, or in human constructions such as holy places or battle memorials. Ross distinguishes nine features of psycho-cultural narratives. He believes that cultural expressions like rituals and performances (festivals, pilgrimages) are important to people as expressions of identity and history. A psycho-cultural drama occurs when there are conflicts between groups over competing claims which are perceived as threats. According to Ross, objects and symbols can take on a strong emotional meaning and become focal points of intergroup conflict, acting either as exacerbators or inhibiters. In his view, group narratives acted out in daily life and in a city's sacred rituals are very relevant, not only in terms of explaining the start of conflicts, but also in terms of finding solutions or mediating a conflict. Cultural performances, narratives and symbols form a symbolic landscape that constructs identities. In Ross's view, governments play a small role in cultural contestations.

THE CONFLICT OVER NAGORNO-KARABAKH

Disputed TerritoryAfter a short period of de facto independence after the Russian Revolution in 1917, it was decided during the Paris Peace Conference that Karabakh was going to be part of Azerbaijan, despite the protests by the Armenian National Council of Karabakh and the attempts to negotiate a grant of 'territorial autonomy for all Karabakh and national-cultural autonomy for its Armenian population' (Altstadt 1992: 101; MacMillan 2002; Hille 2010). When Armenia and Azerbaijan were incorporated into the Russian Federation in May 1921, it was first decided that Karabakh would be united with Armenia, but later it was concluded that Karabakh would be part of Azerbaijan (Kaufman 2001: 49–83; MacMillan 2002: 388, 453). Karabakh officially became a constituent part of the Azerbaijan SSR on 24 November 1924 with the status of an Autonomous Oblast (NKAO). This situation did not change until the late 1980s, when there was a reappearance of the conflict in 1987–1988 with large demonstrations by Armenians in Armenia and Mountainous Karabakh, followed by petitions to the central authorities for the transfer of the territory to Armenia, which petitions were rejected. This was followed by an outburst of ethnic violence and ethnic cleansing in both republics, which led to the fleeing of Azeris from Karabakh and Armenia and of Armenians from Azerbaijan. In December 1989, the Armenian SSR unilaterally annexed the NKAO to Armenia, followed by abolishment of NKAO's autonomy by the Azerbaijani SSR in early 1990. This escalated into an armed conflict between paramilitary groups, which led to the gradual loss of control over the NKAO by Azerbaijan. After the collapse of the USSR, a full-scale war broke out in 1992 (Map 9.1).

The Azeris speak a Turkic language. They are Muslims with a Shi'a denomination. The Azeri Turks are the largest ethnic group in the Caucasus (close to 7 million) (Cornell 2002).The Azerbaijanis have a long literary tradition dating back to the sixteenth century, but their main identity was either sub-national (khanates, regions or clans) or supranational (Islam) (Cornell 2001a, b; Hille 2010).The Armenian population is around 3 million in the Caucasus. Many Armenians live outside Armenia, mainly in Russia and the USA (ca. 5 million). Their language is Indo-European and they are Monophysite Christians (Cornell 2001a, b).

Map 9.1 Geopolitical situation of the Caucasus region. *Source* https://urldefense.proofpoint.com/v2/url?u=https-3A__commons.wikimedia.org_wiki_File-3ACaucasus-2Dpolitical-5Fen.svg&d=DwIF-g&c=vh6F-gFnduejNhPPD0fl_yRaSfZy8CWbWnIf4XJhSqx8&r=bR7wfrESkspgp-8kVF9EgjR4o9UKvlY8-ALMeDfoCDQD5PxdvD2PjgdeshQSzPwRw&m=9btdqF6Ieq3dfihPGKnk8YyNNsWAUbLZZqG1l6Xl-90&s=CG140v37vodZe-bQsWdvBg96ecRHj7WxmyoK74lI91LQ&e=

Afflicted Cultural Property

In the build-up to and during the conflict, heavy artillery and comparable conventional weapons were used, as well as air strikes, Grad and other missiles by all actors in the conflict. Destruction, looting and pillaging of properties, including cultural heritage, took place in all districts.

It is not easy to visit NK and the occupied territories and hence it is difficult to make a precise assessment of the afflicted cultural heritage. The information provided by the national authorities and diverse reports, literature and statements gives some information on the present status and condition of the afflicted cultural heritage. Also, the Fact-finding mission reports of the Human Rights Watch/Helsinki (1992; 1994), the International Committee of the Red Cross (ICRC) and the Organization for Security and Co-operation in Europe (2005; 2010) (OSCE) have contributed to understanding the status of built monuments in the area. However, international cultural organizations have not been able to execute Fact-finding missions to the occupied territories.

All the reports on the human rights situation mention indiscriminate attacks on civilians as well as wide-scale looting and destruction of civilian property, buildings and monuments. Houses have been reconstructed on the ruins or new ones built. Some areas, like Agdam, are now deserted and difficult to enter, among other reasons due to landmines. The Field Assessment Mission 2010 with experts from UNHC and the UN Refugee Agency showed the same outcome (OSCE 2010). It was recommended that measures be taken to preserve cemeteries and places of worship. Also, according to the International Crisis Group (ICG)[1] the once relatively prosperous regional towns of Agdam, Kelbajar, Jebrail and Fizuli had been methodically dismantled or destroyed. The building materials in these areas, such as bricks and street lamps, were pillaged, moved to other regions or sold.

According to the Azerbaijan authorities, the cultural heritage in NK, the seven adjacent districts, as well as in seven villages of the Gazakh district and the Karki village of Nakhichevan, consists of 1891 cultural resources, comprising 738 monuments, 28 museums with more than 83,500 exhibits, four picture galleries, 14 memorial complexes and 1107 cultural establishments (Azerbaijan Center for Strategic Studies 2007). Most of this cultural heritage, being historical/architectural monuments, archaeological monuments, museums, memorial complexes and monuments of arts and crafts as well as cultural establishments, are destroyed or their fate is unknown, according to the Azerbaijan Center for Strategic Studies (2007). For example the Azykh cave, in Martuni/Khojavend, registered as an archaeological monument of global significance, was used as an arsenal for Armenian forces and served as a target in the training base.

On the website of the Ministry of Culture and Tourism information is also given on the cultural heritage of Karabakh, and via a virtual tour an idea of the former situation in the area is presented.[2] The figures of monuments and museums mentioned on the website are comparable to those mentioned by the centre, but as different descriptions of categories are used and, for example, different numbers of exhibits, there is no overall clear picture of the amount of afflicted cultural properties and the damage thereto.[3]

The number of affected cultural properties is contested by Armenia. In a Motion for a Recommendation to the Parliamentary Assembly of the Council of Europe (PACE) (2001b), Armenia denies the figure of 500 historical and cultural monuments by Azerbaijan (PACE 2001a), because at an earlier registration in 1988 the number of monuments in NK was put at 282 (Schmidt 1990). According to the Armenian delegate, there was 'never a comprehensive and proper registration of monuments; the historical monuments and Christian heritage in Karabakh were deprived of state care and during Azerbaijan rule left in a neglected state. There are 10,000 Armenian historical and cultural monuments in NK, and only five Azeri historical monuments. Armenian Christian monuments are presented by the Azeri authorities as Caucasian Albanian' (PACE 2001b). Armenia also stated in the Motion that khachkars were used as construction stones and that several monuments were destroyed by the local Muslim population.

Both Armenia and Azerbaijan claim that (parts of) their cultural heritage have been destroyed not only in the occupied territories, but also outside their respective countries, and moreover that cultural remnants have been erased. This is, for example, the case with the Goy mosque in Erevan (Armenia), which was turned into the Museum of History during the Soviet period and after 1991 was restored and presented as the 'Blue Mosque', a Persian Mosque (Azerbaijan Center for Strategic Studies 2007: 265). Another case is the 'Aga-Dede' mosque and cemetery in the Masis region of Armenia, which was totally destroyed by Armenian forces.[4]

According to the Research on Armenian Architecture (RAA) Foundation, on the territory of Azerbaijan, including NK, Nakhichevan and Shahumyan, Armenian historical monuments (Karapetian 2011) have been dismantled or reused, both during the Soviet rule and as a result of the conflict situation. In particular, cross-stones and construction inscriptions from monuments have disappeared. Several reports mention the removal and destruction of fifteenth-century and six-teenth-century khachkars in the town of Julfa or Jugha (Armenia), in the south of the exclave Nakhichevan (Petzet and Ziesemer 2008; PACE 2006). According to the overview not only tombstones, but also churches and cloisters in the area were destroyed.

The information provided by the Tourist Department of the self-de-clared Republic of Nagorno-Karabakh shows that several museums in NK have been renovated and were reopened since the ceasefire, for example in Stepanakert/Khankendi, Shusha, Tigranakert and in Kashatagh. The website mentions that the Museum to the History of Shoushi City 'illustrates the centuries-old past of the ancient city-fortress with rich archaeological material from the Hellenistic period that has changed the former ideas about the time of Shoushi foundation in 18 c'.[5]

Not only has (im)movable cultural heritage suffered much damage from the war, but also intangible cultural heritage. The Chovqan, a tradi-tional Karabakh horse-riding game in Azerbaijan, was placed in 2013 on the List of Intangible Cultural Heritage in Need of Urgent Safeguarding. One of the reasons for placing it on this List is the shortage of Karabakh horses due to, *inter alia*, the closure of the Agdam horse-breeding farm in Karabakh in 1993, which had been an important centre of Chovgan transmission and breeding.[6] According to information by the Department of Tourism (via the Ministry of Culture in NK), in a village nearby Shusha horse-breeding activities have been taken up.[7]

The Myth-Symbol Complex in the Cultural Landscape

In the conflict over Nagorno-Karabakh, religion and language do not seem to be the decisive factors (Cornell 1998, 2001a, b; 2006). According to Cornell (2001a, b), the conflicts are above all political con-flicts over territory and over its ownership. The conflict is first and fore-most about the control over a certain territory based on ethnicity, and a security dilemma based on fear.

If we follow the arguments by Kaufman and Ross, the destruction, decay and dismantling of monuments, the wiping out of certain cultural remnants (such as foundation inscriptions in a building), and the quarrels about the number of monuments can be explained from the perspective of the myth-symbol complex. Both the history of the region and its pop-ulation are contested subjects. Central to the debates between Armenia and Azerbaijan are the claims over 'who was first' and 'who has the right to a certain territory'.

A narrative used by both sides focuses on the suffering of both the Azerbaijan and Armenian people and the harms done to them, for example in the massacres in Sumgait (1988), Baku (1918 and 1990) and Khojaly (1992). Both Armenia and Azerbaijan fear and blame each other for the massacres experienced by their people. These feelings of fear and insecurity are kept alive in the collective memories of each side, which results in the strengthening of group-forces against the other party. These events, as well as others, are commemorated on national holidays. In the eyes of Armenians, they were the victims of several wars due to their pioneering Christian faith, like in the Battle of Avarayr in 451 A.D.

In the Soviet period, Armenia regularly complained about the privileged position of Azerbaijan, a pan-Turk policy, and discrimination and oppression. It was also assumed that NK suffered regional economic deprivation compared to urban centres such as Baku or Erevan; core nationalities of the republics were considered superior to the minorities within the same borders (Kaburas 2011; Kaufman 1998; Joffé 1996). For the Armenians, ethnic domination and a minority status were associated with genocide, a fear reinforced by their experiences in 1915. In turn, the Azerbaijanis viewed the Armenians as 'more advanced, dominating the urban professions, civil service, and skilled labour positions', which placed the Azerbaijanis in a backward position (Kaufman 2001).

There is also the fear of losing territory. In Kaufman's opinion the conflict over NK took place not only because of the Armenian myth-symbol complex focused on fears of genocide, but also because of fears of the loss of sovereignty and territorial integrity on the part of the Azerbaijan Republic.

There are several stories wherein Armenians claim their legitimacy as owners of the region based on their long time habitation in Karabakh. One of them is that the Armenians are descendants of the great grandson of the Biblical Noah and that they have been living on the territory since the 4th millennium B.C. (Walker 1996: 89–112, see also Adalian 2002). The Armenians claim that they were a single defined ethnic group with a written language and history and a distinctive religion already by the fifth century A.D. (Kaufman 2001: 49–83). The removal of historic Armenian monuments in Karabakh is thus seen as wiping out their claims to the territory. 'Artsakh' was the Armenian symbol for the political, cultural, spiritual and economic revival of their nation, as is expressed in the writings of the Armenian novelist Sero Khanzadyan (1915–1998).

Armenia believes that the root of its insecurity in the region lies in the persistent attempts of the Azerbaijan (and Georgian) governments to keep their territories together, and so to prevent the just cause of people's right to self-determination (Cornell 2001a, b).

Although the Azerbaijan national identity is recent, modern Azerbaijanian nationalism began in reaction to the 'Tatar-Armenian War' of 1905–1906 and the name Azerbaijan was not widely used until the 1930s, the Azerbaijanis also claim ancient roots in the territory (Wright 1996: 113–133), going back even before the Armenian migration into the region. They claim to have been present in the Stone Age and during the ancient kingdom of Atropatene in the fourth-century B.C. The area did not become ethnically Turkic until after the eleventh-century invasion by the Seljuk Turks (Azerbaijanis argue that the Albanians were assimilated by the Turkic groups, so that modern Azerbaijanis are descendants of the Albanians). For the Azerbaijanis, the city of Shusha, founded in the eighteenth century by Panah Ali khan, was the centre of the Karabakh khanate (De Waal 2010: 103).[8]

According to Kaufman, the question of control over NK became a symbol of national aspirations as well as of hostility towards the other side, which resulted in a security dilemma and violence, as well as in the nationalist extremism that eventually led to war (Kaufman 2001).

Kaufman calls the Karabakh conflict a clear example of symbolic politics and mass-led violence, wherein the hostility and violence started from below, i.e. was not provoked by top-down manipulation (Kaufman 2001). At the start of the conflict in 1988 Armenian, Azerbaijanian and Soviet leaders stood aside, and the police did nothing to protect the civilians. The spiritual leaders of Armenia and Azerbaijan were never at the forefront of the respective movements and seemed to distance themselves from the violence (Cornell 2001b).

But in the early 1990s, one could observe the rise to power of nationalist politicians in both Azerbaijan and Armenia (the Armenian presidents Ter-Petrosyan and Kocharyan came to power on the Karabakh issue). Heydar Aliyev, the third president of Azerbaijan (1993–2003) was a promotor of strong feelings of nationalism in the search for an Azerbaijanian identity, as is also expressed in Azerbaijan's current cultural policy.[9]

Narratives, thus, play an important role in the creation and destruction of the symbolic landscape, in our case, of mainly built cultural heritage. There are, however, strongly held beliefs that legal frameworks should be powerful enough to prevent or halt the destruction of cultural heritage. How does this work and what are the underlying principles? Does it work in practice?

RESPECT FOR CULTURAL PROPERTY WITHIN THE INTERNATIONAL LEGAL FRAMEWORK

The protection of cultural heritage, respect for cultural property and the responsibilities of the actors in a conflict can also be viewed from the legal perspective (see, e.g. Toman 1996; Chamberlain 2004; O'Keefe 2006; Forrest 2010; O'Keefe and Prott 2011; Hausler 2015; Gerstenblith 2016).

Respect is one of the fundamental obligations in international humanitarian law and in the standards established by the international cultural law framework. The obligation to provide respect is a core obligation in the specialized cultural law framework offered by the United Nations Educational, Scientific and Cultural Organization (UNESCO), as are the responsibilities of the national authorities regarding the protection and safeguarding of cultural property, both in peace time and during an armed conflict.

A few months after obtaining membership in the United Nations, Azerbaijan and Armenia joined UNESCO on 3 June 1992 and 9 June 1992, respectively. In 1993, both countries became High Contracting Parties to the 1954 UNESCO Convention and its (First) Protocol, to be followed in a later period by the 1972 and the 1970 UNESCO Conventions.

These UNESCO Conventions place on High Contracting Parties the obligation to respect the cultural property situated within its own territory as well as within the territory of another High Contracting Party by refraining from any abuse of cultural property and its immediate surroundings and by refraining from any act of hostility directed against such property. The obligations also include the prohibition of, and prevention of, and interdiction of theft, pillage, misappropriation and vandalism, as well as the obligation to refraining from taking reprisals against such property. These obligations may be waived only in instances where military necessity imperatively requires such a waiver.[10] An occupying power has an obligation to support the relevant authorities of the occupied country in the safeguarding of their cultural property and to take all the necessary measures for its preservation 'as far as possible'. These obligations also arise in conflicts not of an international character occurring within the territory of one of the parties.

The self-declared Republic of Nagorno-Karabakh, though, is not recognized by the international community. Therefore it is not allowed to enter into international agreements or conventions.

The conflict over NK started as an internal armed conflict between Azerbaijan and its citizens of Armenian origin in the enclave of NK and grew into an internationalized internal armed conflict: a civil war characterized by the intervention of armed forces of other states on behalf of rebels (Human Rights Watch 1992, 1994).

The 1949 Geneva Conventions provide the international standards for humanitarian treatment in war time of prisoners, of the wounded and sick, and for the protection of civilians in and around a war-zone; they also define the rights and protection of non-combatants and their properties.[11] The 1949 Geneva Conventions have attained a nearly universal ratification, unlike the 1977 Additional Protocols. However, many relevant provisions of the Additional Protocols I and II reflect customary international humanitarian law and thus can be applied to all parties to a conflict (O'Keefe 2006). The warring parties are bound by the customary law rules applicable to internal armed conflicts (Human Rights Watch 1992, 1994).

When property is destroyed and such destruction is not justified by military necessity and/or carried out unlawfully and wantonly, the Geneva Conventions are gravely violated.[12] Civilian objects, like churches, are protected by the Geneva Conventions unless they are a military objective. Pillage (including booty or spoils of war),[13] whether in an organized fashion or not, is also prohibited. Communal or state property is protected unless its destruction is absolutely necessary for military reasons (Human Rights Watch 1994: 154).

Also, the rules regarding the protection of objects which are of great importance to the cultural heritage of humankind, as developed by the ICRC, can be seen as customary international law. It is not permitted to expose cultural heritage to destruction or damage, unless such is imperatively required by military necessity.[14] These rules are applicable in international armed conflicts as well as in conflicts with non-state armed actors.

On the basis of customary international law parties in a conflict have to respect as far as possible buildings dedicated to religion, art, science and historic monuments,[15] and it is forbidden to act against cultural goods and places or locations of religious worship.[16] But when the flame of cultural contestation spurts through the roof and ends up in hostilities aimed at wiping out or denying the other's existence on a territory, one can speak of another motive—that of de-identification through the intentional destruction of the symbolical landscape. Legal frameworks provide standards, values and obligations, but they cannot prevent grave hostilities against cultural properties. Historical narratives of pain and fear of the other group can only weaken the legal frameworks that are based on respect.

CONCLUSION

In the conflict over NK heavy artillery has been used with devastating results, and the conflict has included severe forms of cultural contestation. The reports on the Fact-finding missions do not give much hope for the remaining cultural heritage in the area. The destruction of the warring parties has been carried out against both civilian objects and cultural property, and the looting of objects took place even after the ceasefire agreement was concluded. This all has led to a severely affected physical and symbolical cultural landscape, and the overviews of the (afflicted) cultural heritage in the occupied territories referred to above are not even complete.

The war over Nagorno-Karabakh and the adjacent territories has had a lasting effect on the former and present inhabitants of the region. The cultural landscape has changed drastically as a result of the destructive attacks on cultural properties by the warring parties, not only regarding the (im)movable cultural heritage, but also regarding the intangible cultural heritage. The destruction of religious places of worship such as churches, mosques and cemeteries has had a major impact on the people, who are deprived of their social and religious rituals, for example those allowing them to honour their loved ones. Respect for these places and an understanding of their importance for the other party are aspects which should be taken into account, but more often are not.

Selective interpretations of history, myths, symbols and the handling of cultural heritage among the Armenian and Azerbaijan populations are being used by all parties in the conflict in order to prove their existence and their rights over the territory. Feelings of fear and mistrust hinder the dialogue and the search for a solution, which makes the conflict the longest running one in the former Soviet Union and a barrier to economic, social and cultural development in the whole region.

Both countries blame the other for starting the war, and both have developed ethnic prejudices based on long-standing stereotypes. It was once an area with a large ethnic and religious diversity (until the early nineteenth century), a history which stands in sharp contrast to now almost mono-ethnic populations in Armenia, Azerbaijan and NK.

The International Crisis Group (2016) has appealed for 're-energising the Minsk process through sustained, high-level political leadership by its key external actors'. Stuart Kaufman and Ross have argued that diplomacy and economic incentives are not enough to prevent or end ethnic wars, but that they can be helpful in changing hostile attitudes at both the elite and the grass-roots levels. This can be done by encouraging the examination of, and providing keener insights into, hostile myths, fears of extinction, ethnic hostility and emotive symbols. A better understanding of the myth-symbol complexes can also change the security dilemmas. And herein lays a vital role for and a challenge to governments.

Yet, in cases where the contestation is so deeply anchored in societies and where states do not respect the legal framework, the call to respect each other's cultural heritage might seem to be an empty notion when the international level is not present or ignored, thus making it seem unavoidable that intentional destruction of cultural heritage will take place on a large scale.

Notes

1. Policy Briefing no. 67, 27 February 2012.
2. http://www.virtualkarabakh.az/read.php?lang=2&menu=54&id=150#. WX8aJ1FqPDc (accessed 27 December 2017).
3. In 2008 Azerbaijan mentioned, in its National Report for UNESCO on the Implementation of the Hague Convention and its Protocols, the destruction since 1988 in NK of ca. 22 museums with more than 100,000 exhibits, and 600 religious monuments. In the OHCHR Report: 'Information by Azerbaijan to the study of intentional destruction of cultural heritage' (responses to the question by Ms. Karima Bennoune, Special rapporteur in the field of cultural rights), information is also given on the destroyed cultural heritage and the afflicted monuments of world and national importance, http://www.ohchr. org/Documents/Issues/CulturalRights/DestructionHeritage/States/ Azerbaijan.pdf (accessed 27 December 2017).

4. Mentioned in Joint Motion for a resolution by the European Parliament of the EU on 15-2-2006 (B6-0111/06).
5. http://karabakh.travel/en/museums/47/ (accessed 27 December 2017).
6. The List is part of the 2003 UNESCO Convention for the Safeguarding of the Intangible Cultural Heritage. Chovgan Nomination file No. 00905, inscription: 8.COM 7.a.1. Other threats to this game are a decrease in the number of trainers and practitioners and the urbanisation processes within Azerbaijan. According to information by the Department of Tourism, to be reached via the Ministry of Culture in NK, horse-breeding have been taken up in a village nearby Shusha, http://karabakh.travel/en/karabakh-horses/21/ (accessed 31 July 2017).
7. http://karabakh.travel/en/karabakh-horses/21/ (accessed 27 December 2017).
8. In 1977, Shusha was declared a historical and architectural reserve of the Azerbaijan SSR, and in 2001 Shusha was placed on the Tentative List of the 1972 Convention concerning the protection of the world cultural and natural heritage, as a cultural property by the Azerbaijan National Commission for UNESCO. File No. 1574, http://whc.unesco.org/en/tentativelists/1574/ (accessed 27 December 2017).
9. See for example the country reports by the Council of Europe and the Cultural Compendium, http://www.culturalpolicies.net/web/azerbaijan.php?aid=1 (accessed 27 December 2017) UNESCO Country Programming Document for the Republic of Azerbaijan 2014–2017 (October 2013); Azerbaijan Country Report by Damien Helly, 2014, in the series Culture in EU External Relations.
10. Article 4, Convention for the Protection of Cultural Property in the Event of Armed Conflict with Regulations for the Execution of the Convention and its (First) Protocol, The Hague 14 May 1954.
11. Article 53, Geneva Convention IV, Article 27, Hague Regulations, ICTY Case No. IT-95-14/2-T.
12. Article 147, Geneva Convention IV.
13. Article 53, Geneva Convention IV.
14. Rule 38(a) reflects the content of Article 27 of the Hague Regulations in the sense that special care must be taken in military operations to avoid damage to buildings dedicated to religion, art, science, education or charitable purposes and historic monuments, unless they are military objectives; and that property of great importance must not be the object of attack unless imperatively required by military necessity (Rules 38(b) and 39). Belligerents are not allowed to seize, destroy or wilfully damage cultural institutions and monuments, as well as works of art and science (Rule 40(a)); theft, pillage or misappropriation of, and any acts of

vandalism directed against property of great importance to the cultural heritage of every people is prohibited (Rule 40(b)).
15. Article 27, Hague Regulations.
16. Article 53, of Additional Protocol I.

REFERENCES

Adalian, R. P. (2002). *Historical Dictionary of Armenia, Asian/Oceanian Historical Dictionaries, No. 41.* Lanham: The Scarecrow Press.
Altstadt, A. L. (1992). *The Azerbaijani Turks: Power and Identity Under Russian Rule.* Stanford: Hoover Institution Press.
Azerbaijan Center for Strategic Studies. (2007). *War Against Azerbaijan: Targeting Cultural Heritage.* Baky: Ministry of Foreign Affairs, Republic of Azerbaijan; Heydar Aliyev Foundation.
Broers, L. (2005). The Limits of Leadership: Elites and Societies in the Nagorny Karabakh Peace Process. In *Accord Conciliation Resources,* 17. London: Conciliation Resources.
Chamberlain, K. (2004). *War and Cultural Heritage: A Commentary on the Hague Convention 1954 and its Protocols.* Builth Wells: Institute of Art and Law.
Cornell, S. E. (1998). Religion as a Factor in Caucasian Conflicts. *Civil Wars, 1*(3), 46–64.
Cornell, S. E. (2001a). Democratization Falters in Azerbaijan. *Journal of Democracy, 12*(2), 119–131.
Cornell, S. E. (2001b). *Small Nations and Great Powers: A Study of Ethnopolitical Conflict in the Caucasus.* London and New York: Routledge Curzon.
Cornell, S. E. (2002). *Autonomy and Conflict, Ethnoterritoriality and Separatism in the South Caucasus—Cases in Georgia.* Ph.D. thesis, University of Uppsala.
Cornell, S. E. (2006). *The Politicization of Islam in Azerbaijan.* Washington, DC: Silk Road Paper.
De Haas, M. (Ed.). (2006). *Geo-Strategy in the South Caucasus: Power Play and Energy Security of States and Organisations.* The Hague: Netherlands Institute of International Relations Clingendael.
De Waal, T. (2003). *Black Garden: Armenia and Azerbaijan Through Peace and War.* New York: New York University Press.
De Waal, T. (2010). *The Caucasus.* Oxford: Oxford University Press.
De Waal, T. (2017). *The Threat of a Karabakh Conflict in 2017.* Carnegie Europe. http://carnegieeurope.eu/strategiceurope/67774. Accessed 27 Dec 2017.
Destruction and Desecration of Azerbaijani Historical and Cultural Heritage Resulting from the Continuing Aggression of the Republic of Armenia

Against the Republic of Azerbaijan. http://mfa.gov.az/files/file/Destruction_of_Azerbaijani_cultural_heritage.pdf. Accessed 27 Dec 2017.

Forrest, C. (2010). *International Law and the Protection of Cultural Heritage*. London and New York: Routledge.

Gerstenblith, Patty. (2016). The Destruction of Cultural Heritage: A Crime Against Property or a Crime Against People? *The John Marshall Review of Intellectual Property Law, 15,* 336.

Hausler, K. (2015). Culture Under Attack: The Destruction of Cultural Heritage by Non-State Armed Groups. *Santander Art & Culture Law Review, 2*(1), 117–146.

Hille, C. (2010). *State Building and Conflict Resolution in the Caucasus.* Leiden: Brill.

Human Rights Watch. (1992). *Bloodshed in the Caucasus: Escalation of the Armed Conflict in Nagorno Karabakh.* New York: Human Rights Watch.

Human Rights Watch. (1994). *Seven Years of Conflict in Nagorno-Karabakh.* New York: Human Rights Watch.

International Crisis Group. (2016, April 5). *Statement: Responding to the Nagorno-Karabakh Escalation.*

International Crisis Group. (2017, June 1). *Nagorno-Karabakh's Gathering War Clouds* (Europe Rep. No. 244).

Joffé, G. (1996). Nationalities and Borders in Transcaucasia and the North Caucasus. In J. F. R. Wright (Ed.), *Transcaucasian Boundaries* (pp. 15–34). London and New York: Routledge.

Karapetian, S. (2011). *The State of Armenian Historical Monuments in Azerbaijan and Artsakh.* Yerevan: RAA Foundation.

Kaufman, S. J. (1998). *Ethnic Fears and Ethnic War in Karabagh.* Ph.D. thesis, University of Kentucky.

Kaufman, S. J. (2001). *Modern Hatreds: The Symbolic Politics of Ethnic War.* Ithaca: Cornell University Press.

Kuburas, M. (2011). Ethnic Conflict in Nagorno-Karabakh. *Review of European and Russian Affairs, 6*(1), 44–54.

MacMillan, M. (2002). *Peacemakers: The Paris Conference of 1919 and Its Attempt to End War.* London: John Murray.

O'Keefe, P. J., & Prott, L. V. (2011). *Cultural Heritage Conventions and Other Instruments: A Compendium with Commentaries.* Builth Wells: Institute of Art and Law.

O'Keefe, R. (2006). *The Protection of Cultural Property in Armed Conflict.* Cambridge: Cambridge University Press.

OSCE. (2010). *Executive Summary of the "Report of the OSCE Minsk Group Co-Chairs' Field Assessment Mission to the Occupied Territories of Azerbaijan Surrounding Nagorno-Karabakh".*

OSCE. (2005). *Report of the OSCE Fact-Finding Mission (FFM) to the Occupied Territories of Azerbaijan Surrounding Nagorno-Karabakh (NK)*.

Parliamentary Assembly of the Council of Europe (PACE). (2001a). *Document No. 9147 on the Seizure and Destruction of Azerbaijani Cultural Heritage*.

Parliamentary Assembly of the Council of Europe (PACE). (2001b). *Document No. 9256 on the Maintenance of Historical and Cultural Heritage in NK*.

Parliamentary Assembly of the Council of Europe (PACE). (2006). *Document No. 10780 on the Urgency of Preventing the Complete Destruction of the Armenian Mediaeval Cemetery of the Old Town of Julfa in the Autonomous Republic of Nakhichevan of Azerbaijan*.

Petzet, M., & Ziesemer, J. (Ed.). (2008). *ICOMOS World Report 2006–2007 on Monuments and Sites in Danger*.

Potier, T. (2001). *Conflict in Nagorno-Karabakh, Abkhazia and South Ossetia, a Legal Appraisal*. The Hague and Boston: Kluwer Law International.

Ross, M. H. (2007). *Cultural Contestation in Ethnic Conflict*. Cambridge: Cambridge University Press.

Schmidt, A. J. (Ed.). (1990). *The Impact of Perestroika on Soviet Law*. Leiden: Brill/Nijhoff.

Toman, J. (1996). *The Protection of Cultural Property in the Event of Armed Conflict*. Dartmouth: UNESCO Publishing.

Walker, C. J. (1996). The Armenian Presence in Mountainous Karabakh. In J. F. R. Wright (Ed.), *Transcaucasian Boundaries* (pp. 89–112). London and New York: Routledge.

Wright, John F.R. (ed.) (1996). *Transcaucasian Boundaries*. London and New York: Routledge.

CHAPTER 10

Dealing with a Difficult Past: Japan, South Korea and the UNESCO World Heritage List

Ioan Trifu

INTRODUCTION

On 26 July 2017, a South Korean period film opened in cinemas all over the country, quickly attracting more than 4 million spectators. Entitled *"The Battleship Island"* in English, the film depicts the story of a group of Korean people forced to work on a Japanese coal-mine island during World War II and their attempt to escape from their Japanese oppressors. Notwithstanding criticisms of historical inaccuracies, the film was nevertheless promoted as "a fact-based fiction" by its director, Ryoo

The author gratefully acknowledges the generous funding support for this publication provided by the Volkswagen Foundation, issued within its initiative "Key Issues for Research and Society" for the research project "Protecting the Weak: Entangled processes of framing, mobilization and institutionalization in East Asia" (AZ 87 382) at the Interdisciplinary Centre for East Asian Studies (IZO), Goethe University, Frankfurt am Main.

I. Trifu (✉)
Goethe University Frankfurt, Frankfurt am Main, Germany

© The Author(s) 2018
J. Rodenberg and P. Wagenaar (eds.), *Cultural Contestation*,
Palgrave Studies in Cultural Heritage and Conflict,
https://doi.org/10.1007/978-3-319-91914-0_10

Seung-wan (*Yonhap News Agency* 2017a).[1] The island in the film is Hashima Island, more commonly known as *Gunkanjima* or "Battleship Island" in Japanese, in reference to the particular shape of the island with its buildings. From the late-nineteenth century until the early 1970s, the 6.3-hectare island was the home of several thousand people employed by Mitsubishi Corporation to extract coal from the island's undersea mines. During the war, hundreds of conscripted Korean civilians as well as Chinese prisoners of war were also forced to work on the island under deplorable conditions (Siemons and Underwood 2015). Abandoned since 1974, *Gunkanjima* has become a more recognisable site among Western audiences in recent years, notably because of its appearance as the "villain's lair" in the 2012 James Bond film "*Skyfall*" (Schachter 2015).

Two days after the official South Korean release of "*The Battleship Island*", a special film screening was held in front of Korean diplomats and officials from the United Nations Educational, Scientific and Cultural Organization (UNESCO) headquarters in Paris. The intention was to raise awareness about "the dark history of the Japanese island" which, as part of the "Sites of Japan's Meiji Industrial Revolution", was inscribed on the UNESCO World Heritage list in 2015 (*Yonhap News Agency* 2017b). The Japanese nomination of these 23 old factories, shipyards and industrial facilities was seen by Japan to symbolise the nation's rapid industrialisation. However, it sparked an intense worldwide controversy over Japan's use of forced labour during the war.

This research investigates how the nomination of Japan's "*Meiji Industrial Revolution Heritage*" Sites as UNESCO World Heritage became the centre of an international heritage dispute. How should an international conflict regarding cultural heritage be interpreted? Focusing on the actions taken by the Japanese, I argue that this conflict can better be understood as an example of cultural contestation, highlighting a long-lasting lack of recognition on the part of the Japanese government of a core element of South Korea's national identity, a cultural contestation highly facilitated by the development of a new global heritage stage with the UNESCO World Heritage list.

This work is divided into three parts. Firstly, I will present a theoretical framework in order to understand the cultural and symbolic aspects of international heritage controversies in the age of World Heritage. Secondly, I will examine Japan's relation with UNESCO and the World Heritage programme, and how the celebratory narrative of Japan's

Meiji Industrial Revolution Heritage has been constructed. Finally, while recounting the 2015 controversy, I will explain how the exclusive nature of the Japanese narrative led to the confrontation with South Korea.

The Global Politics of Heritage Conflict

Understanding Heritage Contestation at International Level

Heritage contestation at the international level can take a variety of forms. The border dispute and violent clashes between Cambodia and Thailand following the nomination of the Preah Vihear Temple as a UNESCO World Heritage site in 2008 represents, for example, one extreme illustration on how a heritage site can be the trigger of an international military conflict (Silverman 2011). While some international heritage disputes can escalate into violence, many cases seem to be characterised, above all, by a display of colliding narratives, with rather limited tangible consequences.[2]

By focusing on the symbolic dimension of cultural contestation, the theoretical framework developed by Mark Howard Ross provides useful conceptual tools with which to analyse cultural heritage-related disputes. While the material aspects and competition of interests underlying identity conflicts are important (Ross 2007: 28, 2009: 2), Ross argues that "cultural contestation is about inclusion and exclusion from a society's symbolic landscape" (Ross 2009: 1). Narratives are central in these contestations as they act as "reflectors, exacerbators or inhibitors, and causes of conflict" (Ross 2009: 8). For social and ethnic groups, exclusion from a narrative of collective memory potentially fosters psychocultural dramas described by Ross as "conflicts between groups over competing, and apparently irresolvable, claims that engage the central elements of each group's historical experience and contemporary identity" (Ross 2007: 79). One major root of these psychocultural dramas can be found in the struggle for recognition by particular groups and its denial by others.[3] Axel Honneth, in his seminal work on this issue, states how central recognition is for the construction of modern individuals. He identifies three primary modes of recognition (emotional support, cognitive respect and social esteem) and, within these, respectively three forms of recognition: love, legal relations (rights), and community of values or solidarity (Honneth 1995: 129).

Ross' and Honneth's theoretical frameworks were, however, mainly conceived in order to explain conflicts and struggles occurring within one society. How can they be adapted to the specificities of international politics? As Honneth himself explains, the scaling-up process faces more than a few obstacles, including the strong "suggestive power" of the *realpolitik* approach, an inadequate vocabulary to describe the behaviour of nation-states and the difficulties to distinguish the various mode of recognition at the international level (Honneth 2012: 139, 144).

In recent years, and despite the theoretical difficulties expressed by Honneth, an increased number of International Relations scholars have shown interest in the roles played by identity and recognition on the international stage (Murray 2014: 558). Taking inspiration from sociological research, they examine how processes of identity-formation, identity-change and the "international politics of recognition" structure international relations (Ringmar 2010: 3–4). Alexander Wendt, a close reader of Honneth, has elaborated on the desires for recognition by state actors, differentiating between "thin" and "thick" recognition claims: "thin recognition is about being acknowledged as an independent subject within a community of law", whereas "thick recognition is about being respected for what makes a person special or unique" (Wendt 2012: 36–37). In the case of East Asia, Linus Hagström and Karl Gustafsson have built upon these theoretical contributions in their own investigations on how identity-change and recognition issues impact the conflictual relations between Japan and its neighbours. Adopting a relational approach, which "concentrates on how 'Japan' is constructed vis-à-vis particular 'Others'", they analyse domestic and international discussions in order to understand how "identity enables and constrains behaviour" of state actors (Hagström and Gustafsson 2015: 1, 2).

These various works show how narratives and discourses regarding identity and recognition matter in international relations. Combined with Ross' research on cultural contestation, they offer useful theoretical insights for the study of international contestation surrounding heritage sites in the age of UNESCO.

UNESCO and the New Global Stage of Heritage Competition

Over the past forty years, UNESCO and the organisation's heritage programmes (first among them the World Heritage Convention of 1972) have been the main driving force towards the emergence of a global governance of heritage (Labadi and Long 2010: 2; Meskell and Brumann 2015: 22). In late June or early July every year, the selection of World Heritage (WH) sites by UNESCO brings an opportunity for the celebration of national pride among the various countries of the successfully enlisted sites (Brumann 2014: 2176–2177). However, behind the colourful images and displays of self-congratulation lies a particularly controversial aspect of the globalisation of heritage in its UNESCO version: the fierce competition of political and economic interests increasingly taking place within this organisation. More and more states are engaged in a race for the inscription of their cultural items on the UNESCO heritage lists and registers. Ambitions are high among UNESCO state parties that wish to capitalise on this worldwide recognition in order to reinforce their international prestige, improve their public image and build up their soft power on the world stage (Labadi and Long 2010: 6; Nye 2004). At the domestic level, national heritage sites and items listed by UNESCO fortify a government-led approach to heritage and fuel—at varying rates—political and cultural forms of nationalism (Herzfeld 2008: 146). Selected as symbols of national culture, they are usually integral parts of the national narratives which sustain modern nations as "imagined political communities" (Anderson 2006: 6). Finally, economic interests also provide powerful incentives to these competitions for enlisting cultural heritage at UNESCO. With the globalisation of tourism and the growth of heritage tourism,[4] UNESCO labels are highly sought after for tourism development by national and local governments worldwide (Salazar and Zhu 2015: 246–248). The World Heritage "brand" among all has become a powerful "form of tourism-advertising strategy" in recent years (Labadi and Long 2010: 7). Despite UNESCO's constant efforts to defend the "universal" character of its heritage programmes, the fast-growing academic literature on UNESCO tends to agree that it is nation-state agendas that massively dominate the negotiations at UNESCO (Brumann 2014; Labadi and Long 2010; Meskell 2015a, b).

Like other United Nations bodies, UNESCO is an intergovernmental agency, organised around the voluntary participation of nations-states. UNESCO relies on its members states to finance its budget and, lacking coercive powers, for the enforcement of its decisions. With regard to World Heritage, the procedural rules established by the WH Convention of 1972 established an intergovernmental committee—the WH Committee—to vote on the proposals for World Heritage listing filed by the member states. The Committee itself is constituted of 21 state parties in office for four years.[5] This results in an overall institutional framework in which nation-states are the chief actors and where the decision-making process is based upon consensus among the states parties.

For years, consensus has been the norm at UNESCO and (openly) politicised issues or conflictual situations were avoided as much as possible. Despite the recent evolutions, this multilateralist mindset still largely structure behaviour and discourses of the majority of Member States. This is visible in the case of "negative heritage" on the WH List.[6] Negative heritage can be defined as "a conflictual site that becomes the repository of negative memory in the collective imaginary" (Meskell 2002: 558). Examples of negative heritage range from battlefields to prisons or ruins, from the killing fields of Cambodia to the World Trade Center (González-Ruibal and Hall 2015). This kind of heritage has been represented on the WH List as early as 1978 with the Island of Gorée, the historical slave-trading centre located on the coast of today's Senegal. Other WH sites with negative associations include places such as Auschwitz Birkenau (inscribed in 1979), the Hiroshima Peace Memorial (1996) and Robben Island, South Africa (1999). However, it should be noted that UNESCO and its member states display a certain reluctance towards negative heritage sites, with just a few enlisted on the WH List overall, and only under particular or even "exceptional uses" of the criteria for outstanding universal value. Rico suggests that "nations are being taught to present heritage in a manner in which conflict is erased or made to conform to an approved set of political issues" (Rico 2008: 349). The narrative and values projected by these WH sites have to be fully shared by the member states and must aim at universal consensus: denunciation of genocide (Auschwitz) and crimes against humanity (Gorée), the glorification of freedom and democracy (Robben Island), and hope for world peace (Hiroshima).

Historically, UNESCO has relied on scientific criteria in its approach to heritage. This is especially evident with regard to the key concept of outstanding universal value. The WH Convention states that the outstanding universal value of WH is "from the point of view of history, art or science" (UNESCO 1972, Art. 1). These criteria and values are manifested within the UNESCO institutional framework by the decisive role played by advisory bodies of experts, such as ICOMOS[7] on the final decision regarding the enlistment of sites as WH. ICOMOS specialists, for example, are in charge of evaluating WH nomination dossiers and produce scientific and well-documented reports on them prior to the session of the WH Committee. WH Committee votes generally tend to follow the ICOMOS recommendation to inscribe the property on the List, or not, confirming how essential scientific expertise and values are in determining suitable sites for the WH List (Bertacchini et al. 2016: 125). Yet, for scholars such as Lynn Meskell or Christoph Brumann, multilateralism at UNESCO has mostly failed, and the World Heritage Committee, in particular, is becoming "increasingly politicized and confrontational" in the past decade (Meskell 2015b: 226; Meskell and Brumann 2015).

Promoting Japanese Heritage on the Global Stage

Japan and the UNESCO World Heritage Programme

Japan was a relative latecomer in the UNESCO World Heritage programme, signing the 1972 Convention only in 1992. By comparison, Japan's neighbours China and South Korea became State Party, respectively, in 1985 and 1988 (UNESCO 2017). One of the main reasons usually put forward to explain this delay was the divergence between Japanese and Western heritage practitioners regarding the notion of authenticity (Akagawa 2016: 15). Since 1972 and the UNESCO WH Convention, authenticity is a central pillar under the global UNESCO heritage system. Initially defined by the Venice Charter of 1964, the notion relied on a "conserve as found" ethos, which was widely shared among Western-trained specialists, but proved inadequate to encompass fully the diversity of the world's cultural heritage (Smith 2006: 89–90). From the 1980s onwards, UNESCO faced heavy criticism for the overrepresentation of Western and monumental heritage on the WH List, prompting the organisation to search vigorously for solutions that could redress the issue. Around the same time, Japan started to reconsider its cultural diplomacy, gradually involving itself in the global heritage regime notably with the creation of the Japanese Funds-in-Trust for the Preservation of the World Cultural Heritage in 1989 (Akagawa 2014: 107–108). Japanese new willingness on the international stage combined with UNESCO heritage experts' efforts to broaden their view, eventually ease the way for Japan's participation in the WH programme. In 1994, the adoption of the Nara Document on Authenticity, inspired by Japanese heritage practices, opened new and richer understandings of this central concept behind the WH Convention (Akagawa 2016: 15; Neki and Satō 2016: 136).

Since then, the concept of cultural heritage itself has been massively expanded, leading to new institutional settings and complexification of application procedures at the international level. The same year that the Nara Document was adopted, the WH Committee initiated the Global Strategy for a Representative, Balanced and Credible World Heritage List. This Global Strategy intends "to broaden the definition of World Heritage" and correct the imbalance in the WH List with new categories such as industrial heritage, historical itineraries and cultural landscape. Japan was again instrumental in this transformation of the global heritage discourse, particularly by promoting the concept of intangible heritage. At the head of UNESCO from 1999 to 2009, Kōichirō Matsuura, a former Japanese diplomat, advocated for this new understanding of cultural heritage and for a Convention for the Safeguarding of Intangible Cultural Heritage, finally adopted in 2003. Meanwhile, Japan quickly came to be a major financial contributor to the international organisation and its heritage programme,[8] demonstrating how heritage-related diplomacy was perceived by Tokyo as a potential source of soft power for the country (Akagawa 2014: 1).

By challenging the Eurocentricity of the global heritage regime, Japan's increasing involvement in UNESCO heritage programmes helped to re-define aspects of what Laurajane Smith has termed the Western "authorized heritage discourse" (Smith 2006: 29–43, 54–55). In many other instances, however, the Japanese government sustained, and even reinforced, this authorised discourse (Mizuno 2017). Japan's politics regarding WH relied on the substantial financial support to UNESCO and the strict adherence to the formal and informal rules of the international organisation, particularly the professional expertise of ICOMOS. Like other state parties, the Japanese government aimed to use the WH List as a venue to gain recognition and to celebrate the greatest achievements of Japanese culture: the country's first nominees were national symbols, such as the traditional Buddhist temples of Nara (1993), the medieval castle of Himeji (1993) and the historic monuments of Kyoto (1994). In the following years, some efforts were made to include other forms of cultural heritage, such as minority heritage with the nomination of historic remains from the former Kingdom of Ryūkyū (today Okinawa prefecture), which became WH in 2000.[9] Conflicts and tensions were not entirely absent. The enlistment of Hiroshima Peace Memorial was initially objected to by the USA and China, before negotiations let the site joining the list in 1996 (Utaka 2009: 39–40).

Overall, however, it was the attitude of the Japanese government with regard to the UNESCO World Heritage programme which positioned Japan as a model nation while the WH "brand" gained in popularity in the country. In the early 2000s, the WH programme inspired new ambitions for heritage all over Japan. Attracted by the prospect of tourism development and economic growth, many Japanese localities rushed to devise plans to have their own heritage recognised as World Heritage (Yanagisawa 2015: 156–157). It was in this context of a "World Heritage boom" that the idea to promote Japanese industrial heritage worldwide emerged.

Recognition for Japan's Early Industrialisation: The Sites of Meiji Industrial Revolution Heritage

In the beginning of 1999, urban economist and essayist Kōko Katō published a book in Japanese entitled "*The Industrial Heritage: A Historical Voyage through the Life of Everyday Man*" (Katō 1999). The book attracted the attention of Kimiyasu Shimadzu, president of the industrial corporation Shimadzu Limited, who invited Katō to visit him and discuss her ideas. Heir of the Shimadzu clan, a prestigious family which ruled over the southern part of the Japanese island of Kyūshū during feudal times and still personally owns many old industrial facilities in Kyūshū, Shimadzu was extremely interested in Japan's early industrial history and in Katō's depiction of its industrial heritage. Both of them quickly saw the opportunity of working together in order to promote the heritage of Japan's modernisation, focusing particularly on the beginning of the country's industrialisation in Satsuma (the present-day Kagoshima prefecture), the former domain of the Shimadzu clan and key player in the Meiji Restoration of 1868. At the end of 2003, after meeting with several international specialists, the idea emerged that a serial nomination of industrial sites to the World Heritage List was a serious possibility.

In 2005, benefiting from their political connections and influence, Katō and Shimadzu convinced the newly elected Kagoshima prefecture governor Yūichirō Itō to support their idea (Japan's Meiji Industrial Revolution 2015). The project joined with other local initiatives related to industrial heritage, from those of civic groups working to preserve the industrial history of Kitakyūshū to the association for making *Gunkanjima* a World Heritage site, led by a former resident of the island. It also received the support of two major and historic Japanese industrial corporations, Mitsubushi and Mitsui, owners of several industrial sites in Kyūshū. In just a few years, the plan brought together a large variety of stakeholders and supporters, ranging from private citizens, academics and members of international heritage organisations to local and national officials.[10]

In September 2006, Japan's Agency for Cultural Affairs, the governmental entity in charge of cultural heritage, officially opened the selection process for Japanese nominees to the World Heritage List to local projects. Around the same time, several sites located in Hagi city (Yamaguchi prefecture) were added to the Kyūshū project (Japan's Meiji Industrial Revolution 2015). The inclusion of the heritage of Hagi reinforced the early chronology of the nomination file, even though the city is more well-known for its feudal heritage than for its industrial past. It also provided new political support for the project, as major politicians such as Shinzō Abe hailed from the prefecture (Mizuno 2017). By the end of November, the nomination file, now entitled "*Modern Industrial Heritage Sites in Kyūshū and Yamaguchi*", was submitted to the Agency. After an initial setback, it was finally approved by the Agency one year later, in September 2008, leading to the establishment of a consortium to coordinate the project (Japan's Meiji Industrial Revolution 2015).

The Kyūshū-Yamaguchi project was not the only attempt to preserve and promote Japan's industrial heritage, particularly for local development (Kimura 2009: 415). Since the early 1990s, several initiatives have been taken to preserve this form of heritage, both at the local and national levels (Loo 2017). The Tomioka Silk Mill and Related Sites, a Meiji-era industrial complex, were notably inscribed on the World Heritage List in 2014 (UNESCO 2014). The "Meiji Industrial Revolution Heritage" was, however, by far the most ambitious project with eventually 23 sites spread over eight Japanese prefectures and 11 municipalities,[11] mixing a variety of historical remains and facilities linked to the country's industrial history. All of these sites were selected to reflect the three phases of Japan's rapid industrialisation, following a strict chronology starting from the 1850s and ending rather abruptly in 1910, despite *Gunkanjima*, one of the most symbolical sites, acquiring its characteristic architectural features only years later (Underwood 2015a). The narrative was celebrating "the first successful transfer of industrialization from the West to a non-Western nation" (UNESCO 2015a), aiming to obtain worldwide recognition for the heritage of Japan's early modernisation, in order particularly to revitalise both economically and symbolically local communities in steady decline in the post-industrial era.

Despite being advised by a committee of domestic and international experts, the project faced several serious difficulties. For the Agency for Cultural Affairs, the main issue was the preservation of sites and cultural items which were still being used, such as the giant cantilever crane of Nagasaki dockyard, imported from Scotland in 1909, which is still regularly used by its owner Mitsubishi, something which went against the Agency's regular conservation practices. For Japan's Ministry of Foreign Affairs (MOFA), the stories regarding the use of forced labour at several of these sites, notably during World War II, were a concern, even if the choice of 1910, the year of the annexation of Korea by Japan, to conclude the project ought to deflect any controversy.[12]

FORGOTTEN SIDE OF HERITAGE: JAPAN AND THE CONFLICT WITH SOUTH KOREA

Unfolding a Predictable Drama

The MOFA was aware of the risk of conflict with South Korea in the broader context of the political tensions plaguing East Asia since at least the early 1990s. In the past three decades, the region has been the scene of repeated psychocultural dramas involving Japan and its neighbours regarding the history and memories of the colonial and war periods.[13] For South Korea, topics such as the territorial disputes, the return of cultural items, and compensation for "comfort women"[14] and forced labourers remain particularly controversial (Pai 2013: 171). They represent struggles for thick recognition of the nation and are central to its identity. In the case of the Meiji Industrial Heritage nomination file, it is reported that around 60,000 Koreans, along with thousands of Chinese labourers and Allied prisoners of war, were forced to work in seven of the 23 selected components[15] (Underwood 2015b). The failure on the part of the Japanese authorities to address the heart of the matter—the lack of recognition—explains, in large part, the unfolding of the psychocultural drama until the very last days of the 2015 UNESCO World Heritage meeting.

The first warning signs regarding the nominated sites appeared rather early. In August 2007, the South Korean government's Truth Commission on Forced Mobilisation under Japanese Imperialism disapproved Nagasaki city's plan to enlist Hashima Island as a World Heritage site, considering it to be an attempt to whitewash the Japanese past (*The Dong-A Ilbo* 2007). In the following years, objections and criticisms regularly emerged in the Korean press.[16] Yet, despite the concerns of Japanese diplomats and a few discussions between both sides, the Japanese nomination file was never revised to become more inclusive of the complex histories of these sites during this period.

In December 2012, the return of the conservative Liberal Democratic Party in power and the designation of Shinzō Abe as Prime Minister announced a new decisive phase for the Meiji industrial heritage. The nomination file was appropriated by the national government and big corporations in order to attain/make the UNESCO World Heritage List. Close to nationalist positions, Abe was slowly initiating a turn to the right for Japanese politics. The Meiji industrial heritage narrative fitted in with the celebration of Meiji Japan by nationalist groups such as the "Japan Conference" (*Nihon kaigi*): the success story of the first non-Western modernised and industrialised country, leaving aside all reference to colonialism and imperialism.[17]

In order to advance the project beyond the concerns of the Agency for Cultural Affairs and the MOFA, the Japanese Government decided to assign the responsibility of the nomination file to the Cabinet itself, a move criticised as both controversial and highly political by some scholars (Inada 2015: 36–37). In 2014, Meiji Industrial Revolution Heritage was recommended over the "Churches and Christian Sites in Nagasaki" as Japan's nominee for the following year's World Heritage Committee session. The decision of this specific timing was highly strategic in nature. Japan's mandate as member of the World Heritage Committee was ending in 2015, while South Korea was still going to be a member until 2017. In order to successfully bypass South Korea's expected opposition to the bid, 2015 was the best choice for the nomination file (Kiso 2015: 150).

The international heritage conflict between the two nations publicly exploded in spring 2015. At the beginning of May, the Agency for Cultural Affairs announced that the "Sites of Japan's Meiji Industrial Revolution" were recommended by ICOMOS for designation as World

Heritage. The decision was, according to the ICOMOS report, intended to preserve heritage attesting to the rapid and successful modernisation of Japan in the late-nineteenth century and early twentieth century, a transformation which in just a few decades made the nation a rival to Western industrialised countries (ICOMOS 2015: 88–89). The South Korean government very quickly reacted to this declaration by pointing out that no mention was made of the fact that several of these sites were places of exploitation of forced labour.[18] The issue, vehemently pushed by South Korea, attracted a significant amount of international media attention, amplifying the controversy and putting Japan in a difficult position.

For the Korean side, the Japanese bid was a violation of "the dignity of the survivors of forced labour as well as the spirit and principles of the UNESCO Convention", and the "World Heritage sites should be of outstanding universal value and be acceptable by all peoples across the globe" (Quoted in Underwood 2015b). This position was rapidly supported by the Chinese authorities as well as by associations of former prisoners of war and even a group of US congressmen (Ryall 2015; *Yonhap News Agency* 2015). On the other side, that is, for the advocates of the project, the Korean accusations were off the mark. According to them, they were not relevant as the nomination file stated a different time period than the one when the controversial events happened. Moreover, recommended by ICOMOS for its scientific and historical values, the sites were perfectly in line with what is to be expected for World Heritage sites (Kiso 2015: 147–148).

With the World Heritage Committee Session at Bonn just a few weeks away (28 June–8 July), the intense and international public protest campaign led by the South Korean government opened a period of tireless diplomatic moves. Korea's Foreign Minister Yun Byung-se went on a tour among the elected state party members of the Committee. South Korean President Park Geun-hye also discussed the issue during a meeting with Irina Bokova, Director-General of UNESCO (Korean Culture and Information Service 2015). Japanese and Korean officials met several times in Seoul and Tokyo to find a solution which would satisfy both sides. An apparent breakthrough in this diplomatic stalemate seemed in sight after the encounter between the Foreign Ministers of both countries on 23 June. The two ministers agreed to collaborate for the successful enlistment of each country's World Heritage candidate in the next Committee Session (Kameda 2015).

Conflict at UNESCO: Resolution Without Reconciliation?

Yet, less than one week later at Bonn, unsatisfied by the refusal from the Japanese side to produce a written declaration regarding the forced labour issue, the Korean government chose to confront the inscription of the nominated sites as World Heritage directly (*Yomiuri Shinbun* 2015). Such Korean activism, by the government during the Committee session, and by citizens' groups in front of the conference centre, surprised the members of the Japanese delegation.[19] Many of them characterised Korea's negative lobbying as an "irregular move", even for an organisation so full of lobbying and political deals as UNESCO (Kiso 2015: 98–99).

On 5 July, after several days of closed talks between the two parties and the mediation of the German delegation, a compromise was finally obtained. The inscription of the sites as World Heritage was followed by an official statement by the Japanese delegation that "there were a large number of Koreans and others who were brought against their will and forced to work under harsh conditions in the 1940s at some of the sites, and that, during World War II, the Government of Japan also implemented its policy of requisition" (UNESCO 2015b: 222). The ICOMOS recommendations, part of the UNESCO monitoring system of the World Heritage sites, were revised with the "interpretive strategy for the presentation of the property" now requiring "an understanding of the full history of each site" (UNESCO 2015c: 180).

The following day, the major Korean newspapers were prompt to announce that it was the first time that Japan had publicly acknowledged the use of forced labour on the international stage. In Japan, however, facing a far-right outcry and harsh criticisms from within the Liberal Democratic Party itself, the government, through declarations of the Chief Cabinet Secretary and the Minister of Foreign Affairs, refused to acknowledge that the expression "forced to work" was a synonym for forced labour, leaving open the question of how the "interpretive strategy to remember the victims" (UNESCO 2015b: 222) was going to be implemented (*Yomiuri Shinbun* 2015).

As a psychocultural drama, the 2015 World Heritage controversy highlights the division between the two countries, separated by incomprehension and resentment. The long process behind the nomination file, with its blind spots, and the immediate aftermath of the controversy, with its ambiguities and contradictions, indicate that the problem runs far deeper than a competition of national and material interests. The exclusion of the sufferings of Koreans and other forced workers from the main narrative of these heritage sites may be argued upon the basis of the narrow chronology of the narrative. The deliberate choice of this chronology was made in order to celebrate a Japan-first success-story. If Hiromi Mizuno argues that the preservation of industrial heritage by the Japanese government aims "to confirm Japan's place in the world by insisting on its membership in the Euro-centred universality" (Mizuno 2017), the narrative of Meiji Industrial Heritage Sites also expressed an inward turn, facilitated by the project's economic ambitions and the UNESCO institutional settings. By leaving aside the complexities of the history of these sites, the exclusive Japanese narrative instilled resentment among those for whom this past constitutes a core element of their own identity construction. It demonstrates the denial of recognition, in the sense of Honneth, by the Japanese government of these sufferings. This denial and feeling of exclusion provided the motivational and justificatory basis for Korean contestations, from the emotional reactions among civic groups to the more political actions taken by the South Korean government. The conflict dragged on through the Bonn meeting and ended with a compromise, but only because of the intervention of outsiders and the pressures on the Japanese side to avoid a failure with the concomitant political consequences at home.

Conclusion

The resolution of the heritage contestation between Japan and South Korea, during the World Heritage Committee meeting itself, draws ambiguous conclusions. On the one hand, the symbolic Japanese declaration was forced by the circumstances—the urgency of the meeting—without providing the long-awaited recognition from the Japanese government. While the ICOMOS recommendations will probably be fulfilled, the perception of a lack of commitment and sincerity may temporarily undermine the reconciliation process. As depicted in the 2017 film, the forced labour issue continues to be a controversial topic between the two countries.

On the other hand, if reconciliation is "thought of on a continuum, meaning that there can be degrees of reconciliation rather than just its presence or absence" (Ross 2007: 84), the resolution of this issue can contribute to diminishing the tensions in the long term. The introduction of the forgotten, or avoided, "Others" into the Japanese narrative represents a first step towards more inclusive narratives. In order to pursue the reconciliation process, however, genuine transnational collaboration and more grassroots participation are needed in global (negative) heritage-making in order to create public spaces for open dialogue between the various parties, draft new heritage narratives and help achieve thicker recognition.[20]

NOTES

1. The film's historical errors were criticised not only by the Japanese right-wing newspaper *Sankei Shimbun*, but also by Korean spectators; for example, Kwon Yule-jung, director of the Daejeon National Cemetery (Yule-jung 2017).
2. Recent incidents such as Israel's opposition to the Palestinian nomination of "Hebron/Al-Khalil Old Town" to the UNESCO World Heritage List in 2016 or Japan's denunciation of the inscription of the Nanking Massacre Documents on the Memory of the World register in 2015 belong to this category.
3. See Ross (2009): 5.
4. Around one-third of all international tourism in 2009, according to the World Tourism Organization (Salazar and Zhu 2015: 240).
5. The term of office is normally six years according to the Convention but States Parties agree to shorten this period to four years. See UNESCO, "The World Heritage Committee".
6. Many other terms have been proposed to describe this kind of heritage: dissonant, painful, dark, difficult or even undesirable (Park 2013: 78; González-Ruibal and Hall 2015: 150).
7. International Council on Monuments and Sites.
8. UNESCO (2017): Status of contributions to the Regular Budget as at 5 October 2017. Available at: http://www.unesco.org/new/fileadmin/MULTIMEDIA/HQ/BFM/MemberStates-Status-of-Contributions.pdf.
9. See UNESCO website: "Gusuku Sites and Related Properties of the Kingdom of Ryukyu". Available at: http://whc.unesco.org/en/list/972.
10. Interviews with several local government officials involved in the project, October 2015.
11. Two sites outside the Kyūshū and Yamaguchi areas were also added.
12. Interview with a former official of the Agency for Cultural Affairs, October 2015.
13. See Fukuoka (2015). Ross himself often refers, albeit briefly, to the controversial visits of Japan's prime ministers to the Yasukuni shrine which

commemorates the Japanese soldiers who died in war (including some World War II war criminals) (see e.g., Ross 2009: 1).

14. "Comfort women" is the term used to describe women who were forcibly recruited as prostitutes for the Japanese military forces before and during World War II.

15. Yawata Steel Work, Miike Coal Mine, Hashima Coal Mine (*Gunkanjima*), Takashima Coal Mine and three of Mitsubishi Nagasaki Shipyard (*Yomiuri Shinbun* 2015).

16. See, among others, *The Korea Times* (2013).

17. See, for example, the campaign to replace Japan's "Culture Day" (3 November) by a "Meiji Day": *Meiji Day Promotion Council*. Available at: http://meijinohi.com.

18. Less mediatised, the Shôka Sonjuku (Hagi, Yamaguchi Pref.), private academy where many of the major Japanese political figures of the late-nineteenth century and early twentieth century were educated, was also denounced by Korean citizens' groups as being the influential training place of advocates of Japan's expansion policy to Korea such as Hirobumi Itō (Ministry of Foreign Affairs, Republic of Korea 2015).

19. Especially among the local government officials which were invited to the Bonn meeting. Moreover, several of these officials indicated that there was already some recognition of these events near the sites, such as at Ōmuta Coal Industry and Science Museum (Interview with several local government officials, October 2015).

20. See the example of the underground war facilities described in Han (2017).

REFERENCES

Akagawa, N. (2014). *Heritage Conservation and Japan's Cultural Diplomacy: Heritage, National Identity and National Interest*. London and New York: Routledge.

Akagawa, N. (2016). Rethinking the Global Heritage Discourse—Overcoming 'East' and 'West'? *International Journal of Heritage Studies, 22*(1), 14–25.

Anderson, B. (2006). *Imagined Communities: Reflections on the Origin and Spread of Nationalis*. London: Verso Books.

Bertacchini, E., Liuzza, C., Meskell, L., & Saccone, D. (2016). The Politicization of UNESCO World Heritage Decision Making. *Public Choice, 167*(1–2), 95–129.

Brumann, C. (2014). Shifting Tides of World-Making in the UNESCO World Heritage Convention: Cosmopolitanisms Colliding. *Ethnic and Racial Studies, 37*(12), 2176–2192.

Fukuoka, K. (2015). Memory and Others: Japan's Mnemonic Turn in the 1990s. In M. Kim (Ed.), *Routledge Handbook of Memory and Reconciliation in East Asia* (pp. 63–78). London and New York: Routledge.

González-Ruibal, A., & Hall, M. (2015). Heritage and Violence. In L. Meskell (Ed.), *Global Heritage: A Reader* (pp. 150–170). Malden, MA: Wiley-Blackwell.

Hagström, L., & Gustafsson, K. (2015). Japan and Identity Change: Why It Matters in International Relations. *The Pacific Review, 28*(1), 1–22.

Han, J.-S. (2017). The Heritage of Resentment and Shame in Postwar Japan. *The Asia-Pacific Journal: Japan Focus, 15,* 1–4. Available at: http://apjjf. org/2017/01/Han.html.

Herzfeld, M. (2008). Mere Symbols. *Anthropologica, 50*(1), 141–155.

Honneth, A. (1995). *The Struggle for Recognition: The Moral Grammar of Social Conflicts.* Cambridge: Polity Press.

Honneth, A. (2012). Recognition Between States: On the Moral Substrate of International Relations. In A. Honneth (Ed.), *The I in We: Studies in the Theory of Recognition* (pp. 137–152). Cambridge: Polity Press.

ICOMOS. (2015). *ICOMOS Evaluation of Nominations of Cultural and Mixed Properties to the World Heritage List, ICOMOS International.* Available at: http://whc.unesco.org/archive/2015/whc15-39com-inf8B1-en.pdf. Accessed 12 July 2017.

Inada, T. (2015). L'évolution de la protection du patrimoine au Japon depuis 1950: sa place' dans la construction des identités régionales. *Ebisu. Études japonaises, 52,* 21–46.

Japan's Meiji Industrial Revolution. (2015). *Sekai-isan tōroku made no michi-nori* [The Journey Towards the Registration as World Heritage]. Available at: http://www.japansmeijiindustrialrevolution.com/history. Accessed 15 July 2017.

Kameda, M. (2015, June 23). Japan, South Korea Mark 50 Years of Postwar Ties. *The Japan Times.*

Katō, K. (1999). *Sangyō Isan: Chiiki to Shimin No Rekishi e No Tabi* [The Industrial Heritage: A Historical Voyage Through the Life of Everyday Man]. Tokyo: Nihon keizai shinbunsha.

Kimura, S. (2009). Sangyō-isan no hyōshō to chiiki-shakai no henyō' [Representation of Industrial Heritage and the Transformation of Local Communities]. *Japanese Sociological Review, 60*(3), 415–432.

Kiso, I. (2015). *Sekai-Isan Bijunesu* [The World Heritage Business]. Tokyo: Shōgakukan shinsho.

Korean Culture and Information Service. (2015, May 21). *President Park Meets Education Forum Participants.* Available at: http://www.korea.net/NewsFocus/policies/view?articleId=127617. Accessed 11 July 2017.

Labadi, S., & Long, C. (Eds.). (2010). *Heritage and Globalisation.* London and New York: Routledge.

Loo, T. M. (2017). Japan's Dark Industrial Heritage: An Introduction. *The Asia-Pacific Journal: Japan Focus, 15*, 1–1. Available at: http://apjjf. org/2017/01/Loo.html.

Meskell, L. (2002). Negative Heritage and Past Mastering in Archaeology. *Anthropological Quarterly, 75*(3), 557–574.

Meskell, L. (Ed.). (2015a). *Global Heritage: A Reader.* Malden, MA: Wiley-Blackwell.

Meskell, L. (2015b). Gridlock: UNESCO, Global Conflict and Failed Ambitions. *World Archaeology, 47*(2), 225–238.

Meskell, L., & Brumann, C. (2015). UNESCO and New World Orders. In L. Meskell (Ed.), *Global Heritage: A Reader* (pp. 22–42). Malden, MA: Wiley-Blackwell.

Ministry of Foreign Affairs, Republic of Korea. (2015, July 7). *Spokesperson's Press Briefing.*

Mizuno, H. (2017). Rasa Island: What Industrialization to Remember and Forget. *The Asia-Pacific Journal: Japan Focus, 15*, 1–2. Available at: http:// apjjf.org/2017/01/Mizuno.html.

Murray, M. (2014). Differentiating Recognition in International Politics. *Global Discourse, 4*(4), 558–560.

Neki, A., & Satō, Y. (2016). *Bunka-seisaku-gaku yōsetsu* [Outline of Cultural Policy Studies]. Tokyo: Yōkōdō.

Nye, J. S. (2004). *Soft Power: The Means to Success in World Politics.* New York: Public Affairs.

Pai, H. I. (2013). *Heritage Management in Korea and Japan: The Politics of Antiquity and Identity.* Seattle: University of Washington Press.

Park, H. Y. (2013). *Heritage Tourism.* London and New York: Routledge.

Rico, T. (2008). Negative Heritage: The Place of Conflict in World Heritage. *Conservation and Management of Archaeological Sites, 10*(4), 344–352.

Ringmar, E. (2010). The International Politics of Recognition. In E. Ringmar & T. Lindemann (Eds.), *The International Politics of Recognition* (pp. 3–23). Boulder, CO: Paradigm Publishers.

Ross, M. H. (2007). *Cultural Contestation in Ethnic Conflict.* Cambridge: Cambridge University Press.

Ross, M. H. (Ed.). (2009). Cultural Contestation and the Symbolic Landscape: Politics By Other Means? *Culture and Belonging in Divided Societies: Contestation and Symbolic Landscapes* (pp. 1–24). Philadelphia: University of Pennsylvania Press.

Ryall, J. (2015, June 23). *British PoW Families Complain as Japan Asks for World Heritage Protection for Slave Labour Sites.* Available at: http://www.tele-graph.co.uk/news/worldnews/asia/japan/11687308/British-PoW-families-complain-as-Japan-asks-for-World-Heritage-protection-for-slave-labour-sites. html. Last Accessed 11 Oct 2017.

Salazar, N. B., & Zhu, Y. (2015). Heritage and Tourism. In L. Meskell (Ed.), *Global Heritage: A Reader* (pp. 240–258). Malden, MA: Wiley-Blackwell.

Schachter, A. (2015, July 7). *The History of Hashima, the Island in Bond Film 'Skyfall'.* Public' Radio International.

Siemons, M., & Underwood, W. (2015). Island of Horror: Gunkanjima and Japan's Quest for UNESCO World Heritage Status. *The Asia-Pacific Journal.*

Silverman, H. (2011). Border Wars: The Ongoing Temple Dispute Between Thailand and Cambodia and UNESCO's World Heritage List. *International Journal of Heritage Studies, 17*(1), 1–21.

Smith, L. (2006). *Uses of Heritage.* London and New York: Routledge.

The Dong-A Ilbo. (2007, August 15). *Japan Attempts to Put Island Where Koreans Were Worked to Death on World Heritage List.* Available at: http://english.donga.com/List/3/all/26/254515/1. Accessed 11 July 2017.

The Korea Times. (2013, September 22). *Heritage of Shameful.* Available at: http://www.koreatimes.co.kr/www/opinion/2017/10/202_143042.html. Accessed 12 July 2017.

Underwood, W. (2015a). History in a Box: UNESCO and the Framing of Japan's Meiji Era. *The Asia-Pacific Journal.*

Underwood, W. (2015b, June 25). Industrial Story Should Be Told, Forced Labor and All. *The Japan Times.*

UNESCO. (1972). *Convention Concerning the Protection of the World Cultural and Natural Heritage,* UNESCO World Heritage Centre. Available at: http://whc.unesco.org/en/conventiontext. Accessed 11 Aug 2017.

UNESCO. (2014). *Tomioka Silk Mill and Related Sites,* UNESCO World Heritage Centre. Available at: http://whc.unesco.org/en/list/1449. Accessed 11 July 2017.

UNESCO. (2015a). *Sites of Japan's Meiji Industrial Revolution: Iron and Steel, Shipbuilding and Coal Mining.* Available at: http://whc.unesco.org/en/list/1484.

UNESCO. (2015b). *Decisions Adopted by the World Heritage Committee at Its 39th Session (Bonn, 2015).* Available at: http://whc.unesco.org/document/138489.

UNESCO. (2015c). *Summary Records (World Heritage Committee, 39th session).* Available at: http://whc.unesco.org/document/137710.

UNESCO. (2017). *States Parties,* UNESCO World Heritage Centre. Available at: http://whc.unesco.org/en/statesparties. Last Accessed 11 Aug 2017.

Utaka, Y. (2009). The Hiroshima 'Peace Memorial': Transforming Legacy, Memories and Landscapes. In W. Logan & K. Reeves (Eds.), *Places of Pain and Shame: Dealing with "Difficult Heritage"* (pp. 34–49). London and New York: Routledge.

Wendt, A. (2012). Why a World State Is Inevitable. In L. Cabrera (Ed.), *Global Governance, Global Government: Institutional Visions for an Evolving World System* (pp. 27–64). Albany: State University of New York Press.

Yanagisawa, I. (2015). *Meiji Nihon No Sangyô Kakumei Isan* [The Sites of Japan's Meiji Industrial Revolution]. Tokyo: Wani Bukkusu.

Yomiuri Shinbun. (2015, July 6). *'Kyōsei-rōdō' nikkan ga tairitsu sekai-isan shinngi konran* ['Forced Labor' Confrontation Between Japan and South Korea: Confusion at the World Heritage Committee Meeting].

Yonhap News Agency. (2015, July 4). *U.S. Lawmakers Step Up to Oppose Japan's UNESCO Bid.* Available at: http://english.yonhapnews.co.kr/national/2015/07/04/0301000000AEN20150704001000320.html. Accessed 11 July 2017.

Yonhap News Agency. (2017a, June 15). *'The Battleship Island' is Fact-Based Fiction Film,* says Director. Available at: http://english.yonhapnews.co.kr/news/2017/06/15/0200000000AEN20170615007651315.html.

Yonhap News Agency. (2017b, July 31). *'The Battleship Island' Shown to UNESCO Officials, Diplomats in Paris.* Available at: http://english.yonhapnews.co.kr/culturesports/2017/07/31/0701000000AEN20170731005900315.html.

Yule-jung, K. (2017, August 16). After Watching 'The Battleship Island'. *The Korea Times.* Available at: http://koreatimes.co.kr/www/news/opinon/2017/08/137_234857.html.

CHAPTER 11

Lost Temporalities and Imagined Histories: The Symbolic Violence in the Greek-Macedonian Naming Dispute

Biljana Volchevska

INTRODUCTION

Heritage is a category that is well established in both national and international legislation. Whether material or immaterial, it is almost exclusively treated as an explicitly national category. When viewed as a nationalised representation of the past, heritage often fails to represent the collective remembrance of a certain place by favouring certain histories over others for the purpose of articulating one unifying national narrative. Unlike memories, which are often more fluid, open for interpretation, personal and diverse, heritage is well managed, carefully interpreted and state controlled. These mechanisms of control—often by the state—give heritage its potential to deny or hide certain pasts or memories. However, resistance towards these well-controlled narratives of the past can appear on a national level—between different ethnicities or communities—as well as on an international level—where disagreements

B. Volchevska (✉)
Utrecht University, Utrecht, The Netherlands

© The Author(s) 2018
J. Rodenberg and P. Wagenaar (eds.), *Cultural Contestation*,
Palgrave Studies in Cultural Heritage and Conflict,
https://doi.org/10.1007/978-3-319-91914-0_11

can appear in interpretations of the past amongst different countries. This chapter looks at heritage and its role in creating political division and facilitating symbolic violence, in particular in the context of the naming dispute between Macedonia and Greece. The dispute is an example of a recycled heritage that is driven by contemporary political agendas—one that narrates the past in order to illuminate the present in a specific way. The naming dispute between Macedonia and Greece will serve here as my main case study through which I examine symbolic structures and cultural politics as mechanisms for establishing hegemonic histories and oppressive identity politics. Processes of cultural construction such as the monumentalisation of distant pasts and the strengthening of symbolic meaning will be related to political reality and the construction of both dominating and dominated identity.

The establishment of imperial iconographies, the denial of pasts and identities, as well as claims to exclusive ownership of the past occurring on both sides of the dispute will be studied as political rather than historical matters. In order to explore the meaning of the past with regard to the present, I will use Laclau's (1996) concept of the "empty signifier". This concept will assist in gaining a clear understanding of the rhetorical foundations of heritage discourse in this context, thus showing the limitations as well as the impossibility of nationalised heritage when understood and practised as a state-owned culture. By looking at the hegemonic relations created through heritage production and its interpretation, this article aims to study heritage as a top-down curated domain and a valuable political resource that provides more than just a display of material and immaterial culture. By looking at policies of heritage interpretation and management, the article shows the divisive potential of heritage realised via processes of establishing, imagining and defending national identity through historical narratives. The article also addresses the ambivalence between dominant and state-organised heritage on the one hand and other forms of reactive remembrance of denied temporalities on the other.

It should be noted that the concept of memory used here is similar to that of cultural (also called communicative) memory as explained by Halbwachs (2013) and Assman (2008) and stands in opposition to the concept of heritage. Communicative memory does not have one single agency, cannot be state controlled, is not commemorated, and is not legally protected. Assman (2008) characterises communicative memory as recent and lived memory: "It lives in everyday interaction and communication and, for this very reason, has only a limited time depth which normally reaches no farther back than eighty years, the time span of three interacting generations" (111). In contrast, heritage production is directly related to the formation of collective memories—"of how societies remember their past, how they represent it, and lie about it" (Confino 2008: 78)

It is also important to note that, when examining the creation of heritage and historical consciousness, I am not concerned with the scientific reliability of historical images. Instead, as Meyer (2010) has pointed out, the question is "how and by whom, as well as through which means, which intention, and which effect past experiences are brought up and become politically relevant" (176).

THE NAMING DISPUTE BETWEEN MACEDONIA AND GREECE

The political dispute between Macedonia and Greece is widely understood as an identity problem and often unjustly simplified and reduced to a conflict over the name "Macedonia", thus ignoring the complexity and history of the dispute. The dispute begun when Greek politicians raised their concerns over the creation of a country named Macedonia that would also build a Macedonian identity—one separate from that of the Greeks. According to the Greeks, the Macedonian name is part of their own historical heritage and "should not be used to identify, in an ethnic sense another nation" (Skilakakis 1995: 260). The Greeks fear that by recognising the new country under the name Macedonia, they will lose the ownership of the adjective "Macedonian" as primarily Greek. According to Chepreganov (2008: 333), the recognition of a country under the name "Macedonia" for Greece would mean also a recognition of the ethnic identity of the Macedonian minority in Greece, thus also accepting that Greece is not nationally homogenous but rather a multi-ethnic country.

However, the dispute can be traced further back in history to the Balkan wars (1912–1913) when the countries neighbouring Macedonia were claiming territorial rights over the region and thus objected to the formation of a separate Macedonian nation state—each for their own reasons. The territorial pretensions of the different countries triggered the second Balkan War (1913), which was concluded with the Bucharest Treaty in August 1913 and resulted in the partition of Macedonia amongst the Balkan league (made up of Greece, Bulgaria, Serbia and a small part that was given to Albania).

In the early days of establishing their rule, all three countries aimed for a rapid and efficient assimilation of the Macedonians. To this end, Greece and Serbia introduced measures banning (and persecuting) all manifestations of the Macedonian language and wider ethnic characteristics, as well as all contact between Macedonians in the now divided areas of the country (Chepreganov 2008). The silencing of the Macedonian language was especially aggressive in Aegean Macedonia, where the Macedonian language was not recognised by the Greek state and its use was forbidden for any kind of communication: "the Macedonian language was forbidden for private communication, in the family, among the children among the villagers, on weddings, gatherings, or funeral rituals" (Kiselinovski 1990: 43).[1] Public manifestations of the Macedonian language—even in churches, and on monuments and tombs—were also removed. Paramilitary organisations such as "the Greek Macedonian Fist" (Ελληνική Μακεδονική Πυγμή) were formed and terrorised the Macedonians, warning them that the speaking of their language was strictly forbidden and often forcing them to migrate to neighbouring countries. Geographical names in Aegean Macedonia, which were mostly Slavic, were soon renamed with Greek names. Already in the 1920s in the region of Aegean Macedonia, a total of 1666 city, settlement and village names were changed. During the period from 1918 to 1970, and in the twenties and forties of the twentieth century 1487 toponyms were changed (Kulakova 2012). The change of these toponyms is systematic —a strategic duty of the new state of Greece, which was granted "new lands" (Aegean Macedonia) after the Bucharest Treaty (ibid.). Thus, toponym translation, alongside other acts of prohibition of the Macedonian language and folklore, acts as effective mechanisms by which to erase linguistic and cultural memory.

According to the first Macedonian president, Kiro Gligorov (1991–1999), the naming dispute is not so much related to the distant past of Ancient Macedonia. Instead, it is related to more controversial recent histories and what has become known as "The Macedonian Question".[2] "This has weight in Greece because of the enormous number of people who left or were expelled, who are not able to receive their property or compensation" (Gligorov cited in Shea 1997: 283). With such a statement, reference is made to the thousands of Slav Macedonians who were evacuated, fled or expelled during the Greek

Civil War (1945–1949).[3] Some of their homes were left abandoned whilst others were confiscated, thus fuelling an objective fear that thousands of Slav Macedonians might one day return and claim their abandoned properties in Northern Greece. This is the main reason why Macedonian politicians relate the problem, not so much to the ancient past, but rather to the more recent past related to the position of Aegean Macedonia in Greece and the associated Greek denial of the Macedonian Slav ethnic identity amongst the Slavic speaking inhabitants in Northern Greece (Karakasidou 1993).

In the period between 1943 and 1991, when Macedonia had been established as a separate political entity and a republic within the borders of Yugoslavia, Greece exercised restraint by not opposing the existence of Macedonia. Despite the fact that Greece never formally accepted the existence of a country called Macedonia—because of good Greek-Yugoslavian relations—the "Macedonian question" (whilst remaining problematic), was not prioritised. However, this changed in 1991, when Macedonia became an independent country and Greece openly denied the entrance of Macedonia to the UN, and insisted changes of the country's name and flag. In addition to the political measures of 1991, Greece imposed an economic blockade on Macedonia to further weaken the young and already unstable nation, although a few years later under international pressure, Greece lifted the blockade.

It was during the nineties that the Macedonian question gained popularity in Greece, at times almost eclipsing other political and economic questions. Sutton notes how the Macedonian question became the only issue upon which most Greeks could actually agree:

> A few people did express the view that the Macedonian question had been blown out of proportion, to the neglect of more pressing matters of Greek foreign policy. Those who expressed this view, however, did not deny that Greece was "right" in its position. The view that Greece was actually wrong on this issue was extremely rare on Kaymnos. (Sutton 1997: 420)

This position is supported by Boletsi:

> Greece was flooded with posters and flyers declaring that Macedonia is Greek, people in the streets were calling out a variety of slogans on the "greekness" of Macedonia, and teachers at schools were dedicating classes to the "true" history of Macedonia against (what they regarded as) the

ridiculous claims of a group of falsifiers of history. Anyone who would enter Greek airports or other points of transfer would be overwhelmed by official posters spreading the "truth" about Macedonia. Certain places were even renamed, like the airport of Thessaloniki, which was rebaptized as "Macedonia airport". (Boletsi, online)

In the first decade of the dispute, Macedonian politicians have been relatively flexible and open to dialogue, to the extent that the Macedonian government agreed to change the national flag at the request of Greece, which complained that the Vergina Sun is a Greek symbol. Questions surrounding Alexander the Great and Ancient Macedonia were avoided by Macedonian diplomats, and Macedonian identity politics were formulated around the right to self-determination—albeit whilst accusing Greece of violating both UN and EU procedures for denying such right. The condemnation of Macedonians for "stealing", "imitating" or "appropriating" "Greekness" has been rejected both by Macedonian politicians and intellectuals claiming that the dispute should be understood in relation to the more recent past of Aegean Macedonia. However, in the early stages of the dispute Macedonian politicians were not claiming ownership of the Ancient Macedonian past and avoided arguing along historic lines. This has been clearly articulated by the Macedonian president:

I believe that the ancient Macedonians were a special ethnic entity, which does not necessarily mean they were Greek. As to the Greek historical heritage, we do not wish to steal it. We settled this region in the 6th and 7th centuries AD. Unlike other tribes, we took the name of the territory we settled, Macedonia, and that does not mean we have any pretensions to the history of ancient Macedonia. We have our own history and our own heritage. (Gligorov cited in Panov 1994, online)

A closer look at the rhetoric around which the dispute is centred could lead us to a better understanding of how the past is conceptualised and politicised. Central to the Greek rhetoric is the phrase "falsification and stealing of history". According to official Greek narratives, the young nation that calls itself Macedonia is stealing Greek history. This claim gives rise to a series of questions: Who has access to historical symbols and narratives? Who has the right to identify with them and how is that right legitimised? Who controls the boundaries of historical images and how is the ownership of such boundaries settled within (and across) the borders of modern nations?

According to Greece, the dispute is not only a contestation of histori-cal symbols and what they call "stealing of history", but also a realpolitik threat that could result in the claiming of resources and territories. The Greek government based its position on the claim that in using the name "Macedonia: FYROM was declaring its future expansionist aims on the neighbouring Greek Province of Macedonia" (Sutton 1997: 418). This Greek fear is clearly grounded in the annexation of the Aegian part of Macedonia in 1913. At the time of annexation, the majority of people living in what is now Northern Greece were Slavic Macedonians (Rossos and Evans 1991). In its effort to solve the naming dispute with Greece, the Macedonian government has invested a lot of effort in proving that the young nation state has no territorial pretensions towards the annexed Aegean part of Macedonia. The Macedonian government has dealt with accusations of these irredentist claims by making constitutional changes that explicitly outlaw any territorial pretensions towards neigh-bouring countries.[4] Accusation by the Greeks continued, until finally being rejected in the Badinter report on Macedonia part 6: "The name Republic of Macedonia cannot be treated as a basis for any territorial claims and irredentism (...) and thus an obstacle to the recognition of the new state" (Robert Badinter, cited in Frchkovski 2016: 41).[5]

Macedonian diplomacy which had been largely open to dialogue and negotiation during the early years of the dispute drastically changed its approach following the 2008 NATO Summit in Bucharest at which Greece vetoed the Macedonian accession, suggesting that the country's name implies territorial aspirations against its own region of Macedonia. At this point, Macedonian diplomacy gave up on negotiations and instead sued Greece at the International Court of Justice,

> claiming that Athens unilaterally broke a 1995 treaty and asking the court to order Greece "to cease and desist from objecting in any way, whether directly or indirectly, to (Macedonia's) membership of the North Atlantic Treaty Organisation nor any other international multilateral and regional organisations and institutions of which (Greece) is a member". (The Hague Justice Portal 2011, online)

Although Macedonia won the case in 2011, the bilateral relationship between Greece and Macedonia only worsened. Moreover, the momen-tum for joining NATO was lost, whilst European diplomacy remained neutral to the dispute, but supportive of Macedonia's EU integration processes. At this point Macedonian cultural politics—now lead by the right-oriented VMRO DPMNE (Internal Macedonian Revolutionary Organization—Democratic Party for Macedonian National Unity)—drastically changed, embracing the "dead status quo" and responding to Greek nationalism and the blockade with equally fanatical nationalism launching a "building bonanza" (Smith 2011, online) that celebrated Ancient Macedonia as national Macedonian heritage. What followed was an intensification of official Macedonian history through the rewriting of history books and a general increase in the production of books, promotional videos and talks related to Ancient Macedonian history. This was also accompanied by a colossal programme of heritage production: of monuments, buildings and fountains—again, most of which were devoted to Ancient Macedonia. The project was called Skopje 2014 and was promoted as the revival of the Ancient, stubbornness, and clinging to the true identity. The term *antiquisation* became one of the most used amongst Macedonian intellectuals, architects and heritage professionals, who often judged the newly completed monuments and buildings of Skopje 2014 as distasteful, badly planned and an embarrassment for Macedonians. *Antiquisation* was used by architectural historians, not only to refer to the "Renaissance practice of giving a city the appearance of ancient Rome" (Tzonis and Lefaivre 1986: 263), but also in a political sense—by using historical themes to define the present.

These changes in Macedonian cultural politics did not only deepen the conflict with Greece, but also introduced a new mode of national self-identification—one that is problematic, not only for Greece, but also for the different ethnicities living in the country. The early political strategy of providing a more amorphous and complex memory narrative that offered other perspectives and appealed to all ethnicities in multi-ethnic Macedonia was exchanged for a static story-centred historical narrative that gave preference to the Ancient Macedonian and ethnic Macedonian past. The attempt of the Macedonian VMRO DPMNE to defend the country's right of self-identification by mimicking and reproducing both its Hellenistic heritage and Greek uncompromising nationalism did not only prove to be disastrous for the country's bilateral relationship with Greece, but also for the internal sociopolitical climate. The impact of these new heritage politics on a national level was bigger than expected, evoking revolt related to symbolic exclusions, amongst others based on gender, race, ethnicity and class. Ultimately, the Skopje 2014 project merely contributed to the end of the ten-year rule of the VMRO

DPMNE and its populist ruling style. However, the direct implications of heritage politics in terms of the sociopolitical climate that was created through heritage production require separate analyses, which lie outside the scope of this article.

THE SYMBOLIC WAR: HERITAGE AS PROPAGANDA

The symbolic violence and aggressive cultural rhetoric framed by the naming dispute have ultimately engulfed both sides, and in the process created two radically different forms of historical consciousness that are not just oppositional—in the sense that they have disagreements—but also antagonistic—in a sense that they are mutually exclusive. Heritage rhetoric of ownership, ancestry and pure identity have been accepted as the only spaces in which new identities can be negotiated and legitimised. The distant past of Alexander the Great has played a special role and has been adopted by both the Slav Macedonians and Greeks as their own—almost mystical—national myth. This raises the question of why such distant history, which has taken place in the territories of both countries, is not accepted as a shared heritage, such as is also an existing category in the World Heritage Convention for the protection of cultural and natural heritage. Further, what prevents cultural heritage from being shaped on the basis of a more hybrid identity? Plamen K. Georgiev (2012) notes that hybrid identity is capable of converting "otherness" into patterns of "mutuality" and thus generating "more or less sustainable forms of coping with the other" (34). Similarly, Ross argues that the rethinking of the cultural and symbolic landscape in more inclusive terms could provide the room "for creative reformulations that can result in new more complex, more inclusive symbolic landscape, and less directly opposed identities" (2007: 27). This however should not be done through direct confrontation and from outside but rather through more careful, inclusive and civil-driven organisation of images, symbols and narratives which will lead to more tolerant narratives, "new experiences and new emotional connections" (Ross 2007: 46).

However, until now not much room for mutuality and inclusiveness has been opened in the Greek-Macedonian dispute, as the exclusiveness of owning the past lies at the core of the conflict. Shifts in (the rather flexible) Macedonian politics and the appropriation of the harsh language of the Greeks have all but blocked any prospect for further negotiation.

As Georgiev (2012) points out, the use of Antiquity by both countries can be compared to the oil business. Oil is discovered by the west and subsequently nationalised by young nation states, who then sell it back to the west. Greece has already profited from its ancient past, as the "Cradle of the European Civilisation", and this has been one of the dominant narratives for its acceptance in the European Union (Frchkovski 2016; Friedman 1992; Herzfeld 1986). Conversely, Macedonian attempts at *antiquisation* have failed and nothing has been more damaging to Macedonian diplomacy than the turn towards antiquity in its cultural politics.

In order to explain the processes of nationalised sanitisation and selection as applied to the past and conducted in such a way that they create a picture or story that can appeal to contemporary realities, Hewison (1987) coined the phrase "heritage industry". Industry of this nature positions heritage as a resource that can provide cultural, economic and political benefit. It is through heritage that we can brand the nation and decide "who a particular community are and who they are not" (Smith 2006: 49). At the same time, it should be understood that the high political potential of cultural heritage is what makes it so contested—not just between different nations, but also between different social groups (divided along the lines of gender and class) within a given society. According to Hewison, it is the politicisation of heritage that determines our relationship with the past:

> What matters is not the past, but our relationship with it. As individuals, our security and identity depend largely on the knowledge we have of our personal and family history; the language and customs, which govern our social lives, rely for their meaning on continuity between past and present. (Hewison 1987: 43)

Being a valuable and easily manipulated political resource, heritage has become a domain often managed and interpreted in a "top-down" rather than "bottom up" manner. Hence, being formed as an elitist memory mechanism, heritage has opened the path for memory activism as a form of social struggle for the recognition of suppressed pasts that oppose privileged, universalised histories.

By borrowing notions such as the empty signifier, hegemonic relationships and the impossible necessity of representation (especially in the Laclaunian political sense), I would like to analyse the role of the distant past—its uses and abuses—in framing the dispute. The fundamental question here is: How and why are narratives of the (ancient) past deployed in shaping the historical consciousness and through which mechanisms do such pasts become powerful political tools? The past has been already recognised as a safe zone and an effective cover for political innovation, instability and insecurity (Hobsbawm and Ranger 2012). The material and symbolic representations of more distant pasts are not burdened with recent remembrance and are thus open to more flexible interpretations. It is the lack of memory of the distant past that makes it eligible for mythologising and mystifying ideological and national motives.

When any given historical epoch, personality, or event is taken outside of its historical context, it becomes an overdetermination and universal representation of a more complex identity. In his conceptualisation of heritage, Kevin Walsh (1992) has borrowed the notion of floating signifiers from the post-structuralist philosophy of language in order to analyse the creation of historical and cultural meanings. According to Walsh, "the signifier has been removed from the referent, the referent being history itself; the free play, or intertextuality, amongst signifiers leaves the referent (history) remaining only as a superfluous notion" (ibid.: 55). Following his analysis, I prefer the Laclaunian term of "empty signifier", which more precisely defines the relationship between the signifier and the referent—the signifier does not float around any content, but rather is fully detached from it. In a strict sense, an empty signifier is a signifier without a signified (Laclau 1996). Being a representation of the past (symbol, name, personality, object, etc.) in the process of becoming a national heritage, the empty signifier renounces its particularity as a differential historicity within more complex historical interrelatedness in order to represent what Laclau calls "the purely equivalent identity of a communitarian space as such" (ibid.: 41). Thus, if a signifier stood for a concrete historical content, it is now elevated to a dominant signifier, which is emptied from the initial referent in order to assume the representing function for the totality of national identity. Being attached to universal value, historical symbols and images need to become ahistorical in order to participate in "the mediation of the past into myth" (Walsh 1992: 281).

One of the main ideological purposes of nationalised heritage is the unification of a group of people under one symbol. The concept of the empty signifier is helpful in understanding the formation of nationalised heritage as an ahistorical, universal, but also inadequate representation of national identity. Whether a historical event, symbol, name or personality, different signifiers are meant to encapsulate national identity as well as the complexity and interrelatedness of the past. The impossibility of a signifier to encapsulate an identity in its entirety leads inevitably to an inadequate representation. All differential identities that a national identity attempts to unify through one well-controlled historical consciousness are something "which cannot have a signifier on its own" (Laclau 1996: 42). "If this impossible object lacks the means of its adequate or direct representation, this can only mean that the signifier which is emptied in order to assume the representing function will always be constitutively inadequate" (ibid.: 40). This process of emptying the signifier allows for past symbols, events, and personalities to lose their direct historical significance and meaning, as well as to become ahistorical in the sense that their symbolic potential is utilised for contemporary purposes and ideological needs.

However, the national identity project demands that different histories, memories, stories, and interpretations of the past need to be unified under one national story that will be represented in one unified heritage. That is how heritage has become simultaneously a necessary and impossible project for every nation state. Laclau (2000) suggests that it is through that impossibility that we can understand the hegemonic nature of such signifiers: "The state presents itself in the language and culture of specific epochs" (48). Collective memory as a necessity for identity formation thus becomes possible only when historical knowledge is served as a simplified narrative or pamphlet propaganda. According to Laclau, this lies at the root of hegemonic relations. By singling out historical personalities and events, ideology is communicated and the ruling style is normalised. Fountains portraying mothers' breastfeeding, warriors on horses, kings and emperors—as represented in the project of Skopje 2014—communicate very specific images of femininity, ruling style and heroism. A good example of hegemonic heritage and the emptied signifier is the revival of the personality of Alexander the Great, which has been done with a complete lack of consideration for any historical accuracy. Alexander the Great has become a branding figure for the Macedonian national campaign for tourism promotion: "Macedonia Timeless". A huge statue of the great warrior was erected in the middle of the city of Skopje, and historical books were amended in a way that will give more space to the Ancient Macedonian past. However, such promotion expresses little concern for any deeper or more profound understanding of the promoted epoch:

> The video clips portrayed Alexander as a brave warrior who never backs off, saying that it is not "Macedonian" to retreat. He is represented as a macho man, despite the historical accounts of his fluid sexuality. His conquest is interpreted as the "liberation" of the oppressed people of Asia and Africa, although it was carried out in the age of slavery when huge portions of the populations held the status of slaves and servants regardless of political developments. His realm is displayed as a unitary and sovereign empire, although it fell apart shortly following his death. (Vangeli 2011: 18)

In Greece, the distant past has been accepted as confirmation of a long national existence that has been kept away from more recent memories that might compromise the fixed and pure character of this national past. By clinging to the metanarrative for their own political reasons, these antagonistic historical narratives provide a "counterbalance against the necessarily reductive and restrictive drive of the working memory" (Assmann 2008: 106). In the Macedonian case, more recent memories related to the Yugoslav past are denied access to the new Macedonian identity, as are the histories of Albanians, Roma, Vlachs and other minorities.

When there are different historical struggles—memories and symbols that compete for recognition—it is the political and ideological interests that determine which past will be universalised and hence through which certain identities will be legitimised. The establishment of identity on the basis of a universalised history is fundamentally hegemonic in nature because it stands as a privileged particularity in relation to all other epochs that are not given this signifying capacity. It is through such universalisation of particular epochs and the establishment of metanarratives that processes of strategic forgetting are facilitated.

CONCLUSION

The Greek-Macedonian naming dispute exemplifies how historical domination can lead towards political subordination—both between nation states and within a single nation. In such cases, notions such as shared or mutual heritage are disabled by the rigid cultural boundaries produced through the simplification and universalisation of historical narratives.

Unlike memories—which are private, unstructured, subjective and often not included in official history—heritage stands as a direct representation of one closely controlled unified national history. It is through memories that the unresolved difficulties of history are revealed, thus representing "the most efficient protest against suffering and justice" (Fortunati and Lamberti 2008: 128).

Furthermore, it has been shown that Greek politics of negation, as have been applied to Macedonian identity and ethnicity, attempt to suppresses or ignore certain pasts cannot be contradicted simply through mimicry. During the last decade, Macedonian cultural politics has decided to mimic its national obstructer by adopting the same national fanaticism and imitating the Hellenistic heritage. It is a type of relationship that the suppressed adopt in order to oppose the suppressor or a more powerful opponent. Grossberg (1996) argues that such imitation and misappropriation of the dominant discourse "locates the power of the subaltern in a kind of textual insurrection in which the subaltern is defined only by its internal negation of the coloniser" (358). However, such intentional misappropriations of dominant discourse have their own hegemonic ideals that mark internal subalterns. Promoted as a mono-ethnic identity, the new Macedonian identity does not just disable more transformative memory practices that could potentially shed a different light on the name dispute, but also deny the multi-ethnic character of the country, thus causing dissatisfaction amongst other ethnic groups.

Hegemonic histories are created and function in such a way that memories do not precede, but follow history, thus helping "speculative history to be integrated in the symbolic universe" (Ricoeur 2004: 161). Representations of the past, whether they are symbols, toponyms, monuments, buildings or customs, gain their meaning through their performance: either spatially or visually. As such, heritage goes beyond the purpose of remembrance and rather participates in the shaping of the sociopolitical contexts themselves. In this way, heritage has become a political, rather than historical, affair. The danger of the symbolic violence executed through heritage is an identity issue is not easily resolved and often precedes—and legitimises—a more structural violence. Symbolic violence does not harm people directly, but it can provide the ideological ground for more structural or direct violence that harms and threatens citizens very directly. By presenting certain groups of people as the enemy, silencing their past, or imagining them in a certain way, their invisibility and discrimination become justified. Therefore, heritage and culture are far from innocent and apolitical; they matter very directly in setting the scene for more tangible and warring political problems.

NOTES

1. "In 1913, Greece acquired Aegean Macedonia, at about 34,000 square kilometres the largest piece of Macedonian territory" (Rossos 2013: 2). Aegean Macedonia refers to the region of Macedonia in Northern Greece. The Greeks avoid the term, as it implies that Aegean Macedonia together with Vardar and Pirin Macedonia constitutes what was known as the region of Macedonia during the Ottoman Empire
2. "The Macedonian question" is a dispute that has dominated politics in the southern Balkans from the late nineteenth century onwards, through to the early twenty-first century. Initially, the Macedonian question involved Greece, Bulgaria, and, to a lesser extent, Serbia in a conflict over which state would be able to impose its own national identity on the ethnically, linguistically and religiously diverse population of Macedonia (Danforth 1993).
3. The Greek Civil War (1946–1949) resulted from the conflict between Greek Governmental Army forces supported by the UK and USA, and the Democratic Army of Greece (DAG), led by the Greek communist party and supported by Bulgaria, Yugoslavia and Albania. The final victory of the Greek government has helped to guarantee a NATO membership for Greece. The Macedonians of Aegean Macedonia took the side of the DAG, seeing it as an opportunity for "national liberation of the Macedonians in Aegean Macedonia" (Rossos 1997: 42). The Macedonians had around 20,000 casualties, as opposed to the 50,000 on the DAG side (Kirjazovski 1989). After the defeat of DAG and the end of the war, thousands more Macedonians were forced to migrate to neighbouring communist countries.
4. The decision of the Macedonian government has sparked dissatisfaction amongst the Macedonians living in Northern Greece (Aegean Macedonia), who feel forgotten by their motherland. Macedonia's new-found independence did not give much hope to displaced Macedonian refugees and immigrants. "The Macedonian constitution has removed any immediate hopes among the exiled Macedonians of a possible return or even the continued existence of a Macedonian homeland, in Greece" (Kolar-Panov 2003: 74).
5. The Badinter report is the Report of the Arbitration Committee of the Conference on Yugoslavia (1991). The committee was chaired by Robert Badinter, President of the French Constitutional Council. Its task was to

provide legal advice for the disintegration of Yugoslavia. "They were concerned with the question of whether the republics of Croatia, Macedonia and Slovenia, who had formally requested recognition by the Community and its Member States, had satisfied the conditions laid down by the council of Ministers of the European Community on the 16th of December 1991" (Pellet 1992). According to the final report, only Macedonia and Slovenia have fulfilled all the conditions.

REFERENCES

Assmann, A. (2008). Canon and Archive. In E. Astrid & N. Ansgar (Eds.), *Media and Cultural Memory* (pp. 97–109). Berlin: Deutsche Nationalbibliothek.

Assman, J. (2008). Communicative and Cultural Memory. In E. Astrid & N. Ansgar (Eds.), *Media and Cultural Memory* (pp. 109–119). Berlin: Deutsche Nationalbibliothek.

Boletsi, M. *The War of Words: When Butler's Excitable Speech Meets Injurious Speech in Greece (A Case Study)*. Amsterdam: University of Amsterdam. http://www.rpe.ugent.be/Boletsi_paper.doc.

Chepreganov, T. (2008). *Istorija na Makedonskiot Narod*. Skopje: Institut za Nacionalna Istoriaja.

Confino, A. (2008). Memory and the History of Mentalities. In E. Astrid & N. Ansgar (Eds.), *Media and Cultural Memory* (pp. 77–85). Berlin: Deutsche Nationalbibliothek.

Danforth, L. M. (1993). Claims to Macedonian Identity: The Macedonian Question and the Breakup of Yugoslavia. *Anthropology Today, 9*(4), 3–10.

Fortunati, V., & Elena, L. (2008). Cultural Memory: A European Perspective. In E. Astrid & N. Ansgar (Eds.), *Media and Cultural Memory* (pp. 127–137). Berlin: Deutsche Nationalbibliothek.

Frchkovski, L. D. (2016). *Restless Nationalism*. Skopje: Kultura.

Friedman, J. (1992). The Past in the Future: History and the Politics of Identity. *American Anthropologist, 94*(4), 837–859.

Georgiev, P. K. (2012). *Self-Orientalization in South East Europe*. Dordrecht: Springer Science & Business Media.

Grossberg, L. (1996). Identity and Cultural Studies: Is That All There Is? In S. Hall (Ed.), *Questions of Cultural Ideniity* (pp. 87–107). London: Sage.

Halbwachs, M. (2013). Les cadres sociaux de la mémoire. Paris: Albin Michel.

Herzfeld, M. (1986). *Ours Once More: Folklore, Ideology, and the Making of Modern Greece*. New York: Pella Publishing Company.

Hewison, R. (1987). *The Heritage Industry: Britain in a Climate of Decline*. London: Methuen.

Hobsbawm, E., & Ranger, T. (Eds.). (2012). *The Invention of Tradition*. Cambridge: Cambridge University Press.

Karakasidou, A. (1993). Politicizing Culture: Negating Ethnic Identity in Greek Macedonia. *Journal of Modern Greek Studies, 11*(1), 1–28.

Kirjazovski, R. (1989). *Makedonskata politička emigracija od Egejskiot del na Makedonija vo istočnoevropskite zemji po Vtorata svetska vojna.* Skopje: Kultura.

Kiselinovski, S. (1990). *Egejskiot del na Makedonija 1913–1989.* Skopje: Kultura.

Kolar-Panov, D. (2003). *Video, War and the Diasporic Imagination.* London and New York: Routledge.

Kulakova, K. (2012). Enforced Linguistic Conversion: Translations of Macedonian Toponyms in the Twentieth Century. In S. Stojmenska-Elzeser & V. Martinovski (Eds.), *Literary Dislocations* (pp. 28–43). Skopje: Institute of Macedonian Literature.

Laclau, E. (1996). Why Do Empty Signifiers Matter to Politics. *Emancipation (s), 36*, 46.

Laclau, E. (2000). Identity and Hegemony: The Role of Universality in the Constitution of Political Logics. In J. Butler, E. Laclau, & S. Žižek (Eds.), *Contingeny, Hegemony, Universality.* London and New York: Verso.

Meyer, E. (2010). Memory and Politics. In E. Astrid & N. Ansgar (Eds.), *Media and Cultural Memory* (pp. 173–181). Berlin: Deutsche Nationalbibliothek.

Panov, L. (1994). The World Reacts to the American Recognition and Greek Embargo of Macedonia. *The Macedonian Tribune (2-c/3).* https://groups. google.com/forum/#!topic/soc.culture.bulgaria/6rQm6sqkIBI.

Pellet, A. (1992). The Opinions of the Badinter Arbitration Committee a Second Breath for the Self-Determination of Peoples. *European Journal of Inational Law, 3*, 178.

Ricoeur, P. (2004). *Memory, History, Forgetting.* Chicago: University of Chicago Press.

Ross, M. H. (2007). *Cultural Contestation in Ethnic Conflict.* Cambridge: Cambridge University Press.

Rossos, A. (1997). Incompatible Allies: Greek Communism and Macedonian Nationalism in the Civil War in Greece, 1943–1949. *The Journal of Modern History, 69*(1), 42–76.

Rossos, A. (2013). *Macedonia and the Macedonians: A History.* Stanford: Hoover Press.

Rossos, A., & Evans, P. H. (1991). The Macedonians of Aegean Macedonia: A British Officer's Report, 1944. *The Slavonic and East European Review, 69*(2), 282–309.

Shea, J. (1997). *Macedonia and Greece: The Struggle to Define a New Balkan Nation.* London: MacFarland.

Skilakakis, T. (1995). *Sto Onoma tis Makedhonias* [In the Name of Macedonia]. Athens: Greek Europublishing.

Smith, H. (2011, August 11). Macedonian Statue: Alexander the Great or a Warrior on a Horse? *The Guardian*. http://www.guardian.co.uk/world/2011/aug/14/alexander-great-macedonia-warrior-horse.

Smith, L. (2006). *Uses of Heritage*. London: Routledge.

Sutton, D. E. (1997). Local Names, Foreign Claims: Family Inheritance and National Heritage on a Greek Island. *American Ethnologist, 24*(2), 415–437.

The Hague Justice Portal. (2011). *International Court of Justice Starts Hearings in FYR Macedonia v. Greece*. http://www.haguejusticeportal.net/index.php?id=12493.

Tzonis, A., & Lefaivre, L. (1986). *Classical Architecture: The Poetics of Order*. Cambridge, MA: MIT Press.

Vangeli, A. (2011). Nation-Building Ancient Macedonian Style: The Origins and the Effects of the So-Called Antiquization in Macedonia. *Nationalities Papers, 39*(1), 13–32.

Walsh, K. (1992). *The Representation of the Past: Museums and Heritage in the Post-Modern*. London and New York: Routledge.

PART III

Government Mitigation in Cultural Contestation

CHAPTER 12

Of, By, and for Which People? Government and Contested Heritage in the American Midwest

Elizabeth Kryder-Reid and Larry J. Zimmerman

INTRODUCTION

"Government of the people, by the people, for the people, shall not perish from the Earth." When President Abraham Lincoln spoke these final words of his address at Gettysburg in November 1863, the audience was reportedly unimpressed by the two-minute speech. But over the years this phrase has come to symbolize the ideals of American democracy. The USA is, in Lincoln's words, a nation "conceived in liberty, and dedicated to the proposition that all men are created equal." Heritage practices, however, often complicate such high ideals in the face of competing interests and political power. Democracies require both representative and participatory governance, but which voices are represented and who participates? State-sponsored heritage sites, particularly those involving contested heritage, expose the fissures and frictions of

E. Kryder-Reid (✉) · L. J. Zimmerman
Indiana University School of Liberal Arts at IUPUI, Indianapolis, IN, USA

© The Author(s) 2018
J. Rodenberg and P. Wagenaar (eds.), *Cultural Contestation*,
Palgrave Studies in Cultural Heritage and Conflict,
https://doi.org/10.1007/978-3-319-91914-0_12

government roles in managing and interpreting the past, and they may also demonstrate the strategies of resistance that influence governmental decisions.

Examined in this study are two contested heritage sites located in central Indiana, just north of Indianapolis, Indiana, in the heart of the American Midwest.[1] Mounds State Park (Mounds),[2] as the name implies, is one of the twenty-five parks owned and operated by the state of Indiana, while Strawtown Koteewi is one of the eleven public parks operated by the Hamilton County Parks and Recreation Department.[3] Mounds was established in 1930 and is listed on the National Register of Historic Places because of its earthworks dating to the late Archaic culture known as the Adena-Hopewell. Archaeologists hypothesize that Native Americans constructed the largest earthwork, the Great Mound, around 160 BC (Squire and Davis 1848; Cochran and McCord 2001). The mounds were primarily used as gathering places for religious ceremonies and probably constructed to align with astronomical events. While the 250-acre park contains a nature preserve and a unique fen environment, a campground, Nature Center, and miles of trails, it was dedicated, as the Interpretive Master Plan notes, "for the purpose of protecting a nationally recognized cultural site" (Mounds State Park 2011).

Strawtown Koteewi is a much newer park, created in 1999 when the county purchased 750 acres from the estate of a local resident. The relatively undeveloped land was known to contain numerous significant archaeological sites, as well as woods, prairies, and 3.25 miles of wetlands along the White River that surrounds three sides of the park. Like Mounds, the park was developed for recreational uses and now contains not only hiking and horseback riding trails, but also an archery range, high ropes course, and zip lines. Strawtown's Native American history is also more recent; while it was likely occupied much earlier, its most significant sites are an enclosed village site dating between 1250 AD and 1400 AD, a period known as the Oliver Phase of the Middle Woodland tradition.[4] Strawtown Koteewi has been the focus of intense archaeological investigation and had an active volunteer archaeology program for a decade (McCullough 2011).[5] In addition to the excavations, the Park runs public programs and maintains a permanent exhibit in the Taylor Nature Center. Both sites are valued as publicly accessible places to connect with nature, as sources of archaeological knowledge, and as places to learn about the past.

Contested Heritage

The parks used today for education and recreation are the homelands of Native Americans who were dispossessed through a series of violent encounters and negotiated treaties as part of the American colonial project, then removed to Indian Territory in what is now the state of Oklahoma. Multiple tribes have cultural affiliations to Indiana including the Miami, Delaware, Shawnee, Wea, and the Potawatomie. In addition, the Pokagon Potawatomi, though technically in Michigan, have large populations in the six Indiana border counties. The official recognition of these tribes is complicated, due to the history of Indian removal by the US government in the nineteenth century, and several of the affiliated groups with federal recognition are based in other states (the Miami of Oklahoma, three federally recognized bands of Shawnee in Oklahoma, the Delaware of Oklahoma, and the Pokagon Potawatomi in Michigan have federal tribal recognition).[6] To further complicate the issue of recognition is that descendants of remnant populations that stayed in Indiana in the 1800s have sought state and federal recognition. One consequence of this history is that the claims to the sites by Native peoples are entangled in broader issues of control, legitimacy, access to resources, and both inter- and intra-tribal relationships.

A second aspect of the contested heritage is that while the sites are valued by some as important sources of knowledge about the deep past, they are also seen by others as sacred sites (Kryder-Reid et al. 2017). The circular mounds at Mound State Park have astronomical alignments to the equinoxes and solstices and are important evidence for understanding the cosmologies of the Adena-Hopewell cultures. Strawtown Koteewi has only recently been available for archaeological investigation and is a significant settlement site from what archaeologists label the Oliver Phase of the Middle Woodland tradition. The sites have also been popular for volunteers, particularly during "Archaeology Week" which is organized each September. The archaeological research was conducted with the knowledge and cooperation of some tribal representatives, but given the complex history of association with the area and changes in elected leadership of tribal governments, others have objected to the excavations. At particular issue is the perception of disturbance of human remains and the belief that the site itself is hallowed ground because of the presence of those remains regardless of the context of intact burials. One outcome is that the Miami of Oklahoma have filed repatriation claims that have resulted in the return of a significant number of artifacts, both those mandated by NAGPRA and additional items falling outside of NAGPRA criteria, but being returned in the spirit of the law. Another outcome is that the NAGPRA claims have generated several stories in local, tribal, and national news media highly critical of park management of archaeological resources (Sikich 2017).[7] Furthermore, even with the resolution of the NAPGRA claims, there remains a conflict among those who use both parks as recreational sites, those who value their potential for scientific and archaeological research, and those who see them as sacred sites of their ancestors.

A third context for understanding the contested heritage of these sites is the tension between preservation and economic development. At Strawtown, the development of the ropes course and archery range, which produce income, has been challenged for the impact on the natural resources such as birds' nesting areas. At Mounds, the debate has centered on where a group looking hopes to stimulate the depressed economy of the region by creating a reservoir. The proposed Mounds Lake project would build an earthen dam on the West Fork White River, backing up water for approximately seven miles into Delaware County and creating a reservoir projected to be 30–50 feet deep, 7 miles in length, with an overall surface area of approximately 2000 acres or more than 800 hectares. The idea was first generated at a Madison County Leadership Academy visioning session in 2010 followed by a privately funded Phase 1 feasibility study that framed the primary purpose of the reservoir as an economic development catalyst. When the state-funded Phase 2 study was being conducted, the developers learned that public waterways cannot be dammed for economic development reasons, and they shifted the purpose of the reservoir to ensuring an adequate and safe water supply for the future, even though no water companies had indicated the need. The proposed dam project would inundate about a third of the Mounds State Park property, and while the mounds themselves would not be flooded, the cultural landscape would be profoundly altered, and the earthworks may become more vulnerable to erosion. The proposed project generated heated public debate about the merits of the proposed project. Some people saw it as a bold but necessary gamble to provide jobs and stimulate the economy in an area hard hit first by the bust of natural gas production and then by the closing of a major manufacturing plant. Others opposed it for its damage to sensitive habitats and rare species, its flooding of low-income neighborhoods, and its impact on valued recreational and cultural resources (Kryder-Reid 2015).

The Role of Government in Contested Heritage

Government is inextricable from cultural contestations about cultural heritage resulting from legislation, policy, and funding, as well as having direct control of, and authority over, heritage resources (Laurence 2010). This case study of Strawtown Koteewi and Mounds State Park exposes the fissures between authorized heritage discourse and the paradigms of meaning among the diverse constituencies of the sites, and it highlights the tenuous position of public governance in privileging competing cultural, economic, and social interests. The study also exemplifies the constraints and motivations of the state apparatus of heritage management.

At Strawtown, the NAGPRA claims filed by the Miami of Oklahoma led to a halt in any active excavations. At the same time, in response to a survey conducted by the Hamilton County Tourism office, the Hamilton County of Parks and Recreation constructed a massive, 50 by 50-foot-simulated excavation in poured concrete, complete with inset artifacts and features, and with soil layers indicated by different tints and dated artifacts (Fig. 12.1).

The outdoor exhibit is intended to give visitors the chance to "look through the lens of an archaeologist as they discover historic and pre-contact artifacts. House basins, hearths, and trash pits are only a few of the traces that remain" (Hamilton County 2016). The Parks Department also began constructing what is described as "full-scale, American Indian structures" representing "an American Indian village that was inhabited more than 700 years ago (Fig. 12.2)."

At Mounds, there is a similar disconnect in that when faced with deeply divisive contestation about the Mounds Reservoir project, the position of the Indiana Department of Natural Resources, which owns and runs the park, was officially "neutral." Furthermore, despite a plethora of statements from not-for-profit entities ranging from the Indiana Archaeology Council to the Indiana Forest Alliance, no government agency or entity has publicly spoken against the project (Kryder-Reid 2015).

So, what is to be learned from a county park that builds a mock dig and reconstructs an Indian village while ceasing archaeological excavations and remaining at an impasse after three years of negotiations with tribal communities? What is the significance of a state agency that has remained silent in the face of plans to flood one of the most significant cultural heritage sites in the parks system? What do these two case studies reveal about the role of government in cultural heritage management?

Fig. 12.1 Simulated 50 by 50-foot-poured concrete excavation at Strawtown Koteewi, Hamilton Co., Indiana (Photo: Elizabeth Kryder-Reid)

These cases raise several points that are important for broader investigation of government and heritage. The first is that the notion of "public heritage" needs to be disrupted. Save for rare exceptions, a heritage about which people are the most passionate is usually local, associated with places mostly meaningful to them as members of a relatively small group with well-defined ethnic boundaries and shared historical experience. Information about such heritage and the meaning and emotional responses it generates are often completely inaccessible to outsiders. Heritage is primarily experienced, understood, defined, and shared locally, but when archaeologists or other heritage specialists define heritage without collaboration with local groups it can be seen as colonizing as Smith and Waterton (2009), Zimmerman (2010), Harrison (2012), and others have argued. Furthermore, while heritage professionals and organizations have begun to implement the concepts of shared

Fig. 12.2 Reconstructed Native American settlement with bent pole and bark-covered structures at Strawtown Koteewi, Hamilton Co., Indiana (Photo: Elizabeth Kryder-Reid)

authority (Adair et al. 2011), participatory heritage (Roued-Cunliffe and Copeland 2017), democratization of heritage (Coghlan 2017), and even decolonization (Atalay 2006; Lonetree 2012), government-controlled sites appear slower to embrace these trends. Some resistance may be attributed to the maze of mandated legal and bureaucratic rules in which government institutions operate, but an even more plausible explanation is that sharing control is predicated on questioning the established authority and fundamental principles of state-derived power, particularly in colonial settings. It strikes at the fundamental nature of the relationship between state authority and citizens, and it exposes contradictions between the espoused principles of a presumed "public heritage" and the realities of proprietary and neoliberal practices of government-owned sites.

Government, an Ideology of Public Heritage, and Native Americans

These case studies expose the complexities of assumptions about what "public heritage" means (Holt 2010), and it reveals the ways in which the past as public heritage is simultaneously alienating and democratizing (Zimmerman 2011). Regarding the former, the controversies around the sites are based in fundamental ideologies of settler colonial understandings of cultural heritage and operate in ways that continue to marginalize and exclude Native people. In 2016, the Indiana park system celebrated its centennial. Its founder, Richard Lieber, was concerned that foresting and agriculture were rapidly destroying what he called the state's "original domain"—that is, its pre-European settlement landscape. He wanted to preserve its most pristine areas, which he valued as "not mere picknicking places...." [but] "rich storehouses of memories and reveries. They are guides and counsels to the weary and faltering in spirit. They are bearers of wonderful tales to him who will listen; a solace to the aged and an inspiration to the young" (Smith 1932). In Lieber's view, the parks were unquestioned expressions of manifest destiny tempered with a conservation ethic bespeaking his German origins. The pristine landscape was being preserved for the benefit of the citizens of Indiana. Not only were the origins of the earthworks themselves still being debated, but the Native peoples displaced over the previous century were marginalized from the narratives and from any decision-making process.

The cases of Strawtown Koteewi and Mounds State Park are a microcosm of the intersections of archaeology's origin as scientific colonialism (see Zimmerman 2001: 169; Atalay 2006: 280–284 for discussions) and government endorsement of such archaeological paradigms to frame the rights and responsibilities of controlling cultural resources. Besides taking land and resources as part of economic colonialism, even control of information about colonized peoples shifted to colonizers. Just as they did with land and natural resources, colonizers, acting with and without governmental sanction and support, transformed information about cultural practices, histories, and belief systems into intellectual products they thought more useful or meaningful. In the USA, the idea that the past is public heritage, and therefore part of the role of government to protect and preserve it, also reflects a settler colonial ideology that framed the development of an American identity, and along with it, an American heritage.

Many scholars and politicians have described America as a land of immigrants, which according to a metaphor in use since the late 1700s, created a cultural "melting pot" that eventually stripped away national identities, languages, and heritages in favor of a more homogeneous identity as American. To a degree this seems self-evident as an historical process, particularly among European immigrants. Others argue that assimilation often was forced and that many groups held onto their original cultural identities as long as possible. They offer that a more appropriate metaphor might be a "salad bowl" in which the core ingredients stay the same even though mixed together, with only a thin overlay of dressing that might be considered uniquely American. Others are nativists who generally are against immigration because it destroys or at least disturbs existing American cultural values. Some of them maintain that later-arriving ethnic groups should have lower political or legal status. Ironically, the Indigenous nations of the continent probably were the original nativists. They often resisted immigration, but by the early 1900s were thought to be conquered and soon to be fully assimilated with their history absorbed as part of American history. Certainly, that proved not to be the case, and many still resist when it comes to a wide range of heritage issues including repatriation and even recognition of sites of conscience, which some might think should be noncontroversial (Zimmerman 2007).

During the Progressive Era of the 1910s–1920s, the Cultural Democracy Movement, promoted by such activists as Horace Kallen (1924: 43) and W.E.B. DuBois (1940), advocated cultural pluralism (the salad bowl approach) as a way to counter the demands of Euromerican nativists for a single or "true" American culture, but also assertions of white supremacy. That struggle echoes into contemporary debates about cultural pluralism, and it created puzzling ideological contradictions about heritage. Pluralism pushed for equality and participation in cultural life and policy, that is, cultural democracy. Adams and Goldbard (1995) note that as a feature of American's thematic universe, cultural democracy, created a dynamic interaction between contending ideologies, struggling against racist articulations of monoculture and liberal ideas of the "melting pot." Cultural democracy was always an insurgent notion, pushing against dominant values. The ideas persist because its core resonates with the lived experiences of people who refuse to be dismissed or "melted down." Cultural democracy was promoted as a way to bring Indigenous people into the modern world without damaging their essence. In other words, it wanted to respect Indigenous autonomy, yet it wanted them to be part of the modern world in which everyone could recognize and share elements of identity and heritage. Cultural democracy didn't want to change Indigenous people, but that effectively essentialized them. They became "our Indians" or "America's Indians" in popular media, imagined as primitive and locked in time, and easily understood (compare with Deloria 1969: 12–16).

For many Native Americans, settler value systems associated with democracy, equality, and equal rights sit at the core of public ownership of Native homelands, Native heritage, and access to both, evidence continued colonialization and even seen to contradict the values settlers espouse. Colonization and contradiction symbolize the entire history of Native-settler interactions which has included such settler notions as *terra nullius*, and Manifest Destiny, which were rationalizes for taking Native lands, and the Mound Builder Myth, which sought to create a deep European history for North America while erasing the primacy of Native Americans on the land.[8] Native people also saw their history erased by settler scholars who did not understand the nature of Native oral tradition and assumed because there was little evidence of written language to record tribal histories that Native Americans were peoples without a history or at least were prehistoric. Native peoples developed deep and lingering distrust of anthropological and especially archaeological constructions of Native pasts (Deloria 1995). Coupled with desperate struggles for both physical and cultural survival, removal from homelands, confinement onto reservations, and a wide range of federal efforts to force Native assimilation left little power to challenge settler takeover of their heritage. Thus, Native history became American history. Native ancestral places, artifacts, and human remains became public heritage, not the heritage of particular Native nations whose ancestors were traditional owners (Zimmerman 2016). Federal law and policy supported the concept of public heritage. The 1906 Antiquities Act and creation of early National Parks during the Progressive Era included archaeological sites and objects, and eventually national monuments, historic sites, and historic landmarks, many of them centered on Native archaeological sites.

This indicates that settler society maintained a substantial interest in Native Americans, but what they learned was filtered through non-Native scholarship and popular culture such as books and especially film. During this time, Native American-presented traditional history and detail about their ancestral cultures was mostly silent for settler cultures. These voices were heard in only limited ways starting in the late 1940s with treaty-based land claims, which also proved to be legally problematic. By this time, state park systems had been developed, some of them based on nationally recognized ancestral Indian sites such as Mounds State Park.

By the time of the Civil Rights Movement starting in the early 1960s, there was realization that the American melting pot never really materialized. Ideals about equal rights, largely unmet for minority cultures led to wide-ranging social justice laws. For Indians, this mostly started in the late 1960s with a series of acts with relevance to heritage: Indian Gaming Regulatory Act; American Indian Religious Freedom Act; Arts and Craft Board; National Historic Preservation Act with amendments and regulations providing for Tribal Historic Preservation Officers (THPOs) and recognition and protection for Traditional Culture Properties (TCPs) and then into the early 1990s with the National Museum of the American Indian Act and especially NAGPRA.

What happened was a major shift in which Native Americans became "real" in terms of sovereignty over their heritage, able to tell their own stories about their pasts and able to reclaim ancestral remains, sacred objects, and items of cultural patrimony from any institutions such as museums, universities, and federal agencies. Even though NAGPRA was enacted in 1990, it does not affect private property or entities without federal involvement, nor does it have authority over Native materials held by museums or other organizations outside the USA. Worth noting is that more than thirty states also enacted Native American burial site protection and repatriation, many of them well ahead of NAGPRA.

Mounds State Park was already established and well underway with interpretation and excavation, tourism, and even limited interaction with some of the tribes for ceremonial use of the site. Strawtown Koteewi became a county park almost a decade after NAGPRA, but archaeological excavation of sites in the park and public archaeology programming began with little consultation with tribes possibly affiliated with the sites. Eventual efforts to consult with Indiana tribes, first with the federally unrecognized Miami Tribe of Indiana, which under NAGPRA were not allowed. Eventually, negotiations with the federally recognized Miami of Oklahoma led to issues discussed above. Both parks were by this time well incorporated into the local fabric, incorporating much more than archaeology into park activities and programming, which created varying heritage valuation, and controversy for each park.

GOVERNMENT, CONTESTED HERITAGE, AND STAKEHOLDERS

An examination of heritage and government must take into account the larger context of developments in advanced industrialized democracies over the past 30 years that have led to both internal and external challenges to the traditional bases of their political power. The result has been a rapidly changing political landscape characterized by "an ideological and cultural shift from collective solutions toward individualism and a *Zeitgeist* heralding private enterprise and "the market" as the superior resource allocating mechanism" (Pierre 2000: 2). At the same time, there has been a growing trend to recognize the importance of collaboration, transparency, co-production, and accountability in creating effective governance and building public value, including promoting government-to-government and interagency cooperation, public–private partnerships, and greater citizen participation (Arganoff 2012; Box 2007; Moore 1995; O'Flynn et al. 2014). In both government and for-profit sectors, there has also been a move toward privileging stakeholders in decision-making and planning processes (Freeman 1984; Bonnafous-Boucher and Rendtorff 2016). The heritage sector has similarly embraced concepts of stakeholders and public value (Comer 2015; Magliacani 2015; Manes-Rossi et al. 2016; Scott 2016). In Aotearoa New Zealand, for example, 1840 Treaty of Waitangi and the more recent passage of Treaty of Waitangi Acts of 1975 and 1985 as well as the Local Government Act 2002 helped establish a framework for Maori collaboration in decision making and for developing bicultural museum practices (Bell et al. 2017; Legget 2017; Hong 2014).

At both Mounds and Strawtown, the government officials charged with overseeing the sites were required to navigate diverse stakeholders' interests including those of residents, recreational users, heritage professionals, Native American groups with cultural affiliation to the sites, advocacy groups (e.g., Indiana Forest Alliance, Indiana Archaeology Council, Indiana Wildlife Federation) with interests in the sites' natural and cultural resources, local and state elected officials, governmental agencies (e.g., Environmental Protection Agency, National Park Service), the press, and those with economic development interests, to list only a few. Among these competing interests, there was a tension at both sites between economic development and preservation. The Mounds Lake project is particularly stark in this regard. Although the project promoters have couched the reservoir as a safe, dependable water supply for the future, the impetus of the project was and remains to stimulate the local economy. Opponents are largely preservation-driven, rallying around saving what would be destroyed by the reservoir, whether that is access to a free-flowing White River, protecting the Star Nosed mole, or concern over erosion of the mounds.

The mission of the Indiana DNR is "to manage and interpret our properties' unique natural, wildlife, and cultural resources using the principles of multiple use and preservation, while sustaining the integrity of these resources for current and future generations." But the DNR officials who have expressed opposition to Mounds Lake project off-the-record, however, must also contend not only with the local government entities that prioritize economic development, but also with a state governor and legislature that are pro-business and supportive of neoliberal notions of the role of government. In 2015, then Indiana Governor Michael Pence issued a statement supporting the reservoir project saying that "The vision for that reservoir serves both the long-term water interests of the state of Indiana, ... (and) the opportunity to develop this region in a fresh way that will attract new investment and attract people to the community" (de la Bastide 2015).

The Strawtown Koteewi case is subtler in the tensions between economic development and preservation, but they are still important factors in the Parks Department's management of the site. A closer look at the Department's mission statement is telling. It identifies residents and tourists as the target audience, and it serves their leisure and recreation needs. Staff members do this by preserving parks and offering natural resource education and services. This mission-driven goal to provide recreation for residents and tourists in turn helps drive the economic development of the county by attracting tax-paying citizens and leisure dollar-spending tourists. It enhances the reputation of the county as a desirable place to live and perhaps even helps lure those interested in more sustainable lifestyles to the less developed fringes of this Indianapolis outer suburb. From this standpoint, it is not surprising that in the face of conflict over the control of Native American cultural heritage the county invests in a mock dig and reconstructed Indian village at Strawtown. The needs and concerns of the both archaeological and Native communities have little to do with the core mission of the Hamilton County Parks and Recreation Department. It is also apparent that the logic of governmental control of these sites is predicated on a capitalist assumption of cultural resources as property. These are

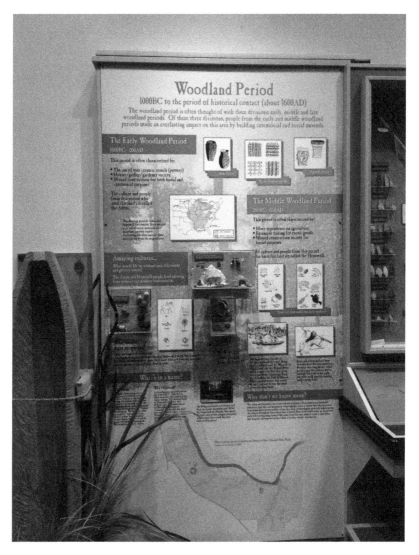

Fig. 12.3 Exhibit at the Mounds State Park Nature Center (Photo: Elizabeth Kryder-Reid)

community assets to be managed within a broader economic exchange between taxes paid by citizens and the amenities and services provided in return.

The discourse surrounding the cultural contestations at the Indiana sites is eerily similar. While the cultural continuity of the "Moundbuilders" and historic Native Americans has been established, the interpretive narratives at the parks embed the Native history in a frozen past, making little connection between the sites and living tribal communities. Furthermore, the parks gloss over altogether the history of warfare and Indian removal that created the "pristine" areas Lieber sought to protect. For example, at the Mounds State Park interpretive center, the exhibit panels tracing the history of Native Americans on the site present a relatively detailed analysis of the Adena-Hopewell cultures of the Middle Woodland. The next panel, however, in typical settler colonial narrative uses passive voice to describe the dispossession of Native lands. Under the heading "Villages, farms, interurban, amusement: this area is full of history and intrigue," the text reads, "Before the 1800s, the Miami Indians controlled much of the northern half of Indiana. By 1794 the Delaware Indians had permission from the Miami to settle on [the] land...In 1821, the majority of the Delaware left the area after the signing of the St. Mary's treaty which gave the land to the United States." The next headline is "Welcome Bronnenberg Family 1820s (Fig. 12.3)."

Given this explicit interpretation in the Mounds site, it is small wonder that the culturally affiliated Native groups have not been an integral part of the site interpretation and were marginalized in the debates over the proposed dam project.

HERITAGE AND RESISTANCE

As Laurajane Smith and other critical heritage scholars have noted, a central issue of heritage is control (Smith 2006: 276–298). In the cases of Strawtown Koteewi and Mounds State Park, we see the complexity of the struggles for control and the ways in which heritage resources materialized broader struggles for recognition, access to resources, and other symbolic representations of power. The cases also reveal the ways in which heritage was deployed as a strategic asset that provided moral weight or political cover for what were more important but less defensible concerns. These contestations also highlight the resilience of both

Native and non-Native citizens to activate heritage as a democratizing force and a form of resistance in the face government authority.

The proposal for the dam project that was promoted by a strong coalition of business and political leaders was opposed by an equally strong coalition of citizens who formed organizations such as the "Heart of the River," turned out in droves for public hearings, and staged protests such as the free-flowing river paddle. They mobilized social media and formed alliances with environmental and preservation organizations. The proposal for Mounds Lake is not dead, but as of January 2018, it has been stalled. Clarke Kahlo, one of the organizers of Heart of the River Coalition, which opposed the dam, explained their strategy, "We used a pretty basic model....You form a group, you name a steering committee, and you start reaching out. It does take a little courage to step forward to critique and then to challenge some of these publicly subsidized projects" (Neal 2015). We (Kryder-Reid and Zimmerman with analysis by Jeremy Foutz) conducted a network analysis of the discourse that reinforced Khalo's characterization of the grassroots opposition and particularly the significance of social media as a powerful communication channel for political action in this battle over local control of natural and cultural resources. A discourse analysis of the texts revealed that most prominent topics were economic development, water, and the role of government (Kryder-Reid 2015).[9] By contrast, as this mapping of the topic networks illustrates (Fig. 12.4), cultural resources had much less weight in the discourse and fewer connections among the topics.

Despite the relatively low frequency and lack of connection of cultural heritage language in the discourse, it was nonetheless deployed strategically as the authorization of the Mounds State Park on the National Register of Historical Places was based on significance of the mounds and related cultural features. An area of legally protected nature preserve and fen, as well as the presence of an endangered bat species, were similarly invoked in opposition to the dam project. Ultimately, heritage became a tool that people opposing the dam project for a variety of reasons used to get what they wanted.

The word frequency tables, network maps, and word clouds (Fig. 12.5) were evocative visualizations of the discourse around these sites, but an equally significant finding of the study was the relative silence of Native peoples both as speakers in the Mounds Reservoir debate and as visibly affected communities.

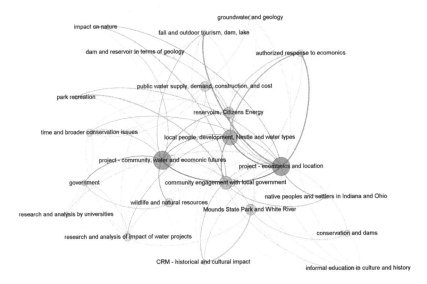

Fig. 12.4 Topic networks map of the Mounds State Park and reservoir discourse analysis (Jeremy W. Foutz, STEAM Workgroup)

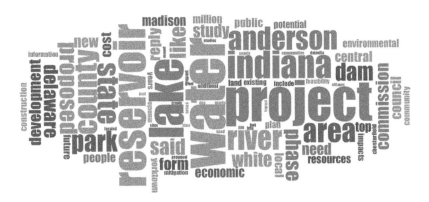

Fig. 12.5 Word cloud of Mounds reservoir project discourse excluding the terms "mound" and "Mounds State Park" (Jeremy W. Foutz, STEAM Workgroup)

Lack of understanding of the culturally affiliated Indigenous groups is reflected in the Phase 1 feasibility study's recommendation to consult "with the Adena and the Hopewell," terms applied to cultural traditions dating from 1000 BC to 500 AD. One of the few sources to call attention to the marginalization of Native people throughout the process was a peer review of the Phase 2 study authored by group of Ball StateUniversity faculty.

> The current Phase II study has not engaged with effected [sic] communities, including those with legal, historical or cultural links to the Mounds sites, additional archaeological sites and the White River watershed. Effected [sic] communities potentially include federally recognized tribes in Michigan, Kansas and Oklahoma and individual tribal citizens living within Indiana…, this is not only a matter of how tribes are treated appropriately under NEPA. It is also an environmental justice issue for the region. (Anderson et al. 2015: 3)

While there will inevitably be other contests over control of Mounds State Park and Strawtown Koteewi, the current situation suggests that citizen and Indigenous resistance has influenced the government's management of the sites. The dam project is not proceeding, at this point, and Hamilton County Parks and Recreation agreed to repatriate 90,000 artifacts to the Miami of Oklahoma, an assemblage that goes beyond the legal mandates of the NAGPRA requirements to return objects that are sacred, of cultural patrimony, or related to funerary contexts and instead honors the spirit of the agreement to return objects because they are significant to the Miami people.

CONCLUSION

The staff of Mounds and Strawtown Koteewi are dedicated heritage professionals who have committed themselves to preserving and interpreting the sites. The Hamilton County Parks and Recreation and Indiana Department of Natural Resources leadership have similarly invested in providing a wide range of opportunities that improve the quality of life of their citizens through access to the sites. The debate around these sites highlights how governmental entities, including tribal, county, and state governments, navigate the often-conflicting agendas and interests of these groups. The debate also exposes the fundamental ideologies that frame a "public heritage" within an unspoken settler colonial narrative and that appear to accede to economic interests consistent with neoliberal trends in government. As well, the case highlights the complex dynamics of resistance to governmental actions as grassroots opponents and tribal representatives mobilized cultural heritage through legal and rhetorical strategies to achieve their aims. These two state and local governmental entities are, like most in the US government-run heritage sector, a long way from the public accountability being implemented in cultural institutions in New Zealand and other parts of the world. But the messy and contentious battles over the value and control of heritage in each case also demonstrate the resilient power of citizens to influence decisions when they feel the government is not acting of, by, or, for the people.

NOTES

1. This project was supported by Indiana University's New Frontiers in the Arts & Humanities Program, a program of the Office of the Vice President for Research funded by the Office of the President. Elizabeth Kryder-Reid is the PI. Co-PIs Elizabeth Wood and Jeremy W. Foutz, principal at STEAM Workgroup, helped to develop the research methodology. Wood facilitated the focus group sessions. Collaborator Larry Zimmerman served as consultant for work with Native American communities. Foutz designed and administered the survey and conducted the statistical analysis of these data. Emma Marston was a graduate research assistant for the first six months of the project. A preliminary version of this analysis was presented by Elizabeth Kryder-Reid at the ACHS Conference in Montreal in June, 2016, in the session "Cultural Contestation: Politics and Governance of Heritage." Zimmerman and Kryder-Reid collaborated on writing this article. We greatly appreciate the assistance of the staff at MSP and SKP, particularly Ted Tapp and Christy Brocken, for generously sharing documents, hosting the focus groups, helping disseminate information and recruit participants, and for their willingness to investigate stakeholder-defined values of the sites they administer.
2. Throughout this chapter, the authors sometimes refer to the parks by common local reference, that is, Mounds State Park will sometimes be shortened to 'Mounds' and Strawtown-Koteewi to 'Strawtown'. Similarly, full site names will be used where a more formal designation is useful.
3. Hamilton County had a population of 274,569 according to the 2010 census and is the fastest growing of Indiana's 92 counties.

4. The terms Adena-Hopewell, Archaic, Late Woodland, Oliver Phase, and the like are archaeological taxonomic labels, not tribal names. Clear links between tribes at the time of European contact and archaeological taxa used in the Eastern USA do not extend earlier than about 800 AD; although tribes certainly moved around before contact, there is no reason to believe that ancestors of the tribes living in the region at the time of contact had not lived in their homelands for millennia as their oral traditions state. See Zimmerman and Makes Strong Move (2008) for a discussion.

5. Funding for the projects included a National Park Service grant for tenth anniversary excavations at Strawtown (over 4300 visitors) and a three-year National Science funded "Research Experience for Undergraduates (REU)" with Indiana University-Purdue University Ft. Wayne (IPFW).

6. As an indication of the complex cultural affiliations with Indiana, under NAGPRA regulations, the Hamilton County Department of Parks and Recreation is responsible for notifying the Absentee-Shawnee Tribe of Indians of Oklahoma; Delaware Nation, Oklahoma; Eastern Shawnee Tribe of Oklahoma; Miami Tribe of Oklahoma; Pokagon Band of Potawatomi Indians, Michigan and Indiana; and the Shawnee Tribe regarding published notices.

7. See Sikich (2017) for a summary story. The online version has internal links to earlier stories, photographs, and video about the issue. Online commenters claimed bias and challenged aspects of reporting in the earlier stories.

8. Discussion of this complex history is well beyond the scope of this paper. See Silverberg (1968), Thomas (2000), and Kehoe (1998: 64–81) for more detail, especially the early development of American anthropology as the primary heritage discipline that documents pre-contact Native American history and culture. For the development of federal law in relationship to Native Americans, see Wilkins and Lomawaima (2001).

9. We collected texts from various sources to define a corpus for our analysis. We then used a Java-based computer program called MALLET (MAchine Learning for LanguagE Toolkit) to determine the discourse topics present in the corpus. Beginning from the assumption of a random distribution of word, the software looks at the frequency, position, and connections to discover which words are used in connection with each other. With each program iteration—standard practice is 500—the program refines a list of associated words around central topics.

REFERENCES

Adair, B., Filene, B., & Koloski, L. (2011). *Letting Go? Sharing Historical Authority in a User-Generated World*. Philadelphia: Pew Center for Arts & Heritage.

Adams, D., & Goldbard, A. (1995). *Cultural Democracy: An Introduction to an Idea*. http://www.wwcd.org/cd2.html. Accessed 30 June 2012.

Agranoff, R. (2012). *Collaborating to Manage: A Primer for the Public Sector*. Washington, DC: Georgetown University Press.

Anderson, B., et al. (2015, March 4). Executive Summary, *Memorandum for Record Subject: Mounds Lake Reservoir Phase II Study Preliminary Peer Review*. Muncie, IN: Ball State University.

Atalay, S. (2006). Indigenous Archaeology as a Decolonizing Practice. *American Indian Quarterly, 30*(3), 280–310.

Bell, R., et al. (Eds.). (2017). *The Treaty on the Ground: Where We Are Headed and Why It Matters*. Auckland: Massey University Press.

Bonnafous-Boucher, M., & Dahl Rendtorff, J. (2016). *Stakeholder Theory: A Model for Strategic Management*. Cham: Springer.

Box, R. C. (Ed.). (2007). *Democracy and Public Administration*. Armonk, NY: M.E. Sharpe.

Cochran, D. R., & McCord. B. K. (2001). *The Archaeology of Anderson Mounds, Mounds State Park, Anderson, Indiana. Reports of Investigation 61*. Muncie, IN: Archaeological Resources Management Services, Ball State University.

Coghlan, R. (2017, June 16). 'My Voice Counts Because I'm Handsome.' Democratising the Museum: The Power of Museum Participation. *International Journal of Heritage Studies*. https://doi.org/10.1080/135272 58.2017.1320772.

Comer, D. C. (2015). Archaeology as a Global Public Good and Local Identity Good. In P. F. Biehl, D. C. Comer, C. Prescott, & H. A. Soderland (Eds.), *Identity and Heritage: Contemporary Challenges in a Globalized World* (pp. 11–26). Cham: Springer.

de la Bastide, K. (2015, June 10). Pence: Reservoir Proposal Has Merit: Anderson Council to Consider Joining Commission. *The Herald Bulletin*. http://www.heraldbulletin.com/news/local_news/pence-reservoir-proposal-has-merit/article_77ec4aca-0f9a-11e5-a0c1-ef404f8243b7.html. Accessed 30 May 2016.

Deloria, V., Jr. (1969). *Custer Died for Your Sins: An Indian Manifesto*. New York: Avon.

Deloria, V., Jr. (1995). *Red Earth, White Lies: Native Americans and the Myth of Scientific Fact*. New York: Scribner.

DuBois, W. E. B. (1940). *Dusk of Dawn: An Essay Toward and Autobiography of a Race Concept*. New York: Harcourt, Brace & Co.

Freeman, E. R. (1984). *Strategic Management*. Marshfield, MA: Pitman Publishing.

Hamilton County Website. n.d. *Koteewi Trace*. http://www.visithamiltoncounty.com/listings/Koteewi-Trace/1854/0/. Accessed 30 May 2016.

Harrison, R. (2012). *Heritage: Critical Approaches*. New York: Routledge.

Holt, S. A. (2010). The Past as a Place: Challenging Private Ownership of History in the United States. In L. Jensen, J. Leerseen, & M. Mathijsen (Eds.), *Free Access to the Past: Romanticism, Cultural Heritage and the Nation* (pp. 279–289). Leiden: Brill.

Hong, B. (2014). National Cultural Indicators in New Zealand. *Cultural Trends, 23*(2), 93–108.

Kallen, H. (1924). *Culture and Democracy in the United States*. New York: Boni & Liveright.

Kehoe, A. B. (1998). *The Land of Prehistory: A Critical History of American Archaeology*. New York: Routledge.

Kryder-Reid, E. (2015, November). *Caring About and Caring for Heritage Landscapes: Two Contested Sites in Indiana*. Paper presented at the American Anthropological Association Annual Meeting, Denver, CO.

Kryder-Reid, E., Foutz, J. W., Wood, E., & Zimmerman, L. J. (2017, June 22). 'I Just Don't Ever Use That Word': Investigating Stakeholders' Understanding of Heritage. *International Journal of Heritage Studies*. https://doi.org/10.1080/13527258.2017.1339110.

Laurence, A. (2010). Heritage as a Tool of Government. In R. Harrison (Ed.), *Understanding the Politics of Heritage* (pp. 81–114). Manchester: Manchester University Press.

Legget, J. (2017). Shared Heritage, Shared Authority, Shared Accountability? Co-creating Museum Performance Criteria as a Means of Embedding 'Shared Authority'. *International Journal of Heritage Studies*. Published online [date TBA].

Lonetree, A. (2012). *Decolonizing Museums: Representing Native America in National and Tribal Museums*. Durham: University of North Carolina.

Magliacani, M. (2015). *Managing Cultural Heritage: Ecomuseum, Community, Governance and Social Accountability*. New York: Palgrave Macmillan.

Manes-Rossi, F., Allini, A., Spanò, R., & Dainelli, F. (2016). Changing Performance Measurement Towards Enhanced Accountability: Insights from the British Museum. *International Journal of Public Sector Performance Management, 2*(4), 331–347.

McCullough, R. G. (Ed.). (2011). *Tenth Anniversary of Archaeology in a Public Venue at Strawtown Koteewi Park, Hamilton County, Indiana: 2010 Archaeological Investigations at the Strawtown Enclosure (12H883) and 12H1052. Reports of Investigations 1101*. Washington, DC: U.S. Department of the Interior, Historic Preservation Fund.

Moore, M. H. (1995). *Creating Public Value: Strategic Management in Government.* Cambridge: Harvard University Press.

Mounds State Park, Interpretive Master Plan. (2011). http://in.gov/dnr/park-lake/files/sp-Mounds_State_Park_IMP_2011.pdf. Accessed 17 May 2016.

Neal, A. (2015, October 12). From the South Wall: Watchdogs Win. *Indiana Policy Review.* http://inpolicy.org/2015/10/andrea-neal-watchdogs-win-against-favored-projects/. Accessed 30 May 2016.

O'Flynn, J., Blackman, D., & Halligan, J. (Eds.). (2014). *Crossing Boundaries in Public Management and Policy: The International Experience.* London: Routledge.

Pierre, J. (2000). Introduction: Understanding Governance. In J. Pierre (Ed.), *Debating Governance: Authority, Steering and Democracy* (pp. 1–12). Oxford: Oxford University Press.

Roued-Cunliffe, H., & Copeland, A. (Eds.). (2017). *Participatory Heritage.* London: Facet Publishing.

Scott, C. A. (Ed.). (2016). *Museums and Public Value: Creating Sustainable Futures.* New York: Routledge.

Sikich, C. (2017, June 17). Hamilton County to Return Artifacts Excavated from Strawtown Park to Miami Tribe. *Indianapolis Star.* https://www.indystar.com/story/news/local/hamilton-county/2017/06/07/hamilton-county-return-artifacts-excavated-strawtown-park-miami-tribe/373209001/. Accessed 11 Jan 2018.

Silverberg, R. (1968). *Mound Builders of Ancient America: The Archaeology of a Myth.* Greenwich, CT: New York Graphics Society.

Smith, D. (1932). *The Mound Builders of Indiana and the Mounds State Park in Madison County Near Anderson, Indiana.* Indianapolis: Department of Conservation, State of Indiana, Division of Lands, and Waters.

Smith, L. (2006). *The Uses of Heritage.* London: Routledge.

Smith, L., & Waterton, E. (2009). *Heritage, Communities, and Archaeology.* London: Duckworth.

Squire, E. G., & Hamilton Davis, E. (1848). *Ancient Monuments of the Mississippi Valley.* New York: Bartlett & Welford.

Thomas, D. H. (2000). *Skull Wars: Kennewick Man, Archaeology, and the Battle for Native American Identity.* New York: Basic Books.

Wilkins, D. E., & Lomawaima, K. T. (2001). *Uneven Ground: American Indian Sovereignty and Federal Law.* Norman: University of Oklahoma Press.

Zimmerman, L. J. (2001). Usurping Native American Voice. In T. Bray (Ed.), *The Future of the Past: Archaeologists, Native Americans, and Repatriation* (pp. 169–184). New York: Garland Publishing.

Zimmerman, L. J. (2007). Plains Indians and Resistance to 'Public' Heritage Commemoration of Their Pasts. In H. Silverman & D. F. Ruggles (Eds.), *Cultural Heritage and Human Rights* (pp. 144–158). New York: Springer.

Zimmerman, L. J. (2010). Archaeology Through the Lens of the Local. In A. Stroulia & S. B. Sutton (Eds.), *Archaeology in Situ: Local Perspectives on Archaeology, Archaeologists, and Sites in Greece* (pp. 473–480). Lanham, MD: Lexington Books.

Zimmerman, L. J. (2011). *Is the 'The Past is a Public Heritage' Democratizing or Alienating?* Paper presented at the American Anthropological Association Annual Meeting, Montreal. http://www.academia.edu/16637059/Is_The_Past_is_a_Public_Heritage_Democratizing_or_Alienating. Accessed 11 Jan 2018.

Zimmerman, L. J. (2016). Repatriating Buhl Woman, Keeping Our Word, and Making NAGPRA Work. In M. J. Trubitt (Ed.), *Research, Preservation, Communication: Honoring Thomas J. Green on his Retirement from the Arkansas Archeological Survey. Research Series, 14.* (pp. 9–17). Fayeteville: Arkansas Archaeological Survey.

Zimmerman, L. J., & Dawn Makes Strong Move. (2008). Archaeological Taxonomy, Native Americans, and Scientific Landscapes of Clearance: A Case Study from Northeastern Iowa. In A. Gazin-Schwartz & A. P. Smith (Eds.), *Landscapes of Clearance* (pp. 190–211). Walnut Creek, CA: Left Coast Press.

CHAPTER 13

Ethno-Nationalism Revisited? A Journey Through the New Estonian National Museum (*Eesti Rahva Muuseum*)

Emilia Pawłusz

INTRODUCTION

One of the signs that a significant amount of time has passed since Estonia became an independent westernized state is the growing number of modern buildings in the skyline of the capital city of Tallinn and the second largest city Tartu. Most of these new buildings house hotels, shopping malls, and multinational corporations. It is definitely prestigious to have an office in one of them, as they stand for innovation and the successful transition of this once Soviet country into a modern, fast-growing, and digitally advanced economy. Early in the nineties Estonian political elites took the fast transformation of the country into a western liberal economy as their primary strategic goal. The transformation was rather successful with Estonia joining the NATO and EU in 2004 and having a well-functioning, stable state. The notion of innovativeness, progressiveness, and modernity, propagated in its nation

E. Pawłusz (✉)
Lodz, Poland

© The Author(s) 2018
J. Rodenberg and P. Wagenaar (eds.), *Cultural Contestation*,
Palgrave Studies in Cultural Heritage and Conflict,
https://doi.org/10.1007/978-3-319-91914-0_13

branding campaigns, as well as its main political figures like the former President, Toomas Hendrik Ilves is what defines the image of Estonia over the last 20 years. At the same time, independence also brought a turn to cultural nationalism, the notion that the newly recovered state belongs to and protects the Estonian nation, its language, and cultural heritage. This created an ongoing tension between a romantic ideology of an old nation defined through its history and peasant heritage and a democratic, fully transformed state of liberal values. Some called it an "ethnic democracy" that ignores the de facto multicultural and multinational composition of the country. One-third of Estonia's population are Russian speakers, the majority of whom had migrated to Estonia during the Soviet period. In some areas, Russian is the most heard language of communication. Against this backdrop, it is interesting to look at the new Estonian National Museum in Tartu. It is one of the three great modern buildings for cultural and educational institutions (next to KUMU Art Museum and the Estonian Academy of Music and Theater in Tallinn) erected in recent years. The Estonian National Museum (ENM) as an institution was established before Estonia's first statehood in 1918. It was partly dismantled during the Soviet times and reopened in 1994 as an ethnographic museum housing material objects of Estonian peasant culture, the basic element of national romantic imaginary. In October 2016, the museum was moved to a newly built structure, designed by a team of international architects. The new building with its sharp edges and forms makes a bold architectural statement, as do the new permanent exhibitions. In this paper, I will discuss the remade national narratives presented in the museum. Drawing from a guided visit to the museum as well as a presentation by staff and semiformal interviews with selected staff members, I argue that the new museum is an architectural but also an ideological attempt to catch up with the liberal modernity narrative. It is an attempt to actualize the concept of the Estonian nation and pronounce it through the lens of the present and the lives of ordinary citizens, rather than solely the ethno-national narrative of the nation.

Museums in Identity Making

All museums tell stories. National museums, run by the state, usually tell *national* stories. They are designated sites where national culture and history are defined, and where national heroes, places of importance, and grand events are named. There is an agreement between scholars that museums are embedded in existing structures and discourses but for the most part, they are the sites of creating, rather than simply retelling the national past and heritage (Kaplan 1994; Smith 2006; Knell et al. 2011). Using Pierre Nora's concept (1989, 1996: 6), museums may be called *sites of memory*—"embodiments of a commemorative conscious that survives in a history." They educate about the collective desires of what, who, and how to remember in the current sociopolitical context. Thus museums similarly to archives and libraries are places of political activity, even if this might not be explicitly acknowledged (Brown and Davis-Brown 1998). National museums have been analyzed as sites of symbolic nation-building (Kolsto 2014; Datunashvili 2017), where the boundaries of who we are as a nation are defined and presented with the authority of a public institution (Anderson 1991; Smith 2006).

Since early nineties, museums across the post-Soviet states (as well as monuments and memorials) have formed a part of identity politics, which political elites of the newly emerged states employed to define the gravity of the transition into independence, as well as symbolically reclaim national history, culture, and heritage (Forest and Johnson 2002; Velmet 2011; Tamm 2013; Datunashvili 2017). In countries like the Baltic states, where the tradition of statehood and national museums predated the Soviet times, museum objects and stories serve as evidence of the continuity of the nation and the state, as well as witnesses of Soviet oppression (Velmet 2011; Runnel et al. 2014). Such chronological narratives celebrated the resilience of the nation against all odds but also have a "healing effect": They are a way to commemorate and work through the sense of historical injustice and collective trauma.

This paper looks into the case of the Estonian National Museum, an institution older than the Estonian state itself and which that has been significantly transformed with its reopening in October 2016. The Estonian National Museum is a state institution administered and accountable to the Ministry of Culture. Its main activities (collections and research) are funded by the state. However, since its relocation to the new building and reopening, about 40% of its annual budget are revenues from tickets, services, renting out conference space, etc. Apart from managing its rich collection, the museum aims to be a center for research and education. Its social goals include enhancing democratic dialogue about the past and memory of it, as well as promoting the concept of an open museum, an inclusive institution which takes part in important debates in society. The use of modern technology and focus on innovation are also emphasized in its goals. ENM declares support for the principles of the European cultural policy in developing multicultural diversity and cultural identity. (Estonian National Museum, www. erm.ee). In the context of the Estonian society, this can be read as relating primarily to the issue of integration and equal treatment of Russian speakers. At the moment, the museum formally does not participate in any particular state policy or program related to the issue of minorities integration and increasing social cohesiveness, however as stated in its strategy for development and confirmed by the staff, the museum is actively working with and welcoming Russian language schools and visitors. As the main center for heritage research, it is one of the key state actors *creating* (as opposed to displaying) discourses about national pasts, historical memory, and national culture.

The remaining part of the paper is structured as follows. First, the history of the museum against the backdrop of a common understanding of Estonian identity will be discussed. Next, the museum of today will be addressed, analyzing the change of identity narratives, the role of the museum, and its potential reception in the society.

ESTONIAN NATIONAL MUSEUM IN THE CONTEXT OF THE NATIONAL MOVEMENT

To better understand the National Museum, it is important to set it within a wider concept of nation-building and common perception of national identity in Estonia. Estonia is a country where the ethnic understanding of the nation is strong and is often taken for granted. To a large extent, the formation of the modern Estonian nation followed the model of Ruritania, proposed by Gellner (1983). Namely, a 19th peasant society located within a bigger political entity (Empire of Megalomania) develops a national consciousness conceived by emerging national elites. Under the pressure of industrialization and consequent migration of people to towns, some Ruritanians become teachers, pastors, and scholars who in the spirit of romantic nationalism create the sense of nationhood and shared past amongst Ruritanians. The development of media, public schooling, and national literature supports the process massively creating one national audience. The formerly peasant language becomes elevated to a literary language (Anderson 1991). Folk culture becomes of interest to amateur ethnographers who set off to the country to "collect," describe, and classify songs, dances, beliefs, as well as objects or craft techniques according to their regional provenience. This meticulously collected peasant culture becomes the cornerstone of the future national culture, further elaborated on by the growing cultural and social elites. Finally, in propitious political times, Ruritanians achieve the ultimate goal of national awakening—a sovereign nation-state.

Estonia became independent for the first time in 1918. After 20 years of relative prosperity and development, it was forcibly annexed by the Soviet Union in 1940. In the 20-year interwar time of independence, the notion of Estonian identity has been elaborated and institutionalized through museums, heritage institutions, and public events. One of the major events that shaped the notion of Estonianness for generations to come has been the national song and dance celebration (Kuutma 1996; Brüggeman and Kasekamp 2008; Šmidchens 2014; Pawłusz 2016). It is a nation-wide gathering of (mostly) amateur choirs and folk dancers of all ages during which national songs and dances are collectively performed. The song celebration was first organized in 1869 and since then it gradually became a platform where "the nation meets." In the interwar time, the song celebration was expanded to an institution of national importance. The dance celebration was added and the whole event became the major representation of the nation and its ancient folk heritage.

Another major national institution of the interwar time was the Estonian National Museum. It was set up in 1909 in Tartu, the cradle of the Estonian national movement. The story of the location of the museum has always been very symbolic and provides great insight into how the place is perceived today. In the 1920s, the museum was located in a manor (so-called Raadi manor) that once belonged to a Baltic German family. The manor had been first given to the University of Tartu which shared it with the new museum (Runnel et al. 2014: 21). The first exhibition, in the spirit of the romantic national movement, was ethnographic and pictured the life of Estonian peasants. The placement of the Estonian national museum in a Baltic-German manor had an important symbolic significance: It denoted the end of the cultural and political supremacy of Baltic German elites that had ruled over what is today Estonia for many centuries. Interestingly, the Baltic German former owner of the manor was interested in flying and built a small airfield around it. Years later the airfield made the area militarily attractive to the Soviets. They established an air force base there and closed the site to visitors. Meanwhile, the museum collections were kept in various churches and storage spaces. The museum's work, although scattered, continued in various locations in Tartu. The situation changed during the period of Perestroika. As Runnel et al. (2014: 22) describe, after a public demonstration in 1988 which called for the National Museum to be restored in Raadi, the Soviet army partially withdrew from the site, which was subsequently re-appropriated and turned into the "Estonian National Museum at Raadi."

However, the manor house was long gone as it had been burned down during the war and the site around it was destroyed during the years of its military use. A temporary exhibition of the ENM was opened in 1994 in the center of Tartu. In an official presentation I attended at the new museum in 2016, the staff described the first exhibition as romantic and nationalist. It pictured the Estonian nation as an ethnographic, ethnic group that shares a particular culture visualized in a myriad of everyday objects, clothes, and folklore. The time of the Soviet occupation was not covered. The speaker remarked that "We couldn't have done it otherwise. Back then everybody had to support the nation. There was a lot of enthusiasm." The peasant "ideology," a term used by her, played the central role in the narrative of the exhibition. Such a definition of culture as a static characteristic of a group of people (ethnic or national) perceived as a real community is characteristic not only to the Romantic vision of the nation but also to the Soviet one (Adams 1999; Hirsch 2005; Seljamaa 2012). In the Soviet cultural policies, nations were conceived as tangible, historic communities whose culture was to be preserved in a manner dictated by the state (Adams 2010; Isaacs and Polese 2016). This most often led to a folkloricized and historicized representation of national and ethnic heritages, which the authorities perceived as apolitical enough not to upset the communist ideology. Thus, it can be argued that the first exhibition of ENM was a mixture of the early independence enthusiasm, traces of Romantic nationalism and the Soviet folkloricized concept of the nation.

Contested Remembering: The New Museum Concept

Raadi airfield, as explained by one of the museum staff, for many locals is still a symbol of the Soviet occupation. The area around it is one of the least desired to live in. In the late nineties, it was decided that the new ENM would be built elsewhere, in the city center. The new project was chosen but never realized. Instead, some of the collection was stored at Raadi which, as Runnel et al. (2014) point out, turned the public opinion in favor of rebuilding the museum there. When it was decided to do so in 2003, the decision was welcomed as a sign of justice, reclaiming national memory, and "the museum became now the material, bodily manifestation of the nation" (ibid.: 23).

The architectural competition for the museum building was won by a project named "Memory field" proposed by a team of international architects Dan Dorell, Lina Ghotmeh, and Tsuyoshi Tane. On the museum website, the project is described in the following way,

> The authors of the project "Memory Field" based their idea upon Estonia's dramatic past – by denying signs from this era the Soviet occupation cannot, nor must not be erased from the nation's memory: they should instead be given a new and hopeful meaning. The former runway included in the project area – the sign of occupation – takes the role of a dramatic space. It is not only a runway, but a historic space scarred by military use. In order to give the space a more powerful 'voice', the empty space is extended by the new open building which expands along the runway. Its slightly inclined roof symbolizes rising to the sky, moving towards the future. (ENM, www.erm.ee)

The mission of the new museum is not to negate the Soviet past but to embrace it and discuss it. The project raised a considerable public debate which is presented in detail by Runnel et al. (2014). While some thought it is time to face the negative aspects of the national past, others preferred to stick to the familiar, secure, and idyllic ethnographic narrative of the nation, "unspoiled" by the Soviet occupation. Although the public debate was hot, the "public" as such was not really consulted and the new concept for the museum is primarily the work of museum workers and architects (ibid.: 28–29).

To my question of how the new museum is different from the previous one, one of the staff answered that in the new museum they tried to let go of the romantic, peasant idea of folk and focus on the present. Moreover, the museum wants to be a place of debate, it wants to pose questions to the visitor and make him/her reflect upon the recent past. In that sense, she said, the museum presents positive, neutral but also negative experiences of people who lived in Estonia through different times. She concluded though, that people "do not understand it yet." This passage reveals some discrepancies between the academic, postmodern discourse of museum workers and established national discourses in society. In her view, the museum should be a place of change and reflection, and therefore talking about negative aspects of Estonian recent history is necessary. This approach marks a departure from the grand discourse of Estonian nationalism in the 1990s in which the Soviet times were defined as foreign, illegal, and a violation of the national development (Pettai 2007). Yet, as some ethnographic studies show (Seliverstova 2017; Pfoser 2015; Martinez 2016), the Soviet times are still very present in individual and family memories, in everyday life (think for example of bazaars), in the landscape of Estonian towns. Thus, for some the policy of removing the Soviet times from the national memory is simply alienating and far from their everyday life experience. Perhaps the dialogical attitude of the National Museum is an attempt to reclaim some space for stories, perspectives, and opinions that have been largely silenced in the first 20 years of independence.

Letting Go of the Grand Narrative

The staff of the ENM are aware of their important position in shaping what people perceive as "Estonian." As informal nation-builders, they name heritage, narrate it, and present it in hierarchies of importance. As one museum worker remarked, even if the museum is a state institution, its goal is not to cherish the state. Instead, the new museum puts emphasis on everyday lives and experiences of various peoples that lived in the territory of Estonia throughout the ages. The guide that led my group through the exhibition stressed it even more explicitly, saying that the intention of the museum is to present not only the Estonian nation but other, even the smallest of nationalities that have lived in Estonia. This has an important consequence in how the exhibition is constructed. While the previous museum mainly exhibited objects related to the Estonian rural past and folk culture, in the new one this section is one of many and is significantly less emphasized. Instead, the main exhibition "Encounters" takes a reversed chronological order (from today to the stone age) and focuses on the everyday life of ordinary people in the context of changing political regimes. For example, when one enters the exhibition, one of the centrally located objects is an office chair of one of the creators of Skype who is Estonian. Next to it, information about e-residency and e-governance is displayed, echoing the heavily marketed branding concept of Estonia as an e-state (Pawłusz and Polese 2017).

The focus on ordinary people and the reversed chronology are intended to make the visitor feel closer to the lives and experiences of people in the past. As remarked by one of the staff, the focus here is not on nationality but on human experience as connecting the past and today.

The part of the exhibition with the reversed chronological order is called "Journey in time." It is organized in one hall and the transition between historical eras feels very fluid. Its spatial arrangement decidedly influences the way the exhibition can be read. Objects representing different times are next to each other. The Skype creator's chair, a bunch of valuable objects from Soviet times, a multimedia board with an anecdote about the first president after independence, and an old ATM are only a few examples of objects located in close proximity, but referring to national narratives that are popularly perceived as far from each other. While some of them bring to mind the Soviet occupation, others bring forth an image of Estonia in today's globalized world. The act of placing them next to each other without an explicit linear narrative is rather unexpected and proposes a novel perspective—that they are elements of the same human experience, leaving the national story in the background.

The treatment of the Soviet period deserves some comment. While in the hegemonic narrative the Soviet times are described from the perspective of the corrupt political regime, persecution of opposition and suppression of language and national culture, the ENM offers a much "lighter" take on this time. For example, the alienation of Estonia from the West is shown through an installation resembling a radio which even if turned on to receive Western stations, somehow "automatically" moves back to the East. Another interesting object that has been donated to the museum by a private person is a pair of jeans (Pic. 1). The guide told a story of a young girl whose desire was to have a pair of jeans before joining the university. Below the object one can read about the wider context of informal purchases of jeans in the Soviet period, as well as their symbolic meaning—the capitalist West. The story presents jeans as a symbol of desires and aspirations of Soviet youth. What is interesting is that the stories about the Soviet era are personal, not entirely negative, more pluralistic and sometimes even funny. They are not limited solely to Estonia but refer to a wider "Soviet" experience as in the case of the jeans—a symbol of the West in many communist countries (Fig. 13.1).

The exhibition continues moving backward through history. In Estonian museums which I have during my work in Estonia, the

Fig. 13.1 A pair of Soviet era jeans exhibited at Estonian National Museum. Photo: author

eighteenth and nineteenth centuries are usually pictured as times of Russification, as well as the beginning of the national movement. Again, ENM offers a different angle—the exhibition portrays, for example, ways of spending leisure time in the nineteenth century and early twentieth century to make the point that by then Estonians were no longer serfs tied to their land but had more spare time and moved to towns.

An interesting aspect of the exhibition is its temporal division. According to the standard narrative, it would be subdivided according to who ruled the country ("German times," "Tsarist times," "First independence," "Soviet Estonia," etc.) making it the main factor that defined the lives of the people. In the current exhibition, the context of the political regime is more in the background. While the exhibition mentions all grand political events, it does not use them to construct the main story line as a journey of the nation through times. Instead, it emphasizes cultural and social history, for example food and leisure, religious life, as well as the history of books and literacy in Estonia. For instance, instead of late medieval "German times," the exhibition talks about "the time of books," reorienting the attention again toward the history of human experience, rather than the Estonian nation. Moreover, the emphasis on the written word contrasts the traditional emphasis on the Estonian peasant culture as predominantly oral and reproduced through songs. The exhibition finishes with the Iron Age and Stone Age, which are narrated using mainly archaeological finds from the region presented in an attractive multimedia form.

THE STATE ON THE SIDE

When walking along the "Journey in time" exhibition in the main hall, one can enter several related exhibits arranged in small open rooms within the hall. This spatial arrangement makes it possible to move around the museum freely, ignoring any chronology. These "side" spaces house three sections directly related to the Estonian nation and state. One is the traditional exhibition of material culture of the folk of the nineteenth century arranged in an attractive, dynamic way. The main objects exhibited are folk costumes and decorations, as well as farm objects. The second room allows the visitor to explore the topic of runo singing, a traditional way of singing still practiced in some parts of Estonia and one of the core elements of traditional oral culture. The two sections are the conceptual link between the new and old national museum and echo to the popular understanding of "Estonian culture." The third room exhibits state symbols, from presidential awards and orders to national flags. There is a separate room where the first Estonian flag is exhibited (Fig. 13.2).

The flag is a few meters in length and is the only object in the room. It is displayed in a glass showcase, and the lights in the room are dimmed to preserve the original colors of the flag. This special display of the national flag makes it impossible to miss it. It strengthens the high, extraordinary, and almost sacral status of this object. The caption below the flag tells the story of how the blue–black–white three-color was adapted as the national flag and hidden in a private house during the Soviet times. The original flag is a materialization of the national continuity through time. The way it is displayed makes a strong statement about its value and educates the visitor it is the main national symbol and treasure. This room is the most explicit form of nation-building applied in the museum. At the same time, it is located on the side of the main hall, which corresponds with the idea of the museum staff who emphasized their desire to make the museum focus on everyday lives. The "flag room" definitely makes it clear that the state is not entirely gone from

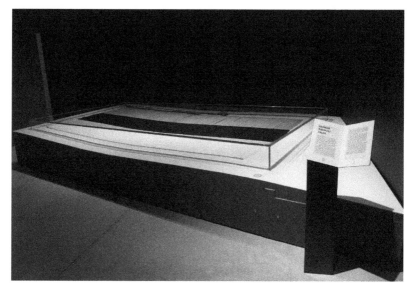

Fig. 13.2   The flag room at the Estonian National Museum. Photo: author

the narrative. Nevertheless, its non-central location in comparison for example with the "Skype chair" suggests an attempt to expand the familiar narrative of "a folk achieving an independent state" with new meanings that refer to recent times.

The new elements ethnically neutral and closer to people experiences might make it easier to relate to the national narrative for those who find the ethnocentric and peasant ideology of the nation too narrow, archaic, and exclusive. This is significant when we take the large Russian speaking population of Estonia into account, who cannot claim "ethnic" Estonian roots and have largely been cast out of the notion of the Estonian nation and pictured as "the other," rather than as someone who belongs to and shapes Estonia's (Pettai 2007; Vetik 2012; Pawłusz 2016). It is also a move toward a more liberal, diverse vision of the society where nationalism is just one of many perspectives on the state. Thus with its new narrative the museum has the potential contribute to building an Estonian identity that is not closed, homogeneous and "frozen" in the past but instead pluralistic and more civic than ethnic-oriented.

The Finno-Ugric Connection

One of the cultural elements of Estonian identity is the Finno-Ugric heritage, constructed on the basis of linguistic commonalities. Finno-Ugranism dates back to the first Estonian Republic but has also gained grounds in current times. In 2011, the Estonian Parliament reintroduced a national holiday called "The Finno-Ugrian day," celebrated for the first time in 1931 (Pawłusz and Polese 2017). In recent branding campaigns, the Finno-Ugric connection is used to contrast Estonia to other European nations and assert its distinctiveness. The following passage from the national newspaper illustrates this intention well,

> Over time, Estonia has become such an integral part of the Indo-European cultural sphere that many tend to forget how much it differs from its neighbours to the west, south, and east. Although grouped with the Baltic states for geopolitical and historical reasons, it serves well to remember that linguistically and ethnically, Estonians are very different from their Baltic brethren. On Saturday, October 17, Estonia is celebrating its own – the Finno-Ugric tribes, their culture and languages. (Estonian Public Broadcasting, news.err.ee, published on 17 October 2015).

A permanent exhibition on the Finno-Ugric peoples in ENM is not sur-prising also because the museum has researched, collected, and exhibited objects of Finno-Ugric cultures since its foundation. The idea of linguis-tic and cultural kinship between Finno-Ugric peoples is the ideological framework on which the Finno-Ugric exhibitions by the ENM have been traditionally prepared (Karm and Leete 2015: 105–106). In the Soviet era exhibitions of kindred peoples fitted the official ideology. An ethno-graphic "static" presentation of nations and ethnic groups that formed the Union was encouraged within Soviet cultural policies and the ENM often cooperated with other Finno-Ugric museums in preparing exhi-bitions of everyday life objects of Finno-Ugric peoples, the majority of whom live in Russia (ibid.). In the last twenty years, the ENM did not abandon the Finno-Ugric theme either. To the contrary, a few tempo-rary exhibitions were organized focusing on the beliefs and indigenous peoples' world views, as well as traditionally everyday life objects and handicrafts. Those few exhibitions have been a preparation for a per-manent exhibition in the new museum (ibid.: 108–109). In contrast to "Encounters" (the main exhibition), the Finno-Ugric exhibition can be described as a classic ethnographic display of life and culture of ethnic groups perceived as historical communities that have a distinctive cul-ture. Rather predictably, it starts with an explanation of a linguistic com-monality between the different Finno-Ugric ethnic groups displayed on a big language tree. Further, in the first room of the exhibition a print of a quote from Matthias Castrén, a nineteenth-century ethnographer of Finno-Ugric and Samoyedic peoples, is given, "The tribe that origi-nated from the empty slopes of the Urals has always been withdrawn and different from the rest of the human kind." This can be interpreted as an assertion of cultural distinctiveness and collective qualities of ethnic groups, characteristic of early ethnography.

The guide led us through the rooms of the exhibition, drawing our attention to the different clothes, decorative patterns, and household items of each tribe (see picture 3). Captions beneath them tell stories about women's and men's chores, life of a household, as well as reli-gious beliefs. Modern technologies, excellent graphic and multimedia effects make the exhibition aesthetically interesting and interactive. What catches attention is that the Finno-Ugric tribes are pictured as living very close to nature, genuine, and authentic. In contrast to how the Estonian nation is created on the exhibition next door, the Finno-Ugrians appear as historical, territorially bounded communities whose culture is being preserved and interpreted exclusively through historical lenses. Leete and Karm, who belong to the new Finno-Ugric exhibition curatorial team, reflected on the process of creating the exhibition a year before the opening in the following way,

> Indigenous cultures are popularly perceived as natural, authentic and "representing alternatives to the negative consequences of a modern, contemporary way of life" (...). We aim to display the Finno-Ugric peoples as normal human beings with a distinctive cultural heritage. The exhibition team avoids overstressing an exotic image of these people but intends to demonstrate that their culture enables us to negotiate cross-cultural human values. (ibid.: 114).

In my view, the exhibition does not quite challenge the romantic view of mysterious indigenous tribes living close to nature on the edges on Europe. There is little in the exhibition that indicates the current social, political, and cultural condition of these people. Interestingly, the assumption of cultural distinctiveness of the Finno-Ugric peoples was simultaneously maintained and challenged by the guide who remarked that "clothing decorations is what connects Finno-Ugric tribes. but yes, actually those are simple shapes and patterns that perhaps can be found elsewhere in the world." Another time she challenged the actuality of the exhibition saying that perhaps these days most people whose ancestors were Komi or Mordvin, today do not identify as such any more (Fig. 13.3).

The latter remark of the guide implicitly points to the overarching ideology of the exhibition—to preserve cultures which do not have political entities, such as states that would take care of the material and symbolic culture of the past. The exhibition does not cover Hungarians, Finns, and Estonians. The guide explained this is because "they have their own states." Indirectly this communicates at least two things. First, that the ultimate stage of national development is an independent state, able to secure a community's heritage and culture. This mirrors the character of the Estonian state, which, already in the Constitution, pledges to protect the Estonian culture and language through the ages. Second, on a more general level, this also communicates to the visitor the naturalness of "a world of nations," making the museum one of the sites where nationhood is banally recreated and materialized (Billig 1995).

Fig. 13.3 The Fino-Ugic exhibition at the Estonian National Museum. Photo: author

CONCLUSION

This chapter discussed the exhibitions of the new Estonian National Museum in the context of nation-building and identity making processes in the country. It has shown that even though there is a continuity in the national narrative the museum conveys, the new exhibitions offer a few innovations and changes in how the nation, its history, and memory are conceptualized.

First, the main exhibition "Encounters" does not present one cohesive grand narrative. Using a reverse chronological order, the exhibition starts with talking about contemporary society, which can be a surprise for local audiences that upsets the expectation of a traditional ethnographic display of Estonian peasant culture applied in previous exhibitions and other museums. Upsetting the chronological order and adding several "side" sections accessible from the main exhibition hall makes it possible to wander through the exhibition, forgetting the temporal dimension. This organizing principle might be confusing to some but intriguing and thought-provoking to others. This is a considerable innovation against the backdrop of the hegemonic narrative in which the nation is the central character that travels through time against all odds.

Second, rather than telling the political history of the nation and the state, the exhibition emphasizes and makes use of life stories, memories, anecdotes, and the like. Although the state is present in stories and in state symbols on display, the political history of the country is told through people's daily life experiences. As a result, the exhibition is less of national pedagogy and focuses on informality and the agency of ordinary people in various political circumstances. This is particularly visible in how the Soviet times are narrated. The Soviet times are not only symbolically brought back as part of national history, but also this exhibition refrains from giving an unequivocal moral judgment of this period.

Third, the museum as promoted by the museum staff, seeks to talk about human experiences without classifying these according to ethnicity or nationality. Rather than talking about experiences of the Estonian nation, it wants to introduce a plurality of voices of people who lived or influenced what Estonia is today. In that way, the "sacral" privileged connection between "ethnic Estonians" and the land is symbolically deconstructed. This move can be read as an attempt to mitigate cultural contestation and symbolic exclusion of Russian speakers from the nation. Seen from the perspective of increased migration in Europe, it can help facilitate a general debate about the role of incomers of different cultural background in the contemporary Estonian society. The main permanent exhibition "Encounters" can be read as a significant departure from ethnically oriented nation-building and a step toward reaching audiences who seek beyond the traditional narrative. This is a positive development as ethnic nationalism which excludes everybody who cannot claim long ancestral roots in the country from the concept of the nation, in particular the large Russian speaking minority, has often been questioned as hindering national cohesion and development (Siiner 2006; Seljamaa 2012; Vetik 2012; Pfoser 2015). It has been observed in qualitative studies that people's identities in practice are rather fragmented and situational (Seljamaa 2012). The state-imposed identity patterns, as well as its interpretation of the Soviet past, often do not embrace the spectrum of experiences of ordinary people (Pfoser 2015). Letting go of the historicized static idea of the nation gives more space for interpretation and reflection to the audience. It can be seen as reflecting the ongoing changes in the society but also as a way to encourage them. The role of change-maker is acknowledged and wanted by the museum staff who sees the museum as a place of thought-provoking dialogue rather than a comfort zone.

At the same time, in the other permanent exhibition located just next door a more static and essentialist concept of ethnicity and culture is maintained. The concept behind the Finno-Ugric permanent exhibition suggests a continuation with the tradition of Finno-Ugric research at Estonian National Museum and amongst local ethnologists. It also taps into the official Finno-Ugrism which has been present in public discourse and in people's popular perceptions. It can be asked why the two exhibitions designed within the same institution are developed in two different directions. A possible answer is that the museum is trying to find a middle way between innovation and respecting well-grounded narratives and familiar forms of display. A sharp departure from the latter could alienate significant parts of the audience and "distort their expectations" (Crane 1997), lowering the chance of the museum to become a frequently visited place of inquiry and reflection. The mixture of conservatism and innovation, communicated through attractive, modern, and interactive designs and spaces allows me to think that the new Estonian National Museum is capable of encouraging dialogue and self-reflection amongst audiences of all ages and backgrounds anticipated by its creators.

REFERENCES

Adams, L. L. (1999). Invention, Institutionalization and Renewal in Uzbekistan's National Culture. *European Journal of Cultural Studies, 2*(3), 355–373.

Adams, L. L. (2010). *The Spectacular State: Culture and National Identity in Uzbekistan.* Durham, NC: Duke University Press.

Anderson, B. (1991). *Imagined Communities: Reflections on the Origin and Spread of Nationalism.* London: Verso.

Billig, M. (1995). *Banal Nationalism.* London: Sage.

Brown, R. H., & Davis-Brown, B. (1998). The Making of Memory: The Politics of Archives, Libraries and Museums in the Construction of National Consciousness. *History of the Human Sciences, 11*(4), 17–32.

Brüggemann, K., & Kasekamp, A. (2008). The Politics of History and the 'War of Monuments' in Estonia. *Nationalities Papers, 36*(3), 425–448.

Crane, A. S. (1997). Memory, Distortion, and History in the Museum. *History and Theory, 36,* 44–63.

Datunashvili, A. (2017). The Georgian National Museum and the Museum of Soviet Occupation as Loci of Informal Nation Building. In A. Polese, et al. (Eds.), *Identity and Nation Building in Everyday Post-socialist Life* (pp. 52–69). New York and London: Routledge.

Forest, B., & Johnson, J. (2002). Unraveling the Threads of History: Soviet–Era Monuments and Post-Soviet National Identity in Moscow. *Annals of the Association of American Geographers, 92*(3), 24–547.

Gellner, E. (1983). *Nations and Nationalism.* Ithaca, NY: Cornell University Press.

Hirsch, F. (2005). *Empire of Nations: Ethnographic Knowledge & the Making of the Soviet Union.* Ithaca, NY: Cornell University Press.

Isaacs, R., & Polese, A. (Eds.). (2016). *Nation Building and Identity in the Post-Soviet Space: New Tools and Approaches.* NewYork and London: Routledge.

Kaplan, F. E. (Ed.). (1994). *Museums and the Making of "Ourselves": The Role of Objects in National Identity.* London: Leicester University Press.

Karm, S., & Leete, A. (2015). The Ethics of Ethnographic Attraction: Reflections on the Production of the Finno-Ugric Exhibitions at the Estonian National Museum. *Journal of Ethnology and Folkloristics, 9*(1), 99–121.

Knell, J. S., et al. (2011). *National Museums: New Studies from Around the World.* London and New York: Routledge.

Kolstø, P. (Ed.). (2014). *Strategies of Symbolic Nation-Building in South Eastern Europe.* Farnham: Ashgate.

Kuutma, K. (1996). Cultural Identity. Nationalism and Changes in Singing Traditions. *Folklore: Electronic Journal of Folklore, 2,* 124–141.

Martinez, F. (2016). *Wasted Legacies? Material Culture in Contemporary Estonia.* Ph.D. dissertation, Tallinn University.

Nora, P. (1989). Between Memory and History: Les Lieux de Mémoire. *Representations, 26,* 724.

Nora, P. (Ed.). (1996). General Introduction: Between Memory and History. In *Realms of Memory. Rethinking the French Past* (pp. 1–20). New York: Columbia University Press.

Pawłusz, E. (2016). The Estonian Song Celebration (Laulupidu) as an Instrument of Language Policy. *Journal of Baltic Studies.* https://doi.org/10.1080/01629778.2016.1164203.

Pawłusz, E., & Polese, A. (2017). 'Scandinavia's Best-Kept Secret.' Tourism Promotion, Nation-Branding, and Identity Construction in Estonia (with a free guided tour of Tallinn Airport). *Nationalities Papers.* https://doi.org/10.1080/00905992.2017.1287167.

Pettai, V. (2007). The Construction of State Identity and Its Legacies: Legal Restorationism in Estonia. *Ab Imperio, 3,* 403–426.

Pfoser, A. (2015). Between Security and Mobility: Negotiating a Hardening Border Regime in the Russian-Estonian Borderland. *Journal of Ethnic and Migration Studies, 41*(10), 1684–1702.

Runnel, P., T. Tatsi, & P. Pruulmann-Vengerfeldt. (2014). Who Authors the Nation? The Debate Surrounding the Building of the New Estonian National Museum. P. Runnel & P. Pruulmann-Vengerfeldt (Eds.), *Democratising the Museum: Reflections of Participatory Technologies* (pp. 19–34). Frankfurt am Main: Peter Lang.

Seliverstova, O. (2017). Keeping Alive the "Imaginary West" in Post-Soviet Countries. *Journal of Contemporary Central and Eastern Europe, 25*(1), 117–134.

Seljamaa, E.-H. (2012). *A Home for 121 Nationalities or Less: Nationalism, Ethnicity, and Integration in Post-Soviet Estonia.* Ph.D. dissertation, Ohio State University.

Siiner, M. (2006). Planning Language Practice: A Sociolinguistic Analysis of Language Policy in Post-communist Estonia. *Language Policy, 5*(2), 161–186.

Smith, L. (2006). *Uses of Heritage.* London and New York: Routledge.

Šmidchens, G. (2014). *The Power of Song: Nonviolent National Culture in the Baltic Singing Revolution.* Seattle: Washington University Press.

Tamm, M. (2013). In Search of Lost Time: Memory Politics in Estonia, 1991–2011. *Nationalities Papers, 41*(4), 651–674.

Velmet, A. (2011). Occupied Identities: National Narratives in Baltic Museums of Occupations. *Journal of Baltic Studies, 42*(2), 189–211.

Vetik, R. (Ed.). (2012). *Nation-Building in the Context of Post-communist Transformation and Globalization. The Case of Estonia.* Frankfurt am Main: Peter Lang.

CHAPTER 14

Acting in a National Play: Governmental Roles During the *Zwarte Piet* Contestation

Pieter Wagenaar and Jeroen Rodenberg

INTRODUCTION

On entering Gouda, one noticed it as soon as one left the train. This was a town that had prepared for serious disturbances. In the hope of preventing hostilities between opposing groups, billboards had been put up just outside the railway station, directing different passengers to different locations. And the police also stopped and questioned visitors. As Gouda used to be a fortified town in the past, a moat still separates its historic center from more recent parts. The police used the bridges across it as checkpoints, trying to prevent unwanted visitors from entering. Downtown Gouda itself was swarming with riot police and with private security firm employees. Yet it wasn't a major soccer match the town was holding itself ready for. Gouda was awaiting the entry of *Sinterklaas*.

'Sinterklaas', 'Saint Nicholas' in English, is the Dutch version of Santa Claus, of which he is a predecessor. His feast is celebrated on the evening of December 5, but preparations start much earlier. Each year

P. Wagenaar (✉) · J. Rodenberg
Department of Political Science and Public Administration,
VU University Amsterdam, Amsterdam, Noord-Holland, The Netherlands

© The Author(s) 2018
J. Rodenberg and P. Wagenaar (eds.), *Cultural Contestation*,
Palgrave Studies in Cultural Heritage and Conflict,
https://doi.org/10.1007/978-3-319-91914-0_14

he enters the country at around the 11 of November, which is a festivity in itself that can be witnessed in every Dutch municipality. One of these entries counts as the national arrival and is broadcast on television. Gouda hosted it on November 15, 2014. Yet, the reason Gouda had so diligently prepared for civil unrest has little to do with the figure of Sinterklaas itself, as that is relatively uncontested. It is Sinterklaas' retinue that is a source of societal conflict. As it happens the good Saint is accompanied by a host of *Zwarte Pieten* ('Black Peters'), dressed in sixteenth-century Spanish costumes, and wearing black makeup. Between November 11 and December 6, these *Pieten* are unavoidable. They are all over the media and can also be encountered in shops, in schools, in hospitals, etc. Some groups in society consider them a racist remnant of a colonial past and of slavery, and an insult to the Afro-Dutch. Other groups, however, see Zwarte Pieten as a touchstone of Dutchness, as a vital part of their identity, and are neither willing to part with them voluntarily, nor to change their color. As Albert van der Zeijden (2012), a scholar studying intangible heritage in the Netherlands, has remarked:

the question where the politicization of Black Pete comes from, is easy to answer. In a multi-ethnic society, where many ethnic groups live together in a more and more globalizing world, a situation emerged where various groups attach different meaning to traditions, to their own and that from others.

As the 2017 Charlottesville riots show, the Zwarte Piet controversy is not unique. Similar conflicts can be found in other societies as well, as is shown in this volume. They are known as 'cultural contestation' (Ross 2007, 2009a, b).

Cultural Contestation

Political scientists distinguish between different ways of looking at conflict. Brubaker, for instance, discerns four: inductive approaches, theory-driven rational action approaches, culturalist approaches, and 'ritual—symbolism—performance' (Brubaker and Laitin 1998). Docherty (2001: 29–35), a student of peacebuilding, prefers to speak of 'worlds': different aspects of conflict that are always there, and that all need to be addressed if conflicts are to be solved. The first of these worlds is 'rational'. It relates to the distribution of power and resources. The second world, the 'relational' one, is about the way opposing groups communicate with each other. In the last world, the 'symbolic' one, the one that concerns Docherty the most, emotions, values, and identities are at stake. 'Cultural contestation' is at its very heart.

Cultural contestation usually takes the form of conflicts over heritage. Yet, heritage conflicts can arise from other sources as well, and it is necessary to make the distinction. Roughly speaking heritage can become the object of dispute for four reasons. It can be contested because there are several parties laying claims to it (the Elgin marbles); it can become a source of conflict when different functions are ascribed to it by interested parties (an agricultural field versus an archeological site); sad memories can be attached to it (former concentration camps); and then, there is cultural contestation. This last form of conflict over heritage arises when practices that are vital to the identity of one group are considered to be highly insulting and threatening to another (the Orange parades in Ulster). The political scientist Marc Howard Ross, who has pioneered the study of cultural contestation, observes that such conflicts can be fierce, as they are 'about inclusion and exclusion from a society's symbolic landscape and that such inclusion or exclusion tells us about the politics of acceptance, rejection, and access to a society's resources and opportunities' (Ross 2009a: 1). In a similar vein, Sharon MacDonald has remarked that 'identity theorists have long argued that collective identities are produced relationally through processes of opposition—defining Us in relation to Them' (...). 'This is then consolidated by identifying content which is taken as marking 'Us-ness'- the construction of differentiating symbols' and what in German are called "Gegenbilder" (counterimages)' (MacDonald 2004: 54). An attack on these symbols can subsequently be perceived as a threat to one's very identity. Obviously, though, these symbols themselves can be equally menacing to others.

THE ROLE OF GOVERNMENT

According to Ross, there is little government can do once cultural contestation arises. It usually simply hasn't the legitimacy to act against it (Ross 2007: 90). Yet, as Ross own work, and that of those he inspired shows, it does try. Great Britain, for instance, has a 'parades commission', that needs to grant permission for contested marches (Ross 2007: 6–7). The British government also subsidizes the painting of murals in Ulster, trying to substitute neutral works of art for controversial ones (Hartnett 2010: 70, 95–96). There thus appears to be a gap in our knowledge of cultural contestation. We know that governments some-times do try to solve it, but these interventions haven't been systemati-cally studied yet. A small body of literature on peacemaking efforts in the 'symbolic world' of conflict does exist, though.

Michelle LeBaron, who has studied the symbolic layer of conflict resolution, stresses the importance of cultural fluency: the ability to see through each other's lenses. Stories, myths, rituals, and metaphors have an important role in this (LeBaron 2003; LeBaron and Pillay 2006: 275–28). Lisa Schirch (2005) has devoted an entire edited vol-ume to the part ritual plays in conflict-solving, and Paul Lederach pays considerable attention to it as well (Lederach and Lederach 2010). Marc Howard Ross asks attention for the role of the contested ritu-als and symbols *themselves*, especially for the degree to which these are inclusive or exclusive. He finds that it quite often is possible to make contested practices more inclusive; even to make these symbol-ize inclusion. As 'more inclusive symbols and rituals can draw former opponents into a new relationship while more exclusive ones harden the lines of differentiation', this is vital (Ross 2007: 3, 16–17, 26–27, 81–82; Ross 2009b: 2, 13, 18). Government, according to Ross, lacks the legitimacy to change (the meaning of) such practices. Yet, civic leaders sometimes can. The outcomes these might be able to real-ize won't satisfy everyone, but they might be a good enough solu-tion for most of those involved (Ross 2007: 125, 284; Smithey 2009: 102–103).

In this chapter, we look into the question of how the Dutch gov-ernment, which found itself forced to handle the Zwarte Piet contro-versy, dealt with cultural contestation. In order to gather data, we have interviewed all parties involved.[1] We have attended (protest) meetings and manifestations, and one of the court cases concerning Zwarte Piet. We've also analyzed everything the media reported on the matter and studied what went on in various social media.

A HISTORY OF CONTESTATION

Where Zwarte Piet comes from nobody knows for sure. Theories abound, but it seems reasonable to assume that the figure—in its cur-rent form—was invented in 1850, by Amsterdam school teacher Jan Schenkman (for a different opinion, see van Trigt 2016: 120–148). In that year, Schenkman published a children's book that would provide a kind of blueprint for the feast of Sinterklaas as it is today. Yet, it took decades before celebrating Sinterklaas Schenkman style had spread through all of the country. In many places, this happened only after the Second World War (Helsloot 2000). It would take equally long before protests against Zwarte Piet were voiced. The journalist Herman Salomonson was the first, in an article in the weekly *De Groene Amsterdammer* in 1930.[2] More than three decades later primary school teacher Arnold Ras followed in his footsteps, actually abolishing the figure's black makeup in the village of Wanroij. He encountered very competent opposition. Writer Godfried Bomans, who, as one of the country's first TV celebrities enjoyed enormous popularity, personally intervened.[3]

Five years later, in 1968, a Mrs. Grünbauer from the town of Leiden continued where Ras had had to give up. It would take until the 1980s, though, until the protest got really underway. The independence of Suriname in 1975 was followed by a wave of emigration to the Netherlands. A few years later, opposition against Zwarte Piet became structural. In the 1990s, these voices were finally heard, at least in Amsterdam. Pieten of many different colors made their entry there, during the arrival of Sinterklaas in 1993, and in 1998, primary schools in one of the Amsterdam neighborhoods received a 'Saint Nicholas code'. The controversy obtained an international dimension in 2003, when the Dutch chapter of the Global African Congress petitioned parliament (Helsloot 2005). Many of these initiatives met with opposition. An anti-Piet exposition/manifestation in the town of Eindhoven in 2008 even elicited such alarming reactions, that it had to be discontinued (van der Pijl and Goulordava 2014).

The current controversy started at the end of 2010. A group of young activists had decided to once and for all put an end to Zwarte Piet and had been brainstorming on possible actions. It finally decided to have t-shirts printed, carrying the text '*Zwarte Piet is racisme*' ('Black Pete is racism'), and to wear these during the national arrival of Sinterklaas in Dordrecht in 2011, as an artistic protest.[4] During this performance, the artists Quinsy Gario and Kno'Ledge Cesare (pseudonym of Jerry Afriyie) were arrested. The police next detained them for seven hours and fined them. Yet, the following day a similar protest was held in Amsterdam (Helsloot 2012a, b). The activists also wrote a letter to mayor Van der Laan of Amsterdam, and one of them, Raul Balai, addressed Van der Laan personally, when he ran into him at a reception.[5]

Heritage Listing

In the meantime, a different development had been set in motion: including the feast of Sinterklaas in the national inventory of intangible heritage. In 2012, the Netherlands signed the 2003 UNESCO-agreement on the safeguarding of intangible heritage. The institute responsible for the Dutch intangible heritage list is the Knowledge Center for Intangible Heritage in the Netherlands (KIEN); not a government body, but a quango-like organization subsidized by the Ministry of Education, Culture, and Science. It had held a survey on the question of which traditions are considered to be most important in the Netherlands in 2010, from which it emerged that Sinterklaas exceeds every other Dutch tradition in popularity (Strouken 2010). Naturally, therefore, it was a prime candidate for heritage listing (van der Zeijden 2014). On December 5, 2012, when the Netherlands signed the afore-mentioned agreement, Sinterklaas, without Zwarte Piet, was presented to UNESCO, in Paris. Ineke Strouken—KIEN's director—explained that Zwarte Piet was absent, because of the contested nature of the figure.[6]

It is not necessarily the KIEN itself, though, that nominates heritage for inclusion in the inventory. 'Communities' who count as the 'owners' of a specific heritage can do so, with the support of the KIEN (Margry 2014). The KIEN has contacts with all important Sinterklaas organizations. It had been warning these about the troubles which might arise from Zwarte Piet for years, when it was preparing the inclusion of the feast on the national heritage list. When it asked an umbrella organization called the Saint Nicolas Society to apply for the heritage listing of the feast, it therefore specifically requested it to write a paragraph on how it would deal with the Zwarte Piet question. Eventually, this would prove to be a reason for the society to not continue with the procedure.[7]

When the debate got truly underway, in 2013, Sinterklaas had therefore not yet been listed. The media attention hit the Sinterklaas organizations 'like a tsunami', according to KIEN director Ineke Strouken. The many thousands of people who thought they were simply involved in the organization of a children's' festivity, now all of a sudden found themselves being accused of racism. They looked to the KIEN for help, but so did many people opposing Zwarte Piet, leading to another tsunami: this time of e-mails sent to the KIEN. The numbers of these ran into the tens of thousands, and they often carried highly insulting and menacing messages. People also contacted the highest civil servant at the ministry, to try to get Mrs. Strouken fired, and activists visited her at her office, to try and bully her into subscribing to their views. At a certain moment, when she was receiving an average of 1.500 hate mails a day, it became impossible for Mrs. Strouken to answer these or to even pick up the phone.[8] Yet, that didn't mean the KIEN withdrew from the discussion, as, indeed, it couldn't. In order to facilitate the societal debate, the KIEN commissioned several publications in 2014. One was an enquiry among the most important spokespersons of both sides to the conflict, to try and find solutions; one was a book on the origins of Zwarte Piet; one was an explanation of the debate for foreign news media; and one was a comic book to facilitate the debate among school children. The KIEN also published educational material on the history of Dutch slavery.[9]

During the controversy, a new umbrella organization for the many local Sinterklaas committees came into being: the 'Sint & Pietengilde' (Saint Nicholas and Peters Guild). It moved into the void the Saint Nicholas Society had left behind and became the community responsible for the heritage listing of the feast. At the start of 2015, it got the feast included in the national heritage list.[10] The ministry, obviously very worried by the way the controversy had spread through the country, had requested the KIEN to have this postponed three times.[11]

The UN

When word got out that the KIEN was trying to get Zwarte Piet heritage listed, Barryl Biekman, a Dutch politician and chairwoman of the National Platform for the History of Slavery, contacted the UN (Wouters 2014). Her protest was supported by UN-advisor prof. Verene Shepherd. In January 2013, prof. Shepherd informed the Office of the United Nations High Commissioner for Human Rights (OHCHR), pointing out that the Netherlands was trying to get a tradition included in the UNESCO intangible heritage list, that her informants considered to be racist.[12] In October of that year, she visited the Netherlands, protesting Zwarte Piet, and in November 2013, the OHCHR itself got involved. That same month, the Working Group of Experts on People of African Descent, chaired by prof. Shepherd, called on the Dutch government to initiate a respectful societal debate on Zwarte Piet.[13] Later, in 2014, prof. Shepherd, together with the working group she had chaired until recently, would meet Dutch Minister Asscher, to discuss the matter. She remained of the opinion that Zwarte Piet, as a hateful remnant of a colonial past, would need to change.[14] A year later, the UN's International Convention on the Elimination of All Forms of Racial Discrimination (CERD) published its periodical report on the Netherlands. It had been informed by the Dutch Section of the International Commission of Jurists, which had presented a report drawn up by 27 NGOs. This shadow report started with Zwarte Piet and with the way the discussion on the figure had progressed in the Netherlands (Nederlands Juristen Comité voor de Mensenrechten 2015). Small wonder then, that many of the questions the CERD addressed to representatives of the Dutch government concerned the figure (Blokker 2015a). The government representatives, in their turn, pointed out that Minister Asscher was already organizing a dialogue between opponents and proponents of Zwarte Piet (Blokker 2015b). Nonetheless, the CERD remained concerned. In its *Concluding Observations*, in articles 15–18, it dealt with Zwarte Piet. Article 18 read:

> Considering that even a deeply-rooted cultural tradition does not justify discriminatory practices and stereotypes, the Committee recommends that the State party actively promote the elimination of those features of the character of Black Pete which reflect negative stereotypes and are experienced by many people of African descent as a vestige of slavery. The Committee recommends that the State party find a reasonable balance, such as a different portrayal of Black Pete and ensure respect of human dignity and human rights of all inhabitants of the State party. The Committee further recommends that the State party ensure non-discrimination in the enjoyment of freedom of expression and association, and that attacks on protesters be effectively investigated and duly prosecuted. (Committee on the Elimination of Racial Discrimination 2015)

Prime Minister Rutte saw no need for government intervention in the appearance of Zwarte Piet, however. The same went for Minister Asscher, although as a private person he was of the opinion that the figure would need to change.[15] Leaving it to society, though, would probably not be a solution to the CERD's concerns. According to a survey, a very large majority of Dutchmen felt that the UN recommendation needed to be ignored, and the Sint & Pietengilde—responsible for Piet's national heritage listing—wrote an open letter to the UN.[16] Yet, the UN's intervention already had had its effect, much earlier.

When prof. Shepherd had visited the country, this had produced such media attention, that Zwarte Piet had finally been put on the societal agenda. For Mandy Roos, a sixteen-year-old girl from The Hague, it had been a reason to organize a massive pro-Piet manifestation; another event the media jumped on. It was also the reason two Internet entrepreneurs from the province of Brabant created a pro-Piet Facebook page, which received over two mln. likes in 48 hours. Mandy Roos later presented these to a politician from the right-wing populist party PVV, another media event.[17] Now nobody could ignore the problem anymore.

Court Cases

In the meantime, a different process had been set in motion. Next to organizing protests, anti-Piet activists had also started legal proceedings. In 2013, Quinsy Gario had begun encouraging people to file objections to the entry of Sinterklaas at the municipality of Amsterdam (Kozijn 2014). These were rejected by the Amsterdam commission of appeal on October 30, 2013. In reaction, on May 22, 2014, the activists took the case to the Amsterdam court of law, and successfully. On July 3, the court ruled that burgomaster Van der Laan should not have granted a permit for the arrival of Sinterklaas without taking the interests of those objecting to Zwarte Piet into consideration, as the private life of these is severely disturbed by the negative stereotypical traits of the figure. Again (international) media attention was massive.[18]

Van der Laan, in his turn, opposed the idea that the municipality was under the obligation to judge the contents of events for which it granted permits before these had even been held. He therefore appealed to the Council of State: the Netherlands' highest court of appeal in administrative law cases. The council heard all parties on October 16 and overturned the ruling of the Amsterdam court on November 12. Its main consideration was that judging the contents of events a priori would go against the constitution. Yet, it refrained from rulings on the exact character of Zwarte Piet and pointed to the possibility of initiating civil law cases (Blokker 2014c). Legists were quick to point out that chances would be limited. To all probability, the law would not provide the means to ban Zwarte Piet.[19] The court cases were to have a different effect, though. They were the main reason for the establishment of the Sint & Pietengilde, that was later to get Sinterklaas heritage listed (van der Zeijden 2014).

And then there were individual law suits. A mother from the town of Utrecht filed a complaint against a primary school at the Dutch human rights council because of Zwarte Piet. She lost her case, on November 4, 2014, but the council did stipulate that in the future the school would need to take care to change all those features of Zwarte Piet that could be considered stereotyping.[20] Quinsy Gario and Jerry Afriyie protested their arrest in 2011 at the national *Ombudsman*, and won, but the police would, in its turn, file a complaint about Afriyie, when he resisted arrest during the arrival of Sinterklaas in Gouda in 2014. This led to the withdrawal of Afriyie's permit to work in private security, and to a lengthy lawsuit.[21] Quinsy Gario, who had received an astonishing amount of death threats and insults in the course of the contestation, filed 771 complaints against the senders of these.[22] And on *KetiKoti*, the yearly commemoration of the abolition of slavery, attendants were called on to file complaints against Zwarte Piet. Hundreds of people did, but in the end this law suit would prove to be unsuccessful too.[23] The media loved it, as they loved everything pertaining to the controversy, and, indeed, were instrumental in keeping it going.

THE MEDIA

After prof. Shepherd's intervention in 2013, the media exploded. From that moment on, Zwarte Piet was on the news always (Slagter 2014; Linders 2016). Every paper reported on the discussion, and talk shows on television devoted considerable attention to the topic as well. The most talked about being a confrontation between Quinsy Gario and Utrecht politician/pop singer/media personality Henk Westbroek on the Pauw and Witteman show.[24] And the international media soon followed suit. Any major event during the Dutch Zwarte Piet discussion was faithfully reported all over the world. In 2015, CNN even broadcast a documentary on the topic, which wasn't the first, as documentary filmmaker Sunny Bergman had already paved the way a year before.[25] According to several of the people who we have interviewed, the media proved to be uninterested in subtle statements, thus contributing considerably to the ongoing polarization.[26]

The social media were quick to follow. Zwarte Piet proved to be an endless source of online debates, which have been dutifully analyzed by scholars studying communication (van Es et al. 2014; Hilhors and Hermes 2016). Often, these posts were of a highly offensive nature.

The 'Contact Point for Discrimination on the Internet' (Meldpunt Discriminatie Internet), which analyzes such posts, noticed a change in the racist slurs it reports on. In the past, anti-Semitism was the most important category, followed by anti-Muslim remarks, while Afrofobia took the third place. Now, all of a sudden, Afrofobia came second.[27]

A very important actor in the world of the media was the so-called Sinterklaasjournaal (Saint Nicholas news flash). The Sinterklaasjournaal is a daily television show, which starts five days prior to the arrival of the good saint, to end when he leaves the country again. It is produced by public broadcasting company NTR, and although it is not the only Sinterklaas TV-show, it is by far the most influential. Each year it is watched by hundreds of thousands of children.

As the Sinterklaasjournaal is so dutifully watched by small children, who still believe the saint actually exists, Sinterklaas committees all over the country keep a watchful eye on it. They try to copy the appearance of Sinterklaas and the Zwarte Pieten as close as possible, so as not to confuse the children when they stage the arrival of the saint locally. Naturally, therefore, what the Sinterklaasjournaal would do with the Pieten was of great importance, a thing all parties involved realized.

Yet, when the controversy gained national attention, in 2013, there was little the Sinterklaasjournaal could still change, as all the preparations for the show had already been made. The following year it organized discussions among its 35 people strong staff, though. Four of these were to decide what would happen with Zwarte Piet (Kuiper 2014). These filmmakers were shielded off from direct confrontation with the various groups of activists, could not read the many e-mails on Zwarte Piet the NTR received, and kept their plans a secret. Paul Römer, NTR's director, claims that not even he could influence the screenplay they were working on.[28] When the actors each received a script—from which the final episode was missing—it was accompanied by a confidentiality agreement (Takken 2014). The evening the show's first episode was aired it turned out that it had attracted 25% more viewers than in previous years (Kuiper 2014). It had a very clever scenario, which was not only full of references to the ongoing Zwarte Piet discussion, but also had a story line explaining why Pieten in different shades of black made their entry in the show. Thus, it enabled every Sinterklaas committee in the country to choose the Pieten it felt best suited its particular points of view. And at the end of the show, the Sinterklaasjournaal even introduced a Saint Nicholas wearing black makeup.[29] Naturally, not everybody was happy with what the Sinterklaasjournaal had done. The chairman of the Saint Nicholas Society, e.g., realizing the impact the show would have, was appalled by the fact that a subsidized broadcasting company tried to influence a discussion society was still deeply entangled in.[30]

GOVERNMENT

People opposing Zwarte Piet had always been of the opposite opinion. They had complained about the lack of government intervention for many years (Knevel et al. 2011; Khaibar 2013; Bijnaar and Maris 2014; Kozijn 2014). Naturally, there had been several politicians who had protested the figure—Amsterdam council member Peggy Burke is a notable example—but these were the exception.[31] When news company PowNed tried to interview Dutch politicians on the controversy many of them shied away or downplayed the discussion; a thing that did not fail to provoke the irritation of Zwarte Piet's opponents.[32] And when television personality Paul de Leeuw sent a copy of Solomon Northup's *Twelve years a slave* to every Dutch member of parliament, to protest Zwarte Piet, he received only three thank you letters (Kozijn 2014: 106; van der Pijl and Goulordova 2014: 269). At the same time, local government was often instrumental in maintaining the tradition, as half of the arrivals of Sinterklaas receive government subsidies (Helsloot 2012b: 139–141). Several mayors also voiced their support for the figure,[33] and right-wing politician Geert Wilders even tried to pass a law protecting it.[34] Prime Minister Rutte's reaction to the CERD report was yet another disappointment to anti-Piet activists.[35] At local government level nevertheless, in Amsterdam, where opposition against the figure was strongest, things had already started to change.

In 2012, anti-Piet activists Quinsy Gario, Jerry Afriyie, and Raul Balai had sent Amsterdam mayor Van der Laan a letter. As a consequence they then had a meeting with him and with the committee that organizes the Amsterdam arrival of Sinterklaas, taking activist Miguel Heilbron with them. The committee was represented by the Mennonite clergyman Henk Leegte, the actor Jeroen Krabbé, and businessman Raymond Borsboom. As a consequence, the committee decided to have the municipality hold an inquiry into the opposition to Zwarte Piet, but for awhile little else happened. Yet, when the activists took the municipality to court, something that received enormous attention of Dutch and foreign media, action was required. Leegte, then one of the two chairmen of the committee, felt contestation was getting to big for a voluntary organization to handle, and asked Van der Laan to intervene. He also asked management consultant Adriaan Krans to succeed him as a chairman of the committee. The mayor, who had already written a letter to the council about the question, now decided to mediate (Broer 2014; Gemeente Amsterdam: Bureau Onderzoek en Statistiek: 2012). On March 24, 2014, all parties involved met in the mayor's official residence, a place Van der Laan uses for officious meetings. Paul Römer, director of broadcasting company NTR, was present as well, but as an onlooker only. This first meeting had a purely exploratory character. It was meant for establishing what the problems were that the different parties wanted to address and for finding common ground. The second meeting, on May 20, didn't lead to closure either. Adriaan Krans, who was intrinsically motivated to change Zwarte Piet, but also realized that something needed to change for pragmatic reasons, then came with a solution he could sell to his constituents. An explanation people in favor of Zwarte Piet often give for his black makeup is that he is black from entering homes through the chimney at night, in order to leave behind presents for the children. Why not change his makeup in such a way that he really looked like he was black from sooth, by giving him a few black smudges in his face only? In that way the figure would still fit all the stories he is surrounded with, and thus be acceptable to his constituents, yet accusations of blackface would become untenable. Krans explained to his constituents—who would be none too enthusiastic—that something needed to be done. One of the arguments he used was that the Amsterdam arrival is dependent on sponsoring from private business. As the tradition was becoming ever more contested, this source of income was drying up. An end to the contestation was not foreseeable, yet if it wasn't ended soon, survival of the tradition would be in danger. This was the reason, he argued, that change was in order. To allow people to get accustomed to the change slowly, the introduction would be gradual: changing 25% of the Pieten into 'sooth Pieten' every year. Part of the deal Krans proposed was also that accusations of racism would be dropped. Van der Laan then had bilateral meetings with the different parties involved and organized a last plenary meeting on August 8. The opponents of Zwarte Piet had not been enthusiastic about the gradualness of the change, but most accepted the compromise. The NTR, which had been an onlooker only, could also work with it. The mayor now proposed to make the deal that had been reached official, by signing a voluntary agreement. The explanations for why he took this step differ. Some say Van der Laan needed to be able to prove to the Council of State that this time he had taken the objections of part of the Amsterdam inhabitants into consideration, in order to prevent being taken to court again over the permit. Others believe that the mayor, who had a background as a lawyer specializing in mediation, was simply used to ending such processes with voluntary agreements. However, it may be, signing a voluntary agreement proved to be a step too far (Broer 2014).[36]

Yet, a compromise had been reached, and a week later the mayor sent a letter to the city council, and briefed the press. He also delivered a motivational speech to the Amsterdam Pieten, part of whom still needed to be convinced that change was necessary (Broer 2014).[37] It had been a bumpy ride, as the activists had used two strategies—negotiating as well as suing—at the same time. This had forced the mayor into a kind of split personality too: suing and mediating simultaneously. Yet, he had the legitimacy to do the latter, as all parties involved accepted his authority. It had meant, though, as journalist Bas Blokker has pointed out, that while claiming in court that he had no authority to influence the contents of the Amsterdam Sinterklaas arrival beforehand, Van der Laan was doing exactly that in a different setting (Blokker 2014b).[38]

Elsewhere, things had been calmer, which is why the city of Utrecht, for instance, got away much easier. It had started a dialogue in 2014, just like Amsterdam, and had changed 20% of its Pieten into 'confetti Pieten'. Resistance in the committee organizing the entry in Utrecht had been manageable, as had been the opposition to Zwarte Piet, and the press had been kept at bay by waiting to the very last before communicating changes. The chairman of the Utrecht committee was a consultant specialized in lobbying and knew how to manage such processes. He kept in close contact with the mayor, but, contrary to Amsterdam, in Utrecht local government mainly played a facilitating role.[39]

The town of Gouda, which would host the national entry, would not be so lucky. When it had offered to host the national arrival of Sinterklaas, it had known about the contestation. Yet, what it had not foreseen is how huge the ensuing societal debate would become. It discussed the problem with proponents and opponents of Zwarte Piet, and with broadcasting company NTR, but obviously could not solve it. The town decided to introduce a few 'themed' Pieten, in the colors of the cheese and the treacle waffles Gouda is so famous for, but this did little to end the dispute.[40] As was to be expected activists of both parties chose to organize manifestations during the national entry. The municipality of Gouda had no legal means of preventing this, but did decide to keep the two groups apart. One group received permission to protest near the Gouda theater, the other near the town hall. For security reasons, the historic city center, where the entry was to be, was off-limits. The anti-Pieten did not agree to this, as it meant they would be kept away from the television cameras, but were warned beforehand that the police would act if they would try to enter the city center. Yet, they did so nonetheless, crossing the moat individually during the national arrival. At one p.m., they then tried to start a silent protest, but as soon as they did they were attacked by pro-Piet protesters, who had slipped through security as well. Now the police intervened, making more than ninety arrests.[41] Yet again (inter)national media attention was massive.

Obviously, the Zwarte Pieten discussion had gotten way too big for local government to handle, which is why central government was already intervening. Minister Asscher had been present at Van der Laan's last meeting in Amsterdam and had now started to organize his own.[42] In September 2014, Asscher invited all parties involved to a roundtable session. The exercise would be repeated at the start of 2015, and in September of that same year. Asscher's intervention was different from Van der Laan's, though. The Minister saw no role for government in coming up with the solution to the problem, but merely wanted to create a forum, where all parties could meet and exchange views. His sole intention was to keep the dialogue going, hoping that the parties would also meet outside of the meetings he initiated, and in this he appears to have succeeded.[43]

Toward Closure?

A few days after Saint Nicholas' entry, mayor Van der Laan thanked Sinterklaas and his Pieten for carrying on in spite of everything they had had to endure, and for the way they had conducted the discussion.[44] A few other municipalities had experimented with untraditional Pieten in 2014 too, but in most places Piet had stayed as black as he had been before (Blokker 2014a).[45] Would 2015 be different? The town of Groningen was quick to announce that in 2015 its Pieten would remain pitch-black, but other large towns declared they were opting for sooth Pieten. Such Pieten would also appear in Meppel, which was to host 2015's national entry,[46] and even in the Belgian city of Antwerp, which has a Sinterklaas tradition similar to the Dutch one.[47] Slowly but surely, therefore, closure seemed to be drawing near. Journalist Bas Blokker (2014d) claims that this had been a result of a deliberate strategy. In a peculiarly Dutch way, government had organized deliberation between all opposing parties, in order to reach consensus among the largest possible group. The aim was to then isolate representatives of the radical fringes, and, as happened in Gouda, simply arrest these if they caused trouble. Several of our interviewees confirm Blokker's claim.[48] Pam Evenhuis, spokesperson of the committee that organizes the Amsterdam arrival of Sinterklaas, has explained how the Amsterdam solution of sooth Pieten was then exported to other towns. He himself addressed local government elsewhere, whereas Adriaan Krans spoke to the organizing committees.[49] Utrecht was one of the cities that followed Amsterdam's lead. It too introduced sooth Pieten and also adopted the Amsterdam percentage, although its organizing committee would have liked to make bigger changes.[50] In 2015, the Amsterdam committee also employed a new strategy: calling attention away from the official entry and its Pieten. It did so by organizing Sinterklaas-related activities for underprivileged children, thus also conveying the message that Sinterklaas is a feast for everybody, and winning the hearts of the Amsterdam inhabitants.[51]

The effects of these initiatives were felt outside of the realm of the official entries too, in primary schools, for instance. As most of these are visited by Sinterklaas and his Pieten in November–December they have found it hard to stay out of the contestation. In 2014, some 14% of them had already changed Piet's appearance[52]; a change that accelerated in 2015. The primary schools in the city of The Hague were the first to announce that they would be using sooth Pieten only, and, although the reactions were furious, schools elsewhere followed their example.[53] This went for schools in Amsterdam, Rotterdam, and Utrecht—the country's other large cities—and even in Groningen.[54] Eventually, about a third of the country's schools would change Piet's appearance. A school in Utrecht even chose to substitute 'Minions' for its Pieten. The driver behind this transition was an action group called 'Nederland wordt beter' (the Netherlands are becoming better), and the Amsterdam committee (Blokker 2015c).[55]

Finally, there was commerce. For many shopkeepers, Sinterklaas is one of the most important events of the year, as their sales volumes so depend on it. The organization of Dutch retail traders was therefore represented at Minister Asscher's meetings. It hoped for a speedy end to the contestation, but in the meantime retail chains in the country needed to act. The strategies they employed differed. The Albert Heijn and HEMA supermarkets still sold products decorated with traditional Pieten, as did the big toy shops, but supermarkets Jumbo and Lidl opted for white ones.[56] Luxury department store de Bijenkorf was a special case. It is famous for its Sinterklaas decorations, consisting of mechanical Pieten who climb ropes, but decided to paint this gold instead of black.[57] Unsurprisingly, then, wholesale window-dressers sold Pieten in every color imaginable, to suit their clients' tastes.[58] Yet, the actual window-dressing proved to be a different matter. All the big retail companies sought ways to remove the Pieten from their showcases. Only small independent shops sometimes displayed them.[59] Behind this transition, there was the activity of an action group as well; this time one called 'MAD Mothers'.[60] Commercial broadcasting companies, who were targeted by MAD Mothers too, differed in their approach. RTL still had black Pieten, but Nickelodeon changed their color to white. Meanwhile, TV presenter Dieuwertje Blok, anchorwoman of public television's Sinterklaasjournaal, publicly stated that Zwarte Piet's appearance would have to change.[61]

However, to the great disappointment of the anti-Piet activists, most of the Sinterklaasjournaal's Pieten stayed as black as they had always been, in spite of the Amsterdam committee's efforts.[62] And at the majority of the arrivals Sinterklaas was also accompanied by classic black Black Pete's. This even went for the entries into the big cities of Rotterdam and The Hague.[63] Unsurprisingly therefore, 2015 again saw protesting. At the national entry in the town of Meppel, there was fierce contestation between supporters and opponents of Piet, some of whom were dressed in Black Panther uniforms. Yet, this time the police managed to keep the two groups apart without having to make arrests (Kuiper 2015).[64] Amsterdam's main arrival went without protesting, but a smaller entry, in one of its boroughs, led to a confrontation. The same went for the Amsterdam 'Sinterklaas departure', one of the events that had been planned to draw attention away of the saint's arrival.[65] A Sinterklaas festivity public television had organized in Utrecht met with protests too.[66] In their turn, supporters of Piet also protested. The Utrecht school that had chosen to have minions accompany Sinterklaas was confronted with angry parents, dressed as Zwarte Pieten.[67]

The real change would have to wait until 2016. That year Minister Asscher held another meeting with the stakeholders, most of whom signed a declaration, in which they promised to refrain from polarization.[68] Amsterdam changed all its Pieten to sooth Pieten, and a small number of towns followed in its footsteps.[69] A similar thing went for the schools: It was especially schools in the west of the country that changed Piet's appearance.[70] A bigger change was that some central government actors finally took a stand. Asscher stated, on television, that he felt that in this case the majority needed to give way to a minority, and that Piet's appearance needed to change. State secretary Van der Steur even wrote a letter to parliament, claiming that the entire coalition was of the same opinion, but the prime minister was quick to force him to withdraw it.[71]

The NTR Saint Nicholas Newsflash, which, as we have seen, plays an extremely important role in the debate, was under fire long before it actually started to broadcast in 2016. In May, three of the Newsflash's most important actors announced they would no longer partake in the show.[72] The same month 120 Dutch celebrities asked the broadcasting company to change Piet, and the Dutch Ombudsman for Children declared that the figure was a violation of children's' rights.[73] In October, a competing Saint Nicholas show, that of commercial broadcasting company RTL, announced that it would modify Piet's appearance. It had been inspired by the Amsterdam approach. Minister Asscher was quick to voice his approval, but leading MP Halbe Zijlstra protested the change.[74] When NTR's Newsflash finally aired it turned out that it made use of Pieten in every imaginable color and pattern.[75] It was now clearly instituting changes itself.

2016's national Saint Nicholas entry was to be held in the town of Maassluis. Opponents of Black Pete were quick to announce that they would be present, and that this time their demonstration would not be peaceful. The NVU, a party on the extreme right of the political specter, made known that it would pay a visit to Maassluis as well.[76] Maassluis mayor Edo Haan then took an active stance. He went to the meeting Minister Asscher had organized, and also had private meetings with the different stakeholders. He personally changed 20% of the Pieten to sooth Petes, and he came up with an innovative idea. Declaring that Maassluis didn't just host the national entry, but also the national discussion, he had an exposition organized on the Dutch Saint Nicholas celebration's controversial character throughout the ages. Naturally, he assigned places for demonstrations, but he made sure that opponents and proponents of Black Pete would be kept apart, and took every precaution to guarantee the safety of the many children who would be present.[77] Maassluis was to be turned into a fortress during the entry. The area where the entry was to be held would be sealed off, and an emergency ordinance was to be proclaimed, making it easier to stop and search people. A day before the entry two people were placed in preventive detention, and the prime minister called for calmness.[78] When we ourselves entered the town, on November 12, we were stopped, interrogated, and frisked already at the railway station. The police also scanned our ID-cards. The same was to happen twice again, as the area was really only accessible to children and accompanying adults. The entry itself proved to be uneventful, as the busses carrying the protesters had stopped in Rotterdam. There the police arrested 197 people, as the mayor of Rotterdam, who had been warned by the secret service beforehand, had forbidden all demonstrations.[79]

And now, where are we now? In 2017, a new status quo appears to have materialized, with the large cities in the west of the country opting for sooth Petes, as do their schools, while the rest of the Netherlands sticks to its traditional ways.[80] In line with this, the Saint Nicholas Newsflash has done away with its multicolored Petes and is now catering to both parties again.[81]

The number of those in favor of change has risen markedly, though, and most people seem to be fed up with the discussion.[82] It is now the fringes of the opposing parties who keep up the fight, which is getting nastier. This year activists dressed up as traditional Petes visited the home of a politician who protests Pete and made a surprise visit to a meeting of the Amsterdam City council, and to a primary school. Pete's opponents, in their turn, made a 'Saint Nicholas house' inaccessible by pouring liquid metal in its lock. A Saint Nicholas circus even had to be closed because of threats.[83] Three buses with protesters tried to visit the national entry in the northern town of Dokkum, for which they had a permit. They were stopped in their way by activists in favor of Pete, who blocked the highway. The mayor of Dokkum, who had received warnings that even greater disturbances were at hand, consequently forbade the demonstration.[84] The highway blockaders, who will probably be prosecuted, were not without sympathizers. A lawyer offered them his services for free, and to pay a possible fine a fundraiser on the Internet collected more than 43.000 euros in a few days.[85]

CONCLUSION

The cultural contestation surrounding the figure of 'Zwarte Piet', which has rocked the Netherlands from 2013 onwards, started with an attempt at heritage listing. It was protests at the UN against placement of the Sinterklaas celebration—of which Zwarte Piet is a part—on the national intangible heritage list, that put the contestation on the societal agenda. In the multicultural city of Amsterdam, civil society was the first to be confronted with the controversy. According to Ross that is where it could have been solved—as in his theory civic leaders can play a role in mitigating cultural contestation—but in this case it wasn't. As the controversy was simply too large for civil society to deal with, government was asked to intervene.

When analyzing the cultural contestation surrounding the symbol of Zwarte Piet, the large number of governmental actors involved in the discussion immediately springs to the eye. They range from the local level, such as the mayor of Amsterdam, to the national level in the person of the Minister of social affairs Lodewijk Asscher, and even to the supranational level in the person of professor Verene Sheperd. They not only include the *KIEN* but also the national ombudsman. Even the judiciary has been forced to take a stance in the debate.

When we take a closer look at these many different governmental actors, it becomes clear that all of them have acted on their own accord, based on their respective interests and competencies. They have reacted to other governmental actors or to requests from civil society. The different backgrounds, interests, and competencies of governmental actors partly define the different opinions they voice. Prime Minister Rutte, for example, took an altogether different stance on Zwarte Piet's attire and makeup, than the Minister of social affairs, or the Amsterdam court of law, and, more recently, the National Ombudsman or the KIEN. This makes an analysis of governmental actions in this case of cultural contestation difficult. Yet, we can still discern three roles they play.

In the first place, government actors act as *facilitators* of the tradition. After all, it is local authorities, most notably the mayors, who are responsible for granting the permits for locally held entries of the Saint and his retinue. Many municipalities also subsidize local associations responsible for the entry.

Secondly, contrary to what Ross writes about the possibilities to mitigate, governmental actors have acted as *passive mediators* in the discussion. Minister Lodewijk Asscher, for instance, has tried to bring parties together and to create a safe space where societal actors could discuss matters.

In the third place, government actors can try to *actively mitigate* the contestation, by not only bringing parties together, but also directing the discussion toward a workable outcome. This was done by Amsterdam mayor Van der Laan, who apparently had clear ideas on the desired conclusion to the discussion, and on the way to end the contestation. Real mitigation, however, seems hard to attain. Several reasons lie at the root of this. In the first place, the cultural contestation surrounding Zwarte Piet is a discussion which is held at the national level, but played out on the local level. That, after all, is the level at which either protests are organized, or everything stays quiet. It is thus the local context that determines the need for mitigation and the room for maneuver. In a left-wing liberal city like Utrecht, little mitigation was needed, as the local population was generally in favor of altering the appearance of Zwarte Piet. In ethnic and culturally diverse cities such as Amsterdam, the need for mitigation was higher, but, at the same time, it was this that created room for mitigation. In small provincial towns such as Dokkum, Maassluis, or Gouda, which have all hosted the national entry recently, the mayors had little room for mitigation and thus needed to restrict the protests. Secondly, the nature of the administrative system, in which different actors based on different competencies and interests act in different ways, hinders mitigation efforts.

On the other hand, it is exactly the fact that contestation is played out at the local level, and the fact that government is fragmented, that might make attempts at mitigation possible. It is at this level, after all, that chances for successful mitigation are highest. The way mayor Van der Laan played his mitigating role during the national play is exemplary. His aim was to find a solution that would satisfy the largest possible group, and in this he eventually succeeded.

Yet, when we zoom out, and take a look at the nation as a whole, we can't but notice that at present contestation is far from over. A recent survey shows that in most municipalities Piet remains as black as he always has been, which also goes for most of the schools. It is especially the larger—multicultural—cities in the west of the country where Black Pete's appearance is changing. The rest of the country is still firmly sticking to its guns.

NOTES

1. We interviewed a considerable number of persons, although not all appear in this chapter. For this chapter, we used interviews with the former director of KIEN Ineke Strouken, Jan van Wijk (member of the Saint Nicholas Association), Raul Balai (involved in one of the protesting groups), Judith van Gameren (member of the organizing committee of the Saint's entry in Tilburg), Riet de Leeuw (policy advisor Ministry of Education, Culture, and Sciences), Paul Römer (director of the NTR), Peggy Burke (former member of the Amsterdam city council), Geert Jan ter Linden (chef de cabinet Mayor of Amsterdam), Luc Dietz (member of the organizing committee of the Saint's entry in Utrecht) Milo Schoenmaker (mayor of Gouda), Edo Haan (mayor of Maassluis), UgoniaTijmensen (policy advisor Minister of Social Affairs) and Adriaan Krans, ds. Henk Leegte and Pam Evenhuis (all at the time of this research affiliated to the committee organizing the Amsterdam entry).
2. http://schrijfsterushamarhe.wordpress.com/2014/11/29/zwartepiet-niet-reeds-in-1930-door-melis-stoke-in-de-groene-amsterdammer-bepleit/.
3. http://www.npogeschiedenis.nl/nieuws/2013/oktober/Pleidooi-uit-1963--schaf-Zwarte-Piet-af.html; http://www.bhic.nl/ontdekken/verhalen/opvoeden-volgens-ras; http://www.npogeschiedenis.nl/speler.WO_VPRO_418222.html.
4. Interview Raul Balai, 5-6-2015.
5. Interview Raul Balai, 5-6-2015; see for a comprehensive overview of protests Euwijk and Rensen (2017) et passim.
6. http://www.rtlxl.nl/#!/rtl-nieuws-132237/f4754cf9-ce39-45ff-b691-bf5dccab67e5.
7. Interview Strouken, 22-09-14; interview Van Wijk, 24-6-2015.
8. Interview Strouken, 22-09-14; Judith Van Gameren, who organizes the entry in the town of Tilburg, also mentioned how shocked she was: Interview Judith Van Gameren, 13-10-2014.
9. Interview Strouken, 10-6-2015; *Immaterieel Erfgoed* (2014: 36).
10. Interview Van Wijk 24-6-2015; http://nu.nl/binnenland/3973474/sinterklaasfeest-nationaal-beschermde-traditie.html; http://nos.nl/artikel/2013511-sinterklaasfeest-nu-officieel-nederlandse-traditie.html; http://m.nrc.nl/nieuws/2015/01/15/sinterklaasfeest-op-lijst-cultureel-erfgoed-in-nederland.
11. Interview De Leeuw, 29-10-2015.
12. https://spdb.ohchr.org/hrdb/23rd/public_-_AL_Netherlands_17.01.13_(1.2013).pdf; https://spdb.ohchr.org/hrdb/24th/Netherlands_10.07.13_(1.2013).pdf.

13. http://www.unric.org/en/latest-un-buzz/28862--un-experts-encourage-respectful-debate-on-dutch-tradition.
14. http://www.trouw.nl/tr/nl/4492/Nederland/article/detail/3679846/2014/06/27/Sint-criticus-Shepherd-met-VN-werkgroep-naar-Nederland.dhtml; http://nos.nl/artikel/670505-vnadviesheroverweeg-zwarte-piet.html.
15. http://nos.nl/artikel/2054617-rutte-zwarte-piet-geen-staatsaangelegenheid.html; http://www.volkskrant.nl/binnenland/asscher-piet-moet-andersmaar-niet-opgelegd-door-overheid~a4131775.
16. http://opiniepanel.eenvandaag.nl/uitslagen/61587/_vn_aanbevelingen_zwarte_piet_niet_overnemen_;http://www.sintenpietengilde.nl/Openbrief-VN.pdf.
17. http://www.joop.nl/leven/detail/artikel/23587_pietitie_bij_demonstratie_aan_pvv_aangeboden; https://www.facebook.com/pietitie.
18. http://uitspraken.rechtspraak.nl/inziendocument?id=ECLI:NL:R-BAMS:2014:3888; http://www.parool.nl/parool/nl/38/MEDIA/article/detail/3683940/2014/07/04/Zwarte-Piet-haalt-internationale-media.dhtml.
19. http://www.trouw.nl/tr/nl/4492/Nederland/article/detail/3788742/2014/11/12/Staan-de-tegenstanders-van-Zwarte-Piet-nu-met-lege-handen.dhtml.
20. http://www.trouw.nl/tr/nl/4664/Mijn-kind-moet-naar-de-basisschool/article/detail/3782420/2014/11/04/Zwarte-Piet-op-school-niet-discriminerend.dhtml.
21. http://www.nrc.nl/nieuws/2014/10/17/politie-arresteerde-in-2011-ten-onrechte-twee-mensen-tijdens-sint-intocht; https://www.nrc.nl/nieuws/2016/09/22/kleeft-er-luchtje-aan-aanhouding-4411871-a1522805https://www.nrc.nl/nieuws/2016/09/22/volg-hier-de-rechtszaak-tegen-anti-zwarte-piet-activist-afriyie-a1522700; http://nos.nl/artikel/2136278-geen-straf-voor-anti-zwarte-piet-activist.html; http://www.nrc.nl/nieuws/2016/10/07/om-gaat-in-hoger-beroep-tegen-uitspraak-anti-zwarte-piet-activist-afriyie-a1525454.
22. http://www.nieuws.nl/algemeen/20141203/Quinsy-Gario-doet-meerdan-771-aangiftes-tegen-racisten [page no longer exists].
23. http://www.parool.nl/parool/nl/4/AMSTERDAM/article/detail/4092978/2015/07/02/Honderden-klachten-over-Zwarte-Piet-bij-meldpunt-Museumplein.dhtml; http://www.ad.nl/ad/nl/1012/Nederland/article/detail/4043079/2015/05/30/Zwarte-Piet-kan-borst-natmaken-nieuw-offensief.dhtml; http://nos.nl/l/2180399.
24. Interview Strouken 10-6-2015; http://www.youtube.com/watch?v=lABvmzPkfUc.

25. http://edition.cnn.com/videos/world/2015/11/11/blackface-pre-view-orig-ff.cnn; http://www.documentairenet.nl/review/2doc-zwart-als-roet-colonial-hangover/.
26. Interviews Strouken, 22-09-14 and 10-6-2015.
27. Stichting Magenta, Afdeling Meldpunt Discriminatie Internet, Jaarverslag 2014, pp. 6–7, 16.
28. Interview Römer, 21-10-2014.
29. http://www.uitzendinggemist.net/aflevering/294777/Het_Sinterklaasjournaal.html.
30. Interview Van Wijk, 24-6-2015.
31. Interview Burke 28-3-2014; speech held by Peggy Burke at her leave from the Amsterdam city council: http://amsterdam.raadsinformatie.nl/notucast/gemeenteraad_26-03-2014 (rond 2U26 min; 26.3.2014).
32. http://www.youtube.com/watch?v=abfalFYs2E8; http://www.joop.nl/opinies/detail/artikel/24051_laten_we_eens_praten_over_racisme/; http://wijblijvenhier.nl/21674/anousha-nzume-fileert-politieke-leiders-zwarte-piet-debat-ontlopen/; http://www.frontaalnaakt.nl/archives/dont-mention-the-racism.html; http://www.vn.nl/Archief/Samenleving/Artikel-Samenleving/Rutte-en-Asscher-moeten-leiderschap-tonen-1.htm.
33. http://www.bredavandaag.nl/nieuws/cultuur/2014-11-06/burgemeester-breda-spreekt-zich-uit-voor-zwarte-pieten; http://regio.thepostonline.nl/2014/11/07/video-annemarie-jorritsma-woedend-vanwege-zwarte-piet-discussie.
34. http://www.pvv.nl/index.php/36-fj-related/geert-wilders/7828-geert-wilders-bij-wnl-vandaag-de-dag.html; http://www.volkskrant.nl/politiek/pvv-wet-moet-zwarte-piet-zwart-houden~a3748093.
35. http://www.joop.nl/politiek/detail/artikel/33574_de_premier_van_wit_nederland/.
36. Interview Krans, 25-11-2014; Interview Ter Linden, 9-2-2015.
37. Interview Krans, 25-11-2014.
38. Interview Ter Linden, 9-2-2015.
39. Interview Dietz, 5-2-2016.
40. Interview Schoenmaker,7-6-2014.
41. Interview Schoenmaker, 23-3-2015; http://nos.nl/artikel/721821-negen-tig-arrestaties-intocht-gouda.html; http://www.nrc.nl/nieuws/2014/11/15/enthousiaste-menigte-en-beveiligers-verwelkomen-sinterklaas-in-gouda/.
42. Interview Schoenmaker, 23-3-2015.
43. Interview UgoniaTijmensen-Kruseman, 21-9-2015; Interview Schoenmaker, 23-3-2015; Interview Strouken, 10-6-2015; interview Krans, 19-1-2016; https://www.rijksoverheid.nl/documenten/kamerstukken/2014/10/23/beantwoording-kamervragen-over-pietoverleg.
44. http://www.nu.nl/amsterdam/3945954/van-laan-bedankt-sinterk-laas-en-pieten.html.

45. http://nos.nl/artikel/716154-intocht-zwarte-piet-verandert-niet.html.
46. http://nu.nl/overig/4130163/groningse-pieten-blijven-gewoon-zwart. html; http://nos.nl/artikel/2062912-sinterklaasintochten-krijgen-schoorsteenpieten.html.
47. http://nos.nl/artikel/2062086-verfijnde-zwarte-piet-in-antwerpen.html; http://www.ketnet.be/kijken/sinterklaas/intrede-2015; http://www.rtvutrecht.nl/nieuws/1400697/sinterklaas-maakt-zich-op-voor-intocht-in-.
48. Interview Römer, 21-10-2014; interview Ds. Leegte, 22-1-2015.
49. Interview Evenhuis, 4-12-2015; interview Krans, 19-1-2016.
50. Interview Dietz, 5-2-2016.
51. Interview Evenhuis, 4-12-2015; interview Krans, 19-1-2016; http://www.nrc.nl/handelsblad/2015/11/13/vergeet-piet-het-hele-festijnverandert-1559183
52. http://www.metronieuws.nl/binnenland/2014/09/zwarte-piet-maakt-het-basisscholen-moeilijk; http://www.nu.nl/binnenland/3926617/zeven-middelbare-scholen-past-zwarte-piet.html.
53. http://www.nrc.nl/nieuws/2015/09/17/zwarte-piet-niet-langerwelkom-op-haagse-scholen/; http://www.ad.nl/ad/nl/1040/Den-Haag/article/detail/4144105/2015/09/17/Woeste-reacties-op-Zwarte-Piet-besluit-schoolbesturen.dhtml; http://www.petities24.com/zwartepietmoetophaagsescholenblijven;https://www.123formulier.nl/form-10827/Aanvraag-Brief-Aan-Directie-Scholen.
54. http://www.parool.nl/parool/nl/4/AMSTERDAM/article/detail/3778233/2014/10/29/Amsterdamse-basisscholen-kiezen-voormodernere-Zwarte-Piet.dhtml; http://nos.nl/artikel/2059284-advies-geenzwarte-piet-op-openbare-scholen-rotterdam.html; http://www.volkskrant.nl/binnenland/zwarte-piet-niet-meer-welkom-op-utrechtse-basisscholen~a4153228/; https://www.youtube.com/watch?v=E1Oxdwsk55g.
55. Interview Krans, 19-1-2016; http://www.nu.nl/sinterklaas/4161804/ruim-derde-scholen-past-uiterlijk-zwarte-piet-aan.html; http://www.trouw.nl/tr/nl/4556/Onderwijs/article/detail/4184577/2015/11/12/Kroeshaar-oorringen-en-volrode-lippen-verdwijnen.dhtml; http://www.nrc.nl/next/2015/11/27/geen-piet-wel-mijter-staf-en-minions-1559819; http://www.nrc.nl/nieuws/2015/11/30/aan-alle-critici-hoe-vier-je-dan-sinterklaas-zonder-pieten; http://nos.nl/artikel/2072999-in-beeld-sinterklaas-bezoekt-basisscholen.html; http://nos.nl/artikel/2072979-zwarte-piet-en-minions-samen-op-utrechtse-school.html; http://www.nrc.nl/nieuws/2015/12/04/en-toen-liepen-de-sint-en-zijn-minions-het-schoolplein-op; https://decorrespondent.nl/3724/Hoe-Zwarte-Piet-langzaam-maar-zeker-van-kleur-verandert/520000006372-1d832692; http://www.volkskrant.nl/binnenland/lespakket-zwartepiet-voor-twijfelschool~a4171537/.
56. http://nu.nl/ondernemen/4131178/winkeliers-willen-duidelijkheid-uiterlijk-zwarte-piet.html; http://www.nrc.nl/nieuws/2015/10/01/win-

keliers-zwarte-piet-verdwijnt-nog-niet-maar-de-discussie-kan-nog-jaren-duren; http://nos.nl/artikel/2060592-albert-heijn-houdt-vast-aan-zwarte-piet.html; http://nieuws.nl/algemeen/20150915/ook-jumbo-gaat-door-de-knieen-witte-piet-op-eigen-merk-snoepgoed.

57. http://nos.nl/artikel/2051311-bijenkorfs-zwarte-piet-wordt-verguld. html; http://nieuws.nl/trending/20150810/voor-en-tegenstanders-niet-blij-met-pietenkeuze-bijenkorf.
58. http://www.metronieuws.nl/binnenland/2015/09/nieuwe-trend-piet-om-zelf-in-te-kleuren.
59. Personal observation, 2015.
60. https://decorrespondent.nl/3724/Hoe-Zwarte-Piet-langzaam-maar-zeker-van-kleur-verandert/520000006372-1d832692.
61. http://nu.nl/media/4130577/rtl-ziet-geen-reden-uiterlijk-zwarte-piet-passen.html; http://www.parool.nl/parool/nl/38/MEDIA/article/detail/4130454/2015/08/27/Ongeschminkte-pieten-in-serie-Nickelodeon.dhtml; http://www.nrc.nl/nieuws/2015/11/04/nickelo-deon-presenteert-ongeschminkte-pieten; http://www.ad.nl/ad/nl/1012/Nederland/article/detail/4178452/2015/11/04/Nickelodeon-presenteert-multicultureel-Pietenteam.dhtml; http://www.nrc.nl/next/2015/11/08/zwarte-piet-op-de-publieke-omroep-heeft-piet-roetv-1556885; http://nos.nl/l/2068922.
62. Interview Adriaan Krans, 19-1-2016; http://www.nrc.nl/nieuws/2015/12/05/sinterklaasjournaal-houdt-vast-aan-zwarte-piet.
63. http://m.ad.nl/ad/m/nl/1012/Nederland/article/detail/4174802/2015/10/30/Onderzoek-in-262-gemeenten-Piet-blijft-zwart.dhtml; http://m.ad.nl/ad/m/nl/33220/Sinterklaas/article/detail/4175250/2015/10/31/Grote-Pietatlas-Nog-zwart-als-roet-en-soms-een-kleurtje.dhtml; http://nos.nl/artikel/2066135-piet-blijft-Zin-meeste-gemeenten-zwart.html; http://www.rijnmond.nl/nieuws/14-11-2015/piet-traditioneel-bruin-zwart-bij-intocht-sinterklaas; http://www.omroepwest.nl/tv/programma/170019163/Intocht-Sinterklaas-2015/aflevering/170019243; http://www.volkskrant.nl/binnenland/roetpiet-komt-uit-de-stad~a4201094.
64. https://m.youtube.com/watch?v=CukEyn5Shk8; https://www.youtube.com/watch?v=yVistqi9D-0; https://www.youtube.com/watch?v=TlQc-QUsyMB8; http://nos.nl/l/2069046; http://nos.nl/l/2068863.
65. http://www.at5.nl/artikelen/149321/nog_geen_aanvragen_voor_demon-straties_tijdens_intocht_sint; http://nieuws.nl/algemeen/20151128/demonstranten-zwarte-piet-willen-aangifte-doen-tegen-politie/; http://nos.nl/artikel/2071911-intocht-sinterklaas-in-amsterdam-zuidoost-ver-loopt-rumoerig.html; http://www.rtvnh.nl/nieuws/175170/protesten-en-opstootjes-bij-intocht-sinterklaas-in-amsterdam-zuidoost; http://www.

at5.nl/artikelen/150414/uittocht-sinterklaas-gepaard-met-demo-te-gen-zwarte-piet-van-der-laan-schaam-je;   http://www.nu.nl/amsterdam/4177842/demonstratie-bij-uittocht-sinterklaas-museumplein.html; https://www.youtube.com/watch?v=f4T-xo6MYfM.
66. http://www.nu.nl/utrecht/4173989/demonstratie-zwarte-piet-bij-sinterklaasfeest-jaarbeurs.html;   http://www.metronieuws.nl/binnenland/2015/11/zwarte-piet-protest-bij-sintfeest-in-jaarbeurs.
67. http://nieuws.nl/algemeen/20151130/boze-ouders-gaan-als-zwarte-piet-naar-school/;   http://www.ad.nl/ad/nl/33220/Sinterklaas/article/detail/4201513/2015/12/04/Minions-en-witte-pieten-bij-Sinterklaas-in-Utrecht.dhtml.
68. http://nos.nl/artikel/2135830-asscher-en-anderen-respectvolle-dialoog-over-zwarte-piet.html; https://www.nrc.nl/nieuws/2016/10/04/katholieken-ondertekenen-verklaring-zwarte-piet-niet-4624250-a1524771;   http://denhaagfm.nl/2016/10/04/nationaal-zwarte-pieten-overleg-in-den-haag/; https://www.rijksoverheid.nl/actueel/nieuws/2016/10/04/verklaring-na-ronde-tafelgesprek-over-defiguur-van-zwarte-piet;   http://www.ad.nl/dossier-sinterklaas/oproep-tot-kalmte-in-discussie-over-zwarte-piet~a373d467/.
69. http://nos.nl/artikel/2141314-geen-zwarte-piet-meer-in-amsterdam-alleen-schoorsteenpieten.html;   https://www.nrc.nl/nieuws/2016/12/02/het-moet-om-sint-gaan-niet-om-piet-5623314-a1534769?utm_source = NRC&utm_medium = banner&utm_campaign = Paywall; http://www.at5.nl/artikelen/161536/sinterklaas-voortaan-zonder-zwarte-piet-naar-zuidoost; http://www.volkskrant.nl/binnenland/steeds-meer-steden-kiezen-voor-roetveegpiet~a4409230/;   http://nu.nl/sinterklaas/4346981/meeste-dorpen-en-steden-houden-vast-zwarte-piet-bij-intocht.html; http://nos.nl/artikel/2141785-piet-blijft-bij-meeste-intochten-helemaal-zwart.html; http://nos.nl/video/2141941-zwarte-piet-verandert-lang-niet-overal.html; https://www.nrc.nl/nieuws/2016/11/07/piet-blijft-zwart-bij-meerderheid-sinterklaasintochten-a1530529; http://www.volkskrant.nl/binnenland/pieten-blijven-bij-meeste-intochten-zwart-of-bruin~a4410284/; http://www.volkskrant.nl/binnenland/van-roetveegpiet-tot-intens-zwarte-piet-dit-doen-de-gemeenten-bij-de-intocht~a4409083/.
70. http://www.nrc.nl/nieuws/2016/11/30/de-roetveegpiet-is-er-voor-de-randstad-5596179-a1534399; http://nos.nl/artikel/2146584-plek-van-de-school-bepaalt-de-kleur-van-piet.html.
71. http://www.rtlnieuws.nl/nederland/politiek/asscher-meerderheid-moet-zich-aanpassen-in-zwarte-piet-discussie; http://nu.nl/politiek/4358531/kabinet-pleit-aanpassing-zwarte-piet.html;   http://www.nrc.nl/nieuws/2016/11/30/kabinet-mengt-zich-in-zwartepietendiscus-

sie-a1534346; http://www.telegraaf.nl/reportage/27142436/__Van_
der_Steur_krijgt_roe_om_bemoeienis__.html.

72. http://nos.nl/l/2106783; http://nos.nl/l/2106843; http://nu.nl/
media/4269988/dolores-leeuwin-vertrekt-bij-sinterklaasjournaal.html;
http://www.nrc.nl/nieuws/2016/05/23/van-muiswinkel-en-myer-
stoppen-als-zwarte-piet.

73. https://www.nrc.nl/nieuws/2016/05/28/beste-omroepbaas-zwaai-zwarte-
piet-uit-2494968-a1287177; https://www.nrc.nl/nieuws/2016/05/29/
zwarte-piet-vertrekt-door-open-deur-1624758-a1106288;
https://www.nrc.nl/nieuws/2016/09/30/zwarte-piet-schaadt-
gekleurde-kinderen-4535244-a1524173.

74. http://nos.nl/artikel/2139373-rtl-kiest-voor-schoorsteenpiet.html;
https://www.nrc.nl/nieuws/2016/10/24/geen-zwarte-piet-meer-bij-
rtl-wel-schoorsteen-piet-a1528112; http://nos.nl/artikel/2139439-vvd-
er-zijlstra-vindt-afschaffen-zwarte-piet-domme-zet.html.

75. https://www.nrc.nl/nieuws/2016/11/09/de-allereerst-piet-in-beeld-is-
wit-de-tweede-is-zwart-5215588-a1531026; https://www.nrc.nl/nieuws/
2016/11/08/sinterklaasjournaal-komt-belofte-na-5202100-a1530850;
http://www.volkskrant.nl/media/achter-de-schermen-van-het-pietenhuis~
a4409166/.

76. http://nos.nl/l/2108767; http://www.nu.nl/binnenland/4324672/
extreemrechtse-nvu-wil-bij-intocht-sinterklaas-demonstreren.htm-
l?kl=771&ku=4193980&utm_source=SIM&utm_medium=email&utm_
campaign = nu%2Enl_berichten_doorsturen_popup_2014&utm_con-
tent = &utm_term = a_226710.

77. Interview Edo Haan, 2-12-2016.

78. http://nos.nl/artikel/2142263-honderden-agenten-om-rust-te-be-
waren-bij-intocht-sint.html; https://www.nrc.nl/nieuws/2016/11/10/
maassluis-doet-alles-om-intocht-leuk-te-houden-5233319-
a1531227?utm_source=NRC&utm_medium=banner&utm_cam-
paign=Paywall; http://nos.nl/artikel/2142598-noodverordening-tijdens-
intocht-sint-in-maassluis.html; http://nos.nl/artikel/2142604-rutte-doet-
oproep-doe-een-beetje-normaal-bij-intocht-sint.html.

79. http://nos.nl/artikel/2142733-200-tegenstanders-zwarte-piet-opgepa-
kt-in-rotterdam.html;http://nos.nl/artikel/2144825-aboutaleb-beperkt-
anti-zwarte-piet-demonstratie.html; http://nos.nl/artikel/2143554-about-
aleb-kreeg-aivd-ambtsbericht-voor-sinterklaasintocht.html; https://www.nrc.
nl/nieuws/2016/12/15/waarom-ik-de-demonstratie-tegen-zwarte-piet-ver-
bood-5807824-a1536904 https://www.ad.nl/binnenland/meeste-ge-
meenten-houden-piet-bij-intocht-zwart-of-bruin~aaef7531/; https://www.
trouw.nl/samenleving/zwarte-piet-verdeelt-stad-en-ommeland~a37409d1;

http://www.duo-onderwijsonderzoek.nl/wp-content/uploads/2017/12/
Rapportage-Sinterklaasviering-in-het-basisonderwijs-december-2017.pdf.
80. https://www.nrc.nl/nieuws/2017/10/05/sinterklaasjournaal-stopt-met-gekleurde-pieten-a1576065.
81. https://www.nrc.nl/nieuws/2017/10/05/sinterklaasjournaal-stopt-met-gekleurde-pieten-a1576065.
82. https://eenvandaag.avrotros.nl/panels/opiniepanel/alle-uitslagen/item/peiling-draagvlak-voor-traditionele-zwarte-piet-loopt-terug.
83. https://nos.nl/artikel/2204140-sinterklaascircus-rotterdam-gestopt-initiatiefnemer-bedreigd.html; https://joop.bnnvara.nl/nieuws/pro-pieten-vallen-basisschool-binnen; http://politiek.tpo.nl/2017/11/30/vergadering-gemeenteraad-amsterdam-kort-stilgelegd-vanwege-zwarte-pieten-op-publieke-tribune/; http://nieuws.tpo.nl/2017/11/22/sinterklaashuis-dordt-gesaboteerd/; https://joop.bnnvara.nl/nieuws/pro-pieten-vallen-sylvana-simons-thuis-lastig.
84. https://www.nrc.nl/nieuws/2017/11/18/fijn-dat-die-demonstranten-er-niet-zijn-vindt-men-in-dokkum-14095190-a1581732; https://www.nrc.nl/nieuws/2017/11/20/veiligheid-stond-even-boven-het-demonstratierecht-14111486-a1581821; https://www.volkskrant.nl/binnenland/zo-wist-het-friese-anti-anti-zwarte-piet-protest-dat-gedoe-uit-de-randstad-te-weren~a4540379/.
85. https://www.doneeractie.nl/boetes-betalen-voor-blokkade-snelweg-anti-pieten/-4928; https://nos.nl/artikel/2203623-steunactie-voor-deelnemers-blokkade-anti-zwarte-piet-betogers.html%3fnpo_cc%3d126&; http://www.dagelijksestandaard.nl/2017/11/friese-zwarte-piet-helden-krijgen-gratis-en-voor-niets-hulp-van-advocaat-na-blokkade-a7.

REFERENCES

Bijnaar, A., & Maris, C. (2014). Zwart als roet Zwarte Piet in de liberale rechtsstaat. *Filosofie & Praktijk, 35*(3), 5–22.
Blokker, B. (2014a). *Zwarte Piet verander je niet zomaar*. NRC, 23–9.
Blokker, B. (2014b). *Burgervader schiet burgemeester te hulp*. NRC, 17–10.
Blokker, B. (2014c). *Burgemeester, geen zedenmeester*. NRC, 12–11.
Blokker, B. (2014d). *Controverse rond Zwarte Piet: hooligan-aanpak blijkt effectief*. NRC, 17–11.
Blokker, B. (2014e). *Politie klaagt anti-Pietactivist aan wegens mishandeling*. NRC, 27–12.
Blokker, B. (2015a). Leg die ongelukkige traditie nu eens uit. *ZP en gouden koets uitgebreid aan de orde geweest*. NRC, 22–8.
Blokker, B. (2015b). *Nederland belooft acceptabele Piet*. NRC, 19–8.
Blokker, B. (2015c). *Hoe denk jij dat het komt dat Piet zwart is?* NRC, 28–10.

Broer, T. (2014). Hoe de roetpiet zijn intrede deed: De inpoldering van Zwarte Piet. *Vrij Nederland, 75*(48), 26–33.

Brubaker, R., & Laitin, D. D. (1998). Ethnic and Nationalist Violence. *Annual Review of Sociology, 24*(1), 423–452.

Committee on the Elimination of Racial Discrimination. (2015). *Concluding Observations on the Nineteenth to Twenty-First Periodic Reports of the Netherlands*. New York: CERD.

Docherty, J. S. (2001). *Learning Lessons From Waco: When the Parties Bring Their Gods to the Negotiation Table*. Syracuse: Syracuse University Press.

Euwijk, J., & Rensen, F. (2017). *De identiteitscrisis van Zwarte Piet*.Amsterdam and Antwerpen: Atlas Contact.

Gemeente Amsterdam: Bureau Onderzoek en Statistiek. (2012). *Hoe denken Amsterdammers over Zwarte Piet?* Amsterdam.

Hartnett, A. (2010). Aestheticized Geographies of Conflict: The Politicization of Culture and the Culture of Politics in Belfast's Mural Tradition. In H. Silverman (Ed.), *Contested Cultural Heritage: Religion, Nationalism, Erasure, and Exclusion in a Global World* (pp. 69–107). New York, NY: Springer Science & Business Media.

Helsloot, J. (2000). De opkomst van Sinterklaas als nationaal feest in Nederland. Een schets op grond van twee volkskundevragenlijsten van het Meertens Instituut. In A. Döring (Ed.), *Faszination Nikolaus. Kult, Brauch, Kommerz* (pp. 104–139). Essen: Klartext.

Helsloot, J. (2005). De strijd om Zwarte Piet. In I. Hoving (Ed.), *Cultuur en migratie in Nederland. 5. Veranderingen van het alledaagse: 1950–2000* (pp. 249–271). The Hague: Sdu Uitgevers.

Helsloot, J. I. A. (2012a). Zwarte Piet and Cultural Aphasia in the Netherlands. *Quotidian Journal for the Study of Everyday Life, 3*, 1.

Helsloot, J. I. A. (2012b). Culture or Commerce: Framing Heritage in the Context of Municipal Subvention. The Case of the Annual St Nicholas Parade in the Netherlands. *Traditiones, 41*(1), 137–146.

Hilhorst, S., & Hermes, J. (2016). 'We Have Given Up So Much': Passion and Denial in the Dutch Zwarte Piet (Black Pete) Controversy. *European Journal of Cultural Studies, 19*(3), 218–233.

Khaibar, S. (2013). Zwarte Piet. Een omstreden traditie. *Nederlands Juristenblad, 88*(43), 3005–3009.

Knevel, P., Polak, S., & Tilstra, S. (Eds.). (2011). *Meerstemmig verleden: persoonlijke verhalen over het Nederlandse slavernijverleden*. Amsterdam: KIT Publishers.

Kozijn, G. (2014). *Zwarte Piet: verkennend onderzoek naar een toekomstbestendig sinterklaasfeest*. Beilen: Pharos.

Kuiper, R. (2014). Interview Paul Römer, NTR-directeur. *Volkskrant*, 6–12.

Kuiper, M. (2015). *Touwtrekken om Zwarte Piet, zonder trauma's*. NRC, 16–11.

LeBaron, M. (2003). *Bridging Cultural Conflicts: A New Approach for a Changing World.* San Francisco, CA: Jossey-Bass.

LeBaron, M., & Venashri Pillay, V. (Eds.). (2006). *Conflict Across Cultures: A Unique Experience of Bridging Differences.* Boston: Intercultural Press.

Lederach, P., & Lederach, A. J. (2010). *When Blood and Bones Cry Out: Journeys Through the Soundscape of Healing and Reconciliation.* New York: Oxford University Press.

Linders, R. T. G. (2016). *News Coverage on the Black Pete Discussion in the Netherlands: Innocent Tradition or Racist Stereotype? A Quantitative Content Analysis of Dutch Newspaper Articles on the Black Pete Discussion,* Master thesis, Groningen.

MacDonald, S. (2004). Commemorating the Holocaust: Reconfiguring National Identity in the Twenty-First Century. In J. Littler & R. Naidoo (Eds.), *The Politics of Heritage: The Legacies of Race* (pp. 49–68). London and New York: Routledge.

Margry, P. J. (2014). Unesco en de paradox van bescherming: immaterieel erfgoed in Nederland. *Ons Erfdeel, 2014*(1), 56–66.

Nederlands Juristen Comité voor de Mensenrechten. (2015). *Joint Parallel Report to the Nineteenth to Twenty-First Periodic Reports of the Netherlands on the International Convention on the Elimination of all Forms of Racial Discrimination (CERD).* Leiden: Leiden.

N. N. (2014). Zwarte Piet. *Immaterieel Erfgoed, 3*(3), 36.

Ross, M. H. (2007). *Cultural Contestation in Ethnic Conflict.* Cambridge: Cambridge University Press.

Ross, M. H. (2009a). Preface. In M. H. Ross (Ed.), *Culture and Belonging in Divided Societies. Contestation and Symbolic Landscapes* (pp. ix–xi). Philadelphia: University of Pennsylvania Press.

Ross, M. H. (2009b). Cultural Contestation and the Symbolic Landscape: Politics by Other Means? In M. H. Ross (Ed.), *Culture and Belonging in Divided Societies. Contestation and Symbolic Landscape* (pp. 1–24). Philadelphia: University of Pennsylvania Press.

Schirch, L. (2005). *Ritual and Symbol in Peacebuilding.* Bloomfield: Kumarian Press.

Slagter, M. (2014). *Want al ben ik zwart als roet,'k meen het toch goed. Hoe de Zwarte-Pietdiscussie geframed wordt in conversaties op Facebook en in praatprogramma's sinds oktober.,* Master thesis, Leiden.

Smithey, L. A. (2009). Conflict Transformation: Cultural Innovation, and Loyalist Identity in Northern Ireland. In M. H. Ross (Ed.), *Culture and Belonging in Divided Societies: Contestation and symbolic landscapes.* (pp. 85–106). Philadelphia: University of Pennsylvania Press.

Strouken, I. (2010). *Dit zijn wij: de belangrijkste honderd tradities van Nederland.* Beilen: Pharos Uitgevers.

Takken, W. (2014). *De man die Sinterklaas zwart maakte.* NRC, 6–12.

van der Pijl, Y., & Goulordava, K. (2014). Black Pete, "Smug Ignorance", and the Value of the Black Body in Postcolonial Netherlands. *New West Indian Guide/Nieuwe West-Indische Gids, 88*(3–4), 262–291.

van der Zeijden, A. (2012). Black Pete and the Negotiating of Identities. Dealing with Controversial Intangible Cultural Heritage. URL: http://www.albertvanderzeijden.nl/publicaties/Black%20Pete%20and%20the%20negotiating%20of%20identities.pdf.

van der Zeijden, A. (2014). Dealing with Black Pete Media, Mediators and the Dilemmas of Brokering Intangible Heritage. *VOLKSKUNDE, 115*(3), 349–360.

van Es, K., van Geenen, D., & Boeschoten, T. (2014). Mediating the Black Pete Discussion on Facebook: Slacktivism, Flaming Wars, and Deliberation. *First Monday, 19*(12).https://uncommonculture.org/ojs/index.php/fm/article/view/5570/4180.

van Trigt, P. (2016). *1000 jaar Sinterklaas.* Volendam: LM Publishers.

Wouters, L. A. (2014). *Zwarte Piet Contested: Tolerance and the (re) production of the Zwarte Piet tradition in the Netherlands*, Master thesis, Utrecht.

CHAPTER 15

Conclusion: Roles Governments Play in Shaping the Symbolic Landscape

Jeroen Rodenberg and Pieter Wagenaar

HERITAGE PRACTICES, CULTURAL CONTESTATION AND THE SHAPING OF THE CULTURAL LANDSCAPE

In this volume, a variety of cases of cultural contestation has been discussed, ranging from the construction of a new national museum to all-out war, and from an attempt at changing a nation's favorite festivity to ethnic cleansing. What all these cases show is that heritage is part and parcel of a society's symbolic landscape. Heritage practices not only give meaning to it, but also construct and re-construct it at the same time. Identity is deeply intertwined with the symbolic landscape, as are the feelings of belonging and exclusion that are expressed by it. Therefore, the effects of the shaping and re-shapingv the symbolic landscape can be severe: When communities do not feel represented by it, emotions run high and cultural contestation can occur.

As the contributors to this volume show, governments play various roles in heritage practices. They articulate and reproduce existing historical

J. Rodenberg (✉) · P. Wagenaar
Department of Political Science and Public Administration,
VU University Amsterdam, Amsterdam, Noord-Holland, The Netherlands

© The Author(s) 2018   315
J. Rodenberg and P. Wagenaar (eds.), *Cultural Contestation*,
Palgrave Studies in Cultural Heritage and Conflict,
https://doi.org/10.1007/978-3-319-91914-0_15

316 J. RODENBERG AND P. WAGENAAR

narratives and heritage discourses in public policies and authorize these. Examples are the conservation plans for cultural landscapes drawn up by the Canadian government or the nomination of a painful historical site as UNESCO World Heritage by Japan. Governments, thus, shape and re-shape the symbolic landscape in different social, cultural, and political-administrative contexts. In the introduction to his volume, we put forward the idea that governments often play a role in cultural contestation and introduced a categorization of roles. Yet, perhaps it is rather the various roles governments have in the shaping of the symbolic landscape that are of importance, than what they do during cultural contestation.

SHAPING AND RE-SHAPING THE SYMBOLIC LANDSCAPE BY AUTHORING AND AUTHORIZATION

Authoring and Authorization for Domestic Purposes

The volume starts with six chapters exploring the ways in which governments are involved in processes leading to cultural contestation. For domestic purposes of identity formation, and the legitimization of their rule, governments use historical narratives—sometimes implicitly, sometimes explicitly—excluding minority communities along the way.

A prime example of the way national governments 'instrumentalize' heritage to strengthen nation-building is China. Maags discusses how contestation is a direct effect of the way the party-state, or central government, uses intangible cultural heritage for nation-building. Due to the bureaucratic organization and the ICH policy design, these attempts give rise to administrative contestation. Central government favors heritage because of its 'fit' with the envisioned national identity. Yet, at the same time lower-level governmental actors articulate their own counter-narratives, trying to shape or re-shape the symbolic landscape at their respective level and in doing so act as authorizer and author too.

Logan discusses the way the governments and military of Myanmar, dominated by ethnic Burmese, shape the symbolic landscape by favoring Burmese heritage over that of ethnic minorities. The teaching of the Shan language and literature under the cover of a training course in Buddhism, for example, is illustrative of how Shan heritage is threatened by a lack of governmental authorization. The absence of the Rohingyas' cultural practices in Myanmar's symbolic landscape is expressed by government's wish not to use their chosen name, but instead to refer to them as the 'Muslim community.'

In Bangladesh, by and large, a situation comparable to Myanmar can be sketched. As Hashem writes, Bengalese central government explicitly favors Bengalese-Muslim cultural and religious practices, instead of appreciating Bangladesh's cultural richness, effectively asking minority groups to give up their identity.

Ikiz Kaya and Calhan, focusing on Izmir, show the historical and present-day role of central governments in the ever-changing shaping of the Turkish symbolic landscape. Illustrative of government's role is the erasure of physical markings pointing to the (past) presence of religious minority communities in the city of Izmir.

Tisdel demonstrates how the Cuban socialist government reproduced existing historical narratives in its cultural policy which excluded Afro-Cuban religions and their practitioners from the country's symbolic landscape. Since the 1990s, state-owned museums tell the visitor a story of Cuban-Religion and its heritage as an inclusive part of the nation's identity while at the same time neglecting the history of its marginalization. This has led to the construction of counter-narratives, by individuals like Fredesvinde Rosell. One easily gets the impression that in authoritarian states like Cuba cultural contestation does not occur. Yet, as Tisdel shows, when one compares the state's official narratives, with individually articulated counter-narratives, cultural contestation does emerge.

That the practice of meaning-giving to landscapes works socially exclusive too is shown by Valadares. While constructing the national park services in Canada, government attributed different cultural and social values to these landscapes, effectively transforming natural landscapes into cultural landscapes. The values attributed to them are intertwined with the processes of identity formation of the colonists and their descendants. The narratives about these national parks are constructed and re-constructed, but still lay bare the core of American and Canadian national identity, in which there is no place for indigenous communities.

Authoring and Authorization in an International Context

In the contributions in the second part of this volume, the effects of governmental heritage practices on a country's international relations are

examined. Governments use heritage to strengthen their national identities, which sometimes leads to diplomatic conflicts with neighboring
countries.

Taking Famagusta as a case, Jaramillo shows how heritage is intertwined with political ideologies in various ways. In itself, cultural expressions such as buildings and cityscapes are a physical effect of politics, as is
the present-day meaning attributed to these. Heritage as a concept, moreover, is highly politicized as well. At the global level, under the umbrella
of UNESCO, member states pursue their respective interests and ideas.
At the local level, communities do the same. As Jaramillo argues, the multi-layered political dimension of heritage makes it difficult to deal with
heritage issues in territories which are under dispute. In fact, it is exactly
the multi-faceted politics of heritage that give rise to cultural contestation
between the states laying claim on these domains, and their heritage.

Van Heese presents the most extreme result of cultural contestation
during the war over Nagorno-Karabakh. She describes how the governments involved took up arms to destroy the symbolic landscape of the
opposing party, as erasing the cultural expressions of the enemy, means
putting an end to his claims on the territory.

Narratives underlying cultural contestation, with a history of violence, suppression and pain at their core, occur in many of the chapters of this volume. This also goes for the diplomatic conflict between
South Korea and Japan, described by Trifu. The cultural contestation
between the two states is caused by the different meanings attributed to
the *Gunkanjima* industrial site. For Japan, it symbolizes the country's
industrialization and its central place in the world. It is a heritage site
that is part of the country's symbolic landscape, expressing the nation's
identity. Central government was keen to underscore it by trying to get
it listed as world heritage. For South Korea, it is a place which stands for
forced labor during the Second World War. In itself, that does not need
to be problematic, as the heritage status attributed to former concentration camps shows. The core of the contestation between the two nations
is the absence of Korean suffering in the Japanese *Gunkanjima* narrative;
Reconciliation between the two states is made difficult by the exclusion
of the dark history of imperialism from Japan's symbolic landscape.

The diplomatic conflict between Greece and Macedonia is quite comparable, as this conflict too has competing claims on history, past suffering and feelings of not belonging at its root. Volchevska examines the
way the Greek government laid claim to Ancient Macedonian history and

its symbols, thus ignoring the Macedonian identity, and past wrongdoings. At first, after the creation of Macedonia as an independent country, its government tried to open up the Greek narrative. When these attempts failed, trenches were dug. Macedonian government claimed the past Greece so desperately sought to protect from it, and started using the exact symbols Greece claimed for itself. This led to intense cultural contestation between the countries.

As these chapters show, governments play the role of authors in the shaping and re-shaping of the symbolic landscape and the role of authorizers when these already exist. By playing these roles, governments are deeply involved in the cultural contestation that might ensue.

Re-shaping the Symbolic Landscape by Mitigation

The third part of the book consists of chapters examining ways in which governments attempt to mitigate cultural contestation. These can be categorized as follows.

In the first place, governments can try to avoid cultural contestation by taking all involved stakeholders and their interests into account, and designing a participative form of decision-making. This, of course, has its limits, for it is often unclear who the stakeholders are. And, when these are defined, will all of them have an equal say in the decision-making process? Moreover, government actors are stakeholders themselves, with their own political ideologies, interests, and competences. Still, attempts are made to mitigate contestation in this manner, as Kryder-Reid and Zimmerman write. They also show the limits of this kind of mitigation. It seems that, if we want to take this approach seriously, government should take a step back as a stakeholder, and be open to formulating new (more) inclusive narratives.

In the second place, governments attempt to mitigate by constructing a more open narrative themselves. Governments of recently independent countries may be faced with the challenges of having to create a symbolic landscape that includes minorities. In such cases, governments sometimes try to avoid contestation, as they understand the threat it poses to a young country. An example of this is provided by the Estonian National Museum. Pawłusz discusses the main permanent exhibition 'Encounters' which can be seen as prime example of a governmental attempt to steer away from a socially exclusive narrative. It presents a more open narrative, including groups who can't claim a long history in the country, instead.

In the third place, governments attempt to mitigate cultural contestation by creating safe spaces for dialogue between the involved communities. The role governmental actors take in such instances is that of a 'compère' or impartial panel chair, bringing contesting groups together, and accommodating the debate. The goal of governments is to let the involved parties voice their feelings and fears, and help them understand those of the opposing parties, which hopefully results in sandpapering the sharp edges of the debate. Governments can do so passively, creating a safe space for debate after a community has asked it to do so. Wagenaar and Rodenberg give an example of this kind of mitigation by describing the attempts of Secretary of State Asscher to create a space for discussion between opponents and proponents of the figure of *Zwarte Piet*.

Lastly, governments play the role of mediator. As they do when they are merely 'compères', governments create safe spaces for dialogue, but they also engage in the discussion themselves. Under government direction, the involved parties together create a new inclusive narrative, to which every party can relate. Wagenaar and Rodenberg illustrate this with the role Amsterdam Mayor Eberhard van der Laan played during contestation. He directed the construction of the 'sooth Pete' narrative, thus re-shaping the symbolic landscape by altering the historical narrative to make it more inclusive.

Mitigation, as many of the authors implicitly or explicitly show, is often hard to attain. The verb 'to attempt' used above in the categorization should be stressed here. Mitigation can be attempted by governments with the best intentions. It often makes the symbolic landscape more inclusive, but just as often it results in new instances of cultural contestation.

Supra-National and Intergovernmental Attempts to Mitigate

One could argue that supra-national and intergovernmental actors, such as the UN and UNESCO, are likely candidates to take up the role as mitigator in cases of cultural contestation. There are international legal frameworks and juridical principles in place as well aimed at preserving heritage and safeguarding human rights. Some of the authors in this volume touch on this. From their work, it becomes clear that it is questionable whether international legal measures and regimes sort any effect in preventing or mitigating cultural contestation, or saving heritage from destruction. As illustrated by Van Heese, when cultural contestation is intertwined with an armed conflict, laws safeguarding the opposing party's cultural rights tend to be disregarded. But even when the international conflict confines itself to a diplomatic conflict, mitigation by UNESCO is hard to attain, as becomes clear from the *Gunkujima* case. As Ross (2007, 2009) noted already, when it comes to successful mitigation, the authority and legitimacy of government is often disputed. The fact that UNESCO is in itself highly politicized, and that international heritage protection regimes are an effect of decision-making at UNESCO, as Jaramillo argues, probably works against the organization too.

Although more research is needed, it is probably safe to say mitigation attempts should be aimed at the level at which the contestation is played out. Perhaps the common truth that all politics is local politics holds value for heritage practices too. Therefore, it might be at this level that chances for mitigation are highest.

Governmental Double-Roles

Understanding the roles governments play in the shaping and re-shaping of the symbolic landscape and the ensuing instances of cultural contestation is not as simple as the above might suggest. As Logan rightly asserts in his contribution, governments often play contradictory roles. Moreover, government seldom acts as a unitary actor. This volume explores cases in which it is exactly this fact that leads to cultural contestation. Maags captures this notion in her chapter, describing the Chinese party-state as 'multi-level governance,' which gives governmental actors the opportunity to pursue their own interests. In a multi-ethnic state, like China, local governments can defend the existing local symbolic landscape as authorizers. On the other hand, chances are that these actions will bring them in conflict with other levels of government, also acting as authorizers and authors of the public landscape.

The chapter by Kryder-Reid and Zimmerman implicitly sheds light on how governments take up contradictory roles as a result of administrative fragmentation. In organizing participative forms of decision-making, the government agency central in the process has to bring together the interests, ideas, values, and ideologies of the stakeholders, acting as a mediator. Yet, often, other government agencies are involved as stakeholders as well.

Administrative fragmentation, thus, is the reason government often plays a double role. In some instances, this might lead to bureaucratic contestation. Yet, on the other hand, states with highly fragmented administrative systems also have possibilities for mitigation, as Wagenaar and Rodenberg demonstrate. In the 'multi-level governance' structure of the Netherlands, with dispersed authority and competence, the Amsterdam Mayor Van der Laan had room to react to local community's demands and act as mediator.

Tabula Rasa?

(Re-)shaping the symbolic landscape is not done from scratch. Newly independent countries may attempt to create an entirely new symbolic landscape, but they always need to deal with existing historical narratives as well, as the cases in this volume make clear. Moreover, their actions are also determined by social-cultural and political-administrative contexts. These affect the various roles governments play, or want to play.

Logan, for example, shows that after the British left their former colony, the new government of Myanmar had the opportunity to shape an inclusive symbolic landscape for the multi-ethnic state. Nonetheless, it mainly authorized the existing Burmese one, as existing social structures and dominant interests still had to be reckoned with. Hashem paints a comparable picture for Bangladesh, where the violent history of fighting for independence made it hard not to favor Bengalese-Muslim cultural expressions over those of others. In an altogether different way, the Netherlands struggles with the social and cultural effects of its shifting demography, as it becomes increasingly multi-cultural. The existing symbolic landscape expressing 'Dutchness' is challenged by 'new' groups, claiming a place for themselves. This changing sociocultural composition challenges the existing symbolic landscape and forces governments to act, although government seems unsure what role it has to play.

The way in which the administrative design affects the role of governments is illustrated by Maags. The administrative design takes the form of 'multi-level governance,' distributing authority and competences horizontally and vertically. In this highly fragmented administrative design, central government can formulate policies, which lower levels of government are obliged to implement, but at the same time, it will always be frustrated by other governmental actors pursuing their own interests. Even more complex, and as influential as the multi-level governance system in China, is the interplay between ethnicity and administrative design in Myanmar. The current government led by Prime

Minister Daw Aung San Suu Kyi grapples with the highly complex political structure and ethnic composition of the Union, and on top of that, the political influence of the Burmese dominated Tatmadaw, influencing the role of central government in heritage praxis. If the current government does intend to mitigate the ethnic cleansing and cultural genocide taking place, it has a hard time doing so due to existing administrative structures.

Ross, and Others

The goal of this volume was to bring together scholars stemming from different academic disciplines and have them shed light on the role government plays in instances of contestation surrounding heritage. To structure the argument and analysis of the volume, we chose to use the theory of Marc Howard Ross on cultural contestation as a red thread, because we believed it could be used by various academic disciplines to study contested heritage. It proved its worth, and, it turned out, can also easily be linked to other theories and concepts, such as the myth-symbol complex, multi-level governance, and the international politics of recognition. Looking at societal conflict surrounding contested heritage through the lens of cultural contestation demands taking the role of government into account. This, and the apparent ease with which Ross' ideas can be combined with theories stemming from a range of disciplines, illustrates the strengths of his work, and its usefulness in public administration science and heritage studies.

Directions for Further Research

Studies on the roles of governments in cultural contestation, we feel, should be focused at a deeper understanding of the roles governments play in the shaping and re-shaping of the symbolic landscape. For further research along this line, we offer a few directions.

In the first place, as this volume demonstrates, in many cases the symbolic landscape has a physical appearance too. Narratives give meaning to something, be it objects, cultural expressions, or a landscape. We feel that this observation can be taken a step further and be linked to the idea of the 'landscape biography' (see, for example, Kolen 2005; Roymans et al. 2009; Kolen et al. 2015). Adherents to this approach examine cultural (urban and rural) landscapes by looking at them both from a historical and a present-day use perspective. They see government as one of the 'authors' of a landscape, together with natural disasters, climate change, daily human use, and the actions of the community involved. In this approach, questions of belongingness and 'sense of place' are part of the equation, which makes it a usable lens for studying the past roles of governments in the shaping and current re-shaping of the cultural landscape. Symbolic landscapes could be approached in a similar fashion.

A second line of inquiry could be the relation between governments and communities. Governments are key actors in the shaping and the re-shaping of the symbolic landscape. They do so together with communities in the societies they govern. Often, government takes a leading role in heritage practices. Yet, it does so in collaboration with communities and sometimes even takes their lead. In instances of cultural contestation, communities often ask governments to mitigate. Government then tries to bring community leaders together, offering them a safe space for debate to re-construct narratives and re-shape the symbolic landscape. Moreover, governments sometimes strive to avoid contestation by making cultural heritage policies inclusive from the start. The relationship between governmental actors and communities in the shaping and re-shaping of the symbolic landscape deserves more attention than it currently receives. Looking closer at it would bring the study of government to the heart of heritage studies, and the study of heritage practices to the heart of public administration science and political science. The 'community approach' advocated in Critical Heritage Studies should be linked to this idea. The call for bottom-up approaches in heritage praxis can't be achieved without an active role of governments, and that role should therefore be central in the study of heritage practices.

CONCLUSION

To conclude, this volume has shown that governments play a major role in the continuing process of shaping and re-shaping of a society's symbolic landscape. The categorization presented in the first chapter was helpful in getting a grip on these roles. What has also become clear is that governments do not act as unitary actors, but play different and often conflicting roles. We should thus speak of 'the roles of governments', instead of 'the role of government.' We have also seen that what is important is not so much the role governments play in instances of cultural contestation, but rather the way they shape the symbolic landscape. As this volume demonstrated, governments always have a part in this, by articulating historical narratives and heritage discourses through policies. The various and conflicting roles governments play in instances of cultural contestation are an effect of their actions in shaping and re-shaping the symbolic landscape.

Understanding the roles government plays during cultural contestation should thus be understood in terms of their conflicting roles as 'authorizers', 'authors', and 'mitigators' in the shaping and the re-shaping of the symbolic landscape. As Ross pointed out in his foreword to this volume, in a globalizing world we will encounter an increasing number of cases of cultural contestation, ranging from the international to the local level. In heritage praxis, governments need to be more self-conscious about their role in the shaping and re-shaping of the symbolic landscape, the effects thereof on feelings of not belonging, and the ever-present danger of cultural contestation. After all, Ross' call to take seriously the emotions of participants in these kinds of conflicts begins with a self-conscious government.

REFERENCES

Kolen, J. C. A. (2005). *De biografie van het landschap. Drie essays over landschap, geschiedenis en erfgoed*. Unpublished Ph.D. thesis, Vrije Universiteit Amsterdam, Amsterdam.

Kolen, J., Hermans, R., & Renes, H. (Eds.). (2015). *Landscape Biographies: Geographical, Historical and Archaeological Perspectives on the Production and Transmission of Landscapes*. Amsterdam: Amsterdam University Press.

Ross, M. H. (2007). *Cultural Contestation in Ethnic Conflict*. Cambridge: Cambridge University Press.

Ross, M. H. (2009). Cultural Contestation and the Symbolic Landscape: Politics by Other Means? In M. H. Ross (Ed.), *Culture and Belonging in Devided Societies. Contestation and Symbolic Landscapes* (pp. 1–24). Philadelphia: University of Pennsylvania Press.

Roymans, N., Gerritsen, F., van der Heijden, C., Bosma, K., & Kolen, J. (2009). Landscape Biography as Research Strategy: The Case of the South Netherlands Project. *Landscape Research, 34*(3), 337–359.

INDEX

© The Editor(s) (if applicable) and The Author(s) 2018
J. Rodenberg and P. Wagenaar (eds.), *Cultural Contestation*,
Palgrave Studies in Cultural Heritage and Conflict,
https://doi.org/10.1007/978-3-319-91914-0